CHAUCER'S KNIGHT'S TALE

AND THEORIES OF

SCHOLASTIC PSYCHOLOGY

D0170814

Chaucer's Knight's Tale and Theories of Scholastic Psychology

—LOIS RONEY—

University of South Florida Press / Tampa

Copyright 1990 by the Board of Regents of the State of Florida
Printed in U.S.A. on acid-free paper

Library of Congress Cataloging-in-Publication Data
Roney, Lois.
  Chaucer's Knight's tale and scholastic psychology / Lois Roney.
    p.   cm.
  Includes bibliographical references.
  ISBN 0-8130-1006-3 (alk. paper).—ISBN 0-8130-1027-6 (pbk.: alk. paper)
    1. Chaucer, Geoffrey, d. 1400. Knight's tale. 2. Chaucer, Geoffrey, d. 1400—
Knowledge—Psychology. 3. Scholasticism in literature. 4. Psychology in litera-
ture. I. Title.
PR1868.K63R66   1990
821'.1—dc20   90-35260

The following illustrations have been reproduced in this volume with the permis-
sion of the rights holders: cover, detail from *The Garden of Eden,* by Pol de
Limbourg, in *Les très riches heures* of Jean, duke of Berry, Musée Condé, Chantilly;
p. xvii, *Three Worlds,* by M. C. Escher, copyright 1990 by M. C. Escher Heirs/
Cordon Art, Baarn, Holland; p. 54, initial D of Psalm 52, Tickhill Psalter, Spencer
Collection, New York Public Library, Astor, Lenox, and Tilden Foundations,
New York; p. 126, self-portrait of an architect or sculptor (Regensburg, St. Peter's
Cathedral), Marburg/Art Resource, New York; p. 148, ivory traveling altar,
Trustees of the British Museum, London; p. 187, zodiac man, *Apocalypsis,* Well-
come MS 49, Wellcome Institute for the History of Medicine, London; p. 263,
the mendicant orders, Book of Hours, MS 1176, Bibliothèque Nationale, Paris;
p. 269, Hoccleve portrait of Chaucer, BM Harley 4866, fol. 88, British Library,
London.

To my daughter,

Deirdre Anne Roney,

and to the memory of my son,

Patrick Daniel Roney

CONTENTS

ILLUSTRATIONS

ACKNOWLEDGMENTS

I have accumulated many debts over the years that this study was in the making. First, it gives me pleasure to thank Jerome Taylor, who gave me encouragement, advice, and help for so long. I am also grateful to Frederic G. Cassidy, Lorraine Stock, Richard Ringler, Sherry Reames, Donald Rowe, Joyce Steward, Alice Doss, Linda Driskill, Jay Dowling, Russell Peck, Donald Green, Melvin Storm, and John McGalliard for help and scholarly advice of many different kinds and in some cases for reading parts of the manuscript as I tried out first one idea, then another, in the course of fitting together the clues of a complex subject; and Fannie LeMoine, Douglas Kelly, Christopher Kleinhenz, Lester Seifert, and Rosemarie Deist for help with translations and scholarship. My further appreciation for explanations and enlightenment on philosophical concepts is due to Paul Spade, Norman Kretzmann, Sten Ebbesen, Seale Doss, and William O'Callaghan. My many debts to other Chaucer scholars, other medievalists, and other literary theorists are enormous, as will be evident in the text and notes, and I wish to acknowledge them here as well. I also thank the Council for Philosophical Studies and the National Endowment for the Humanities for the opportunity to attend the Institute in Medieval Philosophy at Cornell University during the summer of 1980, and the University of Missouri Excellence Fund for a travel grant there. For their conscientious shepherding of my manuscript through the publication process, I thank Deidre Bryan, Larry Leshan, Angela Goodner-Piazza, Roberta Hughey and especially

Walda Metcalf, at the University Presses of Florida. Finally, and above all, I want to thank my patient readers—Jane Chance, Liam Purdon, Martin Stevens, and Julian Wasserman—for their criticism and most excellent advice, given graciously, generously, and often wittily, throughout the writing of this book.

PREFACE

This study was radically inductive. I started with some details of Chaucer's language in the Knight's Tale, found myself drawn by them into the medieval theories of psychology, and came upon, to my surprise, a major Chaucerian defense of pagan poetry.

Initially, my interest lay in Chaucer's ways with words. I concentrated on the two young knights of the Knight's Tale after discovering a large number of unusual and intellectually interesting contrasts by which Chaucer opposed them on every conceivable level of language use. For example, both knights put forward cosmologies, as is well known, but Arcite's is formed deductively, Palamon's inductively. Both knights have about the same number of speeches, as is well known, but Arcite's speeches consist of causes and reasons, Palamon's of choices and moral judgments. Both knights have champions, as is well known, but each champion's description contains two light-reference words: both of Emetreus's flicker ("sparklynge," "glytered"), whereas both of Lygurge's suggest a steady source ("gloweden," "shoon"). And so on. The tale contains a remarkable quantity of these carefully paralleled contrasts. Some meaning must, therefore, have been intended by Chaucer. But, what? What kind of opposition did he embody in these two young men?

At length, after fruitless forays into Ovid, Boethius, the *Timaeus*, Boccaccio, Augustine, and elsewhere, I came upon a map to the mother lode. I came upon a good exposition of the major issues in the great scholastic debate as to which is prior (*nobilior*) among the faculties of the human soul, the intellect or the will. It soon became apparent that the characterizations of the two young knights of the Knight's Tale form one more instance in the vast literature of that pivotal medieval debate. Chaucer had characterized each young knight according to the faculty psychology of one side: Arcite according to the intellectualist theories of the Aristotelian Thomists; Palamon according to the voluntarist theories of the Augustinian Franciscans. Later, as the scholastic references became clearer, it developed that the characterization of Theseus constituted yet a third psychological theory, in fact a Chaucerian resolution to the whole controversy.

At the same time, I was discovering other interesting and unusual language contrasts in the series of long descriptions in Part III. The three temple descriptions are rife with every kind of human suffering, as is well known, but the Venus and Mars descriptions are both shaped as lists of objects, whereas the Diana description consists of summaries of four Ovidian stories. The two champion-kings' descriptions include passages on their companies of a hundred men, as is well known, but Emetreus's men are described only as a group ("al," "al"), whereas Lygurge's men are described one by one ("som," "som"). All five of the long Part III descriptions contain numerous complexly paralleled contrasts just like these. And so, once again, some meaning must have been intended by Chaucer. But, what? Eventually it became clear that even as the subject matter of these five passages is carrying forward the pagan story, the language used to convey it has been carefully shaped to evoke in the reader's mind the scholastic theories of the thinking processes of the human mind. Saturn's monologue concludes the series with a more subjective, and therefore much more realistic, Chaucerian theory of human thinking processes.

And thus, since the Knight's Tale puts forward a new resolution of the great debate over faculty psychology and a new model of human thinking processes, it seemed apparent that Chaucer must have composed the tale in the larger context of trying to work out a more realistic theory of human nature than those of the scholastic thinkers. But, why pagan? Why embed these scholastic theories and Chaucerian resolutions in a story not about fellow Christians but specifically about ancient pagans? Why—apparently to refute scholastic poetics, which, following along with Aristotle's denunciation of poetry as the lowest form of logic, strongly maintained that pagan fictions could not convey truth. Quite the contrary, says Chaucer the Christian humanist, and he proves that they can with his Knight's Tale. The tale puts forward some of the scholastics' very favorite truths—among others, their theories of virtue, of piety, of perception, of reasoning, and of inference—but all these "truths" have been embodied in pagan "lies." How Chaucerian! And how delightful! Read literally, the Knight's Tale is a pagan romance about divine injustice and human suffering, just like the *Aeneid* and the *Metamorphoses*. Read figuratively, however, the Knight's Tale puts forward accurate incarnations of the psychological theories of the scholastics themselves. In this way Chaucer neatly and completely refutes their poetics. Figurative language, even with pagan subject matter as here, is shown to be just as capable of conveying important truths as is literal language.

In his Knight's Tale, therefore, Chaucer has combined elements of the scholastic faculty structure, thinking process, and language use theories into his own, more realistic and more traditional, theory of universal psychology. In Chaucer's theory (as in Boethius's as implied in the *Consolatio*), the human mind is completely free, uses language to think with, and learns from thinking about its own individual experiences. New in Chaucer's theory, as contrasted to those of the scholastics, are the centering on human subjectivity and individual learning, and the inclusion of language as the medium of truly human thought.

The result is that Chaucer opens the *Canterbury Tales* with a story setting forth an important new THEORY of universal psychology—of the faculties and activities of the human mind and the language with which it thinks. In the rest of the *Tales*, I believe, among other things, he is TESTING this new theory against his own superlative understanding of how real people think and behave and of the social contexts in which they actually do exist.

Since this book is proposing an entirely new interpretation for the Knight's Tale, and as a result suggesting a new overall context in which to consider the *Canterbury Tales* as a whole, for clarity's sake let me offer here a brief, more deductive overview.

The title of this book is *Chaucer's Knight's Tale and Theories of Scholastic Psychology*. Scholastic psychologies were universal psychologies. That is to say, they were arrived at deductively, rather like universal grammars. A universal psychology reasons downward from prior notions about the nature of the Creator and his universe to what must therefore be the nature of the creatures who inhabit it. Scholastic universal psychologies concerned themselves with the human mind as bearing God's image and concentrated on the relationship to each other of the faculties of will and intellect. Thinking processes and ordinary language use not being part of their concept of God, they did not connect their theories about them to their theories of faculty psychology. Chaucer, however, makes this connection in the Knight's Tale. So far as I know, this is the first time that a theory just of the mind's faculties, of its processes, and of its language use is put together into a single comprehensive theory of universal *human* nature. For this reason, one sub-thesis of this book might well be recognition of Chaucer as an important scholastic thinker. His universal psychology is presented figuratively rather than literally, in fictional characterizations and descriptions rather than reasoned articles, but the concepts, the methods, and the scope of thinkers like Thomas Aquinas, John Duns Scotus, and William of Ockham are there in it, as well as, of course, the wisdom and concision of Boethius. The Knight's Tale, I will try to show, puts forward an abstract Chaucerian THEORY of universal psychology, one in which human beings are totally free in their minds and learn from their own experiences (including the stories they hear and read); and the rest of the *Canterbury Tales* as we have them, I will suggest, is still in the process of TESTING that theory out, of seeing how it needs to be qualified in order to accord with the dialogue and behavior of real people in the real world.

This book therefore proposes that the Knight's Tale has a two-fold focus: one centering on theories of human nature—Franciscan, Dominican, and Chaucerian; the other centering on theories of valid language use, whether literal alone or figurative as well. The two are not separate, of course: what is a human mind if not the language it uses? Notice that the *Canterbury Tales* as a whole has the same twofold focus: one on the human natures of the pilgrims; the other on the language use in the links and in their tales.

"Allegory" is not the right term for what Chaucer is doing here in the Knight's Tale. Nor is "irony." Veil and truth, husk and kernel, shell and nut, rind and fruit, bone and marrow—these are the familiar terms used to indicate figurative and literal; but, unfortunately, they all imply that once it has been removed, the outer member of the pair is without value. This is not true in the Knight's Tale. Moreover, they can imply that the inner member of the pair is more creatively inferred by the reader than deliberately implied by the writer. This too is not true in the Knight's Tale. Perhaps embedded is the apter term. The Knight's Tale is constructed somewhat like this Escher print of a woodland pond (fig. 1). The brilliant autumn leaves on the surface of the water are the pagan romance surface of the Knight's Tale; the theories of human nature and language use taken together are the shadowy fish below.

Figure 1. M. C. Escher. *Three Worlds*, 1955. Lithograph.

Both leaves and fish are there in the print; both pagan story and scholastic/Chaucerian theories are there in the tale. I believe many among Chaucer's own audience would have seen both.

Further, the Knight's Tale is an extraordinarily rich piece of writing. There is much more in it than this book can even refer to, much less discuss. For reasons of space I am able to do next to nothing here with mythography, with courtly love, or with source studies in Statius and Boccaccio, all fruitful contexts for considering the Knight's Tale. Rather, my purpose here is solely to explicate the use and extensions Chaucer makes in this first *Canterbury* tale of concepts and methods from the formal scholastic philosophy of his own time, concepts and methods that were, I believe (no doubt on varying levels of expertise), well known to many members of his own audience. For my part, I assume my own audience knows the Knight's Tale well—the pagan story of the two young lovers, the descriptions of the temples and champions and Saturn's self-description, and Theseus's efforts to understand and assert some kind of meaning in the universe (also no doubt on varying levels of expertise). From the Knight's Tale the modern reader can learn much that is rich and relevant and satisfying about theories of human nature and language use, and, as a result, about human nature itself and language use itself.

In Chaucer's time, English culture was undergoing profound changes. Many are reflected in the *Canterbury Tales*, as seen through the eyes, language, and values of one of the truly great minds and greatest poets of the Western world. With the tale assigned to his Knight, Chaucer provides for the *Canterbury Tales* collection a traditional, Christian-humanist beginning, as thematically significant as its equally traditional penitential ending. In the first tale human beings are shown that, at least in theory, they are totally free to choose; in the last tale they are shown that, regardless of theory, they must choose. Of all the issues embodied in the Knight's Tale, metaphysical freedom is the most important to Chaucer: freedom of thought, freedom of language use, and (the freedom that cannot exist without them) freedom to choose to be better.

SECTION I

Introduction

Most readers today find the Knight's Tale deeply disturbing—both in itself and in the larger context in which Chaucer places it, as the lead-off tale in his great *Canterbury* collection. In itself, the tale is a paean to suffering and injustice. Two young knights fall in love with the same lady; both suffer for years; a tournament is declared to decide between them; the winner dies horribly and the loser finally marries the lady. The injustice is appalling; innocent people endure constant pain, affliction, and sorrow; and yet, now and then, in the very midst of telling us this stark, blighted story, the knightly narrator inexplicably offers us capricious asides and flippant dismissals that seem to undercut the importance of whatever point he is trying to make about the governance of all things in this wretched world. By itself, the tale is disturbing. And in its larger context as the first of the *Canterbury Tales,* it presents problems of interpretation so formidable they are rarely addressed. Why would the greatest of Middle English poets, a Christian by all accounts, a man trusted and respected by the most powerful figures of his day, a man ordinarily of a sunny, affirmative disposition, a man who greatly admired Dante and who translated Boethius, why would a man such as this give pride of place in the major work of his last twenty years to a story such as this? It doesn't make sense.

The aim of this book is to suggest a new understanding of the Knight's Tale and, as a result, of the beginning of the *Canterbury Tales* as a whole. Chaucer has several purposes in the Knight's Tale. One is a discussion of theories of human nature in this world. Another is a witty and rigorous defense of pagan poetry and, therefore, of all poetry. And there are more. Chaucer's Knight's Tale is high Gothic art at its best—complicated, intellectually intricate, and didactic, crafted with philosophical elegance on the one hand, and good common sense on the other.

The tale's most noteworthy feature, given its romance frame, is its triangle of speech-making characters: Palamon and Arcite forming opposite corners at the base; Theseus standing in judgment at the apex. In this inner three-part form—balanced, orderly, and impartial; the paired protagonists taking turns and speaking at length without interruption; Theseus rendering judgment from a higher level—in this highly rhetorical triangle of characters, more than any other genre the Knight's Tale resembles a university disputation, with a debate at the base and its resolution at the apex. The subject matter of the debate is rival theories of scholastic faculty psychology; the resolution at the apex is Chaucerian.

The tale's second most noteworthy feature, after its triangle of characterizations, is the striking group of long static descriptions clustered in Part III—descriptions of the temples of Venus, Mars, and Diana, of the champions Lygurge and Emetreus, and Saturn's self-description. These six passages form an ordered sequence of scholastic definitions of human thinking processes, presented not literally but figuratively, in the form of university *sophismata,* so as to force their reader to experience vicariously the thinking processes they are defining. The first five definitions are scholastic; the sixth, Saturn's monologue, is their Chaucerian resolution.

Thus, embedded in the Knight's pagan romance is a scholastic inquiry into universal human nature, into the structuring of its faculties and the activities of its mind. Moreover, the two layers—pagan frame and embedded scholastic grafts—taken together constitute a formal disproof of the scholastic denigration of poetry. Rather than lies, here at the beginning of the *Canterbury Tales* is a pagan fiction (the story of Theseus, Arcite, and Palamon) that contains well-known and rigorously demonstrated scholastic truths (the various psychological theories). As a result, the two layers together would have presented any anti-poetry scholastic of Chaucer's time with a wonderfully disabling *insoluble*—either he admit pagan poetry can veil certain truth or he deny his own logical demonstrations. Chaucer leaves him no way to wiggle out.

This is a new paradigm for the Knight's Tale. It establishes a humanist beginning for the *Canterbury Tales,* just as the Parson's Prologue and Tale and Chaucer's Retraction, taken together, establish a penitential ending. Further, it establishes Chaucer as both more polemical and more theoretically minded than, at least until recently, we have been accustomed to think him. The Knight's Tale is a spirited defense of poesy, of the great poems of pagan antiquity and of figurative language use in general, set forth in the concepts of Chaucer's own time. It is at the same time, and equally, a brilliant philosophical presentation of the later medieval theories about the three different kinds of human nature that seem to have always been with us, at least in the West—the intellectualist (Aquinas), the voluntarist (Franciscan), and the humanist (Chaucer).

The purpose of this introductory section is to provide the reader with an overview of the relevant literary, historical, and psychological background for the close look at the Knight's Tale and the Knight himself which comprises the body of this book. This section, therefore, first surveys the present state of Knight's Tale scholarship and the tale's mixture of genres. Then it summarizes the later medieval conflict between humanist and scholastic, outlines later medieval psychological theory, and suggests some implications of this new Knight's Tale paradigm for the *Canterbury Tales* as a whole. It concludes with a brief chapter-by-chapter summary and comments on documentation, terminology, style, and critical theory.

RECENT SCHOLARSHIP

Interpretation of Chaucer's Knight's Tale has been a major activity in twentieth-century literary criticism for two reasons: First, the importance of the tale itself—it is one of Chaucer's longest, most carefully wrought, most philosophical, and, at least on the surface, most serious poems. And second, its placement as the very first tale in the *Canterbury* series—one naturally assumes it will set some sort of thematic context for all the tales and links to follow. For both of these reasons, the Knight's Tale has generated an enormous amount of commentary, much of it very good, some of it of scholarly value far beyond its immediate occasion in the tale itself. One thinks, for example, of John Reidy's eloquent discussion of the background and character development of Theseus, of Peter Elbow's perceptive explication of Chaucerian thought patterns, and of Alan Gaylord's thoughtful and sensible evaluation of the commentary not only on Saturn but on the tale as a whole. Chaucer has been most fortunate in his twentieth-century critics. As a result, in order to make the scholarship more easily accessible, I have organized it by topics—Palamon and Arcite, Emelye, Theseus, the temples, the champions, Saturn, the Knight—and review summaries of the literature on each appear early in the discussion and notes of the appropriate chapters. Since Monica McAlpine's annotated Knight's Tale bibliography will be out shortly, in this introduction my intent is to provide only a brief historical summary of main trends and a sketch of recent work. The summary will also help suggest the problems created by inadequate genre identification, and the sketch will suggest that genre identification is already changing.

In the twentieth century, overall, there have been two interpretative paradigms for the Knight's Tale, the first emphasizing the rivalry of its two young knights, the second emphasizing its orderly structuring. Up until 1949–50, the tale was generally considered to be the story of two knights competing for the same fair lady, and differentiation (or lack of it) between the two was the major critical issue. Early critics like Hoxie Neale Fairchild, Albert Marckwardt, Howard Patch, and J. S. P. Tatlock argued for the most part from instances of psychological realism they found in the text, but since this kind of evidence supported radically conflicting interpretations, it finally became clear that whatever the basis of differentiation was, it was not simply realistic. In 1949–50, with the landmark articles of William Frost and Charles Muscatine, critical attention turned away from the tale's protagonists to focus on its philosophical implications and underlying form. The point of the tale became the order (or lack of it) manifested in its narrative structure and the efforts of Theseus to maintain that order. In the almost forty years since then, a number of critics, although agreeing generally with the structuralist approach, have nevertheless continued to raise the problem of the tale's content—especially the injustice of its ending, the winner dead, the loser blissfully serving Emelye. A few, like Bernard Huppé and D. W. Robertson, Jr., point to the exaggerations, flippant lines, and comic deflations as evidence that, rather than serious, the poem is intellectually comedic. The majority, however, like Joseph Westlund, E. Talbot Donaldson, T. K. Meier, and P. M. Kean, find the principle of order in the poem outweighed by its sense of oppression. Some of these critics argue that the tale is profoundly pessimistic, that it asserts a theme of "divine callousness, even divine injustice."

The most eloquent expression of this bleak view is that of Elizabeth Salter, who stresses the tale's strange, unresolved, double vision, of both darkness and radiance:

> [O]ne of the basic themes of the poem [is] the darkness and suffering which exist at the very centre of [its] radiant chivalric world. . . . The poem portrays many aspects of Athenian life with confident exuberance, [but] it also looks intently at the darker implications of divine and human affairs. . . . Questions are raised about universal order and justice in words of uncomfortable exactness. . . . [In short, Chaucer's] portrayal of the sinister gods and their tormented creatures takes in not only the characters and immediate issues of the *Tale* but the whole human condition: we recall the enlarged scope of the paintings in the temple of Mars, and Saturn's cold revelation of limitless power. This portrayal is so memorably done that it becomes very difficult for us to respond uncritically either to a philosophic statement which largely ignores the prominent issue of divine malice or to a happy ending which gives little sign of recognising the unhappiness it builds upon.[1]

When the genre of the Knight's Tale is taken to be pagan romance, with characterizations intended mimetically and descriptions intended symbolically, Salter's view is certainly just. It seems an odd, deeply disturbing poem. In fact, however, exactly the same questions Salter raises about the Knight's Tale would doubtless be raised about the *Aeneid* had it too been written by a later medieval poet living in a Christian culture. The *Aeneid* too puts forward an unresolved double vision: of darkness, suffering, and divine malevolence on the one hand, and of human courage, endurance, achievement, and transcendence on the other. For that matter, the *Metamorphoses* too, from the Christian point of view, puts forward the same unresolved double vision: of unjust human suffering and divine irresponsibility, and yet of sunlight, gaiety, affection, and love as well. In short, the unresolved double vision that pervades the world of pagan literature generally also pervades the Knight's Tale when it is read literally, as a pagan romance.

This "unresolved double vision" has been for many years the reigning interpretive paradigm for the Knight's Tale, whether optimistic as in Muscatine's persuasive rendering or pessimistic as in Salter's extraordinarily sensitive one. Interpretations within this paradigm always feature some kind of dialectic between order and disorder. According to this view, the Knight's Tale characterizations are flat, the dramatics poor, and the plot not worth close scrutiny, of interest for its symbolic ups-and-downs rather than its particular events.[2] In this view, what is noteworthy about the tale is not its elements themselves, but their extraordinary regularity. Among the lasting benefits of this present paradigm have been its focus on Theseus and its emphasis on order as a cultural value. However, criticism is a matter of trade-offs, and here the trade-off has been neglect of the characters and development of the two young knights. One problem with structuralist interpretations in any field, whether anthropology or psychology or literature as here, is that in going behind surface complexities to get at those underlying cultural regularities, all the vivid particularizing details and moment-by-moment changes in the surface subject matter are leveled out. Recent Knight's Tale scholarship, however, has been either rejecting the structuralist order/disorder reading completely or moving away from it, into the tale's immediate historical context, as with D. W. Robertson and Paul Olson, or—my interest here—into philosophical psychology.

Two recent interpretations that simply reject the order/disorder

format outright are those of Terry Jones and Larry Sklute. For
Jones, who reads every item in the Knight's General Prologue
portrait ironically, Chaucer's Knight is a "shabby mercenary without morals or scruples" and as a result his tale is a dark, disturbing
piece, a "hymn to tyranny."[3] For Sklute, on the other hand, who
takes the details of the Knight's portrait literally, the Knight is one
of Chaucer's "morally ideal characters," and the atttitude toward
the world revealed in his tale is "noble"; the tale itself is in some
ways an epic with "elevated philosophic concerns," and in other
ways "a comedy, cautiously optimistic about man's power to figure
out, and in some ways to control, his own destiny."[4] Thus whereas
Jones subverts the present paradigm with irony, Sklute simply
ignores it.

Three recent critics still within the order/disorder paradigm
but moving away from objectivity into the nature, needs, and
perceptions of the inward human mind, into psychology, are Helen
Cooper, Judith Ferster, and V. A. Kolve. For Cooper, Chaucer's
concern is finally epistemological. For her, the Knight's Tale is the
perfect introduction to the *Canterbury Tales* because it presents the
immense issues "not as complete themes" but as questions which
open out in many directions in the tales that follow it. She concludes
her book with a *Canterbury* world in which "the most one can
achieve is a series of partial and contingent truths, expressed in
fallible language—human truths, not divine."[5] In her view, Chaucer deliberately keeps open as many questions as possible in order
to keep everything full of significance, significances which spill
over into each other, however, and are finally inexpressible because
outward words are inadequate. For Ferster, on the other hand,
Chaucer focuses in all his works on problems of interpretation,
problems caused by the tension between inward self-interest and
outward linkage with others. In the Knight's Tale, Chaucer ex-
plores the paradox of the way selves "isolated from each other"
interpret and thus "define each other." She sees Chaucer himself
caught up, as we all are, in a perpetual process of "interpretive
tangles."[6] For Kolve too, Chaucer's concern is mostly with matters
of mind, like Cooper with epistemology and Ferster with hermeneutics, but Kolve includes freedom as well. Writing within the

order/disorder paradigm, he takes an interdisciplinary tack, exploring Chaucer's use in the Fragment I stories of traditional images from the visual arts. Unlike the other two, he regards the pagan Knight's Tale as a "strange choice" for beginning the pilgrimage, but at length decides it must have been chosen precisely for its exclusion of Christian material. He reads the human need for freedom as one of the tale's motifs: "The two young knights fall in love with Emelye for her beauty, unmistakably, but for the beauty of her freedom most of all." For Kolve, "central to man's nature as it is conceived in this poem are his need to seek freedom and his need to seek love."[7] Thus these three critics, all three starting from the objective structuralist reading, have wound up to some degree inside the mind, with epistemology, with hermeneutics, and with the universal human need for freedom and love.

GENRES

When expert interpreters disagree to the remarkable extent just exemplified by over sixty years of Knight's Tale criticism, the likely reason, suggests E. D. Hirsch, Jr., is widely differing conceptions of a text's genre:

> An interpreter's notion of the type of meaning he confronts will powerfully influence his understanding of details. This phenomenon will recur at every level of sophistication and is the primary reason for disagreements among qualified interpreters.[8]

With respect to genres in medieval literature, which ordinarily come mixed or nested rather than pure, Hirsch's case may be somewhat overstated, but his point is certainly valid: because details become significant only when perceived in a context, proper generic identification is necessary if one wants to "see" the details that are there in a text to be seen.

The Knight's Tale is ordinarily spoken of as a romance. It features knights, love, a lady, a combat, a tournament, a glamorous far-distant setting, and an element of the supernatural. Occasionally, of course, commentators have spoken of its "allegorical implications," or its epic qualities, or its unromantic didacticism, or have referred to it instead as a "pageant" or something akin to a "morality play" or to its style as suitable for a "scholastic quibble."[9] But most of them, and I think most of us, still basically think of and refer to it as a romance, which it most certainly is.[10] At the same time, however, it is a good deal more. The role of its heroine has been reduced, and what has been foregrounded instead is the rivalry of its two young protagonists, not their love of the lady. In fact, one sees very little of the lady in the Knight's Tale. As a result, there is no courting, no dalliance, not one furtive glance or secret meeting. Moreover, there is no real adventure in the Knight's Tale—not a dragon, giant, Saracen, wandering knight, rudderless boat, magic sword, not even a roadside hermit. There are no feats of prodigious bravery, no marvelous conversions, no kidnappings, no stepmothers, no transformations, no great heroics of any kind. Instead, in the place of all these medieval romance conventions, the Knight's Tale features *(a)* some very long speeches and *(b)* some very static descriptions. Given that the larger genre of the Knight's Tale is romance, in these long speeches and static descriptions, I will try to show, Chaucer's primary concern is psychology, the subject area most discussed by the early Knight's Tale critics and raised again most recently by Cooper, Ferster, and Kolve.

In terms of their genres, this book will argue, the three central characterizations of Palamon, Arcite, and Theseus form, within the romance narrative, an embedded university *disputatio*; the six long descriptions in Part III form, within the romance narrative, an embedded sequence of scholastic *sophismata*. Both of these forms were well-known scholastic teaching genres. Often they took place together, the question under dispute being itself a *sophisma*.

First, with regard to the *disputatio,* in the medieval universities from the twelfth century to at least the sixteenth, the two major teaching techniques were the lecture and the disputation. Held perhaps as often as weekly, disputations were "an integral part" of the university curriculum on both undergraduate and graduate levels.[11] Audiences of other students and masters were present, and often a secretary recorded the proceedings (these are the *quaestiones disputatae,* so many of which have come down to us). Ordinarily, a disputation took place over two separated days. On the first day, the master would put up the question to be disputed and possibly give some brief arguments on both sides. Then the bachelor or student would accept and reply to arguments from the audience; or possibly he would offer his own solutions to the question along with arguments refuting the opposing view; and then possibly the master would attack these, the student would reply, and so on possibly again. This first day of the disputation procedure appears to have been quite flexible. Several days later, the second day of the disputation would be held—and here is the point about Chaucer's structuring of the three Knight's Tale characterizations—on this second day, the master would first summarize the positions *pro* and *contra* on the question being disputed, and then he himself would give his own overall solution, his *determinatio*. This university disputation format of question, arguments on two opposing sides, and then resolution seems to have developed out of the needs of the early lecture system to resolve conflicts in textual interpretation (conflicts most famously associated with Abelard but already being formalized before the *Sic et non*). The influence of the disputation format on medieval philosophical literature was enormous: many summas and commentaries were organized analytically into questions (rather than, say, Boethian dialogues or essays or sequential glosses), often with subsidiary articles; frequently each subsidiary article would also be structured like a miniature disputation, starting with the point at issue, then several arguments against the position to be adopted, then an authority in favor of it (*sed contra*), then the central section corresponding to the master's determination (*respondeo*), and lastly some answers to objections. The purpose of these medieval disputations was, at least in principle, not to prove a particular thesis, but to teach students how to harmonize conflicting authorities in order to find truth. The disputation was, thus, a teaching genre. In the Knight's Tale, Chaucer embodies the two conflicting scholastic theories of faculty psychology in his characterizations of Palamon and Arcite, and then puts forth his own harmonizing humanist *determinato* in the characterization of Theseus.

And second, with regard to the ordered sequence of *sophismata* that form the long descriptive passages of Part III, recall that in medieval times, scientific methodology was conceptual and verbal, whether dealing with ethics, with optics, or with physics and mechanics. *Sophismata* were test-case examples, in the form of sentences, which were used by medieval philosophers to gain conceptual entry into abstract problems, usually of metaphysics or natural philosophy. They functioned somewhat like the "thought experiments" of Wittgenstein and Russell. The interest of the sentence lay not in the subject matter expressed, but in the problem which its expression brought to light. Here, from Norman Kretzmann, is an example of a *sophisma* commented on by a number of medieval philosophers.

> The sophisma '*Totus Socrates est minor Socrate.*'
> The Whole Socrates is Less than Socrates.
> Proof. Socrates's foot is less than Socrates, Socrates's head is less than Socrates, and so on as regards his integral parts; therefore each part of Socrates is less than Socrates, and so the whole Socrates is less than Socrates.
> Disproof. The whole Socrates is less than Socrates, but the whole Socrates is Socrates; therefore Socrates is less than Socrates—which is absurd.[12]

For the scholastics, Kretzmann shows, despite its "unpromising appearance," this *sophisma* contained "hidden depths": it exposed problems of at least three types: ambiguity in the use of 'totus', change of subject term (from 'Socrates' to 'part of Socrates'), and ambiguity in the discussion of 'pars,' which can be quantitative or qualitative (e.g., form and matter). Notice that the meaning of this *sophisma* to its own audience had absolutely nothing to do with its subject matter—here it is Socrates, but it could just as well be you, me, or the neighbor's dog. The purpose of the form is its test-case function, and—here comes the point about Chaucer's Part III descriptions—in this genre of writing, the subject matter has one meaning, and the particular way it is expressed has a second, quite different, test-case meaning. In Part III of the Knight's Tale, the first five descriptions (Venus, Mars, Diana, Lygurge, Emetreus) are extended *sophismata* whose subject matter is pagan romance but whose expression test-cases scholastic theories about the thinking processes of the human mind. The sixth description is an extended *sophisma* whose subject matter is Saturn but whose expression test-cases a humanist Chaucerian theory about thinking processes.

In the twentieth century, combining the two unfamiliar-to-us scholastic forms may seem complicated, but in the medieval universities they were in fact closely associated and often combined.[13] Their combination here in the Knight's Tale becomes easily intelligible if one thinks of the two embedded scholastic genres as shaped like the floor plan of a Gothic cathedral, with the *disputatio* characterizations of Palamon and Arcite developing down the two side aisles and that of Theseus developing down the higher central nave; and the Part III *sophismata* descriptions, so different in subject matter and style, cutting across them like a transept. Since Chaucer used the same cruciform shape in the Parson's Tale, inserting the long Seven Sins passage between the shorter penitential passages at beginning and end, perhaps he felt the cruciform shape was a good way to bring together two disparate but closely related subjects. In any event, I will be using the shape to structure my discussion of the Knight's Tale, first the *disputatio* on faculty psychology down the center in Section II, and then the *sophismata* on thinking acts and language use separately in Section III.

In terms of its overall genre, therefore, this new interpretation of the Knight's Tale suggests that the tale is a hybrid, consisting of

(a) a pagan romance story, in which has been embedded
(b) a pair of well-known scholastic teaching forms, one a disputation on faculty psychology and the other a sequence of *sophismata* on human thinking processes.

Further, just as Chaucer took the standard folk genres of fabliau and beast fable and in the *Canterbury Tales* transformed them into great literature, so too with the two scholastic teaching genres. The highest questions of philosophy are the nature of ethics, the nature of freedom, the nature of knowledge, and, perhaps highest of all since it subsumes the others, the nature of the human mind. Chaucer takes the two scholastic teaching genres, which by his time were ordinarily utilized for narrowly technical, forbiddingly arcane, academic exercises, and elevates them into great literature: directly so, in that they put forward a serious discussion of the highest, most noble human concerns; and indirectly so, in that their presence embedded within a pagan romance story constitutes a devastating defense of the figurative language use the scholastics so often attacked. Thus the larger context of the Knight's Tale and the *Canterbury Tales* is Chaucer's own world: a world in which traditional Christian humanism with its traditional ethically oriented focus on individual choice and behavior had been undergoing disparagement for at least a hundred years by the new scientifically oriented scholastics, with their focus on objective logic, speculative metaphysics, and universal causation.

Historical Context

HUMANISM AND SCHOLASTICISM

Renaissance humanism arose suddenly during the second half of the fourteenth century in Italy, whence it spread north and west throughout Europe ejecting all things barbarous and medieval, or so it used to be said. This new humanism stood for the revival of man's ancient rational freedoms (one seldom reads of woman in this context[14]), his freedom to act for himself within nature and society, his freedom to change things if he wished and to make them better. This new humanism rejected asceticism in favor of the active life, rejected metaphysics and physics in favor of moral philosophy, and rejected the arid technical language of the university scholastics in favor of a revival of eloquence. It replaced the old figural sense of time with a new historical perspective; and, recognizing that pagan philosophy and traditional practical Christianity proceeded from the same divine Logos, it replaced narrow Gothic superstition with a more traditional, more ethically oriented Christian piety. All of this used to be thought of as a great new flowering, a sudden rebirth, a re-naissance. Recently, however, scholars have shown that all these humanist touchstones were simply not that new. An emphasis on rationality, on human freedom and responsibility, on moral philosophy, on rhetoric, on historical perspective, and on traditional pastoral Christianity had all been around for a very long time.

R. W. Southern, for example, has shown that if humanism means a strong sense of human dignity, a belief that nature is orderly and the universe intelligible, and a confidence that human reason can understand them both, then the years 1100–1320 were among "the great ages of humanism in the history of Europe." Indeed, on these criteria, according to Southern, Aquinas's two *summae* "mark the highest point of medieval humanism. . . . [E]verywhere [Aquinas] points to the natural perfection of man, his natural rights, and the power of his natural reason. The dignity of human nature is not simply a poetic vision; it has become a central truth of philosophy."[15] In fourteenth-century England, so far as one can tell from its literature, Boethius, Cicero, Quintilian, Macrobius, Virgil, and Ovid were still being read, even if Aristotelian science and method had taken over at the universities. One does not think of Langland and the *Pearl* Poet as Renaissance humanists, yet they both rejected metaphysics for practical theology and rejected the dry scholastic literary style for fictions and eloquence. Langland saves the virtuous pagan, the *Pearl* Poet probably did, and neither seems ascetic. Chaucer too touches all these humanist bases, yet one does not ordinarily think of him as a Renaissance writer. Clearly, humanism in England, and apparently elsewhere in Europe, long predated what we now think of as "the Renaissance."

Further, Concetta Greenfield and others have demonstrated that, although major changes obviously did take place in Italy during the fourteenth century, the battle between humanists and Aristotelian scholastics did not constitute a sudden first eruption by humanists against everything medieval. Rather, it was simply a new phase in a very old war, a phase concentrated once again, as in antiquity, on poetry.[16] During the later medieval period, because of their differing conceptions of theology and philosophy and the differing conceptions of language and truth these entailed, the discipline of *poetica* became a central battleground between the two sides. For both, poetics included not just writing and reading poems in Latin, but also, and much more importantly, reading and interpreting the poems of the ancient pagans. The question was as to their value.

Were Virgil and Ovid to be treasured for their figurative truths or disparaged for their literal lies?

The poetics of the humanists were rooted in the rhetorical, Neoplatonic, and patristic traditions, traditions that emphasized eloquence, moral philosophy, and the inward experience of well-known spiritual truths. These traditions included the notion of poet-as-prophet (divinely inspired), the notion of poet-as-theologian (i.e., as one who writes about myth and sacred allegory—it was in this sense that Virgil and Dante were termed theologians), and the notion of poet-as-philosopher (i.e., as one who possesses great encyclopedic knowledge which he dispenses cloaked in allegory—it was in this sense that Homer and Virgil were termed philosophers). The humanists laid great stress on the fact that scripture and poetry alike utilize figurative language, interpreting this as an indication of their common source. Indeed, Petrarch went so far as to identify poetry and theology:

> Poetics is not very different from theology. Are you amazed?
> Actually I could easily say that theology is that form of poetics
> concerning itself with the godhead. Christ is described now
> as a lion, now as a worm, and is this not a form of poetry?
> It would be a long matter to enumerate all the other similar
> images which can be found in Scripture.[17]

The scholastics, on the other hand, valued poetry much cheaper. Scholasticism was above all rational, and therefore—necessarily—literal. Scholastic methodology consisted of rigorous verbal analysis by means of a semantically based, and therefore determinedly literal, logic. According to these thinkers, not only philosophical but even some theological truths could and therefore should be demonstrated logically rather than simply accepted on faith (for example, the existence, the omnipotence, and the infinity of God). It was the medieval scholastics who, following Aristotle's own style, pared both philosophy and theology down from the semi-fictional poetic dialogue form of Plato and Boethius to the generally literal-minded, logically argued, technically oriented disciplines they remain today. The scholastics rejected metaphoric language and allegorical interpretation as uncertain of meaning and therefore irrational. Scriptural poetry posing an obvious problem, they designated it a special *supra*-rational case. They held that the goal of philosophy and theology was to provide objectively certain, rational answers to questions about being and causes ("causes" in the wide Aristotelian sense of material, efficient, formal, and final). Because the myths and figures of poets support multiple interpretations, they do not provide such answers. Poetry therefore is not scientifically acceptable. Aquinas, for example, although he allowed poetry a moral function, interpreted an unclear statement of Aristotle to mean that because the argument of poetry is not rational, poetry therefore consists of false inventions—"poets are liars."[18] He regarded polysemous biblical interpretation as a special case because in the Bible both things and words have literal meaning;[19] but in secular poetry, he held, only the words have meaning so only their literal sense is objectively there in the text. In Aquinas's system of science, poetry contains the least truth because it functions nonrationally; it therefore constitutes the lowest form of logic and is useful mainly for decoration.[20] Beautiful, perhaps. Pleasantly diverting, possibly. But cognitively useless.

What we have here in this fourteenth-century war over words between humanist and scholastic are two different ways of using language (figurative versus literal) in order to achieve two different kinds of truth (personal versus objective). On the one hand, poetic allegory (the *Aeneid*, the *Thebaid*, the *Metamorphoses*) leads to the truth of inner psychological conviction. The reader enjoys the fiction, ponders it, penetrates its veil by interpretation, and discovers for himself or herself subjectively a new understanding of some traditional moral or spiritual truth. On the other hand, scholastic argument (a *summa*, a commentary on the *Sentences*, a *quodlibet*) leads to the truth of objective scientific demonstration. The scholastic compares his authorities, divides and combines his subject matter, works over his syllogisms and propositions, and discovers some new, previously unrecognized truth about the divine nature or creation. The humanist poet hopes to influence the mind and thereby the behavior of his individual reader; the scholastic scientist hopes to find and demonstrate objectively to his colleagues some new universal fact. Obviously, two different value systems and two different notions of knowledge and truth are at work here. The humanist values the inward ethical kind of knowledge that must be developed over and over again anew, by each individual, in every generation.[21] The scholastic values the factual "expert" kind of knowledge that can be accumulated and built upon by succeeding generations.

Between scholasticism, with its focus on universal abstractions, and humanism, with its focus on individual human beings, the possibility for conflict always exists. Scholasticism reasons about being in general; humanism develops the individual. Scholasticism dissociates itself from the life around it, goes off separately, away from distractions, and focuses on some component of the life left behind (a concept, an object, a process, or a being). Scholasticism then takes that component out of its natural context and subjects it to intense rational analysis, dividing it up into its constituent parts and scrutinizing them acutely, combining its parts in new and unexpected ways, considering them in unprecedented contexts, trying always to discover the general rules by which this particular component exists and functions. Medieval scholasticism is simply one kind of scholasticism. It busied itself abstracting and analyzing metaphysical concepts. Indeed, modern science is simply another kind of scholasticism, busy abstracting physical rather than metaphysical concepts. For that matter, a good part of modern literary theory is simply another kind of scholasticism, attempting to discover the general laws of genre, of closure, of ambiguity, or of the reading or writing process. Humanism, on the other hand, centers itself on promoting the development of the individual human being. As a result, rather than existing as unchanging universal, humanism is always shaped by the particular social context in which it exists. Whether Greek or medieval Christian or Renaissance or twentieth-century Western, humanisms begin and end focused on developing the individual human being, living, learning, and functioning within a particular social setting. Greek humanism focused on perfecting oneself physically and intellectually because those were central concerns of Greek culture. Medieval humanism focused on individual free will and intelligent choice of the good because those were central concerns of medieval Christian culture. Renaissance humanism focused on personal piety, ethics, and classical languages because those were central concerns of its culture. And until recently, twentieth-century Western humanism has focused on the greatest material good for the greatest number because those have been two central concerns of our culture. (Today, when some theorists assert that humanism is dying, what they really mean is that the focus of contemporary humanism is changing as the central concerns of our culture are changing.) But always, whereas the goal of the scholastic scientist is to *discover* a universal nature or law, the goal of the humanist is to *foster* the development of individuals. It is not a simple either/or opposition between these two. Rather, the question is primacy. Which is more important, ballet or the ballerina? the rules of the game or the individual player? Given that both have value, which is or should be subordinated to which?

MEDIEVAL PSYCHOLOGY

In the later medieval period, expressing these two very different sets of priorities were three competing hypotheses/notions/theories as to the innate nature of the individual human mind. As touched on earlier, these theories were universal psychologies. Of these three universal psychologies, two were scholastic (one intellectualist, the other voluntarist), and one was traditional Christian humanist.

First, several definitions. The term "mind" is used here and throughout this book to designate holistically that conscious entity in all human beings which perceives, imagines, reasons, wills, believes, loves, feels, and remembers, that same entity which medieval Christians usually termed "soul" and regarded as immaterial and immortal.[22] In the medieval context, "mind" and "human nature" mean pretty much the same thing, and so the terms will be used fairly interchangeably. Next, the term "psychology" is used to designate systematic studies of and theories about such entities. The term "universal psychology," however, is used to designate psychological theories at a much deeper, much more abstract level than we are ordinarily familiar with today. A universal psychology is very speculative. In principle, it is indifferent to surface particularizations of any kind. It has no concern with the nature or behavior of individuals or groups *per se,* and no concern with predicting local patterns of behavior or development or cause and effect or any such superficial surface-level manifestations or regularities. Instead, it reasons downward, for the most part, from *a priori* assumptions about the nature of reality itself to what the nature of man must therefore be. For example, man being made in God's image, what therefore must he be? What therefore are his powers? What his desires? And what, given the Fall, are his deficiencies and lacks? The object of a universal psychology is a complete theory of man, universal and timeless.[23]

In the twentieth century, by way of comparison, although we have had no universal psychologies, we have had several major approaches toward one—Freudianism, with its focus on the dynamics of the unconscious (but exclusion of cognition); Behaviorism, with its focus on outward measurable behavior (but exclusion of inward thinking, imagining, and feeling); and now Cognitive Psychology, with its focus on knowing processes (but exclusion of emotional and ethical considerations). None, so far as I know, has claimed to be a complete theory of human nature.[24] In the fourteenth century, on the other hand, the speculative situation was far richer. Inspired by the notion that man was made in God's image, every major thinker seems to have had a theory of universal psychology. Indeed, every thoughtful Christian person, simply by reason of his or her spiritual beliefs, must have had at least the rudiments of such a theory. Here we will be concerned only with the three most representative and important: the two major *scholastic* theories, intellectualist and voluntarist, well attested in the works of Aquinas, Scotus, Ockham, and other such thinkers; and the equally major *humanist* theory, apparently derived from traditional Christian humanist values and then worked out in scholastic concepts and put forward by Chaucer in the Knight's Tale, the theory it is the purpose of this book to demonstrate.

In the later medieval period, everybody seems to have been interested in the nature of the human mind. And with good reason. In the Platonic tradition, the mind was to the body as the pilot to the ship; in the Aristotelian tradition, the mind was the body's animating form. As a result, in both traditions, everything the body did outwardly—how it looked, how it spoke, how it behaved—was an output and therefore a revelation of the inward mind. Further, in the Christian tradition, the mind bears God's image. By coming to an understanding of one's own mind and the minds of others, therefore, one can come closer to God. And not only that, the mind is intrinsically interesting in itself. It is what makes others interesting to us, and us interesting to others. In short, with its richness and complexity, its invention and unpredictability, as an object for investigation the human mind has no rival. Seventeenth-century science began the slow turn away from mind to focus on physical matter for many of the same reasons seventeenth-century literature and art began the slow turn away from complexity to focus on unity, one of which was absolute frustration. The mind was too complex. It refused to be pinned down. For people like Descartes, Bacon, and Locke, dealing with the simple, self-evident, and measurable came to seem much more sensible. It promised to be more productive. Only now, in the later twentieth century, with the development of quantum physics and recognition of physical complexity and with the acceptance of universal uncertainty and nonmaterial fields, is the complexity of the cognitive mind again being studied with the fervor it received in the fourteenth century from humanist and scholastic alike.

In figurative literature, exploration of the mind for its own sake appears as early as Chrétien's romances and constitutes the major action of the *Roman de la Rose*. In the rhetorically-centered literature of Chaucer's own time, humanistic theories of mind can be inferred inductively from the dream visions, debates, fabliaux, and romances; indeed, much of twentieth-century literary criticism consists simply of theories as to what kinds of people the characters in these works represent, what are their motives, aspirations, beliefs, moral qualities, and the like; that is, what are their minds? The mind of the dreamer is the central ground in *Piers Plowman* and in *Pearl*. The personalities of the characters is the central focus in *Troilus and Criseyde*.

In scholastic literature, likewise, systematic exploration of the mind begins again at about the same time and produces a great body of speculation. Summing up the "scientific" writing of John of Salisbury, of Abelard, and of the twelfth-century Victorines, for example, Wilhelm Windelband concluded that

> the empirical impulse of the Middle Ages directed its activity to the investigation of the mental life, and unfolded the full energy of real observation and acute analysis in the domain of inner experience—in *psychology*. This is the field of scientific work in which the Middle Ages attained the most valuable results.[25]

Indeed, in the thirteenth century, far more than half of Aquinas's *Summa* is devoted to human psychology—to man's created nature, perception, intellect, acts, passions, habits, virtues and vices and sins, to his religion, his future, his kinds of life, to the sacraments instituted for his benefit and to what he receives from them. The position that from the time of Augustine until the fifteenth century the most valuable and most interesting scientific work produced in the Christian West—i.e., valuable and interesting in living, twentieth-century terms—was its work on universal psychology could, I think, be easily defended.

Today, when one considers the human mind analytically, one naturally thinks in terms of three components: its structure, its processes, and the input/output materials on which it operates. When these three components are converted into the concepts of later medieval psychology, they correspond to the mind's *faculties* (i.e., structuring, the subject of Section II), its *acts* (i.e., activities, processes, the subject of Section III), and, since we are dealing with poetry, its *use of language* (i.e., verbal input/output, also in Section III). Faculties and activities were considered innate (natural, given), use of language free.

First, with regard to the mind's *faculties,* in the medieval period their existence and fundamental nature were unquestioned. The names and number of lesser faculties varied from thinker to thinker, but there was general agreement as to the important ones. The important faculties were those by which human nature images the Divine Nature, namely the specifically human faculties of will (i.e., emotions and choice) and of intellect. In the great scholastic

debate about the nature of human nature, the fundamental disagreement was as to the relationship of these two faculties—will
and intellect—and especially as to which was prime (*nobilior*) in the
human mind. Which is more important, will or intellect? Which
depends on which?

From the decision as to which faculty is or should be prior in
the human mind follow all sorts of implications as to the nature of
perception, knowledge, judgment, freedom, ethics, personality,
individuality, belief, reality, behavior in this world and beatitude
in the next. If intellect is prime—the position of Aquinas, for
example—then the natural (i.e., innate, instinctive) orientation of
the mind is or should be toward truth, knowledge, rational comprehension; in this case the intellect perceives the best means to
achieve something and the will automatically follows along. On
the other hand, if will is prime—the position of Scotus, for example—then the natural orientation of the mind is or should be toward
love and goodness; in this case the will chooses and the intellect
attends. The two competing scholastic systems (Dominican intellectualism and Franciscan voluntarism, generally speaking) agreed
on many other issues, obviously, but their theories of faculty
psychology were fundamentally irreconcilable. In the mind of
God and therefore in the mind of man, for both sides, both faculties—*intellectus* and *voluntas*—were noble. The question in scholastic faculty psychology was as to primacy: which is *more* noble?
which faculty is naturally superior to which in the structuring of
the human mind? In humanist faculty psychology, on the other
hand, the question, at least as Chaucer determines it in the Knight's
Tale, is as to complementarity: since both faculties perform equally
valuable but quite different functions, how will they function together most harmoniously? Thus, on the scholastic side, competition; on the humanist side, harmonious cooperation. Which is it
naturally, in the innate structuring of the faculties of the universal
human mind—rivalry or harmony?

Second, with regard to the mind's *acts,* the natural processes
by which the mind thinks when it is thinking as a specifically
human mind (reasoning, choosing), later medieval thinkers all
accepted and developed further Aristotle's idea that the activities

performed by the mind are of three kinds—Simple Apprehension of Objects, Judgment of Complex Propositions, and Reasoning. However, the scholastics and the humanists did not interpret Aristotle's 3-Acts model in a single way. The scholastic philosophers apparently drew on some of its implications in developing their several theories of science and certitude; the Gothic high artists and poets apparently drew on other implications in developing what we now think of as the Gothic style of art, with its characteristic juxtapositions, compartmentalization, intellectual complexity, and open-endedness.

According to Aristotle's 3-Acts theory (as set forth somewhat fuzzily in the *De Anima*), the mind's understanding of any complex object or event is going to have both objective and subjective components. Act 1—Simple Apprehension of Objects—is the reception by the mind of information from the outward senses. It is completely passive and therefore not subject to error: either the tree is there or it is not there. Act 2—Judgment of Complex Propositions—is the mind's activity of taking apart and putting together into complex propositions (i.e., more than one component) the objects apprehended in Act 1 and then judging them; whether for truth-value or for goodness-value or for both is not clear in Aristotle. Act 3—Reasoning proper—is the mind's reasoning from present objects or events to things about them not necessarily present, for example, to their causes, their consequences, or their implications. Whereas Act 1 is objective, Acts 2 and 3 take place completely within the mind of the individual perceiver. In Chaucer's time, differences in interpretation arose here. Given that Act 2 (judgment of complex propositions) and Act 3 (reasoning) take place totally within the mind, the question arises, is objective certitude possible? The humanists interpreted Acts 2 and 3 as at least partly subjective, so that for them, all human knowledge depends at least to some degree on its knower, the position of Boethius in the *Consolation*. On the other hand, the intellectualist scholastics interpreted Acts 2 and 3 as desirably or essentially rational, so that for them, by means of valid logical demonstration at least some human knowledge can be completely objective and therefore certain, even with respect to some knowledge about God.

The voluntarist scholastics took a middle position between these two; for them some certain knowledge is possible, but, generally speaking, only with respect to some matters within this world.

Thus, by Chaucer's time, if one thought of constructing *ab initio* a theory of the universal of the human mind, one would think in terms of decisions on two givens: First, with regard to the mind's natural structuring, the pivotal question was as to the relationship between its faculties of intellect and will (this is the *quaestio* in the Palamon/Arcite/Theseus disputation). Second, with regard to the mind's natural activities, the pivotal question was as to certitude: can the human mind achieve objective certain knowledge (this is the issue in the Part III sequence of *sophismata*).

The third component of the human mind is the input/output material it processes. In Chaucer's time, in the context of poetry and scholastic philosophy alike, this was language. Ideas. Concepts. Words. Words and more words. Later medieval culture was in some ways much more concerned with words than is our own. Words counted. The Word was ever present. All pre-university education (grammar, dialectic/logic, rhetoric) was verbal, and education in the university consisted of lecture and disputation—again verbal. Scholastic science was verbal rather than physical, scholastic logic was semantic rather than symbolic,[26] and both prided themselves above all on precision with words. Precision and rationality. Further, medieval entertainment seems to have been more verbal than visual, more social than solitary, and more participatory than spectator. Not only are Chaucer's own pilgrims highly verbal, but Langland, the Middle English lyrics, and the cycle plays present us again and again with tenant farmers, peasants, artisans, and members of the middle class far more verbal, far more articulate, than most people of our day. As a result, in this highly word-conscious context, the stakes in the continuing dispute between university scholastic and poet humanist over valid language use—whether literal alone or figurative as well—were high. The stakes were no less than the medium by which each side practiced its art.

For the scholastic philosopher, language constituted his scientific method. Because the objects of his concern were intelligible rather than physical, his analysis was conceptual and his demonstration painstakingly rational and totally verbal. He did his work by reasoning in writing about words—words from the Bible, words from the Fathers, words from other scholastics, occasionally words about his own experience, but always words. Words for the medieval scientist were what mathematical symbols are for the modern scientist—they represent the data that will be manipulated according to the laws of logic. "The scholastic method," says J. A. Weisheipl, "was essentially a rational investigation of every relevant problem in liberal arts, philosophy, theology, medicine, and law, examined from opposing points of view in order to reach an intelligent, scientific solution that would be consisent with accepted authorities, known facts, human reason, and Christian faith."[27] And all of this was done by manipulation of words. Each word, therefore, had to be properly pinned down to a single literal meaning. As Aquinas says,

> Allow a variety of readings to one passage, and you produce confusion and deception, and sap the foundations of argument; examples of the stock fallacies, not reasoned discourse, follow from the medley of meanings.[28]

The underlying assumption here, of course, is that when language is to be used validly, it is to be used rationally. Important appeal is made only to the reason, and this can be done only by means of words used literally.

For the humanist poet, language likewise constituted the medium of his art. However, rather than discovering universal solutions to abstract problems, his goal was to evoke traditional moral or spiritual truths in the minds of his individual readers. So long as his readers profited morally or spiritually from his poetry, what mattered it if they found a "medley of meanings"? Indeed, the more the better. As a result, the humanist poet could validly appeal to both reason and emotions. He could use language literally where he wished, but he could use language figuratively as well—he could delight his readers with the fictional story, exemplum, parable, satire, fable, or whatever itself, and then delight them again with the pleasure they would experience on finding edifying truths hidden beneath his figurative veils. On this basis, the humanist poet could well ask, which is really more effective, more inspiring—experiencing a virtue, or studying its definition? The *Aeneid* or the *Nichomachean Ethics?*[29]

As working courtier, as prolific writer, and as voracious reader, Chaucer could not have been unfamiliar with the issues in this war over the valid use of words.[30] Nor, for the same three reasons, could he have been unfamiliar with the psychological theories of the university scholastics. Indeed, among the major reasons we still read him are his practical use of words and his practical understanding of human psychology. The difference between abstract speculative theory and practical daily experience is, thus, a central concern of the Knight's Tale, as it is of the *Canterbury Tales* as a whole.

The Canterbury Tales: *Both Humanist and Scholastic*

This new two-way paradigm for the Knight's Tale—that it puts forward two central ideas: a humanist defense of the ability of figurative language to convey truth and a humanist theory of universal psychology—naturally suggests a new hypothesis about Chaucer's purpose in putting together the *Canterbury Tales.* As a maker, Chaucer must have taken great pleasure in creating these pilgrims and "retelling" these stories. In addition, however, I would like to suggest that the *Canterbury Tales* also represents a continuing exploration on Chaucer's part into human psychology and into the daily use of language, a continuing, analytic, scholastic-type inquiry seeking new truths about these two subjects. Such a hypothesis would account for many things about the texts, some areas finished, other passages clearly still in the process of being moved around, being tried in more than one context, in the mouths of more than one speaker.[31] Since the *Tales* is unfinished, no hypothesis can ever be demonstrated, of course, but it is possible to show that Chaucer had the knowledge, the interest, the methodology, and the ideas to embark on such a "scientific" exploration. Indeed, what could have been more interesting to a man like Chaucer than attempting to figure out the nature of the human mind and the ways it uses and is influenced by language?

Chaucer had easy access to the theories and goals of the university scholastics. In his time, although few in number even within the church itself, they constituted a politically important and intellectually prestigious group. As this study of the Knight's Tale will show, Chaucer understood their theories well. This should come as no surprise, considering what we know of his friends, his works, and his own personality. With regard to his friends, one of Chaucer's closest was the eminent scholastic Ralph Strode—"philosophical Strode"—to whom, along with Gower, Chaucer offered the *Troilus* to "corecte." Strode, according to J. A. W. Bennett, had "a *mansio* over Aldersgate at about the same time that Chaucer . . . [had] his house at Aldgate, a few hundred yards off."[32] About this time Strode was "common Serjeant," or pleader, of the City of London. Before this he had been a famous teacher of philosophy at Merton College, Oxford. In logic, his books were still being used as texts at schools as far away as Padua in the fifteenth century and were still being reprinted in the sixteenth. In writings on predestination and apostolic poverty, he was opposed (in what Israel Gollancz terms "an unusually friendly and courteous" manner) by his fellow Mertonian John Wycliffe.[33] In semantics, Strode praised Bradwardine, another Mertonian, as "the prince of modern philosophers of nature" because he was the "first to discover something that was valuable concerning insolubles."[34] Besides lawyer, philosopher, and teacher, Strode was also, according to a fifteenth-century Merton College catalog, a poet, a writer of elegies.[35] He sounds, in short, like an extraordinarily interesting man, a man with a lot to say and with the ability to say it. Small wonder Chaucer referred the *Troilus* to him. Two such men, it seems likely, close friends and even neighbors for a time, must have sometimes discussed things like good and evil, free will and responsibility, ethics, individuation, and happiness, *and* things like modes of signification, syncategoremata, universal grammars, and verbal implications—all of these subjects Strode would have pondered and taught at Oxford and all of these subjects Chaucer would have been deeply concerned with in making his poetry. Thus Chaucer's friendship with Strode would have provided him with one access to the ideas of the scholastics, and a most knowledgeable, positive, and friendly one at that. Further, judging from his works, Chaucer was far and away one of the most learned men of his age—in classical and medieval literature and commentary, in Bible and biblical exegesis, in history, in astrology, in mathematics and the physical sciences—comfortably at home in everything to do with books and words. Moreover, he cared enough about the problems of good and evil, fortune, felicity, justice, and free will to translate Boethius's treatment of them into English. (In the *Consolation,* it will be recalled, Boethius's resolution of all of these problems is verbal and psychological; i.e., it all takes place by means of words within the mind.) On the basis of both the learning and the language use displayed throughout his works, therefore, it again seems likely that Chaucer would have been most interested in contemporary scholastic speculations, so much of it on his own favorite subjects.[36] In this regard, as Bennett showed, every astrological allusion in Chaucer leads "to Oxford, and in Oxford, to Merton," to the Merton College Library, which by Chaucer's time had "facilities almost as favorable as those at the Sorbonne itself."[37] Once there, again it seems likely that a man of Chaucer's encyclopedic interests—a man so learned, so curious about everything, so bookish, and already so familiar with contemporary theories of astrology, alchemy, acoustics, rhetoric, physiology, pharmacy, physics, and so on—that at the very least a man like this would have browsed around a bit.

Thus the correct question with regard to Chaucer and the scholastic psychological and language use theories is not whether he knew them, since the probabilities are heavy that he did. The correct question is, how well did he know them, on what level of sophistication and complexity? This book will show that he knew them very well indeed, accepted them in part, and included them within his own broader understanding of human nature, language use, and the purpose of human life in this world.

Most Gothic masterworks are encyclopedic in overall form. This is true of the great stone cathedrals, the huge homemade cycle dramas, the gorgeous books of hours, the filigreed *summas,* and in literature, the *Roman de la Rose, Piers Plowman,* the *Divine Comedy,* and the *Canterbury Tales.* All of these feature a large lucid structure which has been intricately divided and compartmentalized and then stuffed with figures and ideas and events, all shaped with myriad correspondences, variations, and oppositions that proliferate off in every direction in the reader's mind. Given its encyclopedic character, the differentiae of the *Canterbury Tales* are the pilgrims on the one hand and the tales on the other. That is to say, as touched on earlier, the *Canterbury Tales* as a whole exhibits the same two-pronged conception that the Knight's Tale does, two magnetic poles: on the one hand, human nature (the pilgrims); on the other, language use (their tales).

That Chaucer was interested in developing a formal THEORY of language use while he was working on the *Canterbury Tales* is suggested right from the start by the rigorous Knight's Tale defense of figurative language and its equally rigorous attack (set forth in Section III) on the notion that any language use can be completely literal.[38] In the remainder of the *Tales,* the same speculative scientific interest in language use is suggested by its range of literary genres and its range of verbal usages. As it stands, the *Tales* is a collection of pieces of all kinds of writing, on a full spectrum of genres shading from what we now call fiction to what we now call nonfiction (modern categories that are extremely misleading when applied to pre–nineteenth-century literature). The range is from romances, saints' lives, fabliaux, exempla and a fable; through confessions, apologies, a series of biographies,[39] and a kind of sermon; to moral and penitential treatises and finally a retraction. To this list of genres, of course, the Knight's Tale will be adding a scholastic *disputatio* and the *sophismata* sequence. Additionally, on a more general level, the *Tales* itself is a traveler's tale, like the *Commedia,* with a first-person teller who travels, meets up with exemplary figures and events, and tells about them with the kind of truth-affirming detail that urges the reader to seek edifying parallels in his or her own experience. Further, on the same general level, the *Tales* depicts a secular pilgrimage through life in this world toward final judgment. Given the sizable number of literary genres included so far, did Chaucer intend to include for exhibition and examination a sample of every type of writing? Possibly. The difficulty of this question is compounded by the fact that medieval genres are ordinarily mixed, and what we now think of as a separate genre they often treated as a cluster of detachable topoi. Literary genres thus merge into language usages; and of these the *Tales* exhibits a full spectrum, ranging from high courtly to low scurrility as one would expect in such a collection, but also, and unexpectedly, from highly figurative (whether romantic, mystical, allusive, ironic, descriptive, or rhetorical) through various kinds of professional jargon (legal, medical, chemical, astrological and such) and at least two dialects, all the way over to flat-footed scholastic literal.[40] To this already large list of language uses, the Knight's Tale will be adding linguistic logic games and interlocking quantitative imagery. Did Chaucer intend to include in the *Canterbury Tales* for exhibition and examination a sample of every possible language use, an example of every kind of image, locution, and metaphor, a phrase or two of every jargon? Apparently. However, we can never know for sure. Thus, that in making the *Canterbury Tales* Chaucer had a speculative analytic interest in language use, that he was developing a scientific theory as to its nature as well as using it himself on a practical basis, is only a hypothesis. But the Knight's Tale suggests it, and the extraordinary range of genres and usages in the rest of the *Tales* supports it.

That Chaucer was interested in developing a formal THEORY of universal psychology can (and will) be demonstrated from the Knight's Tale alone: the *disputatio* on faculty psychology is argued, figuratively, like a regular scholastic demonstration, ticking off point by point, and its methodology is grounded in logic. That this speculative interest extends on throughout the *Canterbury Tales* is suggested by the importance in the pilgrims' characterizations of the very same concepts that Chaucer added to scholastic psychological theory. For example, in their attempt to achieve a truly universal theory of man, the scholastics wound up positing a creature outside of time, outside of place, outside of social companionship, and for all practical purposes outside of life as any of us know it. In his own universal psychology as put forth in the Knight's Tale, therefore, Chaucer includes specific places and development through time, social give-and-take with other people in the real world, and individual subjectivity, all major topoi in the characterizations of his *Canterbury* pilgrims, and all absent from the scholastic faculty psychologies.

Further, leaving the Knight's Tale and turning to the pilgrims themselves for evidence of a psychological theory in progress, we have no way of knowing, of course, what more Chaucer might have intended. Among the pilgrims as we have them (although these do appear in the stories), there are no small children, no mothers or daughters, no couples, no honest tax collectors, and, so far as one can tell, no real courtiers. Did Chaucer intend to include every type of human being? Possibly. The pilgrims we do have, although limited in rank to two nobles and the rest commoners or clergy, do suggest a spectrum of moral characters, occupations, and personal histories. The manuscripts suggest that more tales and more details were to be written, more links, possibly more pilgrims were to join, that the tales we have were still being moved from teller to teller and position to position, that some things remained to be cut, and that no doubt some of what we have would have been reshaped.[41] Chaucer's wisdom about people, his understanding of how the infinitely intricate, unpredictable, individual human mind really works, is perhaps the main reason we still not merely read but enjoy, study, discuss, and learn from the *Canterbury Tales*. "Thought, as the expression of character, is the art of Chaucer's pilgrimage," remarks Paul Ruggiers.[42] A speculative as well as creative interest in worldly human nature seems likely.

My point here is that in making the *Canterbury Tales,* in addition to the ordinary pleasures of creation and storytelling and the ordinary purposes of *sentence and solas,* Chaucer is also pursuing analytic pleasures and purposes. He is exploring the human mind scientifically, like a scholastic, albeit empirically rather than deductively. As humanist poet, Chaucer generally aligned himself with the older, richer, ethically-oriented tradition of the rhetoricians. In the *Canterbury Tales,* however, he is additionally interested in attempting to discover the nature of the human mind itself, how it perceives, thinks, judges, believes, loves, hates, and learns to be better, and to discover the nature of human language itself and how people use it, both of these being scientific new-truth interests he shared with the university scholastics of his time. Writing is discovery, and this kind of discovery is recursive. When trying to figure out something truly interesting, truly complex, truly rich, only by writing about it can one really work toward understanding it. And what could be more interesting, complex, and rich than human beings, human language, the human mind.

Overview

This book is organized into four sections. The purpose of this first section, the Introduction, has been to provide the literary and historical context for the new view of the Knight's Tale I am proposing. Sections II, III, and IV each contain first a sketch of the backgrounds of their respective subject matters, then two chapters on Knight's Tale material, and a closing chapter on the major theoretical issue raised.

Section II is on the faculty structure component of universal psychology and Chaucer's characterizations of Palamon, Arcite, and Theseus. It begins by defining faculty psychology. Then Chapter 1 shows that Palamon and Arcite embody the two principal theories of faculty psychology of Chaucer's time. Palamon is man according to the theories of the Augustinian Franciscans; he perceives, judges, is free and bound, develops ethically, and so on, according as Scotus and Ockham and their followers conceived to be the nature of all men. Arcite is man according to the theories of the Aristotelian Dominicans; he perceives, thinks, is free and bound, develops ethically, and so on, according as Aquinas and his followers conceived to be the nature of all men. Sadly (or perhaps comically, depending on how one feels about philosophy), the two conceptions of man were in fundamental disagreement. In embodying (incarnating) the two theories of man, however, Chaucer's primary intent is not satire but accuracy. The scholastic material embedded in the Knight's Tale is totally serious philosophy. The stakes, as will become clear by Section IV, could not be higher. Next, Chapter 2 shows the characterization of Theseus as embodying (incarnating) Chaucer's own harmonizing resolution between the two theories. In characterizing Theseus, Chaucer covers the same scholastic issues used to characterize Palamon and Arcite, but he focuses most strongly (in scholastic terms) on demonstrating Theseus's total freedom of both will and intellect, and on showing him learning from personal experience to be a better human being. Chapter 3 concludes this section by considering the problem of the "goal" of the scholastic faculty psychologies as Chaucer himself must have considered it: i.e., the deterministic implications of claiming certitude for any definition of human nature that limits human freedom, suppresses human individuality, and ignores human subjectivity. It then sets forth Chaucer's solution to the question of individuality and the demand of scholastic science that it be universal. Rather than finding his certitude in a universal mental structuring or a universal behavioral pattern, Chaucer's solution proposes to locate his principle of individuation in a universal process that all human beings in this world know and undergo—day-to-day experience with other human beings and the experience of learning from it.

For Chaucer in these three characterizations, a major concern is that the two scholastic faculty psychologies were overdetermined. Palamon and Arcite are rather rigid young men. They are sticklike as often as they are lifelike. One reason for this, Chaucer suggests, is that there is little in the scholastic psychologies to indicate that people learn anything important from living their daily lives in this created world, and even less to indicate the presence of individualized human subjectivity. This is why Theseus seems so much more human. We see his mind in the process of thinking and changing as he responds to the things that happen around him.

Section III is on theories of thinking processes and language use; Chaucer interweaves these two separate-for-us subjects together as comprising the second component of his universal psychology. This section's background discussion begins with language use. It points out the use of language in all specifically human thinking acts, thereby questioning whether completely objective language use is possible. Then it demonstrates that, in some of their own genres (*obligationes, insolubilia,* and *sophismata*) and contrary to their own theories, the scholastics themselves did not use language literally. The background then turns to theories of thinking processes, defining in more detail the traditional 3-Acts mind model and the conflicting interpretations drawn from it, on the one hand by humanist artists seeking to instruct and delight (i.e., to foster), and on the other by scholastic scientists seeking objective certitude for their own new-truth discoveries.

First, Chapter 4 explicates Chaucer's descriptions of the temples of Venus, Mars, and Diana and the champions Lygurge and Emetreus. It shows that these descriptions are *sophismata,* i.e., experiential definitions. The subject matter literally referenced by Chaucer's words is pagan, but his syntax, structuring, and implications will evoke in the reader experientially the scholastic ideas of the three different thinking processes performed by the human mind (Venus and Mars evoke Act 1, simple apprehension of objects; Diana evokes Act 2, judgment of complex propositions; and Lygurge and Emetreus evoke Act 3, reasoning to causes). Next, Chapter 5 explicates Chaucer's concluding *sophisma,* his solution to the deficiencies of the 3-Acts thinking model, in Saturn's monologue. Saturn, with all his affections, pomposities, historicity, and blind spots, adds subjectivity as the larger shaping mental context inside which those three supposedly objective mental activities actually take place. This is why the Saturn description is presented as a monologue.

Overall, since freedom of mind and learning from one's personal experiences are, obviously, functions of one's own subjectivity, the largest difference separating Chaucer's universal psychology from those of the university scholastics is his addition of human subjectivity. In the Knight's Tale resolutions, human subjectivity is the core, the overlap area, uniting the two different kinds of theories, of faculty structure on the one hand (Palamon, Arcite, and Theseus), and of thinking processes and language use on the other (the six Part III descriptions). That overlap is the reason Chaucer's emphasis in the speeches of both resolution figures, Theseus and Saturn, is on their own thinking processes and decisions, i.e., on their subjectivity.

Chapter 6 then sets forth Chaucer's two major criticisms of the scholastics' scientific methodology, namely, their overreliance on logic and their choice of the timeless unchanging aspects of the Divine Nature as model for their image of human nature. His own, more realistic methodology relies on experience as well as logical reasoning, and it takes the behavior of the Divine when he was in this world as a better model on which to base an image of human nature.

And finally, Section IV, "Makers and Contexts," first puts forward as background sketch what seem to be Chaucer's own, highly medieval, ideas about the makers of universal psychologies, from God himself on down to each of us individually, every day, in our own subjective minds; and his own ideas about the contexts in which real universal psychologies are made, whether the world of logical abstraction or the created world in which all of us live every day. Chapter 7, on "The Knight," tries to show that the teller of the Knight's Tale is exactly what his General Prologue portrait says he is (and possibly more)—a worthy, wise, experienced, truly gentle and noble Christian warrior, who has fought actively for many years for what he knows to be good and is still hard at it. Chapter 8, on "The Pilgrimage Reality," shows that Chaucer moves the context for making universal psychologies out from the scholastic cloister and into the real-world pilgrimage of you and me and our neighbors Alison, Oswald, and Huberd, a pilgrimage tangible, temporal, and very social. To the abstract universal psychologies of his time, having already added learning from experience and subjectivity, Chaucer now adds social interaction and friction, all in the context of total freedom of mind and therefore total responsibility. Immediately, however, a problem arises: Is total freedom of mind possible if one learns from one's own experiences in this world-full of fallen other people, some of them powerful? This question, it seems to me, is a major subject of exploration in the rest of the *Canterbury Tales,* and it suggests a degree of immediate personal responsibility toward those right around us that is unusual in a philosophically-based psychological theory. And finally, Chapter 9, on "Chaucerian Didacticism," sets forth the humanist theory of didacticism implied by Chaucer's resolutions in the Knight's Tale, the theory that life in this world is a school, providing real human beings with a benevolent period of total freedom in which to find and serve something higher than their own pagan self-fulfillment.

The conclusions of Chaucer and his Knight are affectionate. They are the conclusions of a person who cares for his fellow human beings and wants only the best for them, but it is a best they must figure out and choose for themselves. Total freedom, total responsibility: that is the theory.

Because the Knight's Tale presents scholastic philosophy figuratively rather than literally, in pagan romance rather than articled treatise, at times it can seem extraordinarily complicated, at least to the twentieth-century reader. In some passages Chaucer is carrying forward the pagan story, exemplifying a scholastic theory, and out-verbalizing the logicians, all at the same time. For that reason, the two chapters explicating Chaucer's use of scholastic ideas are long. (Anything scholastic is long, often fascinating but always long.) For clarity's sake, therefore, in Chapter 1 on Palamon and Arcite and Chapter 4 on the temples and champions, first I pull forward the scholastic issues, then the embedded Chaucerian commentary on them. The verbal features of the Knight's Tale, especially those discussed in these two chapters, may be unique. From a technical point of view they are astonishing. For virtuoso use of the English language, in imagery, syntax, organization, and implication, I know of nothing in Old, Middle, or Modern English as intellectually exciting as the Knight's Tale. Chaucer must have taken great pleasure in it.

DOCUMENTATION, TERMINOLOGY, STYLE, AND CRITICAL THEORY

With regard to documenting the literary scholarship, as mentioned earlier I have classified it by topic—the two rival young knights, Emelye, Theseus, the temples and champions, Saturn, and the Knight—and appropriate critical summaries on each subject appear early in the appropriate chapters and their notes. All quotations from the *Canterbury Tales* identified by line numbers only are from the Robinson edition; those identified by line numbers followed by "MR" are from the Manly-Rickert edition.

Introduction

With regard to documenting the scholastic references, it is always worth a reminder that philosophy is no less subject to interpretation than literature. Theories about reality are fictions too. As a result, using formal philosophy as a context for explicating a work of literature, as I do here, can present a problem of circular or mutually-validating interpretation. This is particularly true when using later medieval philosophy to explicate literature because of its quantity, its complexity, its twentieth-century religious implications, and the state of its texts. Good researchers can ordinarily find citations to support whatever they believe to be the case, because their beliefs arise largely out of the same sources in which they will look for citations. In this sense, interpretation is always to some degree circular, as is documentation; and the question for the writer of a book such as this, a book about literature, is really where to draw the line—where to allow such circularity and where to insist that the evidence one is presenting is outside it.

In this book, I wish to locate the philosophical background I present as being outside the circle of my own interpretation. For that reason, the notes provide references to secondary materials in twentieth-century scholarship as well as references to the appropriate primary materials. For secondary materials I have utilized the scholarship and interpretations of the recognized experts in the field of medieval philosophy, people who have devoted their lives to understanding the scholastic positions in their historical context—Bonansea, Bourke, Gilson, Leff, Moody, and Wolter, among others—and articles from the recognized scholarly journals, encyclopedias, and histories. In this way, by utilizing both primary and recognized secondary sources, I believe I have ruled out introducing, even unconsciously, personal biases or idiosyncratic readings of my own into the scholastic material I am presenting as background for the Knight's Tale. I was pleasantly surprised, in this regard, to discover how very well Chaucer's presentation of scholastic ideas accords with the understanding of modern-day scholars. The only major difference I noticed, a difference of emphasis rather than substance, was that whereas present-day scholarship focuses on the differences between Scotus and Ockham, Chaucer focuses instead on their agreements, combining their

I. Introduction

psychological theories into a single Franciscan embodiment, which he then contrasts to the single Dominican embodiment apparently drawn from Aquinas. Actually, each of these sources, Knight's Tale characterizations and twentieth-century scholarship, tended to validate the other in its depiction of the two great traditions of later medieval thought, the Dominican and the Franciscan. Thus, whereas I am responsible for the literary interpretations and the descriptions of verbal techniques that follow, the philosophical interpretations, as indicated by constant reference to secondary scholarship, are accepted interpretations held today by experts in the field.

Turning now to terminology, throughout this book when talking about theories of psychology and human nature in this world, rather than use the term "soul" with all the complex spiritual and metaphysical implications the word carries for many of us today, whenever possible I have used the term "mind." It expresses more accurately for us, I think, the psychological concepts actually being discussed in the Knight's Tale. Similarly, because the split between philosophy and theology was still taking place during the fourteenth century when Chaucer was writing (the Aristotelian Thomists separating them as two different kinds of reasoning about things; the Augustinian Franciscans refusing to separate them), rather than constantly use the awkward compound "philosopher/theologian" throughout, I have ordinarily used just "philosopher." Again, it expresses more accurately for us, I think, the kinds of concepts Chaucer was actually working with in the Knight's Tale. In like manner, since establishing human subjectivity as a key component of universal human nature was one of Chaucer's aims in the Knight's Tale, a component that always has an influence on one's thoughts and judgments, I have often used the adjective "subjective." Here this term never implies moral relativism or the absence of absolute truths. Rather, it implies influence. Subjective learning, for example, means learning composed of both objective input and subjective shaping; subjective truth, likewise, means truth composed of both objective content and subjective shaping, and so on. The term "Gothic" I have used as Derek Brewer does, to signify the art, literature, and culture of Western Europe (here, mostly England) from the twelfth through the mid-fifteenth centuries; the term "humanist" I have used generally for the poets and artists of the same period, since the didacticism of their output seems to evidence a fostering rather than a new-truth intent; and the terms "scholastic" and "scientific" I have used fairly synonymously for the narrower university culture of the same period, which specialized in the literal, logical, Aristotelian way of thinking and theorizing. The verb "point," one of the very few technical terms we have in which, according to J. A. Burrow, "Ricardian poets thought and spoke about their art," I have used throughout as they used it, to mean an unusually detailed description.[43]

On the subject of style, for reasons both practical and theoretical, this book is not always written in academic style; occasionally it lapses into the personal or figurative. On the practical level, scholastic philosophy presented in undiluted scholastic style is almost unreadable. It overwhelms the reader with details far beyond the reader's need, and it postpones relevance until all but the most tenacious have lost interest. Since this book tries to explain three systems of scholastic psychology and the basic conceptions of scholastic metaphysics as well as to demonstrate their presence and point in the Knight's Tale, written academically it would be three times thicker. At least. And it would probably convey a good deal less to the reader interested in the Knight's Tale or the psychologies. On the theoretical level, the use here of modified academic style is both feminist and symbolic. Feminist critics are often charged with taking literature too personally. "The problematic of a feminist criticism," comments Elaine Showalter on this issue, is "how to combine the theoretical and the personal."[44] At the same time, the problematic of medieval scholastic psychology, in this Freudian Behavioristic age, is how to make it readable. The fact is, it is very good psychology, and yet it is almost totally unknown in the wider academic community. In the Knight's Tale, Chaucer's concern is to bring these scholastic theories of psychology out into everyday life; that is to say, Chaucer takes these theories and makes them both readable and personal. In this book it therefore seems to me appropriate to try to do the same, to make them both readable and personal. I recognize and learn about myself in them; I believe others may also. In a way, therefore, the style of this book is a symbol of its meaning. It is doing what it is saying.

And finally here, with regard to current critical theory, it is now a part of our professional culture. Hermeneutics, dialogics, rezeptionsästhetik, deconstruction, intertextuality, presence, absence, semiotics, signification, discourse, praxis—the terms and concepts are everywhere. The surprising thing is how many of these postmodern concerns were also pre-Cartesian concerns. In his recent book on Chaucer, for example, after defining "poetics" as the search for principles of literariness (as opposed to the interpretation of particular texts), Robert M. Jordan makes a striking distinction between a *realist poetics* (emphasis on reproducing the real world) as opposed to a *rhetorical poetics* (emphasis on language, the act of writing, audience, and meaning and truth as problematic).[45] Notice that all of the current critical-theory terms in the list with which this paragraph opened fit easily under "rhetorical poetics," a term actually coined in connection with a study of Chaucer. In fact, Chaucer shares with Derrida, Lacan, Eco, and Gadamer an interest in how language works. Chaucer shares with Bakhtin and Foucault an interest in the social construction of meaning. Chaucer shares with Gadamer an interest in the effects of historicity. And so on. However, Chaucer also shares these interests with, among others, Boethius, Virgil, Dante, and Jean de Meun. As a result, familiarity with the ideas of these postmodern thinkers cannot but be fruitful when studying any pre-Cartesian literature. I know I have learned to see much that was new to me, especially from the ideas of Gadamer and Bakhtin. On the other hand, there is much in the older literature that the postmodern theories dismiss or may even distort, for example, spirituality, virtue, and metaphysical freedom and responsibility. From the long-known fact that our perceptions of truth may be relative the earlier writers did not infer the nonexistence or cultural dependence of all absolutes. For this reason, in writing this book I have chosen not to use the new theoretical terms; along with their specificity, to the older literature they can bring distortion: Deconstruction for me implies decenteredness, something Chaucer is not (at least as I understand him); praxis for me implies ethical relativism, something Chaucer does not (at least as I understand him). Readers interested in critical theory will, however, recognize when Chaucer's ideas overlap in interesting ways with, for example, Heisenberg's on objectivity, Gadamer's on historicity, and Bakhtin's on sociability. But because this book seeks to illuminate the Knight's Tale by throwing light on the cultural context in which Chaucer wrote it, the context specifically of the medieval theories about human nature and about language use, the special terms and concepts I employ are for the most part those of Chaucer's own time.

SECTION II

Universal Psychologies: Faculty Component

— FROM RIVALRY TO COOPERATION —

CHAPTER 1. Palamon and Arcite:
The Scholastic Will/Intellect Debate

CHAPTER 2. Theseus:
Chaucer's Humanist *Determinatio*

CHAPTER 3. The Goal of a Universal Psychology:
Certitude versus Choice

BACKGROUND

During the past few centuries, the study of psychology has slowly precipitated out from a number of subject areas—ethics, metaphysics, general philosophy, rhetoric, religion, and medicine—into a fully developed discipline in its own right, with parameters ranging from pure science (mathematically based, experimental, predictive), through social and developmental studies, and on into political policy-making and clinical practice. Today, on the clinical and policy-making side, psychologists are primarily concerned with fostering the development of individuals, as humanists usually are; whereas on the pure science side, psychologists are busy looking for general rules and universals, as scientists always are. The opposition of these two approaches to human beings is traditional. One side accords primacy to ethical and mental well-being, essentially individual concerns; the other side accords primacy to discovery

II. Faculty Component

and rationalizing, essentially general knowledge concerns. This opposition goes back at least to the days of the early Greeks, to the Sophist and Socratic focus on the individual as opposed to the Platonic and Aristotelian emphasis on knowing abstractions.[1]

In its medieval appearance, the same opposition shows up in the Augustinian emphasis on introspection and individual choice as opposed to the Thomistic, ultimately Aristotelian, emphasis on objectivity and reasoning. The great medieval debate as to primacy of the will or of the intellect is part of this same traditional opposition, the Augustinian Franciscans holding for primacy of the will (love and choice), the Aristotelian Dominicans holding for primacy of the intellect. For these two rival parties I will use the terms "voluntarist" and "intellectualist." However sweeping and reductive these terms may be, they are traditional, and they do establish the framework necessary to understand the complex interrelationship of the two great scholastic psychologies.

To introduce this section on the faculty psychology component of the Knight's Tale, first, by way of background, I will try to dissipate some of the cloudiness that surrounds the subject today.

The word "faculty" designates a power or agency of the mind. In the medieval period, some faculties were considered immaterial (will, intellect); others were considered physical (imagination, common sense, hearing). The term "faculty psychology" designates a theory that explains all mental phenomena by deductive reasoning from the interaction of such faculties. Today the whole subject is obscured by two confusions: faculties are no longer supposed to exist, yet we speak of them every day; and faculty psychology is supposed to have died out in the seventeenth century with the rise of associationism and empirical thinking, yet its shape and spirit are still everywhere present.

Today, using the word "faculty" for a power or agency of the mind has gone out of style, at least in academic circles,[2] but the notion lives on in our literature, our language, and our thinking. "Will power," "perception theory," "short-term memory"—we all know what these mean, and each of them implies the existence of a faculty. Further, we all know what "id," "collective unconscious," and "I.Q." mean, but far be it from anyone to term them faculties. Academic reluctance to use the word seems to arise from a vague sense allying it with metaphysics, nit-picking, and nineteenth-century phrenology.

For literary historians, the subject is further obscured in that, historically, faculty psychology is composed of two ancient, intermingled streams of thought, that of physicians concerned with healing the physical body, and that of Christian philosophers concerned with understanding the mind (the immaterial soul). The physicians' tradition one sees constantly pictured in those ugly medieval and Renaissance drawings of a man's head divided into four cells, each labeled with its particular powers (faculties): *sensus communis* in front, followed by *phantasia* (or *imaginatio*), then *vis estimativa* (or *cogitativa*), and finally *vis memorativa* in the rear. The word *anima* may appear on any or all of these cells, since it signifies "soul" in the Aristotelian physicians' sense (the animating cause of all life), not in the sense of the Christian philosophers. The philosophers' tradition, on the other hand, one normally studies in treatises rather than sees pictured in drawings, and it is most emphatic that the human soul is immaterial. Obviously, therefore, it cannot be located in any physical bodily organ. The fact is, the two traditions overlap and often conflict.[3]

The illustration in figure 2,[4] dated around 1619 and preserving much of the intellectualist system of Avicenna and Aristotle, is unusual in that both kinds of faculties, physical and immaterial, are shown: the sensible world inputs through the senses; the intelligible world inputs from above through the mind. The complications within the man's head convey the difficulties caused by trying to figure out how the spiritual soul can be in contact with sensible objects.

Starting from the front, data from the sensible world (shown as circles of the four elements) are being transmitted through the senses (touch, taste, smell, vision, hearing) to the *sensitiva,* which quickly passes it back to the *imaginativa* for storage (shown as shadows of the same four-element circles). Notice that these are labeled "hic anima est." In the central cell, the *cogitativa* calls for, combines, and divides the images earlier stored in the *imaginativa* at the request of the *estimativa* directly behind it. The *estimativa* is

Figure 2. Robert Fludd. The Faculties of the Mind, 1619.

the highest power possessed by animals (for example, this is the power by which the sheep discerns the "intentions" of the wolf and thus that it is to be avoided). Notice again, "hic anima est." In the rear cell, the *memorativa* retains the "intentions" apprehended by the *estimativa,* which are summoned up from it as desired at the same time that the corresponding sensible images are summoned up from the *imaginativa.* This last cell also contains the *motiva,* the various powers of will (i.e., desiring, fearing) which direct the powers of local movement (i.e., arouse the *virtus irascibilis* which urges the sheep to run). And again, "hic anima est." In the physicians' tradition, descended mostly through the Stoics, *anima* (or spirit) is physical matter of the most subtle, rarefied kind; it is produced in the heart, whence it spreads out via the arteries to the various bodily organs, which then modify it according to their separate needs. Now, all of these faculties so far discussed are physical, animal faculties, which operate by means of physical animal spirits. They are possessed alike by sheep, wolf, and man.

Above these physical faculties, however, this particular artist has also drawn in the immaterial faculties (in this case according to intellectualist psychology): *intellectus* ruling *ratio,* these in the circle of the mind (*mens*) and ruling the physical faculties below. Above, input rains down from angels, principalities, and so on up to *Deus* himself, all of this labeled *mundus intellectualis.* These immaterial faculties were the powers or agencies by which man bears God's image. Thus these immaterial faculties form the basic subject matter of medieval speculation about universal human nature.

Faculty psychology became important in the West in the twelfth and thirteenth centuries with the incorporation of Aristotelian science into Christian philosophy. Immediately, the problem arose as to what this new notion of multiple faculties implied about the soul's unity. In the Augustinian tradition, the biblical teaching that God created human beings in his image had meant the image of the Trinity.[5] According to this ancient and most basic doctrine, God is utterly simple (i.e., uncompounded, not divisible into parts): "in God every perfection is one with His Being and absolutely identical with each of the three divine Persons."[6] Augustine treated the faculties (will, intellect, and memory) not as separate entities but as different movements of the same entity. Those who adopted the Aristotelian psychology, on the other hand, like Aquinas, treated the human being as a single substance composed of soul (immaterial form) and body (matter), with its faculties/ powers separate, distinct, and hierarchically ordered (vegetative, sensitive, and so on), with the intellect in charge. Aquinas even speaks of the soul as a substance and its faculties as accidents.[7] Conflict between these two opposing notions of the nature of the soul—on the one hand, separate powers; on the other, modes or movements of a single unity—continued throughout the scholastic period (and generated several resourceful arguments intended to bridge the gap[8]). In the Knight's Tale, as one would expect, this is one of the issues Chaucer embodies in his two young knights: in Parts I and II of the tale (to be shown in Chapter I), Arcite's faculties are at war with each other, thus establishing their separateness; Palamon, on the other hand, never undergoes internal struggle, thus establishing his soul's oneness.[9]

However, the unity or plurality of the soul was only one issue among many between those holding with the traditional Augustinian philosophy as opposed to those captivated by the new Aristotelian science. The faculty debate, concludes Wilhelm Windelband, came to symbolize many of their differences:

> [A] special psychological problem . . . was vigorously discussed throughout this whole period, . . . in reference to which the points of opposition between the parties of the time may be recognised upon a smaller scale, but all the more sharply focussed. It is the question whether among the powers of the soul the higher dignity belongs to the will or to the intellect (*utra potentia nobilior*). It takes so broad a space in the literature of this period that the attempt might have been made to look upon the psychological antithesis which unfolds in connection with it as the leading motive of the whole period.

Further, according to Windelband, "the conception of *freedom,* which always involves ethical and religious questions, was looked upon as the point in controversy."[10] As I hope to show, in the characterization debate in the Knight's Tale, freedom is Chaucer's major point too.

Let us therefore consider freedom. What exactly was meant by freedom in Chaucer's time? A brief look will also suggest, at the same time, some of the richness of scholastic thought—the breathtaking scope, the freedom to disagree, the penchant for classification and division. As a discipline, medieval faculty psychology worked within the traditional Augustinian (ultimately Platonic) separation of the spiritual soul from the material world. According to this idea, the spiritual nature of the soul makes it impossible for material sensible objects to sway it against its wishes. As a result, the scholastics associated freedom with immateriality, in the sense of being free from the bonds of nature. Independent action was contrasted with the determining influence of physical matter. In this way of thinking, only God is totally free, that is, omnipotent (except for the limits of logic, another notion that will come up later). Angels naturally are less free, and human beings even less. Now, what is the nature of this limited immaterial freedom we humans can have? And exactly how can we achieve it? Freedom was discussed in many aspects; among them: Freedom from evil in the sense of earthly misery—but this freedom can be complete only in heaven. Freedom from sin—but this freedom can be complete only by grace. Freedom from natural necessities (the appetites, the stars)—yes, this is the freedom we humans can achieve, by means of our reason. This freedom being within man's capacity to choose, medieval philosophers do not speak of free will but of free choice, *liberum arbitrium*.[11] Now, where in man himself, in which faculty, is this freedom of choice located, this freedom by which man can liberate himself from the bonds of physical nature? This being man's highest freedom, whichever faculty it is sited in automatically becomes prime. As a result, some located it in the will, others in the intellect; others regarded it as a combination or arbitration of the two or as a separate and superior faculty altogether, and still others regarded it instead as a disposition (*habitus*). Discussing the subject of freedom in this manner thus illuminated for the scholastics not only the nature of freedom, but also the nature of decision, the nature of the reason (whether active and/or passive, theoretical and/or practical), the nature of the will (whether active and/or passive, natural and/or real), the nature of God, angel, man, and beast. In fact, within the immaterial limits they set for themselves, scholastic speculation was wide-ranging, rich, elaborate, and never-ending.

It was never-ending because, lacking the constraints of empirical testing in the real world, this kind of speculation never stops. The human mind can and will multiply entities (including faculties) and distinctions endlessly. Rather than in worldly testing, the scholastics found their closure-test in logic, in the certitude provided by scientific demonstration from first principles. When we today speak of scientific demonstration, we have in mind a conclusion about something physical that is replicable by other investigators since it resulted from objectively quantified processes taking place under controlled conditions. The scholastics had in mind pretty much the same thing, except their subject matter was metaphysical (i.e., a verbalized concept), their objective process was formal logic (verbal), and their controlled conditions were the rules of valid reasoning. Thus for them a scientific demonstration was a conclusion about something conceptual produced by valid syllogistic reasoning from first principles (i.e., axioms, self-evident truths). Unfortunately, as it turned out, what is self-evident to one person is not necessarily so to all others, and so the demonstrations continued, endlessly.

The first results of this new objective Aristotelian science in the thirteenth century were the great conceptual systems, most notably those of Aquinas the Dominican and Bonaventure the Franciscan. Both were attempting to take from the new science whatever they believed compatible with Christian faith. Among other things, Aquinas absorbed the Aristotelian faculty psychology; Bonaventure, although expressing his in scientific style, essentially retained the traditional Augustinian psychology. The outcome was two comprehensive systems of psychological thought, both encompassing the whole universe, both demonstrated scientifically, yet each conflicting with the other; but both explaining, that is, competing for, the same one great truth. At length this clash of systems was perceived by many as demonstrating the failure, or at least the inadequacy, of logic to provide comprehensive solutions. The second result, in the fourteenth century, was a growing tendency to question the possibility of universal certitudes and to focus instead on pastoral concerns, mysticism, and personal experience, all areas that foreground the subjective and the individual, as Chaucer does. In the fourteenth century, the major philosophic concerns thus became human cognition and human freedom. Is certitude possible? And, in what way are human beings free enough to be justly called to judgment?

Chaucer begins his *Canterbury Tales* with the theoretical discussion in the Knight's Tale of these same two typically fourteenth-century issues: Thinking processes and language use are shaped so as to raise the question of certitude in the *sophismata* sequence in the Part III descriptions—Chaucer says, 'objective certitude is not possible in this world.' Faculty psychology and the ways in which human beings are metaphysically free is the focus in the Palamon/Arcite/Theseus *disputatio*—Chaucer says, 'in theory they're totally free, but let's test it in practice.'

CHAPTER

1

Palamon and Arcite: The Scholastic Will/Intellect Debate

WESTERN CHRISTIAN PSYCHOLOGY begins in many ways with Augustine, with his emphases on the will (love and choice), on obedience, and on the absolute necessity of grace.[12] In the scholastic period, although terminology and details modify somewhat under pressure of the incoming Aristotelianism, and in spite of many differences between the individual thinkers, the basic psychology of the Augustinian Franciscans, Scotus and Ockham for example, remains much the same: the primacy of the will and the affective activities of the soul, especially love, in both God and man;[13] the emphasis on God's sovereignty, authority, and will, and, correspondingly, on man's freedom, dependence, and obedience;[14] and the reduction of secondary causes to a minimal, highly contingent status.[15] In this psychology, humility is a great virtue and theology a practical discipline, something one does, not something one speculates about.[16] The virtuous person here is the person who freely and lovingly conforms his or her will to the will of God.[17]

When Aquinas adopted the Aristotelian psychology in the thirteenth century, a new theory of human nature developed alongside the old. In Aquinas's psychology, as in Aristotle's, the intellect is prime, the appetites (love, joy, fear, and so on) subordinated to it.[18] The emphasis here is on reason and the soul's intellective activities, especially cognition; on natural causes;[19] on being rational more so than being obedient;[20] and on understanding things by understanding their causes rather than by experiencing them. Knowledge is a virtue[21] and theology therefore a speculative science. In this psychology, the person virtuous in nature is the person whose intellect rules his or her appetites rationally; supernatural grace perfects this nature, enabling its recipient to share in God's nature.[22]

These faculty psychologies were philosophical. Rather than clinical, their motivation was theological and ethical; and rather than the individual, their object of study was the universal—that essential inborn nature common to all human beings regardless of time, place, or particular circumstance. Further, in addition to being philosophical, these psychologies were marvelously complex. For that reason, since their "personalities," so to speak, are so very different from the "personalities" of modern psychologies, I think an introductory analogy will prove helpful.

To the twentieth-century observer, the best of scholastic psychology is similar in both its virtues and its vices to the best of later medieval manuscript illumination: On the one hand, both are elegant, ornate, and logically gorgeous, crowded with elaborated concepts and elongated figures in gracefully static symmetrical groupings set amid patterned partitioned backgrounds bordered with forms at once familiar and fantastic. Yet, on the other hand, both are too busy for the modern taste, too repetitious, too divided and compartmentalized, too noisy in their lack of attention to proper emphasis and their compulsion to fill up completely every single hole. As a result, in both Gothic illumination and Gothic psychological theory, the rich complexity of the parts often obscures the simple unities of the whole.

In the Tickhill Psalter at the New York Public Library (Ms. Spencer 26), for example, the initial D for Psalm 52, shown in figure 3, is almost a full-page illustration, stunning in reds, blues and gold.[23] The rectangular center of the D is divided vertically and horizontally to form four small equal rectangles, each containing a little tableau scene of people, each tableau backed with arches and divided from the others by columns and floors, the larger enclosing rectangle surrounded by a scallop-edged oval filled in with four opposing pairs of patterns, this surrounded by a gold background

Figure 3. Initial D of Psalm 52, Tickhill Psalter, fol. 51, c. 1310. Spencer Collection MS 26, New York Public Library.

enclosed in a patterned oval border, this then formed into a circle by crescents added at either side containing leaves and heraldic shields, this then bordered on the sides with reverse scallops and on top and bottom with squared edges, both of these latter filled in with paired contrasting patterns, this then topped with a large leaf-filled spiral off to the left. All this gorgeous artwork actually comprises just a large capital D. To describe it so, however, is to simplify to the point of falsification. Yet, on the other hand, if one wishes to comprehend the manuscript as a unified whole, to see it as a psalter rather than just to admire the individual pages, then such simplification is absolutely necessary, at least at the beginning. So too with Gothic philosophies. One has to see the simplified wholes before one can comprehend the parts. Yet one has to understand the significance of at least the major parts in order to apprehend and appreciate the wholes.

Further, when we today admire the beautiful Tickhill Psalter page, our ignorance of the specific references the artist was making transforms it as a work of art. Rather than conveying to us a powerful spiritual, ethical, political, and cultural message, and making that message *real,* the page conveys instead a feeling of abstract aesthetic beauty, a marvel of form, color, and composition, very elegant and charming, but, alas, no longer powerful, just decorative. In fact, Richard Marks and Nigel Morgan tell us, the Tickhill scenes are from the life of David. In the upper two the Lord instructs David to go to Hebron in Judah. In the lower, on the left David and his wives Ahinoam and Abigail arrive there, and on the right David is anointed King of Judah. In the lower margin David is told that the men of Jabesh-gilead were those who had taken the bodies of Saul and his sons from the wall of Beth-shan and buried them, and on the right David sends messengers to thank them. The outer shields bear the arms of England and France and the Hastings, Clare, and Percy families. Consider the implications, when this page was made (c. 1310), of surrounding these scenes of divine and royal power and devotion to it and reward from it, with both the shields of England and France and the shields of these three magnate families. A fifteenth-century inscription implies that this manuscript was intended for the monastery of Augustinian canons at Worksop in York diocese. All told, this single initial D conveys a powerful message—and a message about power. For us, of course, even with its subject matter identified, the psalter page is still not as forceful as it was for its Gothic audience, but at least now it does mean something concrete and important. It is no longer just an abstract, beautiful, complexly decorated capital D. This is what I hope to do with Chaucer's uses of scholastic psychological and language use theories in the Knight's Tale: raise them from complex and attractive but relatively meaningless details to carriers of powerful, politically and culturally important messages—not only to Chaucer's own Gothic audience, but, I believe, to his twentieth-century audience as well.

As I started the explication above with the human figures to which the eye is most drawn, those of the Lord and David, so I will start the Knight's Tale with the human figures to which the first-time reader is most drawn, Palamon and Arcite. For the past thirty-five years, the majority of Knight's Tale critics, both those who read it as pessimistic and those who read it as comedic, have generally agreed that the two rival young knights are finally not very interesting: "As characters they are scarcely distinguishable."[24] Remarks made en route to this common conclusion, however, vary widely. The two are equally worthy or equally ridiculous; the two are equally noble or equally dishonorable; or, to the degree they are different, each represents half of a two-part standard, for example active/contemplative or lover/warrior or whatever.[25] As will become clear, the interpretation I am proposing will agree with all of these, albeit in different ways. The knights do embody two parts of a single phenomenon, that is, the debate about universal human nature; and although at their best the two are equally worthy, on occasion both of them can be equally ridiculous.

For the educated audience of Chaucer's time, the personalities of these particular young knights would have constituted fairly obvious invitations to think in terms of some kind of debate. The details Chaucer uses for each are very different. Palamon speaks of "crueel goddes," Arcite of benevolent "purveiaunce"; Palamon prays for death rather than disappointment, Arcite promises to cut his hair if he wins; at the end, Palamon is living in all bliss, Arcite is "coold," not in this "registre." Medieval literary debates, unlike modern, were common and were deliberately didactic. Their fundamental purpose was to air the issues. To designate either side a winner or loser was secondary. This is why in so many debates—winter/summer, rose/lily, water/wine—either no winner is declared or else the winner is obvious from the outset. This chapter will set forth the characterizations of Palamon and Arcite as, essentially, a medieval literary debate between equally attractive and equally worthy young opposites, rivals not only in love but also in psychology. My plan is first to air the eight major issues on which Chaucer opposes the two—cosmology, prime faculty, freedom, ethical development, evil, reasoning, piety, and relationship with Providence. After that I will set forth Chaucer's depiction of the two theories as overdetermined, focusing (because Chaucer does) on the restrictions both theories place on human freedom and therefore on individual human responsibility.

The Issues According to the Scholastic Philosophers

By Chaucer's time, these two opposing theories of human nature—one holding for primacy of the will, the other for primacy of the intellect—had been around for several generations. Aquinas died in 1274, Scotus in 1308, Ockham in 1349. So far as one can tell, simplifications of these two great theories as to the nature of the human mind were part of the common conceptual currency of Chaucer's time, just as simplifications of evolution theory and stimulus/response theory are part of the common conceptual currency of our own time.[26] As touched on earlier, Palamon is characterized according to the theory which held that will (i.e., love and choice) is the nobler function of the soul, the theory descended from Augustine and associated with Bonaventure, John Duns Scotus, William of Ockham, and the scholastic Augustinian Franciscans in general. Arcite is characterized according to the theory which held that intellect is the nobler faculty of the soul, the theory derived from Aristotle and associated with Albert the Great, Thomas Aquinas, and Godfrey of Fontaines. In the explication that follows, notice how systematically Chaucer builds these two characterizations, ticking off the topics one by one. As will become clear, both depictions are accurate and objective. Value judgments are neither made nor solicited as to the relative merits of either side. The two young men are treated as equally worthy albeit quite different, and the two theories of human nature as equally valuable albeit in quite different ways.[27]

1. COSMOLOGY

Opposition between the two young knights begins in their first pair of speeches, when each reveals his belief as to the manner in which the universe is run: by means of intelligible natural causes, natural laws that are put into motion at a distance and proceed inexorably in their course; or by a personal divine volition that is present in the world and steps in freely whenever it wishes to change the course of events.[28]

In the intellectualist cosmology, according to whose psychology Arcite is characterized, the fundamental principle is causation. God works in an orderly manner through natural processes of cause and effect. For Aquinas as for Aristotle, one knows an event or a thing by knowing its causes. All of Aquinas's "Five Ways" for showing the existence of God, for example, depend upon reasoning from things in this world back to God by means of chains of causes.[29] When Palamon cries out on first seeing Emelye, Arcite immediately asks after the cause: "Cosyn myn, what eyleth thee, . . . Why cridestow? Who hath thee doon offence?" (1081–83); and when Palamon does not answer, Arcite goes right on to blame a distant natural cause: some "aspect or disposicioun / Of Saturne" condemned us at birth. Later, in his long lament at the end of Part I, Arcite posits an intelligible universe in which the divine principle works indirectly by means of causes, utilizing lesser evils (poverty and prison) in order to prevent greater ones (murder and "greet siknesse," 1251–59).

Palamon's cosmology, on the other hand, is quite different. For the scholastic Augustinian Franciscans like Scotus and Ockham, according to whose psychology Palamon is characterized, the supreme principle in the universe is not reason but will, not regular and therefore intelligible natural laws (causes), but an omnipotent, absolutely free divine will that overrules the order of nature Itself established and steps in directly from time to time.[30] Thus when Arcite advises him to endure their lot patiently, Palamon's immediate response is to drop to his knees to pray: "Venus, if it be thy wil . . . Out of this prisoun help that we may scapen . . . [or] of oure lynage have som compassioun" (1104–10). In a voluntarist universe, the divine may intervene at any moment; hence Palamon prays. Later, in his paralleled long lament at the end of Part I, Palamon posits a voluntarist world ruled arbitrarily (1303–4) by an essentially unfathomable will (1306–24) which makes some things known by positive writ (1305–06) and other things happen by direct intervention (1104–11, 1328–33, 1592). Thus, although the two knights live in the same world, they perceive it very differently.[31]

2. PRIME FACULTY

The same opposition—intellect versus will—is apparent in their personalities. Each knight speaks from, and therefore appeals to in the reader, the faculty of the soul his side in the controversy considered prime.

Every one of Palamon's speeches consists of movements of the will—emotional appeals, moral judgments, and choices—all functions[32] of the will according to scholastic Augustinian psychology. Throughout the tale, Palamon's customary vocabulary is emotional and judgmental. He is, he tells Venus from his knees, a "sorweful, wrecched creature" brought low by "tirannye" (1106–11). It is no great honor, he tells Arcite, to be a false "traitour" to your own "cosyn" and "brother" (1129–31). He considers the gods "crueel" and unjust—in this world serpents and thieves go free while "trewe" men like him suffer in prison (1303–28). You are a "rightful" lord and judge, he tells Theseus, whereas we two "wrecches" deserve to be slain: Arcite because he was banished and has "japed" you; I because I broke out of your prison "wikkedly" (1715–41). And in his final speech he prays devoutly to Venus, "O lady myn," "faireste of faire," and "lady bright," praising her virtue in heaven and asking "pitee" for his "bittre teeris smerte" (2221–31). Further, in addition to emotional and judgmental words, Palamon's speeches constantly proffer disjunctive choices: Help us escape or have compassion on our lineage (1107–10); "Seistow this" in earnest or in play (1124–25); "Forthre" my case with Emelye or be "fals" to your oath (1146–51); either "thow shalt dye, / Or thow ne shalt nat loven Emelye. / Chees which thou wolt" (1593–95); "Sle me first" or "sle hym first" (1721–23); and "Yif me my love" or have Arcite "bere" me "thurgh the herte" (2254–60). Thus, in every one of his speeches, Palamon speaks from and to the function of the will, stirring its emotions and judgments and insisting that it choose.

Arcite's speeches, on the other hand, consist mainly of matters of information that are spoken from and to the intellect—causes and their effects, distinctions, reasons, circumstances of fact or knowledge, and explanatory analogies[33]—and, moreover, his speeches tend to be logically organized into parts and lists. Saturn is the cause of our being in prison (1087–89). If I can't see that lady in the garden, "I nam but deed" (1121–22). "Thyn is affeccioun of hoolynesse," whereas "myn is love as to a creature" (1158–59). We strive as "houndes for the boon" (1177). When Palamon challenges him in the wood, Arcite's angry reply consists of the reasons why he will not fight him now (Palamon is "sik," "wood" for love, weaponless, and mistaken about the oath), followed by the offer of a fair fight consisting again of the reasons for the offer (Palamon is a worthy knight and willing to settle it that way, 1608–9) and then a list of the circumstances under which it will take place (tomorrow, secretly, here; harness, food, drink, bedding; and mortal, 1610–19). In Part IV, when he recommends Palamon to Emelye, his recommendation takes the form of yet another list of reasons: Palamon's truth, honor, knighthood, wisdom, humility, estate, lineage, and so on (2786–95). Arcite's speeches are informational rather than judgmental; and they proceed rationally from part to part in intellectually organized units—lists, analogies, chains of causes.

Thus the speeches of the two young knights are contrasted based on their respective prime faculties. All of Palamon's are spoken from and to the will—its affections, its moral judgments, and its capacity to choose. When Palamon speaks of a cause, as he occasionally does (1328–33, 1591–93), his point is its injustice or its bearing on a choice, not its causation *per se;* that is to say, he subordinates matters of intellect to matters of will. Moreover, he never uses an analogy, nor are any of his speeches organized rationally into lists or chains of causes. Contrariwise, Arcite's speeches are spoken primarily from and to the intellect and always refer to matters of knowledge—causes, reasons, distinctions, analogies, factual circumstances. Because the intellectualist psychology is more complicated, as will be discussed shortly (under ethical development), Arcite occasionally speaks from and to both faculties about equally (for example, "How longe, Juno [cause], thurgh thy crueltee [moral judgment], / Woltow werreyen Thebes," 1543–44); but he never offers disjunctive choices, nor are any of his speeches organizationally undivided. The contrast is particularly clear in their epithets for each other in Part II when they are angry: Each assumes the other should be conforming to his own faculty priority and condemns him for not doing so—Palamon calls Arcite a traitor, impugning Arcite's morals, his will (1580); Arcite calls Palamon a fool, impugning his intellect (1606).[34] In the twentieth century, this distinction between the content of the will and the content of the intellect is rarely drawn, so we do not easily perceive the opposition between these two kinds of speeches; but a fourteenth-century audience, accustomed to the rivalry between voluntarist and intellectualist (between Franciscan and Dominican, generally speaking), would have had no difficulty perceiving what Chaucer was doing. Palamon speaks as an embodiment of the voluntarist psychology, one who assumes everybody is or should be a voluntarist; Arcite speaks as an embodiment of the intellectualist psychology, one who assumes everybody is or should be an intellectualist. A comic but potentially tragic impasse.

3. FREEDOM

Just as the two knights and their two psychologies are opposed as to cosmology and prime faculty, so too are they opposed in their areas of freedom. (In this period, it will be recalled, freedom referred to control of one's appetite or emotion as well as one's thought.)

According to Aquinas, all human beings by nature desire happiness as their final end; presented with a perfect good, therefore, their only freedom lies in choice of the means by which to attain it.[35] This is how Arcite is characterized: End natural (bound, determined); means free. In Part I he perceives Emelye as a vision of perfect loveliness, a "good without blemish" in philosophical terms. As a result, he falls in love with her irresistibly, by natural necessity. As he tells Palamon, "A man moot nedes love, . . . He may not fleen it, . . . Al be she mayde, or wydwe, or elles wyf" (1165–71). For Arcite, love of Emelye is a law of his nature, a natural law, and therefore superior to any positive law such as an oath of marriage or brotherhood.[36] And in Part III, choice of means being his area of freedom, Arcite prays only for the means by which to achieve her, victory in the tournament. He is quite explicit to Mars: "Yif me victorie, I aske thee namoore" (2420). As for the other side, the voluntarist theories about man's area of freedom were in many ways the opposite: For Scotus, every human being is completely free as to both means and end, but if he chooses happiness for his end—and the virtuous man will choose happiness (God)—then he must accept the means determined by the divine to achieve it.[37] And this, of course, is how Palamon is characterized: End free; means obedience (bound). Like Arcite, he perceives Emelye as a good without blemish and falls in love with her immediately, but he does not fall in love irresistibly. For Palamon, love of Emelye is a matter of choice rather than nature, as is shown by his repeated demand that Arcite simply stop loving her (1142–43, 1593–95, 1731) and by his seven-year delay before committing himself completely to her.[38] Not until Part II does Palamon decide that "outher he wolde lese his life, / Or wynnen Emelye unto his wyf" (1485–86); and now at last, having chosen her as his final end, he breaks out of prison. In Part III, given the opportunity to win her in the tournament, he nevertheless prays only for his area of free choice, final end, "fully possessioun / Of Emelye" (2241–42), and explicitly leaves determination of the means up to the divine: "I ne axe nat tomorwe to have victorie, . . . Fynd thow the manere hou, and in what wyse: / I recche nat but it may bettre be / To have victorie of hem, or they of me, / So that I have my lady in myne armes" (2239–47). Thus, as in their cosmologies and prime faculties, so too are the two young rivals characterized as contraries in their areas of freedom. Arcite's final end is determined by his nature; his freedom lies in choice of means—the intellectualist theory of man's freedom. Palamon, on the other hand, is completely free, but once he chooses happiness for his final end, he submits to the means the divine sends him—a voluntarist theory of man's freedom.

4. ETHICAL DEVELOPMENT: PALAMON AND THE *AFFECTIO JUSTITIAE*

Both young knights develop ethically in accordance with the two rival theories they epitomize. Neither is virtuous at the beginning of the tale; by its end both have become truly gentle, truly noble.

In the Augustinian tradition, as mentioned earlier, the virtuous person is the person who freely conforms his or her will to the will of the divine; and this, of course, is how Palamon develops during the tale. Hatred of God is the one intrinsically evil action, according to Scotus,[39] and resentment toward the gods is the major theme of Palamon's cosmology at the end of Part I (1303–24). (In this context, the scholastics regarded all acts of the will as either positive, i.e., love, or negative, i.e., hatred.) Palamon clearly accepts the power and freedom of these "cruel goddes." Indeed, he submits to their "observaunce" because of their power, not freely and not out of love. In his prayer in Part III, however, he has undergone total change. Now he conforms his will fully, freely, and lovingly to the will of the divine. "Mercy, lady bright," he tells Venus with "humble cheere," "Youre vertu is so greet in hevene above, / That if yow list, I shal wel have my love . . . And if ye wol nat so, my lady sweete, / Thanne preye I thee, tomorwe with a spere / That Arcita me thurgh the herte bere" (2231–56). Whatever Venus wills for him—he would prefer Emelye or death, he says, but even if it should turn out to be something else (as it does)—he is completely submissive. Her will is his will. The traditional Augustinian theology of grace combines total submission with total freedom, and these are the qualities that characterize Palamon's prayer, his final speech in the tale.

II. Faculty Component

Justice, in the wide Augustinian sense of "rightly ordered love," of valuing things according to their own intrinsic worth (rather than according to what they can do for you), is perhaps the central concept of the voluntarist psychology. As a result, Scotus rejected the Aristotelian Thomistic argument that man is naturally drawn to his own good, and is therefore free to deliberate a choice only if he perceives an imperfection in the object of his desire, on grounds that it could not explain acts of altruism. Instead, developing further the notion of justice he found in Augustine and Anselm and the Franciscan tradition, he concluded that the human will has an innate twofold inclination toward the good, one passive, the other active: a passive *affectio commodi* which corresponds to the natural appetite by which a creature must seek its own fulfillment and so is not free; and an active *affectio justitiae* by which one is free to do justice to the intrinsic worth of a thing, to love it for its own sake regardless of its effect on or value to oneself. This latter he calls the native freedom of the will. It is a power of *self-determination* with regard to the good known by the intellect. This freedom to do justice to others is, for Scotus, the power that frees one from the necessities of one's own nature and thus makes a genuine Christian ethics possible. By it one is free to love God for himself, to love one's neighbor for himself or herself, and to share one's loves with others.[40] How one judges the good in others can, therefore, indicate one's ethical state. In the Knight's Tale, Palamon's notion of justice expands, from merely demanding his rights according to the oath to freely loving the divine for its own sake, irrespective of its treatment of him.

In Part I, Palamon's first, and inadequate, notion of justice is expressed in his insistence on the simple positive oath between him and Arcite. In it, their treatment was to be equal and responsibility reciprocal (1129–39). When Arcite refuses to honor it vis-à-vis Emelye, Palamon is outraged. He recognizes no natural law that exempts lovers. Obligations freely made are to be lived up to. Arcite's subsequent release from prison convinces Palamon that injustice exists not just between the two of them, but that injustice is the way of the world. Men are not merely treated like beasts; they are treated worse (1315–21). Arbitrary power is what rules this world (1323–27).

In Part II, Palamon has developed a new and larger notion of justice. After sitting in prison for seven years, he emerges with two things: a plan to win Emelye by force and an idea of justice according to which there is nothing wrong with mustering his Theban friends to make war on Theseus, but there is something wicked about breaking out of Theseus's jail or giving him a false name (1735; 1585, 1729). According to this idea, rather than looking to one's equals for justice (since it doesn't work; Arcite reneged), one looks higher, to the figure with positive power. In Athens this is Theseus. This is why, when Theseus stops the fight in the grove, Palamon immediately addresses him as "rightful lord and juge" and spontaneously makes full confession not only of his own crimes but of Arcite's as well. Chaucer must intend Palamon's tone in this speech to be one of repentence, dread, and humility because that is the way Theseus interprets it (1776, 1781). As a voluntarist, Palamon is a man with an innate affection for justice— a natural love of what is right. In his experience he has found no natural law in this world. Therefore only positive law can exist. Theseus is the legitimate ruler of this land. Therefore any decision Theseus makes in it is rightful: Arcite's banishment and his own imprisonment were rightful because Theseus willed them. (Translated into the theological terms in which this position is ordinarily stated, the notion is the standard voluntarist position on morality: Good is good because God wills it, and morality consists of doing voluntarily what one is obligated to do.) Palamon has just escaped from Theseus's prison in order to win Emelye, but he is under no illusions as to the justice of his position on Theseus's lands; as he says, he is wicked and encumbered[41] and deserves death. However, here in Part II, in response to Palamon's insistence on justice-as-enforcing-the-positive-law, death for them both, Theseus considers all the circumstances and gives them justice-as-equity instead, that is, simple fairness, a far wider notion.

In Part III, in his final speech in the tale, Palamon displays an even wider notion: justice-as-love-of-the-divine-for-its-own-sake. Because his affection for justice, his native freedom of the will, frees him from his natural, creaturely drive for self-fulfillment, Palamon can appreciate the divine for its own sake, regardless of what it may or may not do for him (including the disposition of

Emelye); and he therefore submits freely, lovingly, and totally to the will of Venus. In the Augustinian tradition, justice is rightly ordered love. All the cardinal virtues are simply different aspects of the love of God. Ultimately, in Palamon's total accord with Venus here, one feels the old, all-encompassing Platonic concept of justice as transcendent, permanent, harmonious unity.

In Part IV, Palamon remains obedient to the will of the divine as expressed through the outcome of the tournament and makes no further effort to win Emelye. Instead, some years later, Theseus gives her to him because, he says, Palamon deserves her:

> He is a kynges brother sone, pardee;
> And though he were a povre bacheler,
> Syn he hath served yow so many a yeer,
> And had for yow so greet adversitee,
> It moste been considered, leeveth me; (3084–88)

It is true, as Theseus says; Palamon has earned her and giving her to him is the "right" thing to do. On the other hand, the result of this marriage will be renewed Theban "obeisaunce" for the Athenians. Regardless of the rhetoric, therefore, Palamon's world truly is a world ruled by power, not by natural law (whatever that may be, according to this philosophy, and on whatever lower level it may exist). Thus here at the end of the Knight's Tale, justice, equity, mercy, love, power, and expediency all fall together harmoniously for Palamon, as they do generally in the Augustinian-Franciscan tradition.

During the course of the Knight's Tale, Palamon has become a truly virtuous human being, at least from the voluntarist point of view.

5. ETHICAL DEVELOPMENT: ARCITE AND THE *VISIO DIVINAE ESSENTIAE*

Thomistic ethics arrives at much the same result as Augustinian, but via a different process. In Thomism, as mentioned earlier, nature is perfected by grace. The natural virtues have to do with the soul's natural powers, and are achieved; whereas grace has to do with the soul's substance, and is infused. Thus Arcite will first achieve natural virtue in that his intellect will learn to rule his appetites rationally; then he will display the charity that indicates supernatural virtue, that is, the reception of grace and participation in the divine nature.

In Parts I and II, Arcite's intellect and appetites are in conflict. On being released from prison in Part I, Arcite expresses the belief that Providence is benevolent and often gives folk "wel bettre than they kan hemself devyse" (1254), but he does not accept his own release gratefully, as Providence doing "wel bettre" for him. Instead he succumbs to "so greet despeir" (1245, an irascible appetite in Thomism) that, he says, nothing and no one can help him. Likewise, when challenged by Palamon in the woods in Part II, with the same old erroneous (from Arcite's point of view) accusation of falsehood over the oath, Arcite succumbs to anger (another irascible appetite in Thomism) and behaves irrationally, offering to do what he had already explained to Palamon was pointless, to fight like dogs over a lady when the final disposition of the lady was not up to either of them (1617–19). Thus in Parts I and II, Arcite's appetites are able to subvert his intellect, causing him to lose faith and to behave foolishly.

But his Part III prayer for victory demonstrates that his intellect has now achieved proper natural control over his appetites. He organizes his petition logically into four equal parts. Further, each part consists of rational causes—the reasons Mars should accept him as a follower (2373–81), the analogy likening the two of them (2382–92), the chain of causes defining his need (2393–405), and finally the services he will provide in return (2406–20). In short, the "hoote fir" of Arcite's passion now burns with a reasonable flame. He has, therefore, achieved natural virtue according to the letter (if not precisely the spirit) of the Thomist psychology; his intellect is in charge. During his deathbed speech in Part IV, however, he evinces not simply natural virtue, as in his prayer, but its supernatural perfection—true unselfish charity—in his tender regard for Emelye and his loving respect for his cousin, neither of which has been in evidence before this (2765–97).

Cognition is perhaps the central concept in the intellectualist psychology. How one cognizes what one sees can therefore indicate one's ethical state. In the course of his ethical development as an embodiment of the intellectualist psychology, Chaucer indicates the three stages of Arcite's ethical development by changing his cognition of Emelye: Arcite cognizes her first, when his faculties are disordered, as pure form, an immaterial good; then, when his faculties are in proper natural hierarchy, as female common nature individuated simply by her effects on him; and only finally, after receiving grace, does he recognize her as a unique human being, a *compositum,* with her own desires and obligations. The key issue here is the Thomist (and Aristotelian, as set forth earlier) conception of natural hierarchy among the faculties of the soul. In Thomism, man is defined as a unity, a *compositum* of intellectual soul and physical body (a controversial theory at the time, since limiting man's external contact to his senses seemed to despiritualize him).[42] In this psychology, soul and body together make up the man. Man's soul consists of a number of faculties (vegetative, sensitive, intellectual), hierarchically arranged, intellect in natural control. He has two appetites, the intellective appetite or will (its object being the good in general) and the sensitive appetite (its object being sensible bodies), this latter appetite consisting of two kinds, concupiscible and irascible. Irrationality, or evil, results when an appetitive faculty, whether will or sensitive, unnaturally gains control over the intellect.

During Parts I and II, the faculties of Arcite's soul are out of control. At first his will (i.e., his intellectual appetite) is ruling his intellect. From his very first glimpse of Emelye, Arcite desires only the *sight* of her, a satisfaction only of his will:

> The fresshe beautee sleeth me sodeynly
> Of hire that rometh in the yonder place,
> And but I have hir mercy and hir grace,
> That I *may seen hire* atte leeste weye,
> I nam but deed; ther nis namoore to seye. (1118–22,
>   emphasis added)

This is merely the first statement, to be repeated eight times in the next three hundred lines (1231, 1239, 1273, 1346, 1352, 1357, 1397,

1407) that Arcite's great desire is *visual contemplation* of Emelye: "Oonly the sight of hire," "the sighte of hire," "Syn that I may nat seen you, Emelye," "nevere mo he shal his lady see," "But seen his lady shal he nevere mo," "For seen his lady shal he nevere mo," "ne for the dred of deeth shal I nat spare / To se my lady," and "And seen his lady wel ny day by day." As a purely intellectual appetite (in the Thomist psychology), Arcite's will is fully satisfied by visual contemplation. In fact, in this psychology, it is "more perfect and nobler" to possess an object through cognitive knowledge (i.e., through mentally assimilating its form) than through volition (i.e., possessing it as existing outside oneself). Therefore, by contemplating Emelye visually rather than possessing her corporeally, Arcite actually possesses her in a more perfect, a nobler way. The problem is (or at any rate the Thomist problem is), Arcite is suppressing the fact that he is a man, a *compositum,* with bodily appetites as well. Throughout Parts I and II, Arcite's intellect is, wrongly, being ruled by his will, joined at times by one of his sensitive appetites (irascible in lines 1152–61, 1596–1619, 1219–74; and concupiscible in lines 1530–72).

In Part III, however, Arcite's intellect has clearly taken control of his appetites. Not only is his prayer rationally organized, as specified earlier, but Chaucer now gives him an abstractive cognition of Emelye that is, in Aristotelian terms, totally and virtuously self-fulfilling. Rather than (incorrectly) desiring only the sight of her, he now (correctly) desires only the use of her. He now cognizes only the form that animates her matter, her female common nature—"she" (2396), "she" (2398), and "hire" (2399); and her effects on him—the "wo" she does him (2396) and his "peynes smerte" (2392, do not overlook the Latin pun). That is to say, he cognizes her simply as an object that causes a physical need in him only she can satisfy. (By way of comparison, recall Palamon's loving individualized perception of Emelye in his paralleled prayer: "Emelye," 2243; "my lady," 2247; "my lady," 2250; "my love," 2260.) Here in Part III, Arcite has achieved the natural virtue of the intellectualist psychology; he is cognizing as the *compositum* he is, as an abstractive intellectual soul united with a corporeal body and attempting to fulfill its natural corporeal needs rationally by praying for victory in the tournament.

Toward the end of Part IV, however, it is above all the change in Arcite's cognition of Emelye that indicates he has now been infused with divine grace. As he lies dying, he transcends the pagan abstractive epistemology and now, finally, he cognizes Emelye with true charity, supernatural love. He recognizes and values her as a unique individual human being with an intelligible quality all her own. No longer is she just a common nature, she/she/her, to be used. In fact, his magnificent and heartbreaking deathbed speech consists largely of a series of phrases expressing his new cognition of her special individuality: "To yow, my lady, that I love moost" (2767); "To yow aboven every creature" (2769); "the peynes stronge, / That I for yow have suffred" (2771–72); "myn Emelye!" (2773); "myn hertes queene! . . . my wyf!" (2775); "Myn hertes lady, endere of my lyf!" (2776); "my sweete foo, myn Emelye" (2780); "And softe taak me in youre armes tweye, / For love of God" (2781–82). Arcite is now cognizing Emelye in accordance with the distinctively Christian notion that every human soul possesses its own unique metaphysical identity and transcendent value. Moreover, as Arcite goes on to recommend Palamon to her, it is apparent that he now realizes that Emelye has feelings, and he defers to them. She may or may not have a choice about getting married ("shal," 2796), he implies, but if she does, she might consider Palamon. This is the first time in the Tale that anyone has treated Emelye's feelings as real, further evidence that Arcite has received the gift of divine charity.

What happens to Arcite's soul after his death? Whereas the Franciscans taught that man's final glorification is in love, the Dominicans held instead that the final goal for man lies in contemplation, in the cognitive eternal *visio* of God. Nine statements in three hundred lines at the outset of the rivalry that all Arcite desires is the sight of Emelye is extraordinary, and far beyond the number necessary to establish the disorder in his faculties. Couple these nine repetitions with the cognitive teleology that is the very essence of Thomism—"the last end of an intelligent creature is to know

God"[43]—and the implication seems to be that Chaucer intended his readers to have in mind for Arcite from the very first, the *visio divinae essentiae* for his final end. In Chaucer's time, his own audience could scarcely have overlooked the allusion.

Thus the two young men develop ethically, each according to his respective psychology, into "gentil," truly "parfit" knights. Both have been ennobled, albeit in different ways, in accord with courtly romance tradition. In final behavior, it would be difficult to choose between them: Palamon's loving submission to Venus and gentle service of Emelye is just as attractive, but no more, as Arcite's immensely moving questions as to final causes as he dies, with charity in his heart, speaking of the love of God.

6. EVIL

In both philosophical traditions, man's nature was damaged by the Fall, but the two traditions tended to focus on different manifestations of that damage: the voluntarists on wrongful behavioral choices; the intellectualists on deficiencies in being or knowledge. Thus Palamon's negative judgments are polarized on the moral behavior of others, whereas Arcite's negative judgments are polarized on existence or knowledge.

In the voluntarist tradition, evil is choosing not to do what one is obligated to do. From Palamon's point of view, this describes Arcite's behavior exactly; he is choosing not to observe the oath into which he willingly entered. In Palamon's universe, no natural law exists. Because the divine is omnipotent, it does not have to create or act in a manner humans would consider reasonable; thus things could have been ordered very differently than they are. As a result, the only knowable law, the only law that human beings can count on, is positive law—law that has been formally (i.e., positively) agreed to, imposed, legislated, made known, written down. This is the reason for Palamon's strenuous insistence that Arcite fulfill what he (Palamon) regards as the terms of the positive oath of brotherhood between them, an oath which Arcite made freely and is therefore justly obligated to honor; and this is the reason for Palamon's moral outrage when Arcite, placing love above positive law (1165–70), refuses to stop loving the woman Palamon loved first. In Part I, in the course of a single, wonderfully self-convincing, self-righteous speech, Palamon decides that Arcite is a traitor, developing the word "fals" from mere hypothetical possibility in a subjunctive clause—"It nere . . . to thee no greet honour / For to be *fals*" (1129–30)—to a descriptive adverb in a conditional—"And now thow woldest *falsly* been aboute / To love my lady" (1142–43)—to a present epithet—"Nay, certes, *false* Arcite" (1145)—and finally to the negative half of a disjunctive ultimatum—"helpen me, . . . / Or elles artow *fals*" (1149–51). Palamon believes that in loving Emelye Arcite is deliberately choosing to behave in an evil fashion, to be a "false traytour wikke"; and Arcite remains evil in Palamon's eyes until their joint positive oaths to Theseus toward the end of Part II and Theseus's positive decree of the tournament bring to an end the conflict in the tale between natural and positive law. Thus Palamon makes his negative judgments about what he considers to be deliberately chosen, evil actions.

In the intellectualist tradition, on the other hand, evil is caused by deficiencies of one kind or another from the natural good order of things, and, therefore, these deficiencies form the basis of Arcite's complaints. In Arcite's universe, rather than constituting a positive act or thing in itself, evil is caused by the deprivation of some natural good. In Part I, Acite's first sight of Emelye fulfills a natural need for him; that is why he falls in love with her irresistably, and that is why later, when he is deprived of the sight of her, that is, deprived of his natural good, he judges himself sentenced to "helle" (1226). Similarly, in Part IV, the ultimate cause of Arcite's sickness is described as a deficiency in the natural ordering of his body: Arcite's "vertu expulsif" cannot fulfill its natural function of expelling the venom from his chest (2749–51).[44] Further, Arcite's own negative judgments are, consistently, negative judgments not of moral behavior, like Palamon's, but of being or of knowledge: "Allas that day that I was *born*" (1223); "Allas, that evere *knew* I Perotheus" (1227); "Why pleynen folk so in commune / On purveiaunce . . . That yeveth hem ful ofte . . . Wel bettre than they *kan* hemself *devyse?*" (1251–54); "We *witen nat* what thing we preyen heere" (1260); I "hadde a greet *opinioun*" (1268); and so on (emphases added). In sum, whereas the negative judgments of the voluntarist arise from what he perceives as deliberate choices, the negative judgments of the intellectualist arise from what he perceives as errors, defects, or lacks.

The two theories of evil are easily (and traditionally) reconciled on the basis that wrongful choices result from the disorder caused in the soul by the Fall. Yet in the Knight's Tale characterizations, Chaucer consistently depicts the two theories as mutually exclusive, implying once again that both psychologies are one-sided and partial.

7. REASONING

In their paired laments toward the end of Part I, each knight reasons about the nature of the universe with the mode of thinking generally associated in Chaucer's time with his tradition of philosophy. Arcite reasons deductively, Palamon inductively.

On the intellectualist side, the *a priori* theory of essences strongly implies that God wills the good because it is good. The assumption is that God's will, like man's, desires the good naturally and therefore necessarily. God's intellect perceives, so to speak, the best way to attain it and his will naturally follows his intellect. Arcite's cosmology here at the end of Part I simply assumes, takes it for granted, that Providence (or Fortune) gives men "wel bettre than they kan hemself devyse" (1254). In fact, he says, poverty and prison may be lesser evils, actually saving one from greater, such as sickness and murder (1255–58). To this way of thinking, man's suffering is caused by deficiencies in his knowledge rather than by anything positive or real. From here Arcite reasons deductively straight down to the interestingly unrealistic notion that human suffering is really due to human ignorance. Man doesn't suffer; he just can't find the right way home.

Infinite harmes been in this mateere.
We witen nat what thing we preyen heere:

We faren as he that dronke is as a mous.
A dronke man woot wel he hath an hous,
But he noot which the righte wey is thider,
And to a dronke man the wey is slider.
And certes, in this world so faren we;
We seken faste after felicitee,
But we goon wrong ful often, trewely. (1259–67)

If man just understood the whole picture, according to Arcite, he would know better than to feel pain (1268–72). By itself, without constant checking against one's actual experience of the real world, deductive cosmological thinking can lead one into this kind of fairy-tale optimism—an optimism that denies the real pain that does exist in the world (an optimism, for example, that accepts tyrants as a good because they provide the occasion for martyrs). Possibly this is why Chaucer's Arcite undergoes such extended physical torment in Part IV. That kind of suffering cannot be reasoned out of existence, and Arcite dies knowing that pain as well as pleasure does exist in this world.

As for the voluntarist side, much of Ockham's significance as a philosopher lay in his rejection of medieval realism and his "reconstruction of the whole fabric of philosophy on the basis of a radical empiricism" according to which all knowledge is based on "direct experience of individual things and particular events."[45] Thus Palamon's cosmology here at the end of Part I reasons inductively, from his own experience of the world straight up to the nature of the divine. In Palamon's world, human beings really suffer: innocent men are imprisoned, slain in this world and caused to weep in the next. Serpents and thieves and traitors like Arcite go free while he, innocent, languishes in prison tormented by love (1307–33). He says he is leaving the problem of human pain to the clerks (or augurers or gods, "dyvynys," 1323), but actually he has already drawn his conclusion: the gods are cruel. By itself, without constant checking against the fullness of one's experience in the world, inductive reasoning about particular injustices can lead one into this kind of universal nightmare—into denying the real happiness that does also exist in this world. Possibly this is why Providence sees to it that Palamon experiences joy as well as grief.

Both modes of reasoning, deductive and inductive, pertain to the natural power of the human mind. In daily living, the normal mind oscillates constantly back and forth between them. But here again, Chaucer's Knight characterizes the two theories as one-sided, suggesting again that while both can reach some truth, neither can reach all. Both modes of reasoning need constant testing against one's experience.

8. PIETY

In Part III, both young knights express their piety in the course of requesting divine aid, but as they pray to two different kinds of deities, they manifest two quite different modes of reverence. Here the contrast is between humility, pity, empathy, and the mystique of personal relationship on the one hand, as opposed to straightforward rationality, physical strength, businesslike self-fulfillment, and clear cause-and-effect sequences on the other. The contrast is drawn twice: in the way each approaches his divinity, and in the way each prays.

As the knights approach their temples, Chaucer's syntax, tense structure, and organizational clarity evoke the different ways two such different young men would actually move through space and time. Palamon approaches the temple of Venus slowly, with circumlocution, an effect due partly to the convolutions of the syntax. This twelve-line passage consists of one long paratactic sentence in which each of the five main verbs is accompanied by some circumstance of its performance which must be grasped before the sequence can continue, all of these being preceded by a false beginning and interrupted by two lengthy asides. The result is that the reader cognizes Palamon's movement hesitantly, as if in slow motion. Moreover, not only is Chaucer's syntax contorted, but his tense structure slips from preterite to present and back to preterite again, adding an inflectional complexity that contributes to the feeling of haziness:

The Sonday nyght er day bigan to sprynge
Whan Palamon the larke herde synge

Althogh it nere nat day by houres two
Yet song the larke and Palamon right tho
With holy herte and with an heigh corage
He roos to wenden on his pilgrymage
Vnto the blisful Citherea benygne
I mene Venus honurable and digne
And in hir hour he walketh forth a paas
Vnto the lystes ther hir temple was
And doun he kneleth and with humble cheere
And herte soor he seyde as ye shal heere (2209–20 MR, para-
graphing removed)

Thus, with the aid of convoluted paratactical syntax and illogical tense structure, Palamon experiences piety as an elevated, nonrational state of mysticism and sweet solemnity. Arcite's approach to Mars's temple, on the other hand, is forthright and thoroughly rational. No false starts, no extraneous circumstances, no moonlight, no larks, no songs, no rising to go and then three lines later going again, slowly, and no multiple haze-making synonyms as to destination. Instead, the passage consists of two standard straightforward sentences. Their syntax is lucid and regular and their tense structure consistently preterite.

The nexte hour of Mars folwynge this
Arcite vnto the temple walked is
Of fierse Mars to doon his sacrifise
With alle the rytes of his payen wise
With pitous herte and heigh deuocioun
Right thus to Mars he seyde his orisoun (2367–72 MR)

Arcite's is straightforward walking, straightforward praying. Moreover, with regard to organization of ideas, Arcite's approach is structured almost journalistically, When-What-Where-Why-How / How-What. Palamon's, on the other hand, rather than structured at all, is muddled: When-What-When-What-How-What-Why-Where-Who-When-What-Where-What-How-What. One may disagree with a few of the adverbial reductions, but they do show that the contrast here is not just one of length but, more importantly, of organizational clarity. The result is that Arcite's outline is sharper; his movement here, in syntax, diction, and tense and thought structure, is more readily perceptible to the reader's senses and therefore more intelligible than Palamon's. Palamon seems to wend, whereas Arcite really walks. Arcite experiences piety as a serious state of heightened attention and intellect, with his emotions properly subordinated to a self-perfecting telos, "right thus," in "payen wise."

In their prayers, as might be expected, Palamon speaks from the affections, Arcite from the intellect. The conception of Venus suggested by the phrases of Palamon's prayer is that of the blissful lady of heaven, loving, virtuous, merciful, ruling the universe benevolently by means of her power over all the processes of love. (A similar conception of Venus informs the proem to Book III of the *Troilus*.) Thus Palamon's prayer is all piety, praise, obedience, and tender heart.

> Faireste of faire, O lady myn, Venus,
> Doughter to Jove, and spouse of Vulcanus,
> Thow gladere of the mount of Citheron,
> For thilke love thow haddest to Adoon,[46]
> Have pitee of my bittre teeris smerte,
> And taak myn humble prayere at thyn herte. (2221–26)

This reverential mood continues on for thirty-four more lines: "Mercy, lady bright, . . . rewe upon my soore, . . . everemoore, . . . thy trewe servant . . . I kepe noght of armes, . . . [ne] victorie, . . . ne veyne glorie . . . But I wolde . . . dye in thy servyse . . . Youre vertu is so greet in hevene above / That if yow list . . . my lady sweete, . . . thow blisful lady deere." Indeed, even though his prayer is pagan and addressed to Venus, change the pagan names to Christian ones and Palamon's petition could be addressed to the Mother of God. The phrases he uses are the standard phrases of fourteenth-century Marian piety. Arcite's prayer, on the other hand, is a striking combination of rationality and Greek reference. Its division into four equal parts, each part organized by causes, was shown earlier. Equally rational is its approach to love. According to Aristotle, love of anything is an appetite to be satisfied rationally for one's own self-fulfillment, and that is Arcite's attitude here. In this passage Arcite's love for Emelye is an appetite, simply physical and completely self-interested. This is not necessarily bad; it is simply very Aristotelian, very rational: itch / scratch. In Arcite's prayer there is no mysticism of love, no deference to the lady, no caring, no grace, no affection, not even her own personal name. In Part III, Arcite's approach to love resembles his approach to deity—it is business-like. Further, Chaucer closes Arcite's prayer with two specifically Greek references: "The prayere stynt of Arcita the stronge" (2421 MR, the only use in the Knight's Tale of such a locution); and the promise to Mars of Arcite's first hair and beard (a custom particularly associated in antiquity with the Greeks[47]). Thus, in the ways they experience their piety, these opposing embodiments of the scholastic will/ intellect debate remain consistent, the voluntarist side all humility and tender affections, the intellectualist side all reason seeking the means to its end.

In addition, however, the two prayers, taken together, may also constitute another of Chaucer's rare topical allusions. The use of tender Marian-type phrases to express Palamon's affectivity, side by side with the use of several historically Greek-type allusions in Arcite's prayer, may reference the sometimes bitter fourteenth-century polemics between the two fraternal orders. In the high scholastic period, devotion to the Blessed Virgin was particularly associated with the Franciscan Order, whereas pagan Greek metaphysics were particularly associated with the Dominican. With regard to veneration of Mary, from the thirteenth century on, the question of her Immaculate Conception was the topic of heated debate in the West, especially between Dominican and Franciscan. Aquinas objected strenuously that to absolve Mary from original sin would jeopardize the Doctrine of the Redemption, which asserts that Christ saved all men. Scotus, on the other hand, responded strongly that Christ actually saved Mary more than anyone else in that he preserved her from original sin in the first place. In Chaucer's time the subject was a battleground between the two orders (in the fifteenth century Sixtus IV had to forbid both groups from indulging in further charges of heresy; in 1854, after four hundred more years of argument and counterargument, the doctrine was finally defined as dogma, on the basis above proposed by Scotus[48]). However, at the same time that the Franciscans were being forced to defend Mary, the Dominicans were being forced to defend the use of human reason to study the mysteries of the faith. The Augustinian and Franciscan traditionalists were appalled by Dominican rationalizing about the Trinity, the Incarnation, and the Sacraments. In addition, the Greek doctrine of essences, they held, was both an affront to God's dignity and a limitation on his omnipotence and freedom.[49] In both of these controversies—whether Mary was immaculately conceived, and whether universals exist and logic therefore illuminates Christian mysteries—on the Dominican side were reason, consistency, and the demands of the intellect; on the Franciscan side devotion and the affections of the will. Here in the Knight's Tale prayers, Chaucer's contrast of Marian-type diction and Greek allusion, in addition to continuing the tale's psychological debate, may also therefore refer topically to these two theologically explosive subjects. Certainly Chaucer could have made Palamon loving and obedient without using such Marian phrases as "thow blisful lady deere" and "Youre vertu is so greet in hevene above." Similarly, he could easily have made Arcite rational without making him quite so obnoxiously sexist and without the epithet and the pagan offer to cut his first hair. Albeit incapable of proof or disproof, the possibility of topical allusions remains, therefore, a tantalizing possibility.

To this twentieth-century reader, and I think to some fourteenth-century readers as well, both prayers seem a little overdone. Palamon's pilgrimage and prayer are just too touching; one can take only so much sweetness, softness, tearfulness, tenderness, and humbleness. His "werre" on chastity comes as a decided relief. Likewise, Arcite's prayer is just too self-serving. One doubts that any noble young lady with her wits about her, overhearing either prayer, would have given its speaker the time of day. By characterizing the one type of piety as overly sentimental and submissive and the other as overly organized and insensitive, Chaucer again suggests the one-sidedness of both scholastic psychologies.

9. RELATIONSHIP WITH PROVIDENCE

And now the last major contrast to be discussed here between the characterizations of these two theoretical young men is the relationship of each with Providence. This will be a two-step argument. First it will be necessary to show that behind the disastrous events and irresponsible planet-gods of the Knight's Tale is a benevolent Boethian Divine Providence, drawing all things out finally to good. Then I will try to show that both knights do come to final good (in terms satisfactory to the scholastic, if not to many of us): both achieve eternal bliss within the terms of their respective universal psychologies.

In the tale, Chaucer uses the standard epic technique, long familiar from the *Aeneid* and utilized also by Boccaccio in the *Teseida*, of differentiating between the religious beliefs of the characters inside the story as opposed to the reader's perception of the divinities behind those beliefs, so that in all three of these works, *Aeneid*, *Teseida*, and Knight's Tale, there are really two perceptions of the divine—that of the people inside the story, that of the reader outside.

First, the people inside the Knight's story are pagans and perceive the regular polytheistic pagan pantheon; they speak of or recognize or depict at least a dozen gods—Clemence, Mars, Saturn, Venus, Juno, Mercury, Diana, Love, Cupid, Pluto, Jupiter (Jove), Vulcan, and God. Leaving aside all references to God, only Mars, Diana, and Saturn are perceived by these people as having astrological associations (2043–45, 2077–78, 1088); and up until Theseus's final speech, no one seems to regard Jupiter as being particularly in charge. Only at the end of the tale, in his Prime Mover speech, does Theseus come to perceive a One behind the Many, whom he identifies as "Juppiter." The speech shows him to have become a monotheist, but he is still a pagan (i.e., his Prime Mover ordered the elements rather than created them from nothing, and survival is in the species, not for the individual). However, the speech shows that Theseus himself has begun moving toward a better system of belief, a monotheistic natural religion, and he is teaching his Athenians to do the same.[50]

The reader outside the story, on the other hand, who is carefully studying it in the medieval fashion to get at its inner truths,[51] perceives not pagan pantheon but Ptolemaic planet-gods. The seven deities in Chaucer's tale who take active, visible-to-the-reader part in its events are precisely the seven planets of the Ptolemaic system—Diana (2346–60), Mercury (1381–92), Venus (2438–53, 2664–67), Phebus (1491–96), Mars (2438–53), Jupiter (2438–46), and Saturn (2453–78). These are the only gods who actually appear in the tale, and thus the real chain of command in the Knight's Tale is Ptolemaic: Diana is subordinate to the others (2349–54); Venus and Mars are subordinate in position but apparently not greatly in power to Jupiter; and Jupiter is less effectual than Saturn, since it is Saturn, the planet-god farthest from earth, who decides the outcome, or at least he thinks he does.[52]

On still deeper analysis, however, the medieval reader finds yet a third layer of divinity. In addition to these visible planet-gods, the reader perceives at least twice in the tale the actions of a hidden prior Cause, prior even to the planets, a cause perceptible only in its effects (the same way the divine is perceptible in real life). The first time is when Saturnian and Martial champions arrive with Palamon and Arcite before the conflicting prayers are made and granted and before Venus appeals to her grandfather for help. In other words, Saturn's wise 'solution' is being implemented before Saturn is even involved.[53] The second time is when the fires in Diana's temple make their enigmatic prediction (2331–40) before Diana herself appears (2346) and without her knowledge (2355–57), and again some hundred lines before Saturn finds the very solution they predict. When effects twice precede their causes, as here, the medieval reader naturally infers a prior cause, in this case a cause that knows the future, rules the planets, and looks after the human beings on this earth individually (the same cause set forth so eloquently in the *Consolation*). The planet-gods in the tale (like the pagan gods in the *Aeneid*) may believe themselves independent and acting freely, but, at least with regard to Palamon and Arcite, they are not. At best they are merely secondary causes. Thus the earthly fortunes of these two theoretical young men are providential as well as natural. Providence, through the planets, has directed matters to come out as they do. The hidden chain of command in the Knight's Tale is, therefore, standard Boethian cosmology: Providence rules the fates of individuals, and one of its methods is through the influences of the wandering stars.

In the tale, therefore, and in spite of their rival natural psychologies, both young pagans have developed into truly virtuous men with the help of Providence. Palamon in Part III shows himself to have become a "parfit" example of the voluntarist theory of human nature, submitting himself freely and lovingly to the divine will. Arcite in Part IV shows himself to have become a "parfit" example of the intellectualist theory of human nature, his intellect ruling his passions reasonably, the spirit of divine charity informing his relations with others. Both, therefore, according to their respective psychologies, now deserve eternal bliss, and that is just what the Knight gives them.

In intellectualism, God is essentially rational, and it would be irrational (i.e., an imperfection) for such a God to establish an order of grace and then not follow it. Hence, in Thomism the man who receives grace will receive bliss.[54] Notice Chaucer's sequencing: Natural virtue is apparent in Arcite's prayer; then supernatural virtue (i.e., grace) is manifest in his dying speech. Then he actually dies with a *visio*. First the cold of death comes from his feet up to his breast, next he loses strength from his arms, next his intellect begins to fail, and finally,

> Dusked his eyen two, and failled breeth,
> But on his lady yet caste he his ye;
> His laste word was, "Mercy, Emelye!"
> His spirit chaunged hous . . . (2806–9)

(In Boccaccio, on the other hand, Arcita looks at Emilia for a while, but then turns away, loses his eyesight, and dies, *Teseida*, X, 111–13.) When Chaucer's Arcite first evidences natural virtue, then supernatural virtue, then dies receiving a *visio* of the good he has pursued all along, a clear suggestion is being made to the medieval audience that after his death Arcite will receive the *visio divinae essentiae* that is the eternal bliss of both body and soul in Thomism. Given the teleology that is the very essence of intellectualism, no other conclusion for Arcite is possible, at least for the medieval reader pursuing inner truths. In voluntarism, on the other hand, God is essentially omnipotent, and it would be an abridgement of his power for him to be unable to do anything he wishes. Absolutely speaking, God is free to confer grace and not subsequent bliss or bliss without preceding grace. Hence, the voluntarists pointed out, even though God is Omnipotent Love, nothing can be asserted with certainty about the afterlife of any particular man, no matter how virtuous.[55] In his prayer in Part III, Palamon demonstrates the faith and humble loving obedience that indicate the voluntarist relationship of grace with the divine, but the divine is still under no obligation to him. The divine is still, in principle, free to deny him eternal bliss. Therefore the Knight ends his tale with Palamon alive even now, manifestly in bliss for all time, in the emphatically present tense:

> For now is Palamon in alle wele,
> Lyvynge in blisse, in richesse, and in heele,
> And Emelye hym loveth so tendrely,
> And he hire serveth al so gentilly, . . . (3101–4)

Palamon is alive, still enjoying Emelye even "now" in loving service of both body and soul.

Thus, in the course of the Knight's Tale, both of these theoretical young men have become "parfit" according to the terms of their respective psychologies, and so the Knight gives them both what both have "deere aboght": theoretical beatitude. Arcite's bliss is in cognition: he ends up possessing the *visio* of Love. Palamon's bliss is in affection: he ends up serving Love. This is, therefore, the kind of story the Knight approves, as he later tells the Monk, a story in which there is:

> . . . joye and greet solas,
> As whan a man hath been in poure estaat
> And clymbeth up and wexeth fortunate,
> And there abideth in prosperitee.
> Swich thyng is gladsom, as it thynketh me,
> And of swich thyng were goodly for to telle. (VII, 2774–
> 79)

II. Faculty Component

In the tale, having achieved natural virtue, undergone great physical and mental suffering, evidenced the gift of grace and died
immediately, Arcite must necessarily go on to enjoy the contemplation of the divine essence, the unending perfect bliss for which
in Thomism the contemplation of Emelye herself was only an
imperfect fleeting substitute.[56] This is certainly a gladsome thing.
Similarly, having conformed his will freely to the will of the divine,
having lost the tournament, returned home to Thebes, and then
made no further effort to win her, Palamon finally receives Emelye
as a free gift from the powers that be and even now serves her in
bliss. This is another gladsome thing. In their relationships to
Providence, therefore, as in their cosmologies, prime faculties,
areas of freedom, ethical developments, theories of evil, modes of
reasoning, and manifestations of piety, the two young knights are
presented as very different and yet equally worthy, at least in the
eyes of the Knight.

Explicating the characterizations of the two young knights in this
way, by contrasting their oppositions point by point, has possibly
made the two scholastic theories they incarnate seem less realistic,
more artificial, than they actually are. It will therefore be useful, as
well as fair, to briefly put these two rival young men back together
again.

While Palamon is not going to be apprehended as a real human
being, he does have a consistent style and certain beliefs, and he
does undergo development during the course of the tale. Throughout the tale Palamon's style is affective. He always speaks from
and to the will. He appeals to pity, justice, honor, knighthood,
and freedom from tyranny, to mercy, virtue, and brotherly love,
all contents of the will. He generally thinks in terms of disjunctive
choices: "womman or goddess" (1101); "rightful" or merciful
(1719–30); and so on. His speeches proceed by association of ideas
rather than according to any logical structure. With regard to his
beliefs, from the very outset he recognizes the reality and power
of the divine will, and he does not regard it as essentially rational.
He therefore readily accepts the possibility of special divine intrusion into his own everyday life. He himself has total freedom of

will (i.e., total freedom of both emotions and choice); even when presented with a good without blemish, his response is free: his love for Emelye is immediate but not irresistible, and he repeatedly implies that if it were not honorable he would simply cease loving her. He does not perceive any irresistible natural law. As a result, he insists that positive law must be upheld; and when he finally breaks a positive law that others (including Arcite, 1561–62) might regard as unjust and therefore to be broken with impunity, he himself regards his act as wicked (1735). He considers morality a matter of choice. He is aggressive and metaphysically free, making his own decisions spontaneously, until he decides on happiness as his final goal; after that he leaves decisions about means up to higher authorities. This is why he seems so passive in the second half of the tale. In his Part III prayer, his last speech in the tale, his will is freely, lovingly, and totally conformed to the will of the divine; and at the end his final glorification is in outgoing loving service (rather than incoming intellectual cognition). These beliefs and actions of Palamon are all in analogical accordance with the psychological theories of the scholastic Augustinian Franciscans and those others who held the activities of the will to be primary among the functions of the soul. And finally, Palamon's affections (i.e., the content of his will) undergo radical change during the course of the tale: from a man who resents the divine and obeys out of constraint in Part I, he develops by Part III into a man who loves and trusts the divine absolutely and obeys it freely. Palamon is not individualized in the modern psychologically realistic sense. Rather, he is a theoretical construct from the world of scholastic 'scientific' psychology.

Similarly, although Arcite too is a theoretical construct rather than a realistic individual, he too has a consistent style and certain beliefs, and he too develops ethically during the course of the tale. Throughout the tale Arcite's style is intellective. He thinks in terms of causes and explains things (itself an intellectual activity) by means of reasons, analogies, and lists. His speeches tend to be logically organized in sections, and to consist of statements and questions rather than demands, judgments, insults, and ultimatums. With regard to his cosmology, the universe he perceives operates in stable, orderly, predictable fashion by means of natural causes that are intelligible to the human mind. Although essentially benevolent, Arcite's "purveiaunce" aids men by utilizing lesser evils to shield them from greater ones, rather than by intervening directly. Presented with a good without blemish, Arcite is irresistibly attracted by a law of his own nature; natural law therefore takes precedence over positive when the two conflict. Since his area of freedom lies in choice of the means to happiness, in Parts I and II he is passive, counseling acceptance and waiting for Fortune to act benevolently and provide a means to win Emelye. Given the means of the tournament, however, he becomes aggressive, praying decisively and fighting jealously. In his ethics, Arcite undergoes complete development during the tale: in Parts I and II his faculties are in conflict; in Part III he finally has them in the correct natural order, intellect regulating appetites reasonably; and in Part IV his natural virtue is completed by the supernatural gift of grace, evidenced by his display of perfect charity as he dies. And finally, the content of Arcite's intellect undergoes radical change during the action of the tale: from a man who believed he understood the ways of the divine completely, by its end he has learned to approach it with questions rather than causes.

Thus in spite of their common source in the Divine Nature as manifest in the universe, the Bible, and the scholarly church tradition, the two rival philosophic systems generated two conflicting "images" of man. Rather like getting both roses and lilies from the same divine seed.

How careful was Chaucer in working out the details of these two embodiments? He was painstakingly careful. One can see it in the passages already discussed. One can also see it in his intricate reshaping of Boccaccio's plot.[57] Here are some of his more important changes, along with some of their reasons:

(1) Depersonalizing Emelye from her distinctively flirtatious personality in the *Teseida* into a symbol of natural loveliness, in philosophic terms a good without blemish, enables

Chaucer to distinguish between Love as irresistible (Arcite) and Love as choice (Palamon).[58]

(2) Establishing Ptolemaic astronomy explains the additions of the Phebus passage (1493–96), of Arcite's dream of Mercury (1384–92), of the passage on Jupiter's ineffectuality (2438–42), and of the character Saturn (2443–78).

(3) Establishing the hidden presence of Providence as both ruling the planets and guiding the individual fates of Palamon and Arcite causes the reordering of the prayers (from Arcite/Palemone/Emilia to Palamon/Emelye/Arcite), the reverse chronology of Emelye's prayer, and the reduction in number of champions from dozens to only the two as well as their respective astrological characterizations (to be shown in Chapter 4).

(4) Characterizing Palamon as voluntarist causes him to be the first to see Emelye, because the voluntarist loves by free choice. (If Arcite had seen her first, as in the *Teseida,* Palamon would simply have chosen not to love her and that would have been the end of the conflict.)

(5) Characterizing Arcite as intellectualist prevents him from mistaking Emelye for Venus the first time he sees her, as he does in the *Teseida,* because an intellectualist thinks first in terms of natural causes, not divine manifestations.

(6) Establishing Palamon's complete and willing submission to the will of the divine causes the addition of "certeyn yeres" between Arcite's funeral and Palamon's receiving Emelye as a gift from Theseus.

(7) Establishing Theseus's initial polytheism causes him to design, build, and personally approve the lists, whereas in the *Teseida* the structure was already there.

In fact, Chaucer's version of the story of Palamon and Arcite is not only much shorter than Boccaccio's, it is much more complexly plotted and much more intellectually interesting. Pagan romance stories with slots for two potentially equal protagonists are rare. And I know of no other in which the distinction between means and end is key in the action, as it is in Boccaccio's plot and in the scholastic freedom theories. No doubt these aspects of the *Teseida* plot were what attracted Chaucer to "translate" it.

Chaucer's Reaction to the Scholastic Faculty Psychologies

In view of the significant spots of lightness in the tale, how seriously is Chaucer taking the two great scholastic psychologies? The theories themselves were, obviously, completely in earnest, dealing as they attempt to do with the most basic realities of human nature and human existence, and Chaucer depicts them accurately and treats them with both affection and respect. One can respect a theory, however, even while enjoying its occasional shortcomings; and this is apparently how the reader of the Knight's Tale is supposed to react. Of the scholastic oppositions depicted in the tale, I have concentrated so far on eight—cosmology, prime faculty, metaphysical freedom, ethical development, evil, reasoning, piety, and relations with Providence. One can well appreciate the grave ramifications of these issues and still be genuinely amused at times by Chaucer's way of handling them, without in any way depreciating the issues themselves, the attempts of the various thinkers to solve them, or the very real suffering depicted in the tale when the characters are being shown as real human beings. One can truly empathize, for example, with Palamon's bitterness and frustration as he overhears Arcite's complaint in Part II, yet at the same time smile at his totally unrealistic sense of victory as he leaps—completely unarmed—out of those bushes crying, ". . . Arcite, false traytour wikke, / Now artow hent, . . ." (1580–81). The fact that his bitterness at Arcite, his frustration, and his sense of victory all reflect the theory of human nature by which he is being characterized—belief in the inviolability of positive law, in man's freedom to will and to act and his moral responsibility when he does, and in a positive relationship between might and right—in no way detracts from either the sympathy and amusement one feels at his plight or the seriousness of the philosophical issues involved. Similarly, one can be amused at Arcite's total insensitivity to the feelings of others in his Part III prayer—reminding Mars of his most embarrassing defeat while asking for his favor, and regarding Emelye simply as a thing to be won and used—and yet still, at the same time, be deeply moved by the suffering and sorrow of his deathbed speech and the truly unselfish love he finally displays for his cousin and his lady. The fact again that his attitudes are poetic equivalents of philosophical positions does not detract from their aesthetic, emotionally evocative, truth, nor does it demean the positions involved—the beliefs that human reason is superior to human passion, that events have orderly causes, and that there is an element of grace in our love for other human beings. The issues between Palamon and Arcite are not trivial. The scholastic theories attempting to resolve them were certainly not frivolous, and Chaucer treats them with respect. But there is something inherently absurd about the existence, side by side, of two mutually exclusive theories of universal human nature.

The perplexing mixture of tones used in the tale for the two young knights is due to their double natures: romance protagonists *and* abstract scholastic embodiments.[59] By turns the tale is tragic, comic, detached, touching, romantic, inflated, noble, and ridiculous; and by turns it is, philosophically speaking, witty indeed. Although these two theoretical young men, like the two psychologies they epitomize, have absolutely no sense of humor—at all times Arcite is intellectually serious, Palamon morally earnest—the same is not true of their handling in the tale.

There is, for example, as already mentioned, Arcite's surprisingly self-centered characterization during his Part III prayer as the very model of the virtuous intellectualist lover—his passion (morally neutral in Thomism) properly ordered by his reason, his attention totally devoted not to Emelye but to his own self-perfecting telos. There is also Palamon's startling vow to "holden werre alwey with chastitee" (2236). In the medieval period, the word 'chastity' had three kinds of meanings, all pertinent here. It could refer to a physical fact, abstinence from sexual intercourse. It could refer to a spiritual concept, the miraculous purity of both body and mind of the Blessed Virgin. And it could refer to a psychological attitude—one that carries profound philosophical

implications—the attitude that rejects "floures fayre," that spurns
"earthly taint," that turns its back on all the individual creatures
and objects of this beautiful created world as of no real value.[60]
From its inception, the Franciscan Order strongly rejected this kind
of psychological 'chastity.' St. Francis spoke of sun, wind, animals,
and birds as his brothers and sisters, while St. Bonaventure regarded every creature in the sensible world as a reflection of its
Maker. Scotus's doctrine of "haecceity" (by which each individual
thing carries its own unique perfection) and his theory of the
Incarnation (by which Christ would have been incarnated and
come to man independent of Adam's fall), as well as Ockham's
doctrines of the divine liberality (by which people do possess
their goods) and of intuitive cognition (by which individuals are
perceived directly)—all these are but a few reflections of the positive value the Franciscans attached to all of creation. Speaking
particularly of Bonaventure and his "highly developed metaphysics
of exemplarism," Ewert Cousins refers to this whole stream of
medieval thought as "the fecundity tradition."[61] Thus, as an embodiment of the Franciscan psychology, Palamon's vow against
chastity befits his nature—both in the pagan sense of helping his
deity Venus make war on her traditional enemy,[62] and in the
philosophical sense of remaining ever hostile to the idea that the
individual beings and things of this created world have no discernible absolute value in themselves. However, his vow does come at
the end of some twenty-seven heartfelt, deeply pious, mystically
worded lines addressed to the "blisful Citherea benigne." As a
result, the clash Chaucer sets up between spiritual other-worldly
lead-in—

> . . . 'Mercy, lady bright, that knowest weele
> My thought, and seest what harmes that I feele!'
> Considere al this and rewe upon my soore,
> As wisly as I shal for everemoore,
> Emforth my myght, thy trewe servant be,

and physical this-worldly vow to—

> . . . holden werre alwey with chastitee, (2231–36)

is what causes the breathtaking sense of anticlimax the final word in this line produces in the reader.

In the pagan romance story, Arcite's sexually self-centered prayer and Palamon's aggressively fecund vow are simply amusing. In the scholastic debate embedded inside it, however, they also indicate a serious Chaucerian pointing (in the technical medieval sense of an unusually detailed rendering) of the major (and still unresolved) ethical problem in each psychology—in the intellectualist psychology, the problem of loving someone unselfishly; and in the voluntarist psychology, the problem of serving someone intelligently. Chaucer touched on these same ethical problems earlier. In Part I, rationalizing his attraction to the woman Palamon loved first, Arcite pleads irresistible natural law: "A man moot nedes love, . . . Al be she mayde, or wydwe, or elles wyf," claims he (1169–71), thereby legitimizing not only his pursuit of Emelye but any man's pursuit of a married woman and presumably adultery as well if the opportunity should arise. Not exactly unselfish, one might say. Similarly, in the grove in Part II, when asked by Theseus what kind of men the two of them are, Palamon demonstrates his total submission to rightful power by fully confessing the crimes not just of himself, but of Arcite as well:

> . . . For though thow knowest it lite,
> This is thy mortal foo, this is Arcite,
> That fro thy lond is banysshed on his heed. (1723–29)

Confessing his own situation is one thing, but confessing Arcite's? Not exactly praiseworthy, one might say. Thus, even when being amusing about them, Chaucer does take these two psychologies totally seriously. His amusement is at their weaknesses, here their ethical deficiencies, not at their very real strengths.

Next, does Chaucer have a preference? Does he make even a hidden judgment in the tale as to which is the "better" of the two faculty psychologies? In principle, I would like to say no; in practice, I find it difficult to decide. In principle, rather than soliciting a value judgment between the two theories, it seems to me that Chaucer presents them as the two poles of human nature, with facts and reasons and circumstances organized rationally around one pole, and emotions, moral judgments, and disjunctive choices grouped affectively around the other. In real life, of course, these two great polarities in human nature have come down through history into the twentieth century, the intellectualist pole ordinarily associated with the Greek tradition and the achievements of science, the voluntarist pole ordinarily associated with the Judeo-Christian tradition and the achievements of ethics. In everyday life the two polarities are still very much with us, of course, although more often harmoniously combined, one would hope, in individuals in whom intellect and will cooperate freely in accordance with the needs of the particular situation (as they do in Theseus, again anticipating Chapter 2). In principle, it seems to me, Arcite and Palamon are portrayed not as role models to be emulated, but as theoretical extremes to be harmonized. In the tale, both theories contain much truth. Neither contains all.

In practice, however, modern readers often feel a preference for Palamon. Palamon lives on in bliss, whereas Arcite dies. Palamon's loving devotion to Emelye throughout is more attractive than Arcite's self-fulfilling regard for her up until his dying speech. And Palamon's early assertiveness seems more manly than Arcite's passivity in Parts I and II. These all seem good reasons to feel a preference for Palamon. Yet whether Chaucer himself, or whether many among his fourteenth-century readers, would have felt this preference, there is no way of knowing. Evaluation is complicated in that the Franciscan focus on the individual and on the intrinsic value of all beings and things in this world appeals strongly to the modern sensibility, whereas the Dominican metaphysical optimism and interest in formal and final causes is now out of favor. Time passes; preferences change. My own intuitive belief is that Chaucer made every effort to present the two systems as equally valuable although for different reasons and as equally attractive, because he was then going to reject both of them in favor of his own, more traditional and Boethian, less determined system, to be embodied in Theseus.

More important than Chaucer's possible preference for one or the other psychology, however, are his objections to both, objections to what are glaring absences in the scholastic theories, absences that will be filled in his characterization of Theseus. In a nutshell, Chaucer's objections are of three kinds: human subjectivity is ignored; living in this world is accorded no positive value; and human freedom is frittered away.

First, with regard to human subjectivity, the scholastic universal psychologies concern themselves only with the faculties; they seem uninterested in the equally important part played in human nature by the mind's thinking processes and language use. These two subjects, thinking processes and language use, Chaucer therefore inserts forcefully—rams—right into the middle of the century-old scholastic will/intellect debate, with his superlatively scholastic *sophismata* on the gods and champions. These will be discussed in the next section of this book.

Second, the process of day-to-day living in this world is rarely if ever addressed by the scholastics on other than a universal basis, that is, what all men are or what all men perceive. Each person, however, lives in fact in a particular place, during a particular time, in the midst of a particular family or group, under particular circumstances of making a living, getting along with others, and so on. Thus, rather than a simple background place through which we, as completed individuals, pass unaffected on our pilgrimage to a better (or worse) abode, Chaucer posits the world as a learning place. People learn, for good or for ill, from their daily experiences. Preferably they learn to be better. Chaucer makes the process of living in this world with other people, and the effects of daily individual experience on the individual mind, parts of his own theory of universal psychology. This will be discussed in Chapter 2 on Theseus and in the final section on the makers and contexts of universal psychologies.

And Chaucer's third objection to the scholastic psychologies is that human freedom is reasoned away. We have seen this already with Palamon and Arcite. Whether end/free and means/obedience (voluntarist), or end/natural and means/free (intellectualist), the practical result is the same—human beings are not completely responsible for what they do. This subject of freedom is Chaucer's foremost theoretical concern in the Knight's Tale. To it he devotes more poetic attention than to any other single subject. And for it he invents a "poetic logic" that rivals any methodology of the scholastic logicians in rigor. Explication of this system of poetic logic, as Chaucer uses it to illuminate both the nature of human freedom in this world and the importance of language use in this world, will appropriately complete this chapter on the two scholastic theories of faculty psychology in the Knight's Tale.

CHAUCER'S POETIC LOGIC AND THE ISSUE OF FREEDOM

Both poetry and logic depend on repetition with variation. Thus underlying both the literalism of the scholastics and the figures and fictions of the Knight's Tale is essentially the same deep-structure verbal technique. One poetic use of repetition consists of clustering three or four implications of one kind (for example, darkness) and comparing or contrasting them against similar clusters of other kinds (for example, light or brightness). In the Knight's Tale, as must already be more than obvious, Chaucer is unusually complicated in his verbal clusterings, in both quantity and consistency. Rather than three or four implications, Chaucer supplies ten, fifteen, twenty or more; and rather than only simple direct comparisons and contrasts, Chaucer interlocks and even triangulates his clusters (as is done in astronomy, navigation, and surveying), thus providing the kind of quantitative, objectively demonstrable, system-wide consistency any trained logician would have to respect. For example, when a fictional character speaks dozens and hundreds of lines in functions of the intellect (causes, lists, circumstances, analogies), this is an interesting fact, although such a thing could happen by chance. It is only a single character, a single point in space; it can be interpreted in any direction. However, when a second, paralleled character speaks only in movements of the will (judgments, choices), then both facts together become significant. They suggest strongly that the first clustering was not accidental but planned; that the author was deliberately contrasting those two characters on their activities of mind. Two points in space. Then outside historical evidence shows up that the contrast of those particular activities of mind was a significant issue during the writer's own time. Now these two paired together are unlikely to be mere chance. We can speak of interlocking. And then later, a third character, standing in judgment on the other two and already presented in other ways as the apex of a triangle, turns out to speak and think about half in movements of the will and half in functions of the intellect (to be discussed in Chapter 2). Now Chaucer has given us three interlocking points in space. Three characters triangulated. Now, I think, we can speak of author's intention and the like. An interpretation holding these three facts significant cannot be dismissed on grounds of impressionism.

This technique of quantifying, interlocking, and triangulating verbal implications Chaucer uses over and over again in the Knight's Tale: Arcite's seeing, Emelye's name, Palamon's demands for choices, and so on. As a result, at some point, it passes over, for the reader, from ordinary poetic technique to planned poetic logic. The *sorites,* or heap argument, was a favorite medieval logical conundrum: As one places a grain of corn on the ground, and then adds another, and then adds a third, and then a fourth, and so on, at what point do the grains become a heap? So too with Chaucer's quantified, interlocked, and triangulated implications in the Knight's Tale—at what point do they become formal logic? At what point, that is to say, do pagan lies become scholastic demonstration?

For the scholastics, as touched on earlier, a 'scientific demonstration' consisted of valid syllogistic reasoning from true, necessary, and certain premises.[63] What this actually looks like in practice is a string of repetitions of the same type of argument, varying only a term or two, over and over and over again. Dull but convincing. Likewise, a 'poetic demonstration' in the Knight's Tale consists of repetitions of the same kinds of images and contrasts, varying only the subject terms, over and over and over again. Not dull, but just as convincing as if it were. In short, the same logic underlies both methodologies, scholastic literal and Chaucerian figurative.

Logic is study of the rules of valid reasoning. In the medieval period (before symbols were developed), logic was a language art. Together with grammar and rhetoric, it comprised the trivium of verbal arts taught to elementary schoolboys. In addition to theories of nouns and verbs and definition and predication and such, it included philosophy of language and some metaphysics, for example, the notions of genus, species, substance, accidents, and quality, and thus it covered the whole conceptual system of universals and their manifestations in species and particulars. Both Chaucer and the males of his audience would have learned this elementary logic early and automatically as schoolboys. Further, unlike university logic today, the university logic of Chaucer's time was a continuation of this schoolboy logic. Thus scholastic treatises on logic would not have seemed at all forbidding to Chaucer, as they might to some of us today.

The scholastics' belief that the only valuable knowledge is knowledge scientifically demonstrated from first principles made them reject for their research endeavors the Augustinian notion that obscure imagery has positive didactic value. When one is looking for objective fact, no doubt Augustine's shorn teeth are a pain rather than a pleasure.[64] In the Knight's Tale, Chaucer meets the scholastic demand for scientific demonstration if a piece of writing is to be taken seriously—and he wants his Knight's Tale to be taken totally seriously—by inventing this poetic logic. His use of it in the tale is at least as demonstrative, at least as certain, as any literal scholastic logic could actually be. To my mind, with the demonstrations of the contrasted elements in the characterizations of Palamon and Arcite, the reader has already seen a good deal of Chaucer's multiple-interlocking and triangulating verbal implications, enough at least to be convinced she is in the presence of a real scholastic heap. If she decides to examine it further, however, she will soon come upon the most awesomely systematic of all Chaucer's poetic demonstrations: his "making" of human freedom according to the scholastics.

Scholastic conceptions of determinism and freedom differ somewhat from modern conceptions. One major difference is in the notions to which freedom is opposed. We think of determinisms as forces acting beneath a person's conscious knowledge—genes, hormones, childhood abuse, social conditioning, economic or historical circumstances. Medievals, on the other hand, generally thought of determinisms as forces outside one's inner immaterial mind, forces that one could therefore consciously choose to overcome—such as natural appetites and astrological influences. For us, outside forces can affect one's inner consciousness without one's even knowing it. For medievals, one's inner consciousness can always choose to overcome the influence of those outside forces. Thus Chaucer's using poetic logic to point the limits of Palamon's and Arcite's freedom is not in the twentieth-century fashion as to whether or not one is determined in fact, but rather in the four-teenth-century fashion as to whether one does or should submit to an outside power in one's own mind. As to freedom itself, the two scholastic sides defined it somewhat differently: In a Thomist context, freedom is the absence of natural causation in the intellect; in an Augustinian-Franciscan context, freedom is the absence of coercion in the will. From the humanist point of view, however, the difference is not really significant because both psychologies contain areas of submission, and, as a result, in neither can a human being justly be held responsible for all of his or her actions. Chaucer's contrast, therefore, is between any type of *submission* on the one side, as opposed to both types of *freedom* on the other.

I will now argue that throughout the Knight's Tale, the meta-physical status of the two young knights as to freedom or submis-sion is logically pointed by means of the diction associated with each of them. The knight who is free according to the psychological theory he embodies is described with vividly physical attributes and actions. The knight who is submitting, whether to natural necessity or higher direction, is described with attributes and activi-ties that are not outwardly physically evocative. For example, where one knight is "stongen" unto the heart, the other is merely "hurte." 'Stung' evokes a phantasm of skin, sharply perceived puncture, and hot pain. 'Hurt' is generalized; it hardly evokes a phantasm. Again, where one knight "spryngeth up for joye," the other merely "looketh lightly." 'Springs up' evokes bulk, weight, and movement. 'Looks lightly' evokes at most a quick flash of cognition. These contrasts in degree of evoked physicality are both subtle and linguistically fascinating, and they are systematic throughout the Knight's Tale. Let us call these two kinds of diction "physical" and "non-physical."

In Part I Arcite is submitting to natural necessity and receives the non-physical diction; in Part III he is free to choose his means to happiness and receives the physically evocative freedom diction. And vice versa, in Part I Palamon is completely free and receives the physical diction; in Part III he is submitting to higher beings and receives the non-physical submission diction. There are but two qualifications to this logical schema, both also logical: *(a)* potential or actual physical violence is always characterized by the physically evocative diction (for obvious reasons); and *(b)* the word "herte" is apparently not significant in the schema because in Middle English it can cluster on either side: the word can signify the seat of the intellect,[65] the site of the emotions, or the physical organ located in the chest. Here is an abbreviated overview of this 'poetic demonstration.'

In Part I, while Palamon is still metaphysically free, not yet having chosen his final goal, he is described with vividly physical attributes, movements, sounds, and kinds of pain. He roams to and fro in his prison chamber, cries out on seeing Emelye, knits his brows, and makes such sorrow that the tower resounds with his yowling and clamor. His salt tears wet the fetters on his great shins, and the fire of jealousy starts up within his breast and seizes him by the heart. As for the other side, Arcite, who is submitting to natural necessity (at first the planets and later the sight of Emelye), is discussed with diction that is much less physically evocative. He apparently spends his time in prison sitting still, since he starts up on hearing Palamon's cry. He suffers sorrow, rather than making it. He weeps and wails and cries pitifully, rather than making the tower resound. He waits to slay himself, rather than reacting outwardly as Palamon does. He suffers negatively, from deprivation and exile, rather than from having his heart physically grabbed.

In the prayers of Part III, on the other hand, their freedom status being reversed, the diction accorded each young knight is reversed. Now possessed of freedom as to choice of means, Arcite now receives the physically evocative freedom diction. He has youth, might, beard, and hair; he burns (repeatedly) with the hot fire of desire; he heaves his hand up and casts incense into the fire. The doors clatter, the statue rings, and the fires burn brighter. Palamon, conversely, now submitting completely to the will of the divine, is now accorded the slower, quieter, comparatively non-physical diction. He kneels during his prayer. He speaks of the tears he sheds for Emelye, and the arms in which he would hold her. His suffering is generalized into effects and torments and harms. Venus's statue merely shakes and makes a silent sign for him. Here, for comparison, are the two paralleled passages on their rites. The description of Arcite's rites appeals vividly to all five physical senses—sight, smell, hearing, taste, and touch; and Arcite himself is vividly characterized in the full stream of his actions and reactions, right down to that final unforgettable, alliterated, strikingly kinesthetic image of the fowl strutting in the morning sun.

> The preyere stynt of Arcita the stronge,
> The rynges on the temple dore that honge,
> And eek the dores, clatereden ful faste
> Of which Arcita somwhat hym agaste.
> The fyres brenden upon the auter brighte,
> That it gan al the temple for to lighte
> A sweete smel the ground anon up yaf,
> And Arcita anon his hand up haf,
> And moore encens into the fyr he caste,
> With othere rytes mo; and atte laste
> The statue of Mars bigan his hauberk rynge
> And with that soun he herde a murmurynge
> Ful lowe and dym, and seyde thus, "Victorie!"
> For which he yaf to Mars honour and glorie.
> And thus with joye and hope wel to fare
> Arcite anon unto his in is fare,
> As fayn as fowel is of the brighte sonne. (2421–37)

As he appeals here for victory in the tournament, his free choice of the means to Emelye, Arcite is described with the vivid, physically evocative freedom diction. In the description of Palamon's rites, on the other hand, although a good deal of activity is actually going on—a sacrifice, a quantity of circumstances, some observations, a delay, a shake, and a sign, none of it, except perhaps that shake, is going to be physically sensed by the reader. There is no sight, no sound, no sweet smell, nothing to touch. And there is no striking final image.

> Whan the orison was doon of Palamon,
> His sacrifice he dide, and that anon,
> Ful pitously, with alle circumstaunces,
> Al telle I noght as now his observaunces;
> But atte laste the statue of Venus shook,
> And made a signe, wherby that he took
> That his preyere accepted was that day.
> For thogh the signe shewed a delay,
> Yet wiste he wel that graunted was his boone;
> And with glad herte he wente hym hoom ful soone.
> (2261–70)

As he appeals simply for possession of his chosen final end and leaves to Venus determination of the means to achieve it, the submission of Palamon's will is total; and hence he receives the non-physical, non-evocative submission diction.

The preceding overview and examples have by no means done justice to the quantity, consistency, and logic of Chaucer's two dictions. Appendix A, therefore, provides word-by-word lists; the following diagram will sum them up. A fairly neat diagram such as this results when one goes through the whole tale and counts up the kinds of words that appear and do not appear. But when one simply reads the tale as poetry, the striking thing is the exchange of absolute places between Part I and Part III: both the exchange of dictions and the exchange of absolute freedom and absolute submission in the faculty psychologies. In the diagram, freedom and active physical diction appear on the left; the two medieval kinds of submission with their non-physical diction on the right; and the heavy crossed lines indicate the changing dictions accorded each young knight.

The aesthetic result of this remarkably painstaking attention to the evocative effects of even the most ordinary words is that, especially in Parts I and III, the reader perceives the knight who is metaphysically free in what he is doing as an active physical presence, with bones, blood, muscle, and powerful capability. And the reader perceives the knight who is submitting to metaphysical

Palamon and Arcite: The Will/Intellect Debate

Chaucer's Exchange of Dictions
per the Scholastic Conceptions of Freedom

Freedom	Submission	natural necessity
		higher direction

PHYSICAL DICTION		NON-PHYSICAL DICTION
Words referring to corporeal things, perceived first on the bodily senses		Words naming generalizations, abstractions, universals, perceived directly in the mind
Brows, shins, bones, blood, etc.	Physical Attributes	. . . . Few or none
Roaming, riding, casting, etc.	Physical Movement	Subdued . . . . Little or none
Yowling, howling, singing lustily	Noise	Subdued . . . . Little or none
Physically perceived: burn, stab, sting, etc.	Pain	Generalized or . . . . by deprivation

Part I
Part II
Part III
Part IV

Palamon   Arcite

(Qualification: Situations with potential physical consequences—death sentences, duels, tournaments—are described throughout with the physical freedom diction.)

determinism in what *he* is doing as a quieter, more inward, essentially receptive entity, with thoughts and emotions of course, but lacking real physical presence. The scholastic result, on the other hand, is that the reader receives a stunning poetic demonstration that both knights, and therefore both theories of psychology, are rigidly one-sided; and that both restrict about equally their areas of freedom.

The Knight's *determinatio* to this debate will be made in the characterization of Theseus. There, as Chapter 2 will show, Chaucer overrides all the simplistic binary reasoning, all the careful, convoluted, scholastic hedging about human freedom and responsibility. Theseus, an active man in the real world of the Knight's Tale, is demonstrated to be completely free according to the terms in which freedom was discussed in scholastic psychology: free in will, free in intellect; and free in choice of both means and ends.

Although Chaucer himself clearly understood the scholastic psychological theories well, one naturally wonders about the members of his own audience. How much of all this did they see? The two theories were so complex that even today they receive a wide range of interpretation, and in their own time they must have been simplified in many different ways and on many different levels in order simply to be taught and understood. Yet, just as in a Gothic manuscript, an illuminated D is an illuminated D when it has two verticals, two horizontals, something off to the left *and* begins the 52nd Psalm—whether, taking most of the page, it is filled with four rectangular vignettes from the life of David and enclosed ten times over in patterned symmetries; or whether, only two columns high, it is merely a two-color rectangle, enclosing a geometric swirl—so too a voluntarist knight is a voluntarist knight as soon as one perceives some essential voluntarist qualities *and* they are opposed to some essential intellectualist qualities similarly embodied in a rival intellectualist knight. Each characterization illuminates the other. One does not need to understand every single detail, to have every convoluted scholastic qualification spelled out, in order to draw the correct generalization. Chaucer wrote, one assumes, fully aware of the level of understanding of his own courtly and professional audience.[66] He apparently believed he could count on at least some of its members to recognize the psychological oppositions, to generalize them into embodiments of the two rival theories, and then to perceive the implications created by bringing the two of them to life together, competing side by side in this world for the same final goal.

The *quaestio* between the two is, what is the nature of universal human nature? And how does it tell us to live? All the essential positions of either psychological theory are covered and contrasted against those of the other, item by item, issue by issue, accurately and fairly. In fact Chaucer brings both theories to life. Alas, if one accepts the voluntarist psychology, Arcite is not finally a worthy man. He dies with questions in his mind rather than obedience in his heart. Similarly, if one accepts the intellectualist psychology, Palamon never even achieves natural virtue; at no point, so far as I can tell, is his intellect in control of his affections. Yet how can one reject either of these "parfit" young men? They try so hard, they suffer so long, they mean so well. In the characterization of Theseus is presented a truer theory of universal human nature, as it does exist in this real world. When compared with the character-ization of Theseus, both rival scholastic psychologies, although intellectually fascinating and logically elegant, are shown to be overspecified, and as a result unable to generate the variety and complexity of real human nature as we experience it on a day-to-day basis. Chaucer's more general, more generous theory em-bodied in Theseus will be able to include both Palamon and Arcite as the admirable, truly worthy, and wonderful young men they really are.

CHAPTER

2

Theseus:
Chaucer's Humanist Determinatio

IN THE PAGAN ROMANCE NARRATIVE of the Knight's Tale, Theseus is duke of Athens and he is absolutely magnificent—lord, governor, and conqueror—no one greater "under the sonne."[67] At the same time, in the scholastic disputation embedded within it, Theseus embodies the Knight's (and I think it safe to say, Chaucer's) practical *determinatio* as to the two really important points to be included in any adequate theory of human nature in this world: Theseus is free and he learns from personal experience. These two are the aspects of his characterization that Chaucer develops most carefully.

First, with regard to the tale's structuring, whereas the two rival scholastic theories were set forth accurately and objectively in the narrow side aisles of the tale, so to speak, the characterization of Theseus and, as a result, the focus on freedom and on individual learning take place in successive episodes straight down the center of the nave, from elaborate homecoming at the entrance to sensible, conciliatory resolution from the apse. Moreover, with regard to the relationship of his faculties, Chaucer's Theseus is characterized as a man in whom will and intellect complement each other; and therefore, according to the concepts of the faculty psychology of Chaucer's time, Theseus is a man completely free, free as to choice of means and free as to choice of ends. Further, during the course of the tale, because he is free and because he ponders and generalizes

104

Theseus: Chaucer's Determinatio

from the unplanned, unexpected incidents of his own personal experience, Theseus learns to think better and as a result to treat other people better. Chaucer's Theseus is a good man who learns to be better. By the end of the tale he has come to know and honor something higher than his own self-fulfillment.

The Knight covers all the requisite bases of the scholastic philosophy of Chaucer's time. The same eight speculative issues on which I concentrated earlier in explicating the rival theories informing Palamon and Arcite are also used to develop Theseus's character, but in a subtler, more lifelike and practical, this-worldly way. By way of preliminary summary:

Cosmology: his belief develops from polytheism to Prime Mover.

Prime Faculty: his will and his intellect function together as equals from the beginning and throughout.

Freedom: he is free because he believes himself free.

Ethical development: he develops from precipitate and violent to advice-seeking and peaceful.

Evil: he recognizes both deliberate disobedience and deprivation of natural good.

Mode of reasoning: he uses his mind in many ways, including both induction and deduction.

Piety: he supports cultural traditions, tries to be even-handed, and is willing to change beliefs when convinced of a better.

Relationship with Providence: this is convoluted, present but difficult to define, and hence, lifelike.

However, although the Knight uses these same eight issues in characterizing his Theseus, he approaches them from a different direction. Whereas the scholastic philosophers began their speculations with man's likeness to God, the Knight begins his with man's radical unlikeness: at the beginning of the Knight's Tale, Theseus has a lot to learn.

From the Knight's point of view, real human learning and therefore real human change do not take place like a scholastic miracle, with every human being changing suddenly according to a single universal pattern (from active to passive or vice versa), regardless of the facts of his or her own individual life in this world. For the Knight, real human learning and change come slowly; and they come through mulling over one's own personal experiences, through generalizing about what one has seen and heard and felt. Thus, in the Knight's Theseus, real learning and change take place first in the mind, as they do in the *Consolation*. Indeed, if Boethius had ever set himself to demonstrate scientifically, in the concepts of later medieval scholastic philosophy, the theory of psychology one infers from reading his *Consolation*—a theory centered on human thinking, freedom and responsibility, and on faith in ultimate goodness—his theory, it seems to me, would not be unlike the theory Chaucer presents to us embodied in his Theseus.

In this chapter, I will try to show that Theseus is characterized as completely free in scholastic terms (i.e., neither programmed by nature nor constrained by Providence); he is free in his manner of speaking, free in his behavior, and free in his beliefs. Then I will show that during the course of the tale, as a result of his freedom to learn, Theseus changes for the better, developing from a man who responds immediately, physically, and directly to information that reaches him through his physical senses, into a wiser, more thoughtful man, one who searches into the "hidden causes" of things and, as a result, fulfills his responsibilities better. Theseus is a good man at the beginning of the tale and a better man at its end.

FREEDOM

The argument that Theseus is free by nature is scholastic, and it is powerful. In the tale's pagan romance narrative, Theseus is free because he is free outwardly; he is absolute monarch of Athens and does as he pleases. In the tale's embedded humanist *disputatio,* he is also free inwardly.

In Chaucer's time, as already shown in the explications for Palamon and Arcite, freedom was ordinarily discussed by the scholastics in the context of the will/intellect debate and was divided up as to freedom of means (Thomist) and of end (Franciscan). Therefore, to show that his Theseus is free by nature, the Knight must show that in him neither will nor intellect is prime over the

other, that instead the two faculties function together coopera-
tively. This Chaucer does by composing all of Theseus's speeches
about equally of movements of the will and causes of the intellect.

In his very first speech in the tale, Theseus's immediate response
to the ladies in black springs from both faculties. It is both hostile,
a response of the will (they are ruining his ceremonial homecoming), and curious, a response of the intellect (asking for causes—
their names, motives, offender, the reason for their black garb):

> "What folk been ye, that at myn homcomynge
> Perturben so my feste with criynge?"
> Quod Theseus. "Have ye so greet envye
> Of myn honour, that thus compleyne and crye?
> Or who hath yow mysboden or offended?
> And telleth me if it may been amended,
> And why that ye been clothed thus in blak." (905–11)

Similarly, in his second speech, interrupting the fight in the grove,
Theseus begins with a reaction of his will:

> . . . Hoo!
> Namoore, up peyne of lesynge of youre heed!
> By myghty Mars, he shal anon be deed
> That smyteth any strook that I may seen,

and immediately follows it with a query from his intellect:

> But telleth me what myster men ye been,
> That been so hardy for to fighten heere
> Withouten juge or oother officere,
> As it were in a lystes roially. (1710–13)

The rest of his speeches likewise are each mixtures about equally
of causes, questions, and distinctions on the one hand, with judgments, decisions, and emotions (both negative and positive) on the
other. Indeed, his final Prime Mover speech is exactly divided
between the two. The first fifty-four lines (2987–3040), the overall
cosmology, are spoken primarily from and to the intellect: Starting
with the "First Moevere," Theseus reasons deductively from the
universal order of things down a long chain of causes, natural laws,

II. Faculty Component

and explanatory examples of all sorts to the fact of death in this world. The second fifty-three lines (3041–93), his application of this cosmology, are spoken primarily from and to the will: they comprise an appeal to both its affective and elective capacities—to accept rather than reject, to avoid willfulness and resentment, to value the good in things, in this case Arcite's worthy name and the welfare of his soul, to be grateful to Jupiter for "al his grace," and to turn sorrow into joy, concluding with the order to Emelye to take "wommanly pitee" on Palamon and marry him and the assumption that Palamon will "assente," both functions of the will. In short, in the Knight's Tale, intellect and will are separated and one is more noble than the other in the characterizations of Palamon and Arcite, but they are not so separated in Theseus. In Theseus, on the contrary, the two faculties work harmoniously together: at the end, intellect in Theseus is a matter of understanding the causes of things; will in Theseus a matter of desiring a certain end consonant with those causes and of acting toward it and directing others to do the same. So far as one can tell from his speeches, in Theseus neither faculty operates without the other, yet neither faculty is superior to the other. In the terms of the faculty psychology of Chaucer's own time, therefore, both Theseus's faculties of mind are naturally free.

Just as Theseus is free in his speaking (and thinking, 1762–81), so is he free in his behavior, as to choices of both means and ends. Theseus constantly makes spontaneous, apparently free decisions in the Knight's Tale—to listen to the ladies in black, to avenge them, to take his army to Thebes, and so on. The only stronger practical proof of a man's freedom than his ability to make these kinds of decisions, philosophically speaking, is his ability to change such decisions already made. And that is what Theseus does to a degree unusual in medieval literature: he changes his decisions. In Part I, he sets out to do his might on Creon alone, but winds up leveling the city and sacking the countryside as well. He sends Palamon and Arcite to prison "perpetuelly—he nolde no raunsoun" (1024), but at Perotheus's request (1205) he releases Arcite easily. His conditions specify Arcite's beheading if he is ever again found on Theseus's land; yet when he is so found, he is soon forgiven.

In Part II, on breaking up the fight in the grove, Theseus sentences both young Thebans to death (1747), but almost immediately forgives their "trespas" (1825) and decrees the tournament to settle their quarrel instead. His original terms for the tournament are death or total defeat (1859), but a year later he modifies them drastically into the equivalent of a rough contact sport (2542). After the tournament he immediately awards Emelye to Arcite (2658), but some years later gives her to the man Arcite defeated. Similarly, just as he changes his decisions as to means, so Theseus changes his decisions as to ends several times during the course of the tale. He never takes a final goal, in the sense of a single overriding purpose that dominates his every movement, as Palamon and Arcite both do.[68] Instead, in the tale Theseus serves first Mars and then Diana (975, 1682) and he speaks of having served Love in the past (1814). At the end, in the course of praising the First Mover, he speaks of submitting to "Juppiter, the Kyng" (3035–40), and of thanking "Juppiter" for all his grace (3069), but he never considers this First Mover/Jupiter Being as in any way an end to be deliberately chosen. Palamon and Arcite, by way of contrast, each take a final end according to their respective natures—Palamon by choice, Arcite by natural necessity—and once taken, they never deviate from pursuit of it. Thenceforward, every thought, every action, is dominated by love of Emelye. In this regard, they are not free, either of them. Theseus, however, is as free with regard to final ends as he is free with regard to choices of means.

In addition, Theseus is free in other, everyday, recognizably human ways not normally considered by philosophers looking only for likenesses, however remote, between man's nature and God's. Among other things, Theseus is able to change his mood, his point of view, and his level of discourse. He is capable of irony, as when, toward the end of Part II after his anger at the two young knights has ebbed, his eyes light up in seriocomic wonder as he contemplates the miracles performed by the god of love: "Se how they blede! be they noght wel arrayed? / Thus hath hir lord, the god of love, ypayed / Hir wages and hir fees for hir servyse!" (1801–3). He can recognize his own past foolishness in the present foolishness of others and identify with it publicly: "A man moot ben a fool, . . . I woot it by myself ful yore agon, . . . And therfore, syn I knowe of loves peyne, . . . I yow foryeve al hooly this trespaas" (1812–18). He can suddenly drop his level of discourse from serious matters of state to squeaky children's games: after agreeing that both knights are worthy of her in terms of lineage and riches, he points out that Emelye cannot wed two: "oon of you, al be hym looth or lief, / He moot go pipen in an yvy leef" (1837–38). He can understate: at the end of the great Prime Mover speech (and passing up a wonderful opportunity for pomposity), he concludes 102 lines of the highest formality of both style and substance, including a cosmology, an elegy, a eulogy, and a betrothal, with a two-line informal throwaway remark to Palamon: "I trowe ther nedeth litel sermonyng / To make yow assente to this thyng" (3091–92). Theseus, thus, is free throughout the tale in a spontaneous, moment by moment, recognizably human way that Palamon and Arcite are not. So far as one can tell, any humor or irony from Palamon or Arcite is unconscious on their part. They are both completely dedicated young men, Palamon morally earnest (even when betraying his own cousin and when vowing war on Chastity), Arcite intellectually serious (even when empathizing with Mars's famous moment of priapic embarrassment). The only changes that take place in Palamon and Arcite are changes within the parameters of the theories they epitomize: Palamon's will changes from self-righteous hostility in Part I to loving acceptance in Part III; and Arcite's intellect changes from desiring only the sight of Emelye in Part I to correctly cognizing only her formal and material causes in Part III. They are not free to react spontaneously to people and events in the way that Theseus is free. Where they are logically consistent, Theseus is lifelike.

And finally with regard to freedom, Theseus believes himself and all men free. Not only does he himself act freely throughout the tale and hold other men freely responsible for their actions (Creon, Palamon, Arcite), but the Prime Mover he postulates with such care at the end is the ancient Greek conception of a Prime Mover who has no dealings whatsoever with individuals while they are in this world (3013–15, see Appendix B for comparison of Theseus's speech with its Boethian sources). Moreover, in the course of taking well what even he cannot eschew (e.g., praising Arcite's purchase of a "worthy fame" as a way of coping with his terrible death), Theseus advises others also to do the same—"to maken vertu of necessitee" (3042)—implying that he believes they too are free to do so. The Knight thus characterizes his Theseus, his *determinatio* figure, as speaking and acting freely and as believing himself totally free. Theseus can therefore justly be held responsible for his actions.

Is Theseus free in fact, however? In the concepts of fourteenth-century faculty psychology, his mind is free, as I have just shown, both will and intellect. But what about his body? Does he have natural appetites? And do his experiences come to him providentially or randomly? In Part II, while Palamon and Arcite fight up to their ankles in blood, and just before dispatching Theseus to follow the "grete hart" and so to come upon them, at the end of one of those awesomely convoluted Chaucerian sentences so useful for avoiding responsibility, and after bringing up the subjects of both "destinee" (1663) and God's "purveiaunce" (1665), then, Chaucer tells us:

> Yet somtyme it shal fallen on a day
> That falleth nat eft withinne a thousand yeer
> For certeynly oure appetites heer
> Be it of werre or pees or hate or loue
> Al is this ruled by the sighte aboue . . . (1668–72 MR)

Exactly what the first two lines mean in context no one can say because antecedents are uncertain; and "for certeynly" can signify either intensified certainty or real doubt. Either way, however, the result of this famous passage is that in the Knight's Tale we do, in a hazy undefined way, have the presence of natural appetites. Thus, although Theseus's will is free, his body is apparently subject to the pull of natural appetites for war, peace, hate, and/or love. Similarly, although Theseus's intellect is free, Providence does have a hand in shaping the experiences life presents him with: we see, for example, Saturn causing Arcite's horse to founder, and Curry has shown Saturn's hand in the torment and final death of Arcite's body.

II. Faculty Component

Thus, with Theseus the Knight presents us with a third, and determining, theory of human freedom. The Knight's is a practical rather than scientific freedom, a freedom by which, even though one may have natural appetites and providential experiences, nevertheless, one's mind is completely free: with will and intellect functioning harmoniously together, one is free to choose which appetite to satisfy, or none of them; one is free to add one's experiences up and learn from them in any direction, or not at all. In this more realistic, practical theory of freedom, the mind makes many kinds of choices, not simply what to believe and what to do, as in the scholastic theories, but also, and more importantly, what to think and how to think about it. Here, in the Knight's theory, judging from Theseus as exemplum, human beings are free because our minds are completely free. As a result, we are free to learn. Rather than a rational animal, the human being is a learning animal; and, moreover, since knowledge depends partly on its knower (to be discussed in Section III), an animal who chooses what he or she learns. One mind chooses merely to accept and lament Arcite's death; another chooses to try to understand the whole universe by means of understanding it.

LEARNING

Theseus changes in several good ways during the course of the tale. All, however, are actually just different surface manifestations of a single profound change: from a man who responds immediately and unreflectively to outwardly perceived happenings, Theseus learns to search into the intangible, inwardly intelligible, "hidden causes" of things.

Real learning and real change in the Knight's Tale take place slowly, silently, and at first uncertainly, and come out of bad things, as they usually do in life. The hard lessons we learn through suffering. The lesson out of bad things which is repeated at least three times in the Tale is that in this world there can be a large discrepancy between what we intend and the way things turn out. The original noble intention is not always realized in the outcome. The generous impulse can cause chaos; the great and good plan produce pain. In Part I, Theseus's oath to avenge the weeping ladies on that "tiraunt Creon" (959–64) produces ruin far beyond his original good intention. When he gets to Thebes, he not only slays Creon as promised; he goes on to scatter the people, win the city, and raze it, in that order; and the chronological point is made explicitly twice (985–90, 1001–4). Once started, alas, physical violence is difficult to stop. (In Boccaccio, on the other hand, the people leave the city voluntarily before Teseo arrives, *Teseida,* II, 70–72, 77; and the ladies in black are the ones who burn it, II, 81.) Again, in Part IV, Theseus's original good intention to let Fortune make the choice between the two young knights results in the death of one of his dearest friends (1448). Theseus is obviously not responsible; his intention was fair and the rules were modified to avoid just such an outcome. Yet Arcite does die. Moreover, he is the only one to die, and indeed, he dies not as a result of the fighting but as a result of winning and parading along the field. Alas, accidents do happen. (In Boccaccio, on the other hand, fourteen others also die as a direct result of the fighting, X, 8.) Although Theseus is obviously not at fault in Arcite's death—"fallyng nys nat but an aventure" (2722), the fact remains that there is a wide discrepancy between what he intended to achieve by means of the tournament and what actually followed it. Arcite's fall and death may have been *per accidens,* but Arcite is still dead. In both cases, Theseus's intentions were good. Rather than the destruction and slaughter of Thebes, Theseus had intended only to punish Creon; and rather than Arcite's death, Theseus had intended only to betroth Emelye. But undergoing two instances of the same kind of painful experience apparently provokes Theseus to ponder the relationship between good intentions and bad outcomes in this world. From doing so, he learns to look at things no longer as they reflect only his own interests, but to look into them also as they reflect the interests of others and, especially, into their own intrinsic "hidden causes" and inner truths. The result is that his thinking and behavior change for the better—the reader sees improvements in his cosmology, in his statecraft, possibly in some of his values, and in his personal style.

Theseus's new cosmology appears in his Prime Mover speech. His earlier cosmology is depicted in the theater and temples he built, decorated, and explicitly approved in Part III. It was a simple polytheistic cosmology polarized on war, love, and hunting, a little world in which one either suffered passively (as in Venus's paintings) or took up arms actively (as in Mars's paintings), and a world in which there was no meaning beyond the moment and no transcending purpose whatsoever (as in Diana's paintings). In his new cosmology at the end of Part IV, however, the single all-informing thought, the single means by which he resolves the overriding question of the unjust human suffering in the world (such as the destruction of Thebes and the death of Arcite), is a discrepancy between good intention and bad outcome—between the Prime Mover's high first "entente," on the one hand, that fair chain of love which bound the elements into order, as opposed, on the other, to its final outcome of deterioration, decline, and death in this world. By this ordering, nothing "engendred in this place" (oak, stone, river, town, man, woman) can exceed its established duration; thus in this world "al this thyng moot deye" (3034). However, the process is orderly, the Mover is stable and eternal, and all things return to their source. In this new cosmology, the pain and death of individuals in this world—Arcite's for example— are *per accidens* and not *per se*. Side effects, rather than final events in themselves. Now they are part of the orderly process of return to the source. Thus, at the end of the Knight's Tale, Theseus's new monotheistic cosmology of a distant benevolent Prime Mover who originally bound the elements with love and created things "parfit," from which they subsequently declined into corruption and decay, grows out of his own experience of life as it is in this "wrecched world adoun."

And this new cosmology of Theseus is an extraordinarily thoughtful cosmology. In historical fact, it is a combination of the Aristotelian notion of unmoved First Mover who moves all things by desire, with the Platonic notion of God as the intelligent craftsman of order among the elements. (The two notions are similarly combined in several sections of the *Consolation*.[69]) Thus a comparison of the temples he builds and decorates with such care and expense in Part III against his final Prime Mover speech shows that the Knight portrays his Theseus, his *determinatio* figure, as taking the very first steps of the ancient Greeks toward a philosophical conception of the universe, from polytheism to monotheism.[70]

Theseus changes also in his statecraft: at the beginning he is a ruler governing arbitrarily and by force—a "tyrant" (1111, 1562); at the end he is a parliamentary ruler governing also by non-physical, nonviolent means. First, in the early parts of the tale, Chaucer's Theseus believes he lives in the polytheistic world pictured in his temples, a world in which one's choice is either to suffer passively or to fight actively. Accordingly, Chaucer makes his early Theseus much more arbitrary and violent than is Boccaccio's. In Part I, returning home with his army from Scythia, on the very outskirts of Athens, Chaucer's "gentil duc" suddenly learns of Creon's villainous treatment of noble bodies and is so outraged he leaves immediately for Thebes with all his host, without seeking counsel of anyone and without taking even half a day off or allowing his men even half a day off in their home city. (Boccaccio's Teseo, on the other hand, although immediately promising the widows his help, before setting out first asks and receives Hippolyta's pardon and makes a rousingly persuasive speech to his knights, *Teseida*, II, 40–48.) Next, Chaucer's Theseus simply rides to Thebes, alights in the field, fights with Creon, and slays him. (Boccaccio's Teseo, on the other hand, first offers Creon a chance to relent, II, 52.) Further, after the battle, as soon as their bodies are brought to him, Chaucer's Theseus sentences Palamon and Arcite to prison perpetually, for no particular reason so far as one can tell, just arbitrarily. (In Boccaccio, on the other hand, the two are haughty and arrogant to Teseo in spite of his kindness, are first confined to prison along with many others for his triumphal return, and only later in Athens are they condemned to eternal imprisonment in order to prevent future trouble, II, 85–89, 97–99.) Later, in the grove in Part II, on hearing Palamon's confession Chaucer's Theseus immediately sentences the two to death. (In Boccaccio, on the other hand, Pentheus/Arcita easily secures a promise of amnesty before confessing, and afterwards Teseo is only angry for a moment and pardons them almost immediately; no ladies need to plead, II, 84–93). Thus Chaucer has deliberately characterized his early Theseus as hasty and arbitrary, a ruler whose automatic solution to political problems is physical force—war, prison, or death sentence.

At the end, on the other hand, Chaucer's Theseus becomes much more admirable, much more developed and intellectually interesting than Boccaccio's. For one thing, he now has a parliament, a point made twice (and not a small change in Chaucer's time): After Arcite's funeral, Chaucer adds "certeyn yeres" to Boccaccio's story and then an Athenian "parlement," at which "y-spoken was" to have "obeisaunce" from the Thebans; and now, after all this time, Theseus sends for Palamon. Later, speaking to Emelye, Theseus says "this is my full assent, / With al the'avys heer of my parlement" (3076–77), thus specifying explicitly for the second time a parliamentary body in Athens which Theseus now consults before acting.[71] And, of course, his method of ruling here at the end is by peaceful marriage alliance rather than bloody-handed war. (In Boccaccio, there is none of this character development: some days after Arcita's funeral, Teseo simply persuades Palamone and Emilia to marry, and the kings who had come to fight in the tournament and then attended the funeral now stay for the wedding.) Thus, where Boccaccio's Teseo is straightforward but static, Chaucer's Theseus changes during the course of the tale from a well-intentioned but hasty and completely arbitrary monarch, ruling by automatic recourse to physical violence, into a philosophically-minded parliamentary ruler, forming alliances by nonviolent intelligible means.

Theseus's personal values may change likewise. From the beginning of the tale, in his court a man could rise by merit[72] but could not, apparently, marry his sister. In his speech in Part II after he stops the fighting in the grove, Theseus mentions only "roial lynage" and "richesse" as qualifications for Emelye's hand (1829–31). At the end of Part IV, however, in the process of ordering Emelye to wed Palamon, he mentions as well Palamon's long, steadfast, devoted service (3077–88). Interestingly, although he consults his parliament, Theseus still does not consult Emelye in the matter of her marriage (as Arcite had done earlier when he lay dying, 2783–97).

Chaucer also changes Theseus's personal style to accord with the changes in his cosmology, statecraft, and values: In Parts I and II, Theseus is a precipitate, very physical man, responding immediately to outward, physically perceived causes (weeping ladies, unauthorized combats); in Part IV, however, as he becomes more thoughtful, Theseus becomes much less physical—he is characterized with less physical description, less movement, less noise, less tangible power.

In Parts I and II, Theseus's response to every situation is physical and immediate. Touched by the plight of the mourning ladies, he jumps from his horse, comforts them in his arms, and sets off for Thebes. (Boccaccio's Teseo, on the other hand, does not descend from his chariot, nor does he embrace the ladies, II, 25–43.) Chaucer's Theseus gets up early to hunt, delights in the challenge, follows the hart himself, and so comes upon the fight. (Boccaccio's Teseo, on the other hand, is merely one of a large company; Boccaccio's narrative here focuses on Emilia, V, 77–80.) In the grove, confronted with two men fighting furiously, Chaucer's Theseus spurs his horse between them, pulls his sword, and demands an explanation. (Boccaccio's Teseo, on the other hand, watches them for a time from a distance, then rides closer and simply speaks to them; he does not physically intervene, V, 82–84.) Chaucer's Theseus immediately sentences the two fighters to death, then forgives them "al hoolly," and then decrees the physically violent tournament. (Boccaccio's Teseo, on the other hand, pardons them immediately; there is no death sentence; and the question envisioned in the tournament seems to be not death but rather whose company will by force of arms drive the other's out of the theater, V, 82–98.) Thus, in these early parts of the Knight's Tale, Chaucer's Theseus is consistently more physical in his actions and reactions than Boccaccio's Teseo. Where Teseo tends to look on and talk, Theseus responds with his whole body, physically as well as verbally; and in these early parts Theseus's responses consistently entail extreme physical violence and death.

A year later, however, in Parts III and IV, Theseus changes. After spending two days greeting and feasting the two noble companies (and keeping in mind his longstanding affection for Arcite), Theseus modifies his original tournament rules explicitly to pre-

II. Faculty Component

vent bloodshed. In addition, the announcement is made by his herald, while he himself, previously so physical and forward, sits silent and motionless at the window (2523–36). (Boccaccio's Teseo, on the other hand, makes the announcement himself, VII, 7–13.) Confronted here with the impending tournament which he himself had originally arranged, Theseus is not the same hasty, physically inclined, arbitrary man he was in Parts I and II. The long list of weapons he forbids—shot, polax, short knife, short sword, and only one course with the spear (2543–50)—indicates a new concern with the possible outcome of physical violence. (Boccaccio's Teseo, on the other hand, forbids only the lances, VII, 12.) Moreover, during Parts I and III, lack of movement and noise in Arcite and Palamon had indicated inward submission to a higher law. Sitting here motionless and silent at his window like "a god in trone," Theseus may be thinking—and may be intended to make the reader think—of chains of complex hidden causes and potential human suffering. Later, when the tournament is over, Theseus again responds immediately to the physically perceived exigencies: Arcite is carried to the palace and looked after, while Theseus himself honors the visiting lords, decrees an end to the rivalry, feasts them properly, and sees them off. After Arcite's terrible death, however, Theseus's response is delayed. He takes his sister away, the whole town grieves, he listens to his old father, and he comes only to a decision as to where to perform the funeral office. He orders the preparations and he himself lays Arcite's body out, and now "he weep that pitee was to heere" (2878). Almost a hundred lines follow of magnificent funeral rites, but there is no further indication of Theseus's inward feelings, of how he, as opposed to Egeus, the town women, and all the people of Athens, manages to cope with a death such as Arcite's. In a situation like this, what can he do? Whom can this formerly hasty, arbitrary, violent man take up his arms against?

Finally, years later, when in the course of events a need arises for him to bring it to a close, then Theseus speaks about Arcite's death. But first, Palamon is sent for, Emelye is sent for, they all sit, the whole parliament is hushed, Theseus waits for a while, sighs, and finally "right thus" he speaks his thoughts. This is a man of an entirely different personal style from the proud, precipitate conqueror we met at the beginning of the Knight's Tale. This is a man of thought, indeed a man of wisdom, a man who now knows his place in the larger order of the universe, knows his own responsibilities and limits, and freely accepts them.

Thus, at the end of the tale, the Knight's Theseus has become a philosophic man, a man who searches into the hidden causes of things, a man who looks up from the "fool erthe" to the distant stars and behind them to find and honor the "prince and cause of alle thyng."

Does Theseus therefore, like Palamon and Arcite, become "parfit"? No, of course not. One consequence of the notion that man in this world is primarily a learner is acceptance of the fact that he is always going to be imperfect, always one who is learning rather than one who has learned. Magnificent as he is at the end of the tale, Theseus still has a few things to learn. First, there is no way of knowing whether anyone has yet corrected his eye-widening ignorance of the sexual proclivities of hares and cuckoos (1806–10). Emelye may know nothing of serving love, as Theseus says, but hares and cuckoos were proverbial for their expertise at "al this hoote fare."[73] Likewise, in the middle of his magnificent final speech, Theseus twice identifies the Prime Mover, the great motionless Absolute, the prince and cause of all things from whom everything proceeds and to whom everything returns, with that busy ineffectual little planet-god we glimpsed earlier needing Saturn's help to stop the strife between Venus and Mars (2438–46). Theseus is approaching the right conception of deity in his Prime Mover speech, but he still has the wrong name for it.[74] In addition, he still considers it unnecessary to consult Emelye in the matter of her marriage to Palamon. Since the Knight earlier characterized Arcite's reception of divine grace partly by having him do that very thing, speak directly to her and consider her as having real feelings of her own (2796–97), it seems likely that Theseus's lack of human consideration for Emelye here is to be taken as another deficiency, another lesson yet to be learned.[75] Moreover, Theseus's final conception of the universe here at the end, although monotheistic, is still pagan—physically man survives only in the species, mentally man returns to the source. Theseus is, of course, unaware of the Christian revelation, still far in the future; but it is well worth noticing that the Knight had Providence help Theseus along toward discovering the truth of monotheism, a truth that will become Christian truth in time; indeed, a truth that was considered by some medieval thinkers long before Chaucer to have been one of many divine revelations to the pre-Christian pagan Greeks.[76] And finally here, even as he reveals the great wisdom he himself has gained by living his life in this "wrecched" world "adoun" and pondering about it, Theseus nevertheless still sees the struggling and suffering of people on earth, for example the suffering of Arcite, as simply *per accidens,* as simply happenings to be undergone while awaiting return to the source, as lacking meaning or value for the individual personally. The reader, on the other hand, having seen the hand of Providence at work guiding events in the tale, and having seen the changes for the better in Palamon and Arcite and in Theseus himself, knows better. The reader knows that life here really does have a value, that what one does with it does count.

In short, at the end of the tale, Theseus is still humanly deficient; he still has things to learn—about cuckoos and hares, about love, about the Divine Name, and especially about the divine purpose in putting each of us individually into this world. But he has come a very long way. He was magnificent in action at the beginning, sweeping the ladies up in his arms, riding off to Thebes, separating the knights. He is even more magnificent in thought here at the end, revealing the order in the world, the fair chain of love, and the hidden First Cause—still not perfect, still human, but a far better man at the end than he was at the beginning. The Knight's Theseus embodies the best that a human being can be in this world, a person who finds something higher than himself to serve and a person who learns to treat other people better. In this he is more than just a Christian humanist universal; he is a Christian humanist ideal. What Theseus becomes in the Knight's Tale—a person not perfect but improving—is a standard, a universally achievable behavioral ideal, against which all of Chaucer's other characters in the remainder of the *Tales* can profitably be judged.

Chaucer's Changes in Faculty Psychology

In his resolution of the will/intellect debate, Chaucer changes both the principal emphasis and the overall context of the faculty psychology of his time.

First, he changes the emphasis from definition to freedom, that is, from the discovery concern of the scientist to the ethical concern of the humanist. The scholastic philosophers had a passion for definition. This makes sense, because in principle if one can define a thing, one can understand it. The problem with defining human nature, however, is that the more it is defined, the less it is free; and pretty soon there it is, formulated, pinned to the wall like Palamon and Arcite. Although scrupulously evenhanded, the Knight's embodiments of the two scholastic psychologies presents them as extremes, as the two rather rigid poles at either end of human possibility, one *essentially* voluntarist, the other *essentially* intellectualist. Chaucer's faculty psychology is much less defined. Although he does touch all the major scholastic bases (as was shown), in the end, what it all comes down to, simply, is—Theseus is free and he learns to be better. These are the two aspects of his characterization that subsume all the Knight's careful pointings. In a practical sense, of course, the two are interdependent: one cannot learn to be better unless one is free to learn. If one is restricted by one's nature to a single mode of reasoning, whether deductive or inductive, or to a single way of responding, whether rationally or emotionally, one is simply not free. In the scholastic faculty psychologies, human nature was accorded both options, of course, but always with the proviso that one option was naturally more noble, or more direct, or more real than the other. There again, however, if one is restricted by one's nature to a set hierarchy of thinking or of responding to the experiences one has in the world, the fact remains that one is still restricted. One is still not free. The Knight's Theseus is characterized instead by his lack of restriction. He responds with both his intellect and his will. He does everything the two young knights do and more. He perceives, reasons, and responds across a whole spectrum of possibility. According to this way of thinking, the kind of person one inwardly is depends not just on one's own particular givens of appetites, nature, and circumstances; it depends as well on how one responds to them, what one chooses to learn from them. In this view of human nature, regardless of one's particular givens, because one's mind is free one is free to learn to be better.

The fourteenth century was "an age in revolt against Greek necessitarianism," comments Armand Maurer,[77] and that seems to be a major Chaucerian concern in the Knight's Tale. But not just Greek determinism. Chaucer is also concerned with Christian determinism, with blaming God as well as blaming nature. For Boethius, for Dante, and, this chapter has shown, for Chaucer in his theory (to be tested in his other tales), the mind is always free. The mind can make excuses (often with some truth in them), can blame Venus for its "likerousnesse," or Friday for its "meschaunce," or "grisly rokkes" for its unhappiness, or Providence or tyrant or neighbor or priest or spouse or whatever, but the fact remains—and this seems to be one major message of the Knight in his tale—that the mind is eventually going to be held responsible for everything it does, and it would be wise to think now in those terms. Things do happen to one, yes; but one chooses how one responds to them, both mentally and physically. This is the hard edge of later medieval Christianity. Like it or not, this also makes it a very responsible form of Christianity. Dante, painfully, puts Piccarda in the lowest sphere of heaven and Francesca and Farinata and Brunetto Latino in hell. At this time in the medieval universities, on the other hand, under the influence of Greek rationalism, excuses were being made. Coercion, error, tradition, natural incapacity, poor advice, ignorance, innocent intent—as extenuating circumstances were multiplied, individual responsibility was fading away. This is the ethical context in which Chaucer wrote the Knight's Tale. Freedom is the issue to which, in his language use, he devotes the most care. I think it safe to say that on the issue of human freedom, Chaucer considered the scholastic scientists of his time verbally misguided, if not verbally irresponsible. On the other hand, in this context he too is acting as a scholastic scientist, devising a logically coherent theory. His theory opts for traditional

Christian total freedom of choice; yet some of his other tales indicate he too had doubts, or at least questions, about total responsibility for the innocent, ignorant, or coerced.

And second, Chaucer changes the overall context of faculty psychology, from considering human nature in a void to considering it in the context of real lives being lived by real human beings in the real world. Here again, Chaucer's change is from the abstract, rationalizing, new-truth concern of the scholastic to the ethical concern of the humanist. The question here is the value of ordinary day-to-day living for the ordinary day-to-day individual living it. Given the eternity that is to come for the ordinary man or woman, is life here anything more than a pilgrimage of woe or a test to be passed or flunked? If the *Canterbury Tales* as a whole, all the tales and links taken together, can be said to have an overall specific thesis, it seems to me, it is that ordinary (not noble) people learn, for good or for ill, from the unremarkable events of their everyday lives.

In the fourteenth century, this was a most unusual idea. In fact, I cannot recall seeing it anywhere in medieval literature. In Chaucer's time, when one thought of real knowledge, one thought of the eternal, unchanging, universal objects of thought, of the kind of knowledge given by divine illumination, by innate ideas, or by rigorous scientific demonstration from first principles. The kind of knowledge that ordinary everyday people work out informally for themselves from the unplanned transitory events of their day-to-day occupational and social lives was considered opinion and not really worth much.[78] In Aquinas's psychology, for example, one may learn some natural virtues from inadvertent or unplanned daily experience, but no emphasis is laid on it. Rather, natural virtue is a kind of self-perfection by which one deliberately completes oneself, and supernatural virtue is by divine fiat. In Ockham's psychology, on the other hand, virtue is obedience to the divine will; one may or may not learn this from personal experience, but again the role of unmiraculous everyday events is not emphasized.[79] In the high literature Chaucer knew or may have known—the *Aeneid*, the *Metamorphoses*, the *Roman de la Rose*, *Sir Orfeo*, *Piers Plowman*, the romances—unless one is noble, the effect of one's daily way of life and ordinary day-to-day experiences on the workings of her or his mind is rarely if ever addressed. One meets vivid characters to be sure, but they are not made vivid in this way. Noble characters occasionally learn to be better, as do Perceval and Yvain, but what they learn was already theirs by nature. Noble characters occasionally learn a single sharp lesson from a single sharp incident, as does Gawain from the Green Knight's lady. Even in Dante, the moral characters and intellectual qualities of his individuals seem to be givens, from which their experiences appropriately follow.

Chaucer is different. First, his pilgrims are predominantly commoners.[80] Except for the Knight and the Squire, none are noble. And second, their experiences seem to have been on the one hand mostly day-to-day and unexceptional, yet on the other Chaucer seems to use what they would have learned from such experiences to individualize their personalities. It is as if, that is to say, these characters did learn to be some of what they are, good and bad, from some of their own unexceptional, unstructured personal daily lives.[81] The knowledge that they gleaned from these day-to-day experiences (to which, of course, they themselves contributed significantly in interpreting them) may have been uncertain and unreliable in the scientific sense, but it certainly influenced their beliefs and their behavior in the human sense.

A self-conscious presentation of one's own individuality, such as we get from some of Chaucer's middle-class pilgrims, is rare in the medieval period. In visual art the idea of depicting individuality seems to start again in the mid-thirteenth century, but initially its purpose seems to have been the visual excitement individuality adds, rather than our idea of individuality as someone's identity. For example, the unforgettable statues of Uta and Ekkehard at Naumberg Cathedral, so vividly individual that one would recognize them instantly on the street, are actually part of a series of twelve figures carved in 1248–50 to commemorate the founders of the See of Naumberg in 1028, some 200 years earlier. That is to say, the individualities depicted are not those of the two statues' historical subjects. In the fourteenth century, depictions of important people, both saints and rulers, are sometimes individualized, but the artists' purposes still seem to have been excitement rather than verisimilitude. On the other hand, in the beautiful Wilton Diptych from Chaucer's own lifetime, dated around 1400 and pehaps the most famous "portrait" there is of Richard II, the artist seems to have been interested less in excitement and more in aesthetic harmony. Of the sixteen adult figures in the two panels, every face has essentially the same long nose, every hand has essentially the same beautiful long, tapered fingers. With his red hair and youthful features, the Richard depicted accords with what we know of the historical Richard, yet all the angels also have youthful features and red hair. In High Gothic art, depictions of important people are often individualized, but not in our modern sense of showing a real person's uniqueness.

Throughout this whole period, the few peasants and working people one sees in the artwork are duplicated types, their features stamped from the same die, their postures totally engrossed and fulfilled in their particular occupations. What a surprise, then, to find the middle-aged face shown in figure 4, with its wrinkled brow, quizzical eyes, and avuncular mustache, gazing down from the main portal at St. Peter's Cathedral in Regensburg. It is dated 1400–1410. Who is it? Not a saint, not a king, not even a noble to judge from its clothing and posture. As a result, apparently in order to account for the striking sense of intelligent individuality this particular head projects, so vivid that one would recognize the man instantly on a street-corner, art historians identify it as a "self-portrait of an architect or sculptor?" Like Chaucer's pilgrims, this face seems to belong to an ordinary middle-class person who has spent years practicing some skilled occupation, and who has learned in the course of them a certain self-confidence and a particular way of looking at life. To say more than that would be too conjectural, yet how very different this face is from the faces and purposes depicted in the Tickhill Psalter illumination earlier or in the ivory traveling altar shown in the next chapter. This is the face of a skilled middle-class worker, a commoner and knowledgeable about what that means, self-consciously presenting himself to his viewer and to the future as more than just an occupational type, as an intelligent individual in his own right, and as worthy of notice.

Figure 4. Self-portrait of an architect or sculptor, c. 1400–1410. Main portal, St. Peter's Cathedral, Regensburg, Germany.

Theseus: Chaucer's Determinatio

In Gothic literary art one can trace the same kind of development. Nobles and holy people tend to be made exciting, dramatic, or beautiful, but not by means of what we would call personal individualities; peasants and commoners tend to be identical with their occupations. What little autobiography (i.e., self-presentation) we get tends to be what Karl Joachim Weintraub calls "additive," that is, added into a writer's larger account of some accepted social occupation in which the writer presents herself or himself only incidentally and as wholly fulfilled and justified in that occupation—whether of abbot, physician, mystic, teacher, or poet. Abbot Suger, for example, seems to have completely fulfilled what we would call his individuality within the occupational forms his society offered him.[82] The same is true of Julian of Norwich and of Chaucer himself, for that matter. Not so with Chaucer's pilgrims, however. In the *Canterbury Tales,* the middle-class occupational forms presented are not enough to contain completely the private personalities of the people who fill them. The personal histories and interesting particularities of Monk, Prioress, Pardoner, Reeve, Friar, and Miller, to name but a few, spill out all over their set social forms and norms in recognizably self-conscious, surprisingly "modern" ways, personal histories and interesting particularities that seem to have been derived (in varying degrees of tale/teller "adequation," to use Aquinas's term) from the day to day experiences an ordinary individual in that occupation and way of daily life would undergo.

The idea that unplanned unexceptional daily experience is important in shaping the thoughts and judgments of the ordinary human mind is not supposed to appear in modern times until Locke. Indeed, judging from the things we read and look at even now in the course of an ordinary day and evening, the idea is still not accepted. Yet here it is in Chaucer's first, presumably theme-setting *Canterbury* tale, embodied in the figure presumably defining his own theory of universal human nature. Here it is, the theory that every human being gathers and creates important knowledge from his or her own daily life. Indeed, Theseus's Prime Mover speech suggests that behind the ideas of even the greatest of *auctoritees* (Plato and Aristotle and Boethius in this particular speech) lie insights derived from their own individual personal experiences.

II. Faculty Component

In short, what is authority but someone's else's experience and insight written down?

In the Knight's Tale, of course, although Theseus is a pagan, he is noble. From the very beginning, he is noble in nature and noble in behavior. He always reacts and behaves nobly. However, there are many different kinds of "noble," and because he is free and can learn, Chaucer's Theseus becomes the best kind. By pondering the accidents and unexpected outcomes in this world and discerning a natural order within them, he discovers a Being higher than himself with a purpose higher than his own, and he freely accepts his own subordinate position and responsibilities within that Being's "faire cheyne of love." This kind of nobility, the Knight's Tale suggests, is within the choice of every human being.

3

The Goal of a Universal Psychology: Certitude versus Choice

THE TITLE OF this chapter concluding the discussion of the faculty
component of universal psychologies is a gestalt figure. "Goal" can
mean a realizable hope, the culmina-
tion of analysis, planning, and hard
work. It can also mean a prison-
house. A goal can be a boundary
as well as an achievement. For the

Figure 5. Gestalt perceptual choice figure.

scholastic research scientist, always in pursuit of the universal, to
define *correctly* the universal of human nature was a wonderful goal,
a sustaining dream, well worth the devotion of a lifetime. Could
anything be more important than knowing exactly what we are?
Think what it would be to really understand the image (albeit a
fallen one) of the Divine. For the scientist reasoning out his theory,
a universal psychology was the end. Totally abstract. Timeless.
Immutable. For the Christian humanist, on the other hand, a universal psychology, even a correct one, was still only a means. For
the humanist, concerned always with fostering real human beings,
trying always to better their individual conditions in one way or
another, to define *incorrectly* the universal of human nature could
be to build a prison in the mind. A wrong definition could result
in limiting human choices, in restricting human freedom and there-

fore responsibility. For example, when Arcite believes he is not free, he just sits and complains and waits for things to change (1085, 1091, 1238–43). And when Palamon believes he is not free, he just does as he thinks he has been told, accepts the outcome of the tournament and goes quietly home to Thebes until called back by Theseus years later (2967–77). Further, in a Christian rather than pagan context, telling people they are not free, not responsible, can have much more serious results. They can believe it and act on that belief; and only later, say at some distant day of judgment, do they learn too late that they were really free after all and chose to act wrongly because they chose to believe wrongly. The problem here is not with the goal of a universal psychology *per se*. Knowledge is always a good thing, and no one would deny that it would be good to know better what we are. The real problem, Chaucer suggests in the Knight's Tale, is with the scholastic claims of certitude.

Basing their claims on the Aristotelian belief in scientific demonstration (i.e., that valid reasoning from first principles automatically produces universally necessary truths), the scholastics sought and claimed they were achieving real certitude about real human beings. The point originally, of course, had been to bring Bible, Fathers, authorities, and experience together; but by Chaucer's time, after generations of ever-narrower distinctions, the traditional objects of scholastic inquiry had been defined into ossification. Human nature had been codified into, basically, the two competing types, and their faculties and development and especially their areas of freedom and submission had been spelled out inflexibly. Reason, intending to support revelation, had become an object of faith in itself. And by insisting on literality—one word/one meaning—it had shrunk words down from rich signs for complex interpretation to objective mathematical-type symbols for manipulation. In its attempt to achieve certitude, scholastic science had instead cut human nature and human thinking down to a size linear logic could handle. Abstraction, in Christian tradition the servant of reality, was seeking to replace it as master.

The attitude of the teller of the Knight's Tale toward all this endeavor seems to be that abstractions about people can be fun to reason with, rather like playing a good game of chess, but that winning theories from the game of logical abstractions have to be evaluated in terms of their effect on real people. When devising theories of universal psychology, as when devising anything else, intentions are one thing; results may be something else again. The teller of the Knight's Tale seems dubious that rationalizing alone is the royal road to knowledge of human nature. He regards with some amusement the idea that simply by reasoning, by manipulating language, by diddling with a few propositions, one can achieve predictive certitude about the behavior of real people. Predictive certitude is, thus, the target of those surprising Part III prayers.

"Now cometh the point," says the Knight, "and herkneth if yow leste" (2208). First Palamon, with his lark, humble cheer, and sore heart, wends slowly on his pilgrimage to Venus and tearfully utters a mystical prayer of absolute, heartfelt submission. Can this really be the same demanding, defiant young man whose solution to every problem in Parts I and II was physical force? Next, Emelye, "astoned," listens to Diana (a goddess who seems totally unaware of the immediate past, i.e., totally unaware that Providence has just quenched, quickened, and quenched again her own altar fires), set forth the "eterne word" about her future (2350). And finally, Arcite, the young man who in Part I had passively acquiesced to whatever happened to him and in Part II served in the same court with his beloved Emelye for five or six years without making the least move toward her, this once submissive young man now strides "right thus" to the temple of Mars, forthrightly compares his own "peynes" as equal (five "thilke's") to those of his god, and straightforwardly tells his god exactly what he wants, "victorie, . . . namoore." What we have here is not one case of divine foreknowledge flanked by two cases of real human nature undergoing reasonably lifelike development, but three miracles—one of nature, two of scholastic psychology, all three of words.[83]

In real life people do change, of course, sometimes greatly. A self-righteous person occasionally becomes loving and respectful, as does Palamon. An acquiescent person occasionally turns down-

II. Faculty Component

right blunt, as does Arcite. But these scholastic theories were supposedly about universal human nature—about all men of all times and all places. Can one really say that *all* virtuous men conform their wills freely and lovingly to the divine? Can one really say that *all* virtuous men rule their passions reasonably? self-perfectingly? These conclusions are more logical than sensible, not to mention the fact that as behavioral ideals obedience and self-perfection are probably not always compatible. In Chaucer's Knight's Tale rearrangment, these three prayers form an unforgettable triptych: two predictions based on Aristotelian logic frame a third based on fires that "queynt" and brands that whistle. So much for the scholastic claims of universal psychological certitude!

In a traditional Christian context, the end-point should be not universal certitude, but individual choice. Thus Chaucer approached the same psychological problem—the individual's development into a virtuous state of being—from the standpoint of the individual. The philosophical problem as to what makes any person an individual, that is, as to what is the principle of individuation (*principium individuationis*) in all individual beings, arose, like so many other scholastic problems, as a consequence of the universalizing character of Aristotelian-Arabian metaphysics. Before the reception of Aristotle into the West in the twelfth century, the Augustinian tradition just took the individuation of every human soul pretty much for granted. But if, as Aristotelian science taught, all human beings are compositions of form and matter, and if the form (universal) of all human beings is the same, then the principle by which I differ from my next-door neighbor must reside in my particular matter. For most of us this is not a satisfactory explanation of our individual identities. At stake for Christians, obviously, are the personal immortality of the immaterial soul and the doctrine of divine rewards and punishments. As always, the scholastics debated the question in universal terms: does individuality result from aspects of the particular matter in which the human form inheres (the position of Aquinas, loosely speaking); or is individuality the result of an event, a big bang, say, at the moment when substantial form actualizes prime matter in each particular soul (Bonaventure, very loosely speaking); or is individuality (*haec-ceity*, "thisness") something unique that each individual soul is informed with from the start (Scotus, loosely speaking)?[84] Reconciling the existence of universals (genera, species, common natures, types, i.e., class concepts of any size) with the uniqueness of individuals is a major issue in any Aristotelian-based Christian philosophy because Aristotelian science deals with universals and certitudes, whereas Christianity focuses on individuals and contingent choices.

From the common-sense point of view, of course, both individual and universal are really "there," in our minds, in our languages, and apparently in things themselves. The problem for philosophers is getting the common sense and the scientific demonstration to agree. In the mid-thirteenth century, Aquinas, following Aristotle, reasoned systematically about universal human nature, and as one result had to grope around for a principle of individuation compatible with the Christian principle of individual salvation. (He made repeated attempts to locate it in some properties of matter.) In the early fourteenth century, Ockham, following in the Franciscan tradition, reasoned systematically to assert the individual as the primary existent fact in this world, thus dispensing with universals entirely, but as one result had to grope around for a theory of class concepts. (He attempted to locate it in a "confusion" of perceptions.) And so, in the later fourteenth century, Chaucer approached this complex issue from a distinctively new direction. A civil servant and diplomat, accustomed to working with individuals on a day-to-day basis in the real world (rather than reasoning about isolated universals in the quiet of a scholastic study-house), he found his individuating principle not in logic but in living. As touched on earlier, Chaucer's principle of individuation resides, at least in part, not in an entity but in a process—in the uniquely individualizing sum of one's personal day-to-day experiences combined with the meanings one individually makes of them. Chaucer's principle therefore gives value to our own worldly lives and to the way each of us, in the course of our daily living, helps to shape our own individuality and therefore our own salvation. Ideally we learn to be more thoughtful, to search into the "hidden causes" of things, as did Theseus (as did Boethius, *Consolation,* I, m. 2), and as a result to become better human beings.

The goal of Chaucer's theory of universal psychology for the individuals within it, therefore, is both more demanding and more social than the goals of the two scholastic psychologies. Leaving aside the role of divine grace, and considering only what the individual is able to do for herself or himself, one can, like Arcite, get one's faculties into the proper hierarchical order, so that one's reason rules one's appetites. Surely this is virtuous. Or one can, like Palamon, come to love the divine unselfishly and submit to it freely. Surely this too is virtuous. Or one can, like Theseus, come to know and honor a Being higher than oneself and accept the order established by that Being and, in accordance with that order, try to behave better toward one's fellow human beings. Surely this is even more virtuous. The first is a virtue of the self. The second is a virtue between the self and the divine. The third adds behavior toward one's fellows, a more demanding daily goal.

In Chaucer's time, as now, the issue of freedom was often joined with the issue of individuality. They seem, in fact, to be the two bright sides of a single coin. The existence of both is intuitively obvious, yet the existence of neither can be demonstrated, nor can either be positively defined. Freedom can be defined only by absences; individuality can be discussed only as an ontologically questionable metaphysical entity or a jumbled collection of mental contents or processes prior to objectification, or, possibly, only as an "I am" more basic even than thought or feeling.[85] The interesting thing here is that Chaucer settles both concerns, freedom and individuality, psychologically rather than ontologically. That is to say, in Chaucer's universal psychology, both freedom and individuality are subjective. They exist only in the mind. Subjectivity, therefore, judging from the *determinatio* of the will/intellect debate in the Knight's Tale, will have to be included, Chaucer suggests, in any Christian theory of universal psychology. Since the mind chooses what it thinks in response to what happens to it—chooses whether to hate or to love, whether to ignore or understand, whether to hinder or help—the final goal of all human beings will be the result of whatever they themselves, subjectively, choose to think.

Universal Psychologies: Thinking Processes and Language Use

– ADDING SUBJECTIVITY –

BACKGROUND

People use language to think with.[1] They carry on internal mono-
logues while working out their thoughts. They carry on internal
dialogues while working out what they should or should not have
done or said. Struck with a sudden intuition or cognition, they
figure out its significance by means of language in their minds. If
a matter is complex, they write it out in order to figure it out, again
using language to help them think. Further, language is what
enables people to think reflectively, by providing them with a
"chunking" device[2] for pulling out and thus being able to remember
discrete moments, discrete particles of the inexorably passing
stream of events in which, as creatures of time, they are otherwise

immersed. Indeed, it is language that enables human beings to be free, by providing them with the power to form abstract standards of right and wrong and thus free themselves by means of thinking from the impulses and necessities of their own natural drives. Language is, thus, indispensable to human thinking.

Therefore, since thinking is one of the major uses of language (if not *the* major use), to put language in a straight-jacket is to put thinking in a straight-jacket. As a result, when scholastic scientists, attempting to achieve objectivity, disparage the use of figures and the reading of fictions in order to restrict language to literal, the effect on the individuals around them can be, by reason of that disparagement, to restrict thinking to logical, demonstration to scientific, knowledge to certain, and objects of thought to abstract universals. Under such restrictions, the human mind becomes pallid, the created world a paltry place.

The question arises, however, is a purely literal use of language possible? This question Chaucer explicitly raises—and answers—when he chooses to write the six long pagan-romance descriptions in Part III of the Knight's Tale in the form of scholastic *sophismata*. In the fourteenth century, the scholastics' three favorite oral/literary genres seem to have been *obligationes, insolubilia,* and *sophismata*.[3] In none is language used literally. Therefore, bringing any one of these forms into the context of the scholastic/humanist language-use debate constitutes an instantaneous humanist victory. Since all three scholastic genres use language figuratively, all three are eloquent and embarrassing witnesses against their own side.

Until recently, *obligationes* were considered lengthy logical games in the form of nit-picking disputations in which an "opponent" tried to force a "respondent" into a contradiction. Today, however, as research in medieval logic has become increasingly interesting to modern analytically oriented philosophers, it has become clear that the medievals took obligation disputations seriously. Rather than meaningless games, they seem to have been structured situations for rule testing. In them, complicated sets of rules for hypothetical reasoning about deriving consequences and inferences were tested by participants in the rapid-fire *disputatio* format. A favorite trick, for example, was to propose an impossible proposition to begin with, so that the respondent had to double-think every statement. Here is Paul Spade's description:

> "An *obligatio* is an expression by means of which someone is bound to reply affirmatively or negatively to the *obligatum*." Thus, for instance, if the opponent should say "I posit that (*pono quod*) every man runs," and if that *posito* is admitted by the respondent, then the respondent is obliged to reply affirmatively to the sentence 'Every man runs' (the *obligatum*) throughout the disputation. He replies affirmatively by saying "I concede" (*concedo*). On the other hand, if the opponent says "I give it up that (*depono quod*) every man runs," and if that *depositio* is admitted by the respondent, then the respondent is obliged to reply negatively to the sentence 'Every man runs' throughout the disputation. He replies negatively by saying "I deny" (*nego*). The disputation lasts until the opponent says "Let the time of *obligatio* lapse" (*Cedat tempus obligationis*).
>
> After the *obligatio* has been made and admitted, certain sentences are "proposed" by the opponent. The respondent must reply to each of the proposed sentences in turn. He has three replies open to him: he may concede the proposed sentence, he may deny it, or he may doubt it (by replying "dubito"). . . . [and so on.]

As Spade comments, "one would not expect what is said in a *disputatio de obligationibus* to be of much interest to anyone in its own right. And in fact, it appears from the literature that this is so. Interest in such a *disputatio* centers not on the content, but rather on the rules the *disputatio* illustrates."[4] Thus, *obligationes* do not use language literally. "Every man runs" is certainly no more literal than, say, the *Book of the Duchess*. As to the comparative value of the truths the two fictions veil, one scholastic and the other humanist, no doubt that is a matter of purpose and taste.

Then there are the *insolubilia*. These were semantic paradoxes. The most famous is, of course, the Liar Paradox—"A man says that he is lying; is what he says true or false?" That one goes back to long before Aristotle, is mentioned by Cicero and St. Paul, and still exercises semanticists today. The problem with such paradoxes

III. Thinking Processes and Language Use

is that if they are true they are false, and if they are false they are true. Most are generated by self-reference or difficulties in tense or scope. As a group, they pose interesting problems of language use. Here are some scholastic examples from E. J. Ashworth: "I am silent." "No proposition is negative." " 'Socrates knows that he errs,' and this is his sole belief."

> A favorite example [of the crocodile paradox] concerned a bridge whose keeper (often called Plato or Socrates, though Eckius chose 'Eckebertus') said that he would throw anyone who spoke falsely into the water. The man who wished to cross said "You will throw me in the water." Did he speak truly or falsely? Another puzzle concerned a country where all the healthy people, and none of the sick people, spoke the truth. One of their number said "I am ill," thus generating the paradox.[5]

Again, if this is language being used literally, then Socrates is King of Siam.

And last, the *sophismata*. These were defined earlier as test-case sentences used to bring out abstract problems of metaphysics, natural science, or such. Here are two more *sophisma* sentences (from Richard Kilvington, d. 1361) on natural science; the problem being studied is the concept of instantaneous velocity: "Socrates will move faster than Socrates now moves" and "Plato can move uniformly during some time and as fast as Socrates now moves."[6] And notice again: the language is not being used literally. To describe this kind of language use, rather than a term from poetics like "figuratively" or "allegorically," no doubt the scholastics would have used "hypothetically," but the practice in all cases is the same. The meaning intended is other than literal. As a result, the reader must add something subjective in order to interpret it.

Further, as with *obligationes* and *insolubilia* (and as with pagan poems), it was well understood by the scholastics that the abstract questions raised by *sophismata* had no single, correct, objective meaning. These were testing sentences. Just as with interpretations of a poem, additional interpretations were sought and welcomed. The more approaches a *sophisma* could generate, the richer it was considered. Just like a good poem, a good *sophisma* would be commented on for hundreds of years. The whole/part *sophisma* touched on earlier in Section I—"The whole Socrates is less than Socrates"—was commented on by, among others, William of Sherwood (d. c. 1270), Peter of Spain (d. 1277), Henry of Ghent (d. 1293), Walter Burley (d. 1345), William of Ockham (d. 1349), William Heytesbury (d. 1372), Albert of Saxony (d. 1390), and Paul of Venice (d. 1429).[7] Well, so much for purely literal language use, the Knight's Tale *sophismata* suggest. The scholastics preach it, but they don't practice it.

In actual fact, purely literal *use* of a natural language is not possible. The human mind is too rich. Contexts cannot be fully specified; implications will get overlooked; associations and inferences will always be triggered off by something. To achieve the kind of precision and objectivity the scholastics were looking for, they needed artificial technical languages (which, of course, is what they were developing with their constant references to Socrates, Plato, running men, and trips to Rome, and which they did develop in time). In actual fact, the real difference between scientific *sophisma* and pagan poem is not in the literality of the language use, but in the user's goal—objective new universal truth or subjective understanding/appreciation/piety. By means of the Part III descriptions of the Knight's Tale, Chaucer demonstrates, albeit in fourteenth-century terms, that there is always a subjective element to language use, for both speaker and listener, just as there is always a subjective element to thinking, no matter how "reasonable." Subjectivity is, therefore, what the six long pagan-romance descriptions of Part III argue should be added to the universal psychological theory of Chaucer's time.

In Chaucer's time, thinking processes and language use were two separate subjects, and faculty psychology and freedom was a third. Chaucer puts the three separate topics together. Since God was not conceived of as thinking, that is, as taking part in processes (God exists in a single eternal moment, so to speak), the human thinking acts were ordinarily discussed in the context of certitude. Language, on the other hand, was ordinarily discussed in the context of grammatical studies. For Chaucer, however, language is the medium by which the immaterial mind and physical matter (sound waves) interact. Hence in Part III of the Knight's Tale, in some six hundred intricately-wrought lines, he weaves together the later medieval theories of the mind's thinking processes with the controversies between logician and humanist over the valid use of language. Then, having combined language use and thinking processes, he inserts the combination into the heart of his development and resolution of the will/intellect debate, in which freedom was already the central issue. By doing so, he inserted into the traditionally objective study of universal human nature, the whole issue of human subjectivity.

Subjectivity has many aspects. Individuation, daily personal experience, optical point of view,[8] individual learning, inward beliefs about one's freedom and one's personal responsibilities—all of these, in one way or another, are aspects of subjectivity. However, most people would agree, I think, that the fundamental (i.e., universal) character of human subjectivity is going to be best revealed in the mind's thinking processes and language use. No doubt this is why these form the subject of Chaucer's *sophismata* sequence in Part III.

In the remainder of this background essay for the chapters on the gods and champions of Part III, first I will set forth in some detail the so-called 3-Acts Theory of the thinking processes of the mind, accepted as the way the human mind naturally thinks by apparently everybody during the later Middle Ages; and then I will contrast the conflicting interpretations drawn from it by Gothic humanist and scholastic scientist.

Thinking: The Three Acts of the Mind

The 3-Acts mind model had enormous influence during the later Middle Ages. In art and literature it underlies the characteristic juxtapositions, correspondences, compartmentalizations, and open-ended didacticism that set Gothic art apart from all other styles. In philosophy and theology it underlies the characteristic comparisons of conflicting authorities, divisions by intelligible distinction, emphasis on logic, and focus on abstract objects of the mind that set Gothic scholastic style apart from other philosophical styles.

This medieval model of the mind's activities apparently began with a brief, decidedly fuzzy, Aristotelian discussion in Book III of the *De Anima*. Despite great comment and elaboration by the scholastics, it seems always to have retained Aristotle's distinction into basically three different types of thinking. Here, in Richard McKeon's translation, are the pertinent *De Anima* passages:

> The thinking then of the simple objects of thought is found in those cases where falsehood is impossible: where the alternative of true or false applies, there we always find a putting together of objects of thought in a quasi-unity . . . objects of thought which were given separate are combined, . . . In each and every case that which unifies is mind. (Chapter 6)[9]

> To perceive then is like bare asserting or knowing; but when the object is pleasant or painful, the soul makes a quasi-affirmation or negation, and pursues or avoids the object. . . . The faculty of thinking then thinks the forms in the images, and . . . what is to be pursued or avoided is marked out for it, so where there is no sensation and it is engaged upon the images it is moved to pursuit or avoidance. E.g. perceiving by sense that the beacon is fire, it recognizes in virtue of the general faculty of sense that it signifies an enemy, because it sees it moving; but sometimes by means of the images or thoughts which are within the soul, just as if it were seeing, it calculates and deliberates what is to come by reference to what is present; . . . That too which involves no action, i.e. that which is true or false, is in the same province with what is good or bad: yet they differ in this, that the one set imply and the other do not a reference to a particular person. (Chapter 7)[10]

The resulting scholastic model was basically simple—in the process of knowing, the human mind performs three different types of activities: simple apprehension of objects, judgment of complex propositions, and inference. For example, here is Aquinas's well-known description of them from his "Foreword" to his *Commentary on the Posterior Analytics*:

> Now there are three acts of the reason, the first two of which belong to reason regarded as an intellect. One action of the intellect is the understanding of indivisible or uncomplex things, and according to this action it conceives *what* a thing is. And this operation is called by some the informing of the intellect, or representing by means of the intellect. To this operation of the reason is ordained the doctrine which Aristotle hands down in the book of *Predicaments* [i.e., *Categories*]. The second operation of the intellect is its act of combining or dividing, in which the true or the false are for the first time present. And this act of reason is the subject of the doctrine which Aristotle hands down in the book entitled *On Interpretation*. But the third act of the reason is concerned with that which is peculiar to reason, namely, to advance from one thing to another in such a way that through that which is known a man comes to knowledge of the unknown. And this act is considered in the remaining books of logic.[11]

Aquinas's description is much clearer, but given our different modern notions of human thinking processes, still a little terse. I will therefore describe each mental process briefly and then illustrate it with one or two of Chaucer's own examples from the appropriate *sophisma* (examples that will, of course, be more fully discussed later in their actual Knight's Tale contexts).

Act 1: simple apprehension of objects. This is the simple act of perceiving an object, without affirmation or denial. The act is passive and not subject to error: either one perceives the object or one does not. For Aquinas this act was purely abstractive. Sense experience presents the individual objects of the outside world to the perceptions (for example, vision), and the mind abstracts their forms (i.e., their common natures); thus it is their forms that the mind knows directly, not the individual objects or beings themselves. (The reader has already seen this abstraction in Arcite's cognition of Emelye's form during his prayer—"she," "she," and "her," rather than any of her individuality.) It is worth recalling here that "forms" in this sense includes the forms of activities and relationships as well as the forms of entities. Scotus, writing a generation after Aquinas, divided this activity of simple apprehension into two kinds—abstractive cognition of an object, which is indifferent as to its existence or presence; as opposed to intuitive (i.e., experiential) cognition of an object as existing and present.[12]

Chaucer's descriptions of the figures in the wall paintings of the temples of Venus and Mars will illustrate this process of simple apprehension and contrast the two kinds, abstractive versus intuitive. First, both descriptions consist not of actions but of lists of separated objects. The objects in Venus's list are apprehended as if abstractively by the reader because they are already abstractions. Chaucer has formed them of plurals, universals, and generalizations:

> The broken slepes, and the sikes colde,
> The sacred teeris, and the waymentynge,
>
> . . .
>
> Plesaunce and Hope, Desir, Foolhardynesse,
> Beautee and Youthe, Bauderie, Richesse,
>
> . . .
>
> . . . al the gardyn and the lustynesse; (1918–52)

On the other hand, the objects in Mars's list are apprehended as if intuitively by the reader because each is a separate individual person or thing. Moreover, Chaucer has further particularized each of them with some concrete physical detail, so that the reader's physical senses experience them as if existing and present:

> The smylere with the knyf under the cloke;
> The shepne brennynge with the blake smoke;
>
> . . .
>
> The sleere of hymself yet saugh I ther,—
> His herte-blood hath bathed al his heer. (1996–2035)

In other words, both temple descriptions consist of lists of objects which will be apprehended simply (i.e., separately) by the reader, according to Act 1 of the 3-Acts thinking model; but in addition, the objects in the two lists will be apprehended in the two different ways, Venus's objects abstractively (as if present within the mind) and Mars's objects intuitively (i.e., concretely, as if present to the bodily senses).

Act 2: judgment of complex propositions. This is the mind's activity of combining and dividing the separate objects which were apprehended by means of Act 1 (hence the term 'complex', i.e., more than one), and here is where the possibility of error first arises. (Notice that Act 1 is objective, according to this theory; Acts 2 and 3 subjective.) For Aquinas, judgment here is as to truth value.

Chaucer's descriptions of the wall paintings in Diana's temple (2056–72) will illustrate Act 2. The separate objects in each of the four little stories are combined into sentences (complex propositions)—some true, some false—which are presented to the reader for judgment. For example, here is the first story:

Ther saw I how woful Calistopee
Whan that Diane agreued was with here
Was turned from a womman til a bere
And after was she maad the lodesterre
. . .
Hir sone is eek a sterre as men may see . . . (2056–61 MR)

With regard to its truth value, for the reader who knows the story of Callisto well, the convoluted implications of Chaucer's first sentence here are false (according to Ovid, she was turned into a bear by Juno and then stellified by Jove); the second sentence is true. Mistelling a traditional story like this will ordinarily activate any reader's faculty of judgment. (A similar effect might be elicited from the modern reader by asking Snow White to let down her hair.) Judgment of complex propositions takes place whenever one object is juxtaposed with another. The ultimate product of this thinking act in Aquinas's interpretation is a judgment in which the mind affirms or denies the composition as true.

Act 3: reasoning, or inference as to causes. In the De Anima, this is the mind's act of moving from an understanding of one thing to arrive at a new understanding of something, as in, for example, proceeding from what is present so as to calculate what is to come.[13] Aquinas uses the term *ratiocinando* for this activity of the mind; but because the nature of scientific activity has changed so much, the clearer rubric in Modern English for his thought here would be "inference as to causes," using 'cause' in the broad scholastic sense of any influence of any kind on a thing's being. For Aquinas as for Aristotle, "full-fledged scientific knowledge of something requires understanding its necessitating causes."[14] (By way of example, in the case of this page, the paper and ink would be among its material causes; myself, my own sources and teachers, and my typist would be among its efficient causes; and so on for its many and various formal and final causes according to Aristotle's unsurpassedly flexible analytic system.)

Details from Chaucer's portraits of the two champions, Lygurge and Emetreus, will serve to illustrate this Act 3 of inferring from something present to something not present. For example, the astrological allusions in their descriptions will lead the reader from material causes in present objects (them) to efficient causes not present, namely Saturn and Mars, under whose signs respectively these two great kings were born. As Curry showed in his ground-breaking study of Chaucer's use of medieval physical science, the Saturnian man's hair is black, his complexion "swartish or maybe honey-colored," his eyes red, and his shoulders broad.[15] Thus Chaucer's description of Lygurge enables the reader to infer his astrological "cause":

> Blak was his berd, . . .
> The cercles of his eyen in his heed,
> They gloweden bitwixen yelow and reed,
> . . .
> His lymes grete, his brawnes harde and stronge,
> His shuldres brode, his armes rounde and longe; (2130–36)

Similarly, the Martial man's hair is usually crisp or curling, ranging in color from brown to yellow or white; his face is round, his eyes varying from hazel to yellow or light green. Thus Chaucer's description of Emetreus enables the reader to infer Emetreus's astrological "cause":

> His crispe heer lyk rynges was yronne,
> And that was yelow, and glytered as the sonne.
> His nose was heigh, his eyen bright citryn,
> His lippes rounde, his colour was sangwyn. (2165–68)

Inference as to causes, Act 3 of the medieval thinking process model, takes place whenever one reasons *about* a thing or being or event.

The Aristotelian 3-Acts thinking model started out simple and not very clear, but its implications changed as it was transplanted from a pagan to an Islamic to a Christian context, and then changed again depending on the goal of the Christian context surrounding it, whether a renewed sense of charity in the believer's heart, or a rational objective understanding of some article of faith.

First, I shall draw out some humanist implications of the 3-Acts model, in the context of the later medieval love of order and intelligibility, as to what, based on their art and literature, the model apparently implied to people in the thirteenth and fourteenth centuries about how the human mind works. In the course of doing so, I shall be suggesting that attempts by Gothic artists both to cope with and to capitalize on this conception of the mind's thinking processes underlie the peculiarly rich content and the peculiarly intellectual appeal of the high art of the later Middle Ages—the great encyclopedic stone cathedrals with their ranks of sculptures and glorious jewel-like windows, the bursting manuscript illuminations, and the conceptually-crowded dramas, dream visions, debates, and framed story collections. Then I shall draw out some very different scholastic implications of the same 3-Acts model, implications which apparently inspired the scholastic philosopher/theologians to their pursuit of perfect truth, and especially to the notion that given necessary and unchangeable premises followed by valid reasoning, they could enjoy in this fallen world the blissful state of perfect certitude.

IMPLICATIONS—HUMANIST

The influence of the 3-Acts thinking model on Gothic art and literature was enormous.[16] Consider: on the surface level of subject matter and composition alone, Gothic art is especially characterized by separated objects (Act 1), by combination into groups and partition into compartments (Act 2), and by inference from what one sees to what caused it (Act 3). These connections are intuitive and obvious. The slightest mental reference to the *Divine Comedy,* the *Canterbury Tales,* or any cathedral or cycle drama will reveal them, as will the briefest glance back at the Tickhill Psalter page reproduced in figure 3.

Further, they appear in minor art as well as major. For example, the small fourteenth-century ivory traveling altar shown in figure 6 depicts on its left wing the separated figures of St. Peter (upper) and St. Stephen, and on its right wing St. Paul (upper) and St. Thomas à Becket. Each figure is separate, each is fitted into its own highly decorated architectual compartment with its own haloing arch, each is intended to evoke from its viewer an inference to its Cause. In the center panel, the lower compartment features the figure of Christ on the cross in the center, separating two subgroups of three harmoniously drooping figures on either side, the upper torso and head of the central figure of each subgroup leaning away from the center in sadness so as to both frame and isolate in space the figure of Christ in the center. The upper compartment depicts the Virgin with Christ in glory, the two figures leaning harmoniously towards each other yet separated by the carved architectural armrest between them and the downpointing of their separating, haloing arches. And again, the intent of these center-panel figures, both separately and as grouped, is to lead the mind of the viewer back to their causes, to their Cause. In fact, almost any reasonably ambitious Gothic art work of any kind will display these same three characteristics: separated objects, as in the altar; compartmentalization, as in the altar; and appeal to the viewer's knowledge of causes, as in the altar.

In addition, on the deeper level of artistic conception and out-

Figure 6. Ivory traveling altar, mid-fourteenth century. British Museum, London.

look, the influence of the 3-Acts model was equally great. Several of its deep-structure implications, which I will now develop at some length, are: *(a)* that what people know depends on themselves as well as on what they perceive, that is, that knowledge is a function of the knower as well as the object known; *(b)* that people's minds are constantly active, constantly absorbing information and converting it to knowledge, whether good or bad; and *(c)* that people have a natural capacity to think intelligently about things, rather than simply accept them uncritically, if they are presented with alternative views. As I will show, each of these implications contributes in its own way to the logicality and exuberance of Gothic high art.

(a) Knowledge depends on both known and knower. This is the philosophically difficult problem of accuracy: How close is the mind's perception to whatever it is that is "out there"? Does the mind contribute to its own perceptions (in a pre-Kantian sense); and if so, how?

The medieval thinking model has both objective and subjective components. Act 1—simple apprehension of objects—guarantees (at least according to the medieval way of thinking) that, barring some physical disorder in the perceiver, there will be at least some objective reality to the complex object (proposition, poem, personage, event) as known. Aquinas, for example, speaks of a true understanding as the "adequation" of the thing-which-is to one's understanding of it *(adaequatio rei et intellectus).*[17] At the same time, Acts 2 and 3—judgment and inference, both of which take place completely within the mind—guarantee that there will be at least some subjective component to the complex objects, judgments, and inferences as known. Thus any complex object will always provoke a range of interpretation among different perceivers. And this seems sensible. How often do any two or three people agree exactly about anything complex? Thus here, in the later medieval conception of the mind thinking, interpretation of any complex object will always display a subjective range within objective limits.

This Gothic solution to the problem of accuracy does accord with our thoughtful everyday experiences, "naive" though they may be, that on the one hand, given a single event with multiple witnesses, the witnesses will always differ about some details even as they agree about others; as well as that, on the other hand, given multiple identical events with a single witness, for example, repeated readings of the same poem, the witness's understanding of it will change over the years (or at least one hopes it will change, deepen, possibly even grow wiser) even though the words on the page have not changed. According to this medieval model, knowledge of complex objects or events will always depend on both the knower and the object known. This solution to the problem of interpretational accuracy goes back at least to Boethius, who used it in the *Consolation,* most notably to show that knowledge of good and evil depends on the knower (Book IV) and that divine foreknowledge entails no restriction on human freedom (Book V).

In fact, when one thinks about it today, the truly naive realism is not the medieval kind, which does allow for subjectivity in knowledge if not in initial apprehension. The truly naive realism is the kind we encounter in the humanities classroom almost every day, an unfortunate carry-over from math, logic, and science classes, that says that we all do or should perceive exactly the same thing "out there," that we all have or should have exactly the same perception of a poem, character, event, or life as a whole. At the same time, of course, the polar opposite notion that anything goes since it is all "in here," in totally-responding reader or creatively-misreading critic or pre-determining language, seems equally absolutist and naive since we are always able to agree on at least some important facts or aspects. Today, the more complex kinds of interpretive theories, those that seek to incorporate both objective and subjective components, seem more in accord with the facts of everyday life; and, of course, this is what accounts for the great persuasiveness of eclectic pluralism, in both its medieval variety and its present-day manifestations in some reader-response and hermeneutic systems.[18] As the only sure basis for toleration, for listening to the viewpoints of others, for truly humane discourse, the notion that knowledge depends on both known and knower will have to be a major component of any workable solution to the problem of accuracy. It does not deny the possibility of absolute truth; it simply accepts the fact that our perceptions of it will differ.

It is this notion, apparently drawn from the 3-Acts mind theory, that underlies much of what we call Gothic "open-endedness."

(b) The human mind is constantly adding to its knowledge. A second implication of the 3-Acts thinking model is that the human mind is constantly active and innately knowledge-seeking. In this model, the mind does not simply respond to outside stimuli, nor is its search for real knowledge doomed to futility.

During Act 1, simple apprehension, the mind is essentially passive, a receiver of impressions from its outward senses.[19] In Acts 2 and 3, on the other hand, the mind itself actively combines and divides the objects (whether abstracted species or intuitive cognitions) achieved by means of Act 1, and then goes on to judge and reason and recombine and judge and reason again about the resulting propositions. Indeed, the mind is conceived as a kind of appetite (potency) which craves satisfaction (actualization) in the form of knowledge. In this sense for Aristotle the mind is not an entity but rather a capacity for thinking whatever is thinkable; when it thinks something (i.e., abstracts the form from the image), it becomes it (i.e., it actualizes itself): "In every case the mind which is actively thinking is the objects which it thinks."[20] Similarly for Aquinas, in the process of cognition the form (i.e., the real being, the essence) of the object being perceived is impressed in one's mind and becomes intentionally one's own, and one becomes intentionally what one knows. For both Aristotle and Aquinas, the more one knows, that is, the more forms one's mind possesses (or, more accurately, is), the better. Since in Thomism God is both being and knowledge, the more knowledge one has, the more being one has; and the more one has of both, in principle at least, the closer one is to God.[21] A most beautiful expression of this idea is in Dante's last canto, during which he receives the Vision of the Divine Essence and finds, among other things, that the Vision itself is unchanging, whereas he changes as he gazes up into it, becoming more as he sees more.

> Now in my recollection [of the Vision] . . .
> I have less power to speak than any infant
> wetting its tongue yet at its mother's breast;

and not because that Living Radiance bore
    more than one semblance, for It is unchanging
    and is forever as it was before;

rather, as I grew worthier to see
    the more I looked, the more unchanging semblance
    appeared to change with every change in me. (*Paradiso*,
    33, 106–14)[22]

When one thinks today about all this mental actualizing, a curious fact emerges: in this model of thinking, no distinction is being drawn in our terms between perceiving, knowing, and learning. We tend now to think of learning as something acquired in youth and at second hand, so to speak, from study and books; and of knowledge as something which is acquired more actively and directly and which possesses more mental surety. According to the 3-Acts model, however, as soon as something enters one's perceptions, it enters one's mind permanently (in fact one becomes it). This conception of the mind has unusual educational implications, at least from our point of view. Apparently on the basis that people will acquire forms—that is to say, acquire more knowledge—that is to say, learn—every day of their lives, the medieval system of education was conceived on a principle quite different from ours. Dorothy Sayers points out that the great distinction between medieval education and modern is that the goal of medieval education was to teach pupils how to think actively, how to use their minds on the objects in them, whereas the goal of modern education is to have them absorb "subjects." Our children learn everything, she says, "except the art of learning":

The whole of the Trivium was, in fact, intended to teach the pupil the proper use of the tools of learning, before he began to apply them to "subjects" at all. First, he learned a language; not just how to order a meal in a foreign language, but the structure of a language, and hence of language itself—what it was, how it was put together, and how it worked. Secondly, he learned how to use language: how to define his terms and make accurate statements; how to construct an argument and how to detect fallacies in argument. Dialectic, that is to say, embraced Logic and Disputation. Thirdly, he learned to express himself in language—how to say what he had to say elegantly and persuasively.

At the end of his course, he was required to compose a thesis upon some theme set by his masters or chosen by himself, and afterwards to defend his thesis against the criticism of the faculty. By this time he would have learned—or woe betide him—not merely to write an essay on paper, but to speak audibly and intelligibly from a platform, and to use his wits quickly when heckled. There would also be questions, cogent and shrewd, from those who had already run the gauntlet of debate.[23]

To learn "six subjects without remembering how they were learnt does nothing to ease the approach to a seventh; to have learnt and remembered the art of learning makes the approach to every subject an open door."[24] In this context, the various medieval systems of biblical and literary interpretation—Hugh of St. Victor's threefold, Dante's four, and the others—may profitably be regarded not as mandatory prescriptions to hold in every case, but as optional tools to be learned and applied according to the reader's skill and discretion. Bersuire, for one, is quite clear that he is *adding to* Ovid, not finding some meaning implicit in Ovid's text.[25] In other words, not only was the medieval reader expected to contribute to the text, he was taught how to do so. People read this way because the important thing was not "out there." Out there was only sensory data, whether leaves on trees, pictures on walls, sounds in the air, or black marks on the page. The important thing was the meaning inside their individual heads, what they—as knowers— were making of the objects they were knowing. In our own time, some educational theories are recovering this notion of the mind as active and contributing, a rediscovery most strikingly evidenced by the various reader-response theories of literary interpretation.[26] But as for life outside the classroom, the generally accepted medieval notion of the mind, unlike ours, contained the idea that increase in knowledge goes on whenever sense perception goes on. The mind is by nature active and knowledge-seeking. No doubt this notion, apparently drawn from the 3-Acts mind model, under-lies the exuberant richness of allusion characteristic of all Gothic arts. Of course, what one actually learns from any particular paint-ing or story—how one puts one's perceptions together, what one infers from them, what one makes them mean—depends on one's own capacities as a knower.

(c) Human beings have a natural capacity to think intelligently (rationally, analytically) about things when they are presented with more than one viewpoint to compare. A further implication of the 3-Acts thinking model is that, when given several ways of looking at a thing, the human mind will consider it rationally. In this regard Raymond J. McCall, writing in the scholastic tradition, makes a useful distinction between two kinds of logic: *natural* logic, our native or inborn power of judgment and inference, as opposed to scientific or *acquired* logic:

> natural logic in some sense stands to the developed art and science of logic as any native ability (for instance, singing) stands to that same ability as perfected by training and criti-cism. By natural logic we are able to perform correctly and readily those primary acts of judgment and inference without which our later scientific and philosophical reasoning could not be valid. It seems to be, in truth, what St. Thomas called the "habit of first principles" as applied to the operation of reason itself. Just as we recognize naturally that a thing cannot both be and not be at the same time, that a physical whole is equal to the sum of its parts, that if something happens it requires a cause, so we recognize readily and without special training that it is wrong to contradict ourselves, that affirma-tive premises require an affirmative conclusion, that what is true of a given universal is true of a particular coming under that universal, and the like.[27]

Thinking as a twentieth-century humanist, I find myself just natu-rally questioning some of these particular "first principles" that McCall lists, but the key idea here is the useful distinction between natural and acquired logic and, even more important, the underlying assumption that all people, regardless of class, culture, or formal education, possess a natural ability at the fundamental principles on which scientific logic was erected.

The point I am working toward now is the possibility that this medieval model of the mind as naturally active, naturally knowledge-seeking, and possessing a natural logic, combined with the notion that knowledge is both subjective and objective, is what brought forth the rich profusion of content and surprisingly intellectual appeal of the high literary and visual art of the later Middle Ages.

According to the 3-Acts model, a single isolated figure, concept, object, event, whatever, will be accepted simply and uncritically by the mind. Only when it is combined with some other figure, concept, etc., or when it itself is divided into parts (Act 2), can discursive analytic thought begin. The other object(s) with which it is paired may come from memory, imagination, experience, or perception; the point here is the logical necessity for *at least two objects* for a mental proposition to function. As in formal logic, where at least two instances are necessary to form a generalization, so here with this natural medieval model—the mind is not able to function as a specifically human mind unless it has at least two objects to work with, to form into a complex proposition of some kind which then it can evaluate and make inferences from.[28] The principle of Gothic juxtaposition, of course, leaps immediately to mind.

When setting forth a concept, the Gothic high artist ordinarily gives us at least two objects, two events, or two points of view. His intention, apparently, judging from the mind model, was *(a)* to encourage us to react to them intellectually, to form them into a proposition rather than just accept each one uncritically; and *(b)* by specifying both terms, to give us the context, if not the explicit proposition, in which to think. In literature, in art, everywhere we look in the later Middle Ages, we meet with at least two sides of a contrast, two figures, or two different viewpoints, which we, the audience, are to resolve. We are constantly presented with explicit alternatives, with multiple approaches to complex human situations, with at least two instances, possibilities, aspects, correspondences, or varieties, of intellectual, ethical, or spiritual oppositions which we presumably are to consider and compare, and about which (knowledge depending partly on knower) we are to generalize and judge for ourselves.

In visual art the viewer is ordinarily presented with angel *and* gargoyle, with the orderly ranks of the blessed *and* the contortions of the damned, with Virgin and Christ-child inside the gilded historiated capital *and* dog pursuing hare out in the margin. It is the fact that, unlike modern art, later medieval art usually presents the alternative viewpoints *explicitly* that I am concerned with here, not with the difficulty or ease or even the foregone quality of any particular judgment or inference.

In literary art, of course, the alternatives could be considerably more complex, but here again the audience is ordinarily presented with several variations on each important theme and then left to make many of the connections and judgments for themselves. Sometimes the contrasts are explicit. Sometimes they are unstated, left for the reader to find and ponder. For example, Dante places three imposing figures in complexly corresponding positions in each of the three cantica, Farinata in canto 10 of the Inferno, Sordello in canto 6 of the Purgatorio, and Cacciaguida in cantos 15 through 17 (especially 16, i.e., 10 + 6 and overflowing out) of the Paradiso. Why do this? What is their correspondence? Farinata is in Hell, sixth circle (Heretics) to be exact. He has dignity, power, and majesty; he is a larger man than most; yet he *is* in Hell. Considering him by himself, we accept him uncritically, as a simple, symbolic object, noble and rather tragic. (Possibly we wonder for a moment why he is there, since so many lesser human beings are working their way around Mount Purgatory—but notice, this is already a comparison utilizing other instances; i.e., our minds have automatically gone on to Acts 2 and 3 of the model.) Once Farinata is paired with Cavalcanti, however, once we are confronted with two instances juxtaposed, our minds are naturally engaged, actively seeking comprehension; and eventually we come to understand that the evil trait they share, the reason Dante must have juxtaposed them (Act 2), is the sin of factionalism: Both are still completely consumed with their special personal loyalties to family and party. Later, in the Purgatorio, we meet a second solitary figure with dignity and majesty. This one, unlike Farinata, not only greets Virgil with a special affection for their mutual city but actually extends it outward. Sordello includes his special loyal affection for Mantuans within his love for the whole Latin race.[29] And later still, in the Paradiso, we meet the third imposing solitary figure (actually a magnificent shooting star, which streaks alone from the right arm of the great heavenly cross down to Dante and Beatrice at its foot). Cacciaguida's special gladness on greeting Dante is compared to that of Anchises beholding Aeneas in Elysium. But Cacciaguida's love exceeds even that of Sordello; he joyously includes his special loyal affection and delight in his own lineage within his greater outflowing love for the Trinity itself.

This kind of slow, subtle definition by multiple instances—of wrongful and rightful partisanship, wrongful and rightful love, so to speak, wrongful when it shows indifference or hatred to those outside its circle, rightful when it extends its love in ever-widening circles to those beyond—is typical Dante and quintessential Gothic. Chaucer too constantly presents his characters, actions, and themes in two's and three's, as does Langland. January has two advisers. Alisoun has two admirers (three if one counts John). Griselda faints twice. Pardoner is paired with Summoner, Pardoner's Tale with Physician's, Miller's with both Knight's and Reeve's. Knight begins, Parson ends. Why? Will is faced at the outset with two striking women. Dowel, Dobet, and Dobest are defined at least half a dozen times (Passûs 8, 9, 10, 12, 13, and 19) and differently each time. What is the point? The Gothic reader was apparently expected to read and reread and to make the connections and the judgments and to do so finally on the basis of thinking rather than feeling. This is the reason Gothic high art often insists on the hard decisions: Dante, for example, returns his beloved Virgil to Hell as soon as his job is done.

In actual fact, I believe, even the most illogical, sentimental kind of subject matter will evoke in us an intellectual-type response of comparison, judgment, and/or inference when presented to us by means of at least two different instances. It is the nature of the human mind, according to this model, to compare, for

III. Thinking Processes and Language Use

instance, the Prioress's sentiments about mercy in her own prologue with the quality of mercy in her tale, and these two together with the mercy she shows in the General Prologue portrait. The rich conceptual multiplicity of so much Gothic high art, its insistent repetition, variation, and explicitness, and, at the same time, its ordered yet surprisingly open-ended quality, whereby the most important as well as the most subtle of moral or spiritual questions may be left to the individual reader to resolve, certainly accords with and may well be due to this general later medieval understanding of the thinking processes of the human mind.[30] In this view, the mind is innately active and hungers for knowledge (actualization), and when given at least two objects will compare them and ponder them and arrive at some understanding from them. (Farinata alone is imposing; paired with Cavalcanti, however, he is flawed as well, a man finally to be rejected.) At the same time, the understanding the mind will reach will be only partly due to the objects; part of it will be due to the mind's own prior content and to its own acquired habits of thought and to its own choices.

For those of us today who were raised on the notion that differences in interpretation are due to error, that the meaning is objectively in the piece of work rather than constructed in our minds, it is still difficult to appreciate that the high art of a great culture may have flourished on the belief that the meaning of something is not—indeed, cannot be—wholly specified within the work; that high artists—Dantes, Chaucers, and the like—may therefore have set out to give their readers two, three, or four instances with which to form their ethically or spiritually or intellectually valuable meanings, trusting that their readers would find and form for themselves the meanings they were able to understand. According to this model, human beings are lifelong learners. If the viewer or listener or reader doesn't get the correspondences this time, perhaps he or she will the next time. Or the next.

IMPLICATIONS—SCHOLASTIC

All this, however, is a far cry from the use the university scholastics made of the same 3-Acts model. Some scholastic scientists drew the implication that all truly human mental activity was or should be essentially logical. Aquinas himself certainly interpreted Aristotle's model in this way. In his "Foreword" to his *Commentary on the Posterior Analytics* (quoted at the beginning of this section), for example, Aquinas likens Act 1 (simple apprehension of objects) to the *Categories,* Act 2 (judgment of complex propositions) to *On Interpretation,* and Act 3 (inference) to the remaining books of Aristotle's logic, thus corresponding all the human mental activity envisioned in this model, at least ideally, to Aristotle's version of all logical activity. In fact, even today the accepted divisions of traditional logic still correspond to these same three kinds of thinking activities: *analysis of terms* deals with defining and classifying the separate objects of thought; *principles of predication* deal with forming and judging propositions; and *inference* covers reasoning and demonstration proper.

The notion that the human mind is essentially rational has persisted throughout history, of course, but it was the scholastic scientists who first seem to have identified (rather hopefully) natural rationality with basic logic. Judging from the *Rhetoric,* Aristotle himself did not do this. Today, only a moment's reflection will persuade most people that not all logic is reasonable, nor is all reasoning rational. Yet the scholastic identification persists. For example, some years ago when Ernst Cassirer was attempting to establish the existence in human beings of a symbolic mode of thought entirely different from and prior to the mode of "facts, reasons, and discursive logic," that is, a mode of thought not simply prelogical in the way that Act 1 seemed simply prelogical to the scholastics, he described the generally accepted mode (the notion of knowledge as "philosophers had developed it since the Middle Ages" which he was trying to show incomplete) in terms strikingly similar to a description of the medieval 3-Acts model: "The aim of theoretical thinking, as we have seen, is primarily to deliver the contents of sensory or intuitive experience from the isolation in which they originally occur [i.e., Act 1]. It causes these contents to transcend their narrow limits, combines them with others, compares them [i.e., Act 2]. . . . It proceeds 'discursively,' in that it treats the immediate content only as a point of departure, from which it can run the whole gamut of impressions in various directions [i.e., Act 3]."[31] Thus, although human rationality is not necessarily to be restricted to (or even conflated with) logic, there has been a powerful urge in Western science ever since the scholastic period to claim that because the mind possesses a natural rationality (a "natural logic" in McCall's sense), it therefore should be only logical.

The scholastics themselves, from about the middle of the thirteenth century on, were captivated by the prospects they glimpsed in Aristotelian speculative science of achieving absolute natural truth—i.e., absolute certitude by reason alone, without appeal to divine ideas or divine illumination. As a result, many simply abandoned the practical realm for the speculative. Practical knowledge concerns itself with doing things in this world, and therefore has to pay attention to uncooperative individuals, fuzzy particulars, and sloppy accidents. Moral philosophy, medicine, teaching, the arts—these are all practical sciences in the Aristotelian scheme. Speculative knowledge, on the other hand, concerns itself with truth for its own sake. In the speculative realm, real knowledge, as discussed earlier, is objectively demonstrated knowledge, achieved by *a priori* reasoning from self-evident first principles, and the objects with which it deals are unchanging and universal. As a result, this kind of knowledge is necessary knowledge. It *has* to be true. This kind of knowledge, obviously, results only from Act 3 of the 3-Acts model. Act 1, simple apprehension of objects, is left far behind in the realm of practical apprehension. Too many uncertainties are involved for it to be intellectually interesting. Act 2, judgment of complex propositions, tends now to concentrate on the formal aspects of being (dividing and composing). It leaves behind the practical ramifications of judgments by real people about real events in the real world. For the scholastics, the exciting act, the prestigious act, was Act 3, inference to causes. Pure reasoning. Unchanging universals. Certitude. Bliss. In the *Summa,* for example, Aquinas seems to limit all human knowledge to certain knowledge, that is, knowledge produced only by the rigorous, highly circumscribed exercise of Act 3. About this, Paul Durbin, the careful translator of the Human Intelligence section (Ia, 84–89) of the Blackfriars edition of the *Summa,* comments:

> The almost total absence, throughout the six questions in the treatise, of any reference to less-than-certain knowledge is striking. *Opinio,* in the sense of a probable assertion (even allowing for such a synonym as *conjectura*) appears no more than four or five times,★ and *fides,* in the sense of knowledge on the authority of another (human or divine), even fewer times. Intellectual knowledge is virtually equated with *scientia,* usually to be translated as 'demonstrative knowledge.'[32]

★Aside from references to 'the opinion of Plato,' etc.

Thus, by Chaucer's time, interpretation of the Aristotelian 3-Acts mind model had developed in two different directions, both wielding tremendous influence. Gothic high artists and writers were utilizing its implications for traditional humanist didactic purposes; university scholastics were utilizing its implications in pursuing the goals of their scientific theology. Because the Gothic artists, sculptors, and poets were seeking to develop subjective convictions of truths already known, so to speak, they could appeal to their audiences' perceptions, memories, emotions, and introspections. They could picture a griffin and assume most of their audience would be reminded of the twofold nature of Christ. They could retell the story of patient Griselda and have confidence that at least some of their audience would call to mind the virtue of perfect obedience. They could carve the beasts of the zodiac over a lintel and count on most of the viewers to perceive in them the marvelous ordering of the cosmos. The scholastics, on the other hand, regarded such appeals as illogical, definitely second-rate as far as truth value was concerned. For them, the meaning of a treatise was to be found objectively in the treatise. Because it was written literally and demonstrated scientifically, it did not depend at all on the mind of the reader for interpretation, or so the scholastics liked to think.

Given this background, we are now ready to consider these two subjects together—thinking processes and language use—in the

Knight's Tale descriptions of gods and champions. As we examine these descriptions, we will see Chaucer muster every resource of language against those in his time who were seeking to deprive human languages and thinking processes of their natural richness. Each of these six Part III descriptions contains *(a)* an experiential definition of a thinking process *(b)* presented in the form of a *sophisma* for test-case consideration *(c)* couched in the pagan-romance subject matter the scholastics disparaged. Thus, in this sequence of six descriptions, in addition to carrying forward the romance narrative, Chaucer's point is again twofold:

> *On language use:* that language use and thinking processes interact together to form/reveal the subjectivity of the individual human mind.
>
> *On psychology:* that human subjectivity must therefore be included in any theory of universal human psychology.

Gothic high art is indeed complicated. Readers brought up on the Bauhaus have to relook and rethink at Canterbury. Readers who relate intuitively to Georgia O'Keeffe may relate intuitively to the Limbourg Brothers too, but to perceive what the Limbourgs really wrought they have to consciously s-l-o-w themselves down, look again at those details, rethink their implications, identify the allusions, and conceptualize according to some ancient and unfamiliar principles of structuring. Readers brought up on Ernest Hemingway have to do the same with Langland and the *Pearl* Poet. After a century (it seems like three) of cultural literalism, we are all in this bind.[33] Some of us more, some of us less, but all of us, no doubt, are relooking at and rethinking the language use and thinking processes of our pre-Cartesian forebears.

4

Temples and Champions: Sophismata *Sequence on the Scholastic Thinking Acts*

PART III OF the Knight's Tale "feels" different. Cramped, closed in, lacking air and light, it keeps blocking the forward progress of the story of Palamon and Arcite with great chunks of static description, descriptions formed of myriad details that pattern off in unfamiliar directions in the reader's mind, much as the myriad details in the great Canterbury picture windows pattern off in unfamiliar directions in the modern viewer's mind. Instead of ongoing, outward, narrative events, Part III presents the reader with stationary objects to examine and develop inwardly.

Part III consists of the nine lengthy set pieces—three temple descriptions, two champions' portraits, three prayers, and Saturn's monologue—all joined together by means of brief narrative transitions covering Theseus's building and approving the lists and feasting the strangers and the strife in heaven after the two conflicting prayers have been granted. These nine passages portray persuasively the four essential subjects of the world of pagan literature: human suffering, human rivalry, human piety, and divine machination. Little else goes on in the *Aeneid* or the *Metamorphoses*. Chaucer gives us three pagan temples: inward emotional suffering of all kinds is depicted in Venus's temple; outward physical suffering of all kinds is depicted in Mars's temple; and suffering at the hands of the divine is depicted in the temple of Diana.[34] Chaucer gives us two pagan champions: Human rivalry of all kinds, geographical, cultural, and generational, is epitomized in the striking contrast of the barbarian king Lygurge of Thebes, with his long raven-black hair, his ponderous slow-moving ox-chariot, his heavy black bearskin and huge vicious dogs; as opposed to the glittering, highly civilized, young Indian king Emetreus, with his curled hair, laurel green garland, sparkling ruby mantelet, tame white eagle, and heavily armored warhorse.[35] Chaucer gives us three pagan prayers (discussed earlier): In the petitions of Palamon, Emelye, and Arcite, the whole spectrum of human piety is covered, in terms of attitudes (mystical, ritualistic, rational); of requests (end, whatever is best, means); of secrecy of rites (undescribed, partly described, fully described); and of reactions (inward gladness, astonishment, outward preening). And finally, Chaucer gives us the person and contrivances of one pagan divinity: Saturn's behavior well typifies that of the irresponsible, all-too-human, immortal gods of pagan antiquity. All this, however, rich as it is in terms of human multiplicity, is simply the ornate pagan romance surface of Part III of the Knight's Tale.

Of these nine passages, the six not yet considered are constructed as a *sophismata* sequence, in verse paragraphs rather than brief sentences, on the thinking acts. Here is an overview of the five to be discussed in this chapter:

Venus and Mars: Act 1, simple apprehension of objects
Diana: Act 2, judgment of complex propositions
Lygurge and Emetreus: Act 3, reasoning, or inference to
    causes

The sixth, the *sophisma* in Saturn's monologue, is Chaucer's humanist resolution to the sequence; it will be discussed in its own chapter following this one.

Earlier, after quoting Aquinas, I defined the dry scholastic interpretation of the 3-Acts model literally; in these five *sophismata* Chaucer defines it figuratively, so as to enable the reader to experience for herself or himself exactly how it feels to think according to each of these processes when they are interpreted as essentially logical. Just as when reading the *Aeneid,* one experiences and thereby learns to recognize and understand what is really meant by such terms as "courage" and "pity" and "blood lust," so too here. When reading these five descriptions, one experiences and thereby learns to recognize and understand what is really involved when *all* human thinking processes are defined as being subsumed by these three acts and the second and third are restricted to logical. These five descriptions thus test-case the scholastic interpretation of the 3-Acts model.

For each of the three processes, first I will show that Chaucer's passages were indeed written not only as description but also as *sophismata*; then I will suggest Chaucer's reaction to the logic.

Venus and Mars: Act 1, Simple Apprehension of Objects (Abstractive and Intuitive)

Exactly how the immaterial human mind is able to perceive the material objects and beings which surround it in this world has always presented an interesting problem to philosophers. This is what "simple apprehension of objects" is all about. Anciently, the immaterial was separated from and valued far above the corporeal, causing a problem as to how, then, inferior corporeal objects could act upon the mind and cause it to perceive them. Augustine solved this problem of sense-object perception by putting a mechanism in the mind to call its attention to the particular corporeal object. Aristotle solved it by putting a mechanism in the mind to abstract the sense-object's immaterial form, or *species*. Thus in the Augustinian tradition of perception as it came down, the mind directly cognizes individuals; in the Aristotelian, it directly cognizes abstractions. By the early fourteenth century, as mentioned earlier, these two different theories as to what the mind directly apprehends of sensory objects—individuals or abstractions—had been elaborately defined, divided, combined, and multiplied, in the usual scholastic fashion; and by Chaucer's time the important cognition theories contained both kinds of apprehension depending on which aspect of an object was being perceived. Intuitive cognition was directly of the individual corporeal object as existing and present. Abstractive cognition was of *species,* generalizations, and universals.

III. Thinking Processes and Language Use

When one looks again at the paired Venus/Mars wall paintings in the context of Act 1, simple apprehension of objects, one quickly sees that both descriptions were written as long lists of simple (i.e., uncombined) objects. In neither list do the individual items (figures, objects, events) interact with each other. In both, each item is a separate object for apprehension. Here, for examples, are the first five lines from the two passages:

First in the temple of Venus maystow se
Wroght on the wal, ful pitous to biholde,
The broken slepes, and the sikes colde,
The sacred teeris, and the waymentynge,
The firy strokes of the desirynge . . . (1918–22)

Ther saugh I first the derke ymaginyng
Of Felonye, and al the compassyng;
The crueel Ire, reed as any gleede;
The pykepurs, and eek the pale Drede;
The smylere with the knyf under the cloke; (1995–99)

Venus's list of objects is twenty-nine lines long (1918–46); Mars's list of objects is thirty-six lines long (1995–2030). Depending on how one counts them, Venus's list contains at least thirty-nine separate objects for apprehension, Mars's list contains at least thirty-one.

Further, and again as touched on earlier, simple apprehension of objects was of two types: abstractive and intuitive. The same is true of Chaucer's lists. Both descriptions list essentially the same subject matters for their respective deities: principal dwellings, customary personifications and pains, a few victims, and concluding remarks on their respective powers. But the two passages will be apprehended by the reader in the two contrasting ways. The Venus passage will be apprehended inwardly; it consists of the abstractions, generalizations, and universals that, according to the traditional, ultimately Platonic, theories of knowledge, are perceived directly inside the mind. The Mars passage, on the other hand, will be apprehended outwardly; it consists of the physically particularized individual figures and events that, according to the theories, are perceived on the outward bodily senses as existing and present. In short, these two descriptions confront the reader with the complete range of objects that, according to the theories, the human mind can apprehend, those of inward experience and those of outward.

Venus is accorded her usual garden, in this case on Mount Citheron, but its description here is extraordinarily abstract: just "al the mount of Citheroun . . . / With al the gardyn and the lustynesse" (1936–39). "Al the mount" and "al the gardyn" are summary generalizations; "lustynesse" is a universal. Everything in this description has been abstracted from its physicality; there is nothing for a reader to see, hear, taste, smell, or touch, nothing to arouse his bodily senses. Chaucer does the same with her traditional personifications:

Plesaunce and Hope, Desir, Foolhardynesse,
Beautee and Youthe, Bauderie, Richesse,
Charmes and Force, Lesynges . . . (1925–27)

Modern grammar and punctuation may designate these words as personifications, but actually they are abstractions, that is, universals. According to the traditional theories of rhetoric, without a vivifying attribute of some kind, the reader does not personify words in such a list. So too with Venus's traditional emblems and activities—Chaucer just names them; he does not depict them in action.

Festes, instrumentz, caroles, daunces,
Lust and array, and alle the circumstaunces
Of love, . . . (1931–33)

Again, names in a list. The only two activities depicted, if one can call them activities, are "sittynge" (Jealousy's cuckoo) and "caught were" (the people in Venus's "las"); in neither case is there any physical movement to evoke any response from the reader's senses. In addition, the individuals specifically mentioned as present in these paintings are all mentioned negatively, so as to render them imageless in the reader's mind. As a result, in spite of their names, the reader still has nothing to see, hear, taste, touch, or smell.

Nat was foryeten the porter, Ydelnesse,
Ne Narcisus the faire of yore agon,
Ne yet the folye of kyng Salomon
Ne yet the grete strengthe of Ercules—
Th'enchauntementz of Medea and Circes—
Ne of Turnus, with the hardy fiers corage,
The riche Cresus, kaytyf in servage. (1940–46)

These people are "not forgotten," rather than actively present doing something. Further, the activities one ordinarily associates with Idleness, Narcissus, and Croesus are without outward physical movement (being idle, gazing at one's reflection, and waiting in chains). Of the other named individuals—Solomon, Hercules, Medea, Circe, and Turnus—it is actually their typifying qualities, their folly, strength, enchantments, and courage, that are not forgotten, rather than they themselves, a syntactic arrangement that removes them even further from physical particularity than merely being not forgotten does. Further, even the pains in Venus's description are abstracted. The following lines contain the three words closest to being physically evocative of all the words in her paintings (broken, cold, and fiery), yet the pains they modify are not themselves active—they are the passive *results* of inward sorrows, not their causes; and Chaucer has generalized them into plurals so that they too are difficult to visualize or mentally personify:

The broken slepes, and the sikes colde,
The sacred teeris, and the waymentynge,
The firy strokes of the desirynge . . . (1920–22)

Thus there is little in the Venus passage to arouse the reader's outward physical senses. Rather, the reader will apprehend its contents—its generalizations, common noun names, summaries, universals, negations, and plurals—inwardly, directly within his or her mind.

At the end of Venus's description comes the explicit statement as to how she wields her powers over humans: she is all-powerful inwardly. Notice the phrasing: another vast generalization, consist-

ing again of a list of universals, and again stated negatively, so as
to arouse no responses from the reader's bodily senses:

> Thus may ye seen that Wysdom ne Richesse,
> Beautee ne Sleighte, Strengthe ne Hardynesse,
> Ne may with Venus holde champartie,
> For as hir list the world than may she gye. (1947–50,
>   capitalization added)

This generalization about her absolute power is followed by another generalization summarizing its results:

> Lo, alle thise folk so caught were in hir las,
> Til they for wo ful ofte seyde "allas!" (1951–52)

Like all results, hers can only be 'shown' outwardly, as here, but
her power is inward. Her victims are again motionless, caught in
her snare. Moreover, she herself had to do nothing physical, nothing outward, to trap them. Her power apparently works directly
in the mind of her victims, in the same way her diction works
directly in the mind of her reader.

Whereas the objects listed in Venus's paintings will be apprehended by the reader as if abstractively, the objects listed in Mars's
paintings will be apprehended as if intuitively. The reader will
apprehend the individualized objects in it vividly and directly, as
if they were existing and present to his bodily senses.

The description of Mars's dwelling is strongly particularized—
a "grisly place" in "thilke colde, frosty regioun" of Trace. Chaucer
devotes twenty-five lines to making the reader see and feel the
barren forest, the twisted trees and sharp stumps, the rumbling
wind, the cold drafty hall, and the thin winter light. So too with
Mars's traditional personifications. Chaucer gives every figure in
the list some vivifying physical detail so as to cause in the reader
a phantasm of a particular individual or activity present and existing
in the flesh.

> The Tresoun of the mordrynge in the bedde;
> The Open Werre, with woundes al bibledde;
> Contek, with blody knyf and sharp manace;
> Al ful of Chirkyng was that sory place. . . .

The nayl ydryven in the shode a-nyght;
The colde Deeth, with mouth gapyng upright. (2001–8,
some capitalization added)[36]

And so on. The figures are identified by their activities, by what they do, and are also phrased in the singular number, so that the reader perceives them as particular individuals existing and present in the flesh: "The pykepurs, . . . the smylere with the knyf, . . . The sleere of hymself, . . . The barbour, and the bocher, and the smyth, / That forgeth sharpe swerdes on his styth" (1998–2026). Even the plurals and negations in Mars's paintings are particularized: "A thousand slayn, and nat of qualm ystorve" (2014); "The toun destroyed, ther was no thyng laft" (2016). Likewise, the victims in Mars's paintings are all individual and are sharply physicalized: "The careyne in the busk, with throte ycorve" (2013); "The hunte strangled with the wilde beres; . . . / The cook yscalded, for al his longe ladel" (2018–20); "The cartere overryden with his carte: / Under the wheel ful lowe he lay adoun" (2022–23). People are knifed, burned, crushed, scalded, strangled, nailed, and worse in the temple of Mars. Pain here is vivid, violent, and acutely present. It is inflicted directly on the outward physical bodies of its victims, and, according to the traditional theories, it will be perceived by means of the outward physical senses of the reader.

At the end comes the statement as to his power over humans. Mars is all-powerful outwardly. He rules over the physical bodies of his victims by means of the stars, which rule over the universe of physical matter. Chaucer individualizes the statement of his power by naming three historical people—Julius, Nero, and Antony—and by predicting their individual slaughters astrologically. Thus, throughout Chaucer's description, Mars's power works directly on the physical bodies of his victims, as his diction works directly on the physical senses of his reader.

In this pair of *sophismata* on Act I of the thinking processes, even the reader's own point of view and own kinesthetic phantasms are drawn into the contrast between the quiet inward abstractive cognitions in Venus's temple as opposed to the active outward intuitive cognitions of Mars's. The reader does not move through space at all to get to Venus's temple and, once inside, does not move around at all in it. The paintings are described as "wroght on the wal" (1919), "peynted on the wal" (1934), and "shewed on the wal in portreyynge" (1938); and the subjects are lumped together in groups rather than individually singled out. As a result, the reader "sees" all of Venus's paintings while standing motionless in one place. The contrary is true in the passage on Mars. First, the reader has to go through that hideous landscape to get to the temple. Then, on going inside, he or she finds that the paintings themselves are clustered into little groups, so that as the teller moves from one group to the next, the reader too has some feeling of moving from one group to the next: "First on the wal was peynted a forest" (1975); "And dounward from an hille, under a bente, / Ther stood the temple . . ." (1981–82); "Ther saugh I first . . ." (1995); "The sleer of hymself yet saugh I ther,—" (2005); "Amyddes of the temple sat . . ." (2009); "Yet saugh I . . ." (2011); "Yet saugh I . . ." (2017); "Ther were also . . . (2024). And so on. The reader is even asked, after looking down at the carter under the wheel, to look up "al above," at the tower, then at Conquest sitting in it, then at the sharp sword over *his* head, adding a three-dimensional verticality to what he is apprehending. In short, as in the paintings themselves, so with their reader's mind and body: quiet and motionless in Venus's temple, active and outward in the temple of Mars.

With Venus all-powerful inwardly and Mars all-powerful outwardly, Chaucer's reason for including the single individualized, intuitively apprehended figure of Jealousy, with her garland of "yelewe gooldes" and her "cokkow," in Venus's otherwise drab paintings becomes clear. Jealousy is what drives a person from Venus's jurisdiction to that of Mars. In the Knight's Tale, people dead for love are in Mars's temple, not in Venus's (2038). Jealousy is how they get there.

This, then, is Chaucer's *sophisma* on Act 1 of the 3-Acts mind model. Here in the Knight's Tale, the subject matter has been pagan romance suffering, but it could just as easily have been pro football or foreign cuisine. For purposes of constructing a *sophisma* on simple apprehension of objects, the key terms are:

—Objects, lists of.

—Cognitions, abstractive versus intuitive.

Difficult to do? Not very. A standard schoolroom exercise? It wouldn't surprise me.

SOME CHAUCERIAN COMMENTARY ON LOGIC

Sophismata provide a means to look at abstract problems concretely. Chaucer's purpose in the Venus/Mars *sophisma* is to provide for his reader a concrete experiential definition of Act I of the 3-Acts model, since he wishes to include thinking acts (and eventually subjectivity) within his own universal psychology. At the same time, of course, in composing this *sophisma,* Chaucer is once again formally disproving scholastic poetics, by once again embedding scholastic truths within the pagan lies of his story of Palamon and Arcite.

Today, the veneration that formal logic inspired in the scholastic mind seems scarcely believable. Chaucer was apparently deeply concerned about its real-life effects: On language use, the logician's insistence on literality is devastating. Fictions, figures, metaphors, rhetorical shaping, personal stylistics of any kind, are totally denigrated. On thinking processes, the logician's insistence on objectivity and scientific demonstration completely devalues any operations of the mind that are not one hundred percent rational and thereby objectively replicable. Emotions, value statements, insights, moral judgments, hunches, shaping metaphors, and, above all, personal experience, are held irrelevant to any serious enterprise. What is a poet to do? Chaucer apparently decided to take on formal logic itself, with truly remarkable results. Each of the Part III *sophismata* is, therefore, constructed like a nest of Chinese boxes, the innermost containing what appears to be an elaborate schoolboy joke demonstrating the deficiencies of formal logic in the real world. Possibly such deconstructive jokes as these were standard grammar or rhetoric class exercises. Possibly they were the extracurricular activities of logic students themselves (fourteenth-century versions of computer hacking). Possibly they are ordinary Chaucerian undercutting. In any event, rather than "saving the appearances," these jokes cave them in.

Each act of the 3-Acts thinking model had a logical technique proper to it. According to the scholastic way of thinking, the certitude of one's simple apprehension of the objects of both inner and outer experience was guaranteed by the law of contradiction. (Either the object is a horse or it is not a horse, H or not-H). The only perfect "all-or-nothing" contradiction in traditional logic consisted of a universal negative and a particular affirmative (No horses are there; a horse is there—clearly this is a contradiction, no Hs and an H). In this *sophisma,* Venus's temple description closes with a universal negative about her absolute power in this world:

> Thus may ye seen that Wysdom ne Richesse,
> Beautee ne Sleighte, Strengthe ne Hardynesse,
> Ne may with Venus holde champartie,
> For as hir list the world than may she gye. (1947–50,
>   capitalization added)

This is a truism: those six qualities rule the world and Venus rules them as she pleases; who would disagree with this? Some eighty lines later, however, the temple description of Mars closes with a particular affirmative asserting that Mars, through the stars, does wield power in this world:

> Depeynted was the slaughtre of Julius,
> Of grete Nero, and of Antonius;
> Al be that thilke tyme they were unborn,
> Yet was hir deth depeynted ther-biforn
> By manasynge of Mars, right by figure.
> So was it shewed in that portreiture,
> As is depeynted in the sterres above
> Who shal be slayn or elles deed for love. (2031–38)

Logic teaches that only one of these statements can be true. Either nothing in this world shares power with Venus, or Mars has power in this world through the stars.[37]

We all know enough Roman history to know that there is no problem with the Mars paintings, so we look back more carefully at the claim made for Venus, and suddenly we realize it is absurd. Actually, "to hold champartie" does not mean "to share power."

III. Thinking Processes and Language Use

It means "to share in the proceeds."[38] So the claim being made here in Venus's temple is that intelligence, money, looks, cunning, power, and persistence receive no shares in the proceeds of love, no rewards from Venus. Balderdash! The claim is patently false. The Knight's Tale itself begins with a marriage by Strength, culminates in a tournament for Beauty, and ends with a marriage by Wisdom (or Sleight, depending on one's point of view). We turn again to reexamine the Mars conclusion, and suddenly realize that it too is false—partly. Julius certainly was slaughtered, but Nero and Antony are the two most famous suicides in Roman history. However, the claim here is in the form of a future contingent;[39] it will not become even one-third true until Julius is born and slaughtered. So, what is its truth status until then? Is it temporarily false? And what will it be after Antony's suicide? two-thirds true? And after Nero's? Further, since the truth of any proposition implies the falsehood of its contradiction, what does this do to the truth status of the Venus claim? And vice versa. Explaining this headspinning system-breaker takes the fun out of it, of course, but Chaucer's point is valid—in the real world the forms of traditional logic are not universal; they are subject to time.

Further, the problem in the Mars prediction seems to be with the law of excluded middle. According to this law, a thing must be either H or Not-H; it cannot be a little of both. Now then, testing the Mars prediction against future Roman history: *(1)* Julius will be slaughtered, or "S"; *(2)* Antony will be not-slaughtered, or "Not-S"; *(3)* Nero, however, will in fact be a little of both, "S" and "Not-S," slaughtered and not-slaughtered. According to Suetonius, first Nero armed himself with poison, but his servants stole it, along with his linen. Then he called for a gladiator to come kill him, but no one appeared. Then he ran out toward the Tiber as if to drown himself, but changed his mind. Then he took up two daggers, but after testing their points decided he was being premature. At the last, hearing the Senate horses, he drove a dagger into his throat, but his hand faltered, and finally one of his freedmen helped him press the point home.[40] In short, both slaughter and not-slaughter, both S and Not-S. Thus, in the Mars passage, Nero's death is one of those excluded middles that cannot take place.[41] Fourteenth-century schoolboys must have loved this sort of thing. Its presence here in the Knight's Tale, however, also makes a serious point: The world of logic is an artificial, binary world. In the real world, excluded middles exist in the contexts of their own particular time and place and circumstances, all of which are subject to change, possibly changing them. In the real world, Chaucer comments, relying on predictions based on logical operations can be a mistake.

By way of concluding summary here, in these descriptions of the paintings in the temples of Venus and Mars, Chaucer has presented us with—in the subject matter, surveys of inward and outward pagan suffering; in the scope, qualifications, and relationships of the terms he uses, an experiential *sophisma* on simple apprehension of objects, Act 1; and in the conclusions of both passages, witty but rigorous demonstrations of the inadequacy of formal logic to deal with the complexities of life in the real world. In short, pagan suffering, scholastic definition, and comic refutation. The Diana passage immediately following is set up in exactly the same way.

Diana: Act 2, Judgment of Complex Propositions

The second type of thinking the human mind is capable of, according to this model, is judgment of complex propositions—i.e., combining and dividing those objects of thought apprehended by Act 1 into propositions (statements), and then judging them.

Because the mind is now active, present for the first time are the alternative possibilities of true or false. Formal logic attempts to escape the possibility of the false by discovering rules (i.e., forms, structures) of reasoning such that true premises will always and necessarily produce true conclusions. Now then, as mentioned earlier, in the scholastic interpretation of the 3-Acts mind model, each act had a logical technique proper to it. Just as Act 1 was guaranteed by the law of contradiction (either the object is or it is not), so Act 2 was guaranteed by truth functions (either the proposition is true or it is false). Truth functions were worked out for all the major connectives ("and," "or," "not," "if-then," and

III. Thinking Processes and Language Use

"if-and-only-if"), the idea being that if the truth value of each part of a sentence is known, then when the parts are put together by means of some connective, the truth functions for that connective will show whether the sentence as a whole is true or false. In order to visualize the function easily, truth tables were made up for the various connectives.[42]

Here, for example, is the truth table for the connective conjunction "and." It shows that there are four possible combinations of truth-values for the conjunction of two propositions P and Q; and it further shows that when both P and Q are true (the notation being T and T), the compound proposition P and Q is true. The other possible combinations, T and F, F and T, F and F are all false, as the table shows. Thus, when given something really complicated to judge, one simply figures out which parts are true and which are false, refers to the tables, and correct judgment of the whole follows automatically. What a wonderful invention! The procedure reduces tiresome complex thinking acts to simple, purely formal operations, without any sloppy subjectivity and so without possibility of error.

P	Q	P and Q
T	T	T
T	F	F
F	T	F
F	F	F

Turning back again now to the Knight's Tale, immediately following the temple descriptions of Venus and Mars, the reader comes upon that of Diana. The subject matter is again human suffering, but Chaucer's writing style here is entirely different. Whereas the Venus/Mars descriptions had consisted of lists of beings and objects but without any indication of how they came to be that way, the Diana description consists precisely of the stories of how things came to be the way they are. The narrator summarizes four—the stories of Callisto, Daphne, Actaeon, and Meleager. Each little summary seems to contain both a cause and its baleful effect. Collectively, these four stories show human beings as passive, innocent, and totally at the mercy of a powerful and unjust divinity. The active agent throughout the passage is Diana herself, her vengeance and ire. She was aggrieved with Callisto; Actaeon was made a hart for her vengeance; and she wrought Meleager care and woe. The human beings here are more acted upon than acting. They are turned, are made, are caught and "freten," are wrought care and woe. All this is very pagan—in life is suffering, in death is no transcendence, and in the divine is no comfort at all.

But for the reader outside this pagan romance, something is very wrong with the way these four stories are being presented. The description fastens on Diana the blame for everything in it, yet any reader reasonably acquainted with Ovid knows, at the very least, that Callisto was turned into a bear by Juno, not by Diana, as the passage implies. In this description, rather than straightforward summaries, Chaucer has deliberately mistold the *Metamorphoses* stories in order to rouse the reader's mind to making judgments. In short, this passage is another *sophisma,* this one an experiential definition of Act 2, judgment of complex propositions. First I will summarize the four stories as Ovid himself tells them, so that truth values can be properly assigned to the parts. Then I will show that Chaucer shaped each story in the form of two complex propositions, some true, some false,[43] so that, as a whole, in addition to presenting the pagan suffering, the Diana description also forms the truth table for the conjunction "and."

Chaucer's first summary is the story of Callisto:

Ther saugh I how woful Calistopee,
Whan that Diane agreved was with here,
Was turned from a womman til a bere,
And after was she maad the loode-sterre;
    Thus was it peynted, I kan sey yow no ferre.
Her sone is eek a sterre, as men may see. (2056–61)

According to Ovid, Callisto, a favorite of Diana, was raped by Jove, was so innocent herself she felt guilt about it, was expelled by Diana from the company of nymphs when her pregnancy became evident, gave birth to a son, and then was turned into a bear by Juno for punishment. Fifteen years later her son chanced

III. *Thinking Processes and Language Use*

upon her while hunting and was about to spear her when Jove, to prevent such a monstrous crime, metamorphosed the two of them into neighboring stars in the heavens. In Ovid, all Diana herself does is expel Callisto from her company. Here in the Knight's Tale version, however, the implication is that Diana caused everything: after she became angry with Callisto, Callisto was turned from woman to bear to lodestar. Chaucer's sequence of events here is correct, but by omitting the names of Juno and Jove and naming only Diana as cause, he implies that Diana did it all. In terms of its truth value, then, the first sentence of Chaucer's summary is false; the third sentence—that her son is also a star—is true.[44]

Next is the story of Daphne, daughter of the River Peneus:

Ther saugh I Dane, yturned til a tree,—
I mene nat the goddesse Diane,
But Penneus doghter, which that highte Dane. (2062–64)

As Ovid tells it, the story of Daphne is more complex. Apollo in his pride insulted Cupid, who in retaliation shot him with the arrow that kindles love and shot Daphne with the arrow that puts love to flight. She wished to emulate Diana both in her hunting and in her desire for permanent chastity, so she fled to the woods. Now Apollo truly loved Daphne, according to Ovid, since he wanted to marry her, but finally, his patience exhausted, he gave up his coaxing words and chased her. About to be caught, she cried to her father to destroy her beauty, and he changed her into the laurel tree. Literally, the Knight's Tale lines seem merely to betray an overly punctilious narrator who wants to be sure the reader understands that he saw Daphne, not Diana, in Diana's paintings. Actually, however, his remark puts Diana squarely into the middle of Daphne's story, a story in which in Ovid she never appears, a story which therefore either should not be or is not depicted in her temple. The rhetorical technique here, juxtaposing two statements without a transition, ordinarily will cause a reader to infer some connection between them, usually one of cause and effect, and that is how these statements will work in the mind of the Knight's Tale reader. Unless she or he knows the Daphne story well, the reader will infer that Diana had something to do with Daphne's suffering.

Thus both statements in Chaucer's summary are false, since any depiction of Daphne, or report of a depiction of Daphne, in paintings done to honor Diana, would be out of place and therefore false.[45]

Next comes Actaeon:

> Ther saugh I Attheon an hert ymaked,
> For vengeaunce that he saugh Diane al naked;
> I saugh how that his houndes have hym caught
> And freeten hym, for that they knewe hym naught.
>   (2065–68)

Actaeon, like Callisto and Daphne, was innocent. According to Ovid, he happened to stumble into a grotto where Diana was bathing, whereupon she turned him into a hart so that he might not tell he had seen her naked. Thereafter he was caught and torn to pieces by his own hunting dogs. This is the only story of the four that is accurately summarized in the Knight's Tale description. Notice, however, that the summary does not actually state that Diana turned Actaeon into a hart. Literally, any god could have done it. But, as in the two previous summaries, Chaucer's juxtaposing two ideas without a transition leads the reader to infer a causal connection, in this case, however, correctly. Thus, in terms of their truth value, both sentences here are true.[46]

And finally, there is Meleager:

> Yet peynted was a litel forther moor
> How Atthalante hunted the wilde boor,
> And Meleagre, and many another mo,
> For which Dyane wroghte hym care and wo. (2069–72)

Diana sent the great boar to ravage Calydon because the king neglected to do her honor, and during the ensuing hunt, Meleager, the king's only son, fell in love with Atalanta. Atalanta drew first blood from the boar, and so when Meleager finally brought it down, he presented her with the skin and head. But the other hunters begrudged a woman the spoils, and Meleager's two uncles took them from her, thereby taking from him the right of giving them. He became enraged and slew them both. His mother, torn between love for her brothers and love for her son, finally chose to avenge her brothers by burning the billet of wood on which Meleager's life depended. At the end, Diana, satisfied at last with the destruction of the house of Calydon, metamorphosed his grieving sisters into guinea hens. In this long story in Ovid, Diana is actually mentioned only four times: she sends the terrible boar; during the long hunt she once protects the boar by removing the head from a spear traveling toward it; one of the hunters boasts he will kill the boar even if Diana herself tries to protect it and he subsequently dies violently, although nothing is said about her role, if any, in his death; and finally, after Meleager's death, she turns his sisters into birds. Meleager himself slays his uncles, and his mother causes his death. With regard to Chaucer's summary, therefore, it is true that Atalanta hunted the boar along with Meleager and many others, and therefore the first part of the summary is true. But in Ovid, Diana wrought none of them, not even Meleager, care and woe for this. The hunter who made the insulting boast against her dies horribly on the tusks of the boar, but in Ovid he apparently dies because of the boast, not because of the hunt. Literally, as in the other summaries, the Knight's Tale lines *seem* correct: Atalanta, Meleager, and many others hunted the boar, and Diana (apparently) wrought a "hym" (the boaster) "care and wo." But the direct cause-and-effect implication in the second part of the summary as Chaucer tells it here—that Diana wrought Melager woe for hunting the boar—is wrong, so the second part is false.[47]

The result is, when one judges Chaucer's retellings, the Callisto truth values are FT, those of Daphne FF, those of Actaeon TT, and those of Meleager TF. Since Chaucer's description contains, therefore, every possible combination of truth values for the conjunction "and," it is a perfect truth table. It will activate the reader's mind fully to judgment, by causing him or her to experience the full range of possibility of Act 2 of the 3-Acts mind model.

This, then, is Chaucer's *sophisma* on Act 2, judgment of complex propositions. Here in the Knight's Tale, of course, the subject matter has been four pagan myths, but it could just as easily have been Mother Goose rhymes or Norse sagas. For purposes of constructing a *sophisma* on Act 2 so as to arouse the full spectrum of true/false judgments in a reader, the key components are:

—A well-known collection of stories.

—Truth functions for the chosen connective.

Difficult to do? Not with incentive. As a schoolroom exercise for advanced trivium students, I would guess two hours would about do it.[48]

MORE CHAUCERIAN COMMENTARY ON LOGIC

Recognizing the description of Diana's paintings as a *sophisma* depended on distinguishing between T and F in the retellings of the four stories. Recognizing Chaucer's attack on the logic underlying it depends, on the other hand, on distinguishing between T and F in the real world. Let us, then, judge for truth value first the description of her paintings against its real world implications, and then the description of her statue against *its* real world implications.

All the mistellings in these four summaries have been shaped toward one rhetorical end: blame Diana. Blame the divine for human suffering. Yet even according to Ovid, the truth about human suffering is not nearly so simple as this passage implies. Of the four summaries, the implications as to Diana's part are true only for the lines on Actaeon. Of the others, Diana was in no way involved in Daphne's suffering; she caused no suffering to Atalanta; she was only indirectly involved in Meleager's suffering; and she merely expelled Callisto from her company. However, Theseus's temple paintings blame her for everything. Ovid's complex interweaving of gods, humans, deeds, motives, innuendoes and silences, and shared divine and human guilt, has been reduced here to a simplistic either/or human judgment totally blaming the divine. In this passage, humans are innocent and suffering, Diana vengeful and blameworthy. Indeed, the rhetoric is persuasive. Even a reader who knows the *Metamorphoses* stories well and may pause on the sweeping indictment of Diana will still find the facts too complex to easily distribute the blame. Faulty human judgment about the relationship between human pain and the divine purpose is, therefore, the intelligible real-world focus of the Diana passage.

III. Thinking Processes and Language Use

So, in the Knight's Tale as a whole, what is the relationship between human suffering and the divine? In the pagan narrative, Venus's paintings have set forth a full spectrum of inward emotional suffering; and Mars's paintings have set forth a full spectrum of outward physical suffering. These are things all human beings apprehend (Act 1). But judging from the sweeping indictment in Diana's paintings, often they do not evaluate correctly the reasons for such suffering (Act 2). The real-world question raised by the Diana paintings is, therefore, about how human beings judge all the suffering, all the "care and wo" life presents them with—as in the razing of Thebes, as in the terrible suffering and death of Arcite. At the end, as already discussed, Theseus's Prime Mover speech will put forward the better judgment he will come to about the nature of the divine and the cause of human suffering—the Prime Mover's high intent, the fair chain of love, the corruption of all things in this world, but their final return to the source. Moreover, it will be a judgment derived from pondering long and hard and silently the facts of his own worldly experience and his own responsibility in them, not from reducing those facts to bits and pieces to fit a truth table.

Immediately following Diana's paintings comes the description of her statue. Let us now judge it against its real-world implications. On the pagan narrative level, the statue's subject matter is again faulty human judgment of the divine. Diana sits high on her hart, dressed for hunting, looking down toward Pluto's reign (2075–82). A woman in hard labor lies before her, pleading for her help (2083–88). As they are juxtaposed here, Diana seems to look down indifferently right past her pitiful petitioner. The poor woman has apparently never reflected on the contradiction whereby the goddess of virginity is also supposed to be the one "best of alle" able to help in childbirth.[49] It is a historical irony that the cold unforgiving classical goddess of chastity and the hunt, who expelled Callisto simply for looking pregnant, somehow also became a fertility goddess and in this aspect one of the goddesses of childbirth. (This aspect of Diana never appears in the *Metamorphoses,* nor is Emelye in the Knight's Tale familiar with it, 2310.) Chaucer's description, however, is pitiless. His stony Diana will never bend down to help the poor woman suffering before her. The woman is praying to the wrong goddess; she has misjudged the divine.

At the same time, on the scholastic truth function level, in this description Chaucer is again taking on formal logic, again shattering the "appearances," again demonstrating that formal logical operations do not work in the real world. Notice that the description of Diana's statue actually consists of two complex propositions, as did each of her painting summaries, although here they are visual rather than verbal: Diana herself high on her hart; the woman pleading before her.[50] Taken separately, both visual propositions are true: Ovid's Diana is a huntress; and everyday experience teaches that one childbirth in seven is very hard. However, the implication their conjunction produces in the mind of the viewer is false. Nowhere in the *Metamorphoses* is the goddess of chastity conceived as a goddess of childbirth; indeed, she expelled Callisto for being with child. And, further, real world experience teaches that people who mandate virginity, like Diana, rarely show compassion toward women not virginal. Thus, in this statue, although P and Q are both true, their conjunction produces a false in the mind of the real world viewer. On the other hand, the truth table for "and" teaches us that the conjunction of True and True necessarily produces a True.[51] Something is wrong. In the real world, Chaucer's Chinese-box statue suggests, judgment of complex propositions (Act 2 of the mind model) is by no means a simple, purely formal, procedure reducible to truth functions. As with the law of contradiction and the law of excluded middle, so here with truth functions: real world judgment (i.e., thinking process 2 in the real world) is considerably more complex than these simple logical operations would have it.

By way of concluding summary, here again, as in the Venus/ Mars passage, we have pagan-romance subject matter, a scholastic definition, and its drastic refutation. In the description of Diana's paintings, Chaucer has presented us with—in the subject matter, stories of innocent human suffering and implied divine guilt; in their division, composition, and mis-implication, an experiential *sophisma* on judgment of complex propositions; and in the concluding image of Diana's statue a visually painful and philosophically rigorous demonstration that in the real world, simplistic binary thinking, as in the operations of formal logic, can produce tragically wrong, humanly devastating errors.

Lygurge and Emetreus: Act 3, Reasoning, or Inference to Causes

In a culture in which the distinction between terms and propositions was highly significant, Chaucer's lists of specific objects (terms) in the Venus/Mars descriptions, and his set of complex propositions in Diana's, would have stood out like beacons. His own audience (and any educated audience until the demise of the trivium) would have known automatically what was to come next, what would complete the sequence—reasoning. Like Harry after Tom and Dick, and superego after id and ego, reasoning from what is present to what is not present, that is, inference to causes, completes the 3-Acts mind model.

Today the notion of "causes" has narrowed down to signify efficient causes only. In scholastic times, as touched on earlier, the notion was much broader; a "cause" was more like a principle of explanation. Writing in the scholastic tradition, B. M. Ashley defines a cause as "that on which something depends for its existence in any way."[52] Among the causes of a garden, for example, would be not just the gardener, but also his catalogs, the seed store with its employees and delivery van and advertising (efficient causes); plus the flowers, trees, insects, dirt, light, water, and fertilizers (material causes); plus the idea of any garden in the gardener's mind, the idea of this particular garden, and the ground plan for this garden (formal causes); plus its beauty, the flowers and fruits it produces, the pleasure it gives, the oxygen it gives off, and the psychological benefits to the gardener's soul and the physical benefits to his body (final causes). According to this way of thinking, any object or event is going to have many, many different causes, depending on the particular aspect of its being under examination. In principle, by means of this kind of thinking it is possible to figure out every aspect of a thing's being and thus to know it *totally*. For Aristotle, one knows a thing by knowing its causes, and every effect has its cause. But stop now, for a moment, and notice the universal determinism implied in this idea of reasoning. If every effect has its cause, then every cause can be traced back to its cause, and so on back (infinite regress). Aristotle ended this chain of causes with his Prime Mover, the First Cause, totally self-moved and totally self-absorbed. Christian thinkers adapting the Greek notion of First Cause to the very different conception of Judeo-Christian Deity, thus had a problem. Where, in this universe of totally interlocking, ever retreating chains of causes, is freedom? If every cause is intelligible, how can man be free?

The older medieval notion of freedom, discussed earlier and ultimately Platonic, was that freedom is liberation from our own materiality. In this way of thinking, all humans, Christian and pagan alike, were made in God's image, but this image was damaged by the Fall, so that since then man has been dominated by the need to satisfy his own natural appetites, to fulfill only himself. According to this idea, such worldly rights as to own possessions and to hold sovereignity and jurisdiction are natural powers that have been open to all men since the Fall. The freedom of Christians must, therefore, be in addition to these, and as a result is spiritual. For it to be otherwise, Ockham was fond of arguing,[53] would be to make the liberty of Christians less than that of pagans. The freedom of Christians, thus, is a liberation in the mind. Christian grace is liberation from the domination of natural appetites. Grace gives one the power to throw off the chains of one's own damaged nature; and, hence, Christian freedom is the freedom to desire something better than oneself, to love, know, and serve something higher. This difference between the universal causation and natural self-fulfillment of the pagans as opposed to the higher spiritual freedom of Christians is the larger context of the *sophisma* on reasoning in the portraits of Chaucer's two rival pagan kings. When, by means of reasoning to their causes (Act 3), every detail in these two portraits is traced back link by metaphysical link to its source, by the end of the process the reader has come to know both champions *totally*. And it has become clear that they both act

III. Thinking Processes and Language Use

according to their own natures. They *are* totally what they *are* naturally. They do not enjoy/exercise the freedom to choose to be other than what they are. The Knight's larger point here is that differences of culture, homeland, generation, physical stature, possessions, *and* of faculty structuring, religious expression, and friends are not what Christians are going to be judged on (and so should not be what Christian philosopher/theologians should spend their time arguing about). All these differences pertain to pagans and Christians alike.

By way of illustration, we are all familiar with medieval drawings of the "Zodiac Man." Zodiac men are merely one type of a large group of medieval medical drawings of the natural structures, influences, and disabilities of the body. Other types include the "Wound Man," usually a placid-looking individual with swords, knives, arrows, spears, and a mace puncturing his body; the "Blood Letting Man," who stands often with one foot in a bowl while thin streams of blood fan out from the various blood-letting points of his body to appropriate medical information in the margins; the "Disease Man" or "Disease Woman," with arms and legs outstretched and labeled all over with names of the different diseases to which the parts of the body are subject; the "Muscle Man," who displays with labels the body's different muscle bunches, and so on. All such drawings pertain, obviously, to Christian and pagan alike, because everything they indicate is physical and therefore natural. Figure 7 shows a Zodiac Man, from the Wellcome Manuscript in the Wellcome Institute for the History of Medicine in London. This one is especially interesting in that it relates the particular parts of the body not only to the zodiacal signs (in the fixed stars) believed particularly to influence them, but also to the movements of the seven wandering stars, depicted in the appropriate Ptolemaic sequence so as to enable one to calculate also the influence of their positions on the body. Drawings such as these were used by physicians to compute when medicines and surgical procedures would be most beneficial or hazardous in terms of natural influences on the body. And natural influences were, of course, exactly the same for Christian and pagan. As will be shown, in the Knight's Tale Chaucer depicts his two champion kings as

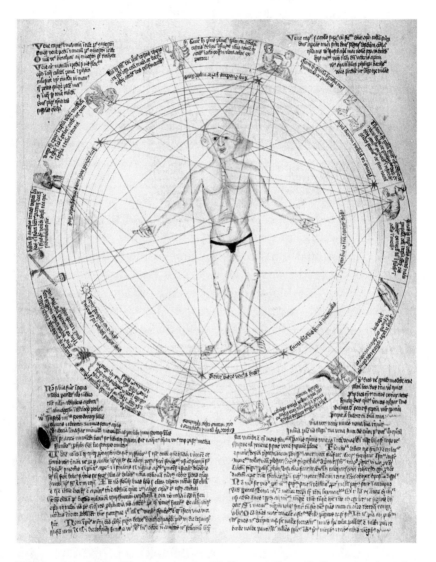

Figure 7. Apocalypsis, fifteenth century. Wellcome MS 49, Wellcome Institute for the History of Medicine, London.

totally natural men. In their choices of clothing, gear, men, and pets, they follow the dictates of their own natural (and fallen) natures; among other things, they fight for primacy.

In addition, their descriptions are *sophismata* on Act 3, the reasoning process. If the reader becomes intrigued with the intricately crafted details of these two portraits and tries to reason them out in order to make sense of them, that is, tries to infer all their many causes, she will be *experiencing Act 3 of the mind model*. If she keeps at it systematically, sooner or later she will find that Chaucer's contrasting details fall into paralleled hierarchical groups: Each portrait contains details of three types: *(1)* personal appearance, *(2)* possessions, *(3)* company of men. Further, each type has its subtypes: personal appearance consists of *(a)* astrological, *(b)* animal, and *(c)* light causes. Possessions consist of six subtypes, each item of which is constructed according to the four Aristotelian causes. And similarly with the company-of-men subtypes and their details. If the reader continues to persist (as Curry did with such success on the astrological details), eventually she comes to something wonderful. In making these two portraits, in the briefest number of lines, Chaucer has formed the chains of causes of their concrete details to lead back to an accurate statement of the positions of the two sides in the major metaphysical discussions of his day, including both their immaterial riches and their pagan rivalries. Just as Palamon and Arcite embody the rival voluntarist and intellectualist psychological theories, so their champions Lygurge and Emetreus embody the rival voluntarist and intellectualist metaphysical systems on which they were based. In just seventy-three lines, Chaucer's double *sophisma* on the Act 3 reasoning process guides the interested reader through the underground foundations of the entire scholastic enterprise. (This is no mean feat when one considers the length of the average *summa*.) In fact, these two portraits are magnificent verbal emblems of the three main topics of medieval metaphysics: Causation, Being, and Reality. Solving the double *sophisma* is both demystifying (they are in the vernacular) and enlightening (they are graspable). In the same way that a topographic map makes sense of a complicated countryside, these two portraits make sense of scholastic metaphysics. Here is how Chaucer has organized the descriptive details in the portraits of these two rival kings:

(a) Their physical appearances—these details lead to an understanding of the metaphysics of *Causation* (whether natural or free, as just discussed).

(b) Their possessions—these details lead to an understanding of the metaphysics of *Being,* i.e., substance and accident theory (Aristotelian Thomist versus Augustinian Franciscan).

(c) Their companies of men—these details lead to an understanding of rival perceptions of *Reality* (realism versus nominalism).

Human rivalry is the specific subject of these two pagan portraits. These two kings epitomize basic human antagonisms. In culture, Lygurge is barbarian, Emetreus civilized. In age, Lygurge is mature, Emetreus only twenty-five. In homeland, Lygurge is from Thebes in the cold unfriendly North, Emetreus is from sunny India.[54] On the pagan narrative level, these two rival kings have come together in a love tournament to fight to the death. On the scholastic debate level, they are rivals as well, come together in a truth tournament to fight for . . . one hesitates to say it . . . primacy. As in the struggle for Emelye's hand, no compromise between the two systems seems possible.

(a) **Physical appearance: Causation.** Today, we ordinarily infer a person's physical background from what he or she looks like. People's physical characteristics imply their ethnic heritage and where their far-distant forebears came from. To specify this far-distant kind of physical information about these two kings, Chaucer provides astrological, animal, and light references.

The physical appearances of these two kings lead back to their astrological causes. As mentioned earlier, Curry long ago showed that Palamon's Lygurge, by reason of his black hair and beard, his red and yellow eye circles, his heavy brows, and his muscular build, is to be recognized as a man born under the influence of Saturn; and that Arcite's Emetreus, by reason of his curly yellow hair, citron eyes, round lips, and sanguine complexion, is to be recognized as a man born under the influence of Mars. Thus, the two kings differ in astrological cause. Yet, at the same time, both alike bear its marks. Both alike have been physically shaped by the stars of the created universe. The chronological impact of their entry here in Part III was also mentioned earlier: since at this point in the tale there is no indication as to which young knight will pray to which deity, or that later one of the deities will appeal to Saturn for help, the fact that Arcite arrives with a Martial champion and Palamon not with a Venerian but with a Saturnian champion indicates that events and even choices in the lives of both young knights have already been determined/foreseen not by the wandering stars themselves, but by the power that stands behind them and determines *their* movements. Thus, with regard to these two rival kings, their astrological markings, combined with their appearance in the tale before the astrological strife in heaven which 'causes' them, indicate that both come from and manifest the same far-distant First Cause.

The paired animal references in their "lookings" lead back to the same Cause. Recently John Friedman has shown that medieval physiognomists believed a person's eye movement indicated his inward psychological state.[55] In the Knight's Tale, as Chaucer's Lygurge rides along standing high on his chariot, he "looked" about him "lik a grifphon" (2133). And as Emetreus comes riding on his great steed bay, he casts his "lookyng" like a "leon" (2171). Further, these two animal references are not only verbal and apparently psychological, they are also visual, as Beryl Rowland showed: the two champions seem to resemble visually the two animals to whose glances their own are compared.[56] Lions and griffins traditionally have the same bodies; the point here is their heads. With red and yellow eye circles glowing under bristly brows and black feather-like hair shining down his back, Lygurge's head does faintly evoke the eagle's head of the griffin. Likewise, with crisp rings of glittering yellow hair, bright citron eyes, high nose, round lips, and black and yellow freckles, Emetreus's head does faintly evoke that of the lion. Reasoning from Chaucer's references and these resemblances back to their causes (Act 3), in the medieval period, griffins were associated with justice; lions with hierarchy;

and both with strength and ferocity. In addition, in pagan as well as Christian times, both animals were widely accepted resurrection emblems. Griffins, as strong, high flyers, literally carry people to heaven, as they did Alexander, and figuratively carry the soul to God. Indeed, the extraordinary number of "griffin eggs" in later medieval English inventories testifies to their unusual popularity as rebirth symbols in England. The 1382 catalog of reliquaries of Durham Cathedral, for example, lists no less than eleven "ova griffina"[57] (today, much less spectacularly, they are identified as ostrich eggs). As for lions, their cubs seem to be dead when born, according to the pagan natural histories, but after three days their father awakens them with a mighty roar. This story obviously presented remarkable opportunities for allegorical interpretation, and it was embellished accordingly by medieval Christian thinkers.[58] Thus, here in the Knight's Tale, the animal resemblances of both champion-kings lead back to different aspects of the same First Cause—the griffin to its justice (the voluntarist emphasis), and the lion to its hierarchy (the intellectualist emphasis). In addition, their lookings lead back to a possible harmony, to the promise of resurrection for both.

The far-distant source of these two kings is similarly identifiable by the quality of light associated with each of them—steady as opposed to sparkling. In the medieval period, ontologically speaking, light was a substance both metaphysical and physical: The Light was to the context of knowledge as the Word was to the context of truth. Chaucer puts two explicit light references in each portrait, and the quality of the light associated with each king implies he has the kind of direct, personal relationship with God that is natural according to his side in the metaphysical debate. In the Augustinian tradition, whether the mind turns toward him or away from him, God is always present inside the mind. He is the Light (*lux, lumen*) which makes all knowledge possible, and he is always there. Thus, appropriately, the two light references in Lygurge's portrait are to a steady-source kind of light: the circles of his eyes "gloweden" and his black hair "shoon" (2132, 2144). In the Aristotelian tradition, on the other hand, knowledge is a completely natural mental activity; no divine illumination is needed; and so a new and different theory of the Divine Presence in the mind developed among the German Dominican mystics, that of the *scintilla animae,* the spark of the soul. In Eckhart's psychology, for example, above the usual Thomist hierarchy of vegetative, sensitive, and rational levels, there is an uncreated element, essence, or spark, the *vünkelin* or *scintilla* of the soul, which bears the image of God and unites with him in mystical union.[59] Thus, appropriately, the two light references in Emetreus's portrait scintillate: the rubies of his mantelet are red as fire "sparklynge" (2164) and his hair "glytered" as the sun (2166). In sum, their paired contrasted light references associate Lygurge with the steady, constant, Augustinian kind of Divine Presence in the soul and associate Emetreus with the sparkling Dominican kind. At the same time, however, both kings are alike bearing witness—"shoon" and "glytered," another harmony—to the touch of the Divine on their heads.

So in spite of their very different present-to-us personal appearances, inferences from their astrological and animal markings indicate that these two kings proceed from the same far-distant source. This is because planets and animals, by the thinking of Chaucer's time, act only according to nature, that is, in accordance with natural and therefore ultimately divine laws. They are not free. In addition, and again in spite of their different personal appearances, both kings alike evidence the present approval of that same far-distant source. This is because light, by the thinking of Chaucer's time, acts in accordance with metaphysical law and therefore by reason of the Divine Presence. It is not free to humans. With regard to human freedom, therefore, Chaucer's overall point here is that natural human multiplicity—of coloration, build, texturing, facial structure, temperament—derives from the Divine and bears the Divine's present seal of approval. Differences of this sort pertain to pagan and Christian alike. They have nothing to do with Christian freedom.

As a result, by reasoning from the details of physical appearance in these two portraits to their various causes (Act 3), the reader can achieve a real understanding of the medieval metaphysics of Causation. These two rival portraits show what is natural (i.e., caused by stars, physical matter, bodily appetites, and such) for pagans and Christians alike.

(b) Possessions: Being (substance and accident theory). The later medieval science of metaphysics covered study of all things non-physical: the existence and nature of God, of first causes, angels, the human soul, and the amorphous immaterial substance underly-ing the physical universe. Substance/accident theory was a funda-mental concept, comparable in implications and importance per-haps to our own theory of atomic structure. It constituted the medievals' notion of basic being, of the underlying manner in which all existing things are formed.

By this notion, every object is a substance, resulting from the union of form with prime matter. The form of human beings is the soul. Thus every human being—you, me, the man next door—is a substance. Likewise, a tree, a rock, a sheep—each is a substance composed of the appropriate form for tree, rock, or sheep, combined with prime matter. Prime matter (a metaphysi-cal substrate underlying physical matter) is the same for every object; the specifying into human, tree, rock, or sheep is totally accomplished by the appropriate form. Accidents, on the other hand, are the fortuitous, contingent, nonessential properties of things. Beautiful, green, American, modern, hungry, rich—these are accidents. A man's possessions, such as his crown, pets, and gems, are accidents; they are not part of his essential being. However, they can *reveal* his essential being, his substance, especially if he is a king and can have whatever he pleases; and that is the notion Chaucer is working with in specifying the possessions of these two kings. From their possessions we can infer what these two men *are*. In fact, we can infer their substances. For each king, Chaucer's particular choices of acci-dents can lead our reasoning unerringly back to his kind of form, his kind of prime matter, and his kind of combination of the two. Lygurge's substance, it will turn out, is one hundred percent voluntarist; Emetreus's, one hundred percent intellectual-ist. Judging from their possessions, both men are completely natural. They completely fulfill the natural needs/desires of their own respective substances.[60]

We still use the same reasoning process: we still infer what people are from the possessions they choose to surround themselves with. Chaucer provides each king with six kinds of possessions for the reader to compare and reason from: gold, gems, crown, conveyance, cote-armure, and household pets. He shapes most of their descriptive details on two basic contrasts: primacy of an item's *workmanship,* whether physical force or intellect; and degree of an item's *alteration* from its original natural state, whether little or much. These two contrasts are actualized as contrasts between weight, mass, and physical force on the one side, as opposed to lightness and sparkle, layer, and absence of physical restraint on the other.

First, with regard to his form (mind/soul), Lygurge's possessions characterize him as a formidable adversary. They give the viewer an impressive sense of his power, weight, and mass, and his inclination and ability to use brute force to achieve his purpose, whatever it might be. Given the circumstances of an impending tourney, all are functional. His chariot is of gold, and is apparently of tremendous weight, since it is pulled by four bulls. There is not a hint of decoration or embellishment. His crown is an incredibly thick, incredibly heavy wreath of gold, set with rubies and diamonds which are first described as "stones brighte." For cote-armure he hangs over his harness a heavy bearskin with polished claws. His household animals are great steer-sized dogs, kept for practical purposes like hunting large game, and are savage enough to require muzzles when on show. Alaunts were notoriously vicious by nature,[61] and those of Lygurge retain their original state. The narrator's/reader's eye notices first their color and breed, "white alauntz," then the size of the pack "twenty and mo," then the size of each individual hound "as grete as any steer," and then thinks of their fearsome capabilities—"to hunten at the leoun or the deer," and now, fully aware of them, he devotes two lines to checking safety precautions, the muzzles and ringed collars (2148–52). As with his dogs, so too with his gems, gold, bearskin, and bulls—Lygurge's possessions have been altered only slightly from their original state, only enough to perform the practical functions, both direct and symbolic, for which he keeps them. What little change they have undergone has been by physical strength rather than sophisticated technique. His gold is in lumps and dog collars; his gems are bright stones; both have been altered only as much as is necessary for them to symbolize his power. Compared with Emetreus's warhorse, Lygurge's chariot and bulls harken back to an earlier stage in the technology of war; little skill is expended in training bulls to pull, and not much more is required for their traces. His bearskin is "col-blak for old," implying it has changed color with age and therefore was cured by fairly simple techniques. The overall point here is power: the power of raw human and animal brawn and of great primitive wealth.

Lygurge's possessions will animate the affective will (in their owner, their viewer, and the Knight's Tale reader) but leave the intellect cold. The will's response will be twofold: at the same time it is attracted by the richness, the weight, and the slow-moving primitive splendor of Lygurge's chariot and crown, it will be repelled, threatened, by the tangible savagery of his clawed bear-skin and muzzled dogs. Reasoning back from his possessions to the man who chose them, the reader infers that Lygurge is a king in whose soul will is prime. He is interested in brute power, in imposing his own purpose. Intellectual delight in beautiful decoration or fine workmanship is not a part of his personality.

As for the form (mind/soul) of Emetreus, on the other hand, all of his possessions have beauty. They all give aesthetic pleasure on being perceived, the medieval pleasures of order, hierarchy, pattern, and rapidly changing light and color. They characterize him as a man highly civilized, a man who delights in the exercise of the intellect. His precious metals and gems seem to have little weight or mass of their own; and they impress more by reason of the skilled technical craftsmanship they display than the wealth they represent. Some of his gold has been beaten into leaf to cover his saddle. Other gold has been made into thread and woven into cloth to cover his horse. His gems, great round white pearls and rubies faceted to sparkle like fire, have been used to decorate his clothing rather than to impress on their own. The total effect is one of glittering, highly refined beauty. He rides a "steede bay," but it impresses more by reason of its diapered gold cloth than its "horseness." Diapered cloth had a small uniform pattern made by weaving the threads to cross diamond-wise so as to reflect light differently from the different surfaces. The diamond-shaped spaces so made were filled up randomly with parallel lines, dots, and simple patterns. Ordinarily such cloth was made of linen. But here, rather than showing off its own mass and muscle, the slightest movement of his horse would reflect instead a remarkable amount of rippling light. His cote-armure is "cloth of Tars," a rich, costly Oriental fabric woven of silk and cashmere (which Chaucer pointedly contrasts to Lygurge's black bearskin). His household animals are kept for pleasure: Tame lions and leopards for whom no practical purpose is given surround him "on every part," and he bears a tame eagle on his hand simply for "deduyt." His eagle, lions, and leopards, all animals notoriously difficult to tame, have been altered so far from their natural wild state that even under stress conditions, for example during a ceremonial entry into a strange city, they require no muzzles, no collars apparently, no physical restraints of any kind. The narrator's/reader's eye hardly pauses on them. Like his pet animals, so too his gems, gold, horse, cote-armure, and crown—all of Emetreus's possessions have been greatly altered from their original states, so as to perform not only practical and symbolic functions, but so as to be decorative as well. And all the changes they have undergone have required much more intellect, much more planning, skill, dexterity, and finesse, than brute strength. The laurel wreath seems his least demanding possession to make; in fact, however, its significance is due not to its own natural matter, but to the human intellect that created, maintained and handed down over centuries a rich intellectual tradition. In short, Emetreus's possessions are all works of sustained human artifice. The overall effect of his description is one of great decorative beauty.

As objects of beauty, Emetreus's possessions will first arouse in their viewer an intellectual response. For Aquinas the beautiful was that which gives pleasure when perceived, and the pleasure it gives is cognitive and disinterested.[62] Some of Emetreus's possessions may arouse the appetite as well, since the beautiful is often identical (in this tradition) with the good, but they will arouse the appetite only secondarily, after their nature has first been cognized by the intellect. For example, one may desire to own a huge lump of gold immediately on perceiving that it is a huge lump of gold without examining it further, but in the case of works of real art, whether fine fabrics or tame leopards, ordinarily one first regards these disinterestedly; one grasps their fine materials and admires their extraordinary workmanship. Then one may or may not feel a desire for possession. Moreover, for Aquinas, the shining forth of "bright color" was one element of the beautiful;[63] and most of Emetreus's possessions reflect bright color: his horse's cloth of diapered gold, his cote-armure couched with lustrous pearls, his beaten gold saddle, his mantelet with rubies "rede as fyr spar-klynge," and even his curled glittering yellow hair. Thus Emetreus's possessions will animate first the cognitive intellect (in their owner, their viewer, and the Knight's Tale reader), after which they may or may not animate the appetite/will. The resulting inference is that Emetreus is a king in whose soul intellect is prime. He likes civilized beauty; he appreciates intellectual skill; he loves patterned decoration. His possessions are all functional or capable of being functional, but it is their beauty, their *ratio,* that shines out, not their function.

In sum, in the terms of fourteenth-century metaphysics, reasoning from their accidents to their causes has revealed that Lygurge's form is voluntarist, Emetreus's form is intellectualist. But what of their respective prime matters? And what of the manners of their respective combinations? One needs to know all three—form, prime matter, and method of their combination—in order to truly *know* a thing's substance.

Metaphysically speaking, prime matter is the passive recipient of form. It is a kind of potentiality, that out of which a thing is made, except that it has no shape, no mass, no extension. Rather, it underlies the shape, mass, and extension of what we now think of as physical matter. Here again the two scholastic sides differed, and Chaucer depicts their difference in the two kings' possessions by converting this notion of underlying prime matter into images of a thing's original natural matter. On the intellectualist side, Aristotle speaks of prime matter as "substrate for being." He regarded it as pure potentiality, and the Thomists followed him: prime matter is in no way actual or real; it is simply substrate for change. As a result, Chaucer characterizes Emetreus's possessions as lacking mass or weight. Instead, visually, they are all light, glitter, insubstantial layer, and glancing movement. Further, the natural matter of every one of Emetreus's possessions has been either covered over with gold or gems or changed by technology, tradition, or training into something of a substantially different kind. Indeed, Emetreus's own natural body is not visible to the reader; and just as his cloth of Tars is patterned over with pearls and his mantelet with rubies, so too is his face patterned over with freckles. Emetreus is a man who regards natural (created) matter as potential rather than actual, as something which, in addition to being made useful, is also to be made beautiful, to be decorated or tamed so as to form objects of "deduyt." Judging from his possessions, for him natural matter is simply substrate for change. As for the voluntarists, on the other hand, the Augustinian Franciscans held that since God created it, prime matter actually does exist to some degree, however minute, and it is therefore positive, real, and good to the degree that it exists. As a result, Chaucer characterizes Lygurge's possessions as having bulk, body, and weight, and their natural matter is actual, positive, and visible to the viewer's eye. Further, although the faces of both kings are visible, Lygurge's body is visible as well, and Chaucer makes it markedly solid and weighty:

> His lymes grete, his brawnes harde and stronge,
> His shuldres brode, his armes rounde and longe. (2135–36)

Judging from his possessions, Lygurge is a man who regards natural matter as actual and good (i.e., attractive, desirable, useful) in itself. He likes his gold, gems, dogs, and bearskin to remain close to their original state, changing them enough to be functional, but always retaining their own special natural qualities.

To conclude here, reasoning back from their possessions to their causes has revealed that Chaucer's two champion-kings bring to the aid of their young protégés the appropriate kinds of form and prime matter, one voluntarist, the other intellectualist. (See Appendix C for sample four-cause analyses.) For their complete metaphysical definition as substances, there remain only the different ways in which their respective forms and prime matters are combined.

The key terms here are *plurality* versus *oneness.* The question was, how many forms combine to shape the substance? Since the Aristotelian Thomist notion was that a substance is shaped by a single form, any substantial change involved the total substitution of a new form for the old.[64] Thus visually the forms of the things associated with Emetreus have been totally changed from their original manifestations. What was once gold is now perceived, in terms of its form, as cloth or saddle; what was once eagle is now perceived, in terms of its form, as harmless pet. And so on. The Augustinian Franciscan notion of the combination, on the other hand, was that a plurality of forms combined with prime matter to bring a substance into being. Different thinkers utilized different forms, but a form of corporeity was standard. As a result, with a plurality of forms, major change in an object is not necessarily instantaneous and total; one of an object's forms can pass away and another take its place without necessarily altering the character of the object as a whole. Thus, with regard to the things associated with Lygurge, precious gems can be set in a gold crown and still retain their original character as bright stones; alaunts can be used for hunting and still retain their original vicious natures. And so on with his other possessions. The result is, the different kinds of possessions these kings have chosen for themselves (as described by Chaucer) reveal the rival scholastic theories as to the manner in which form combines with prime matter: Lygurge's reveal the Augustinian-Franciscan plurality of forms; Emetreus's reveal the Aristotelian-Thomist substantial unity of form.

Reasoning, therefore, from the accidental possessions of these two rival kings back to their causes (i.e., Act 3 of the mind model) has taken the reader into the heart of scholastic metaphysics, the nature of Being itself. Instead of the unity he expected, however, the reader has found the same diversities in the nature of things that

he found on the pagan surface. And so once again, the differences
between these two kings are natural. They are part of their very
substance. Not being free, they are not blameable. The result is,
differences in personality, culture, and taste—whether one prefers
one's gems rough or faceted, whether one prefers one's gold in
lumps or filigreed—are not ethically important. Christian freedom
does not pertain to differences such as these.

*(c) Companies of men: perceptions of Reality (realist versus nomi-
nalist).* Intellectualist perception focuses on the group, on the
common nature and the common purpose. That this perception
constitutes an objective reality is medieval realism. Voluntarist
perception, on the other hand, focuses on the individual, on individual experience and individual concepts. That this perception
constitutes knowable reality is medieval nominalism. Reasoning
back from Chaucer's descriptions of the two rival companies of
one hundred men each to their perceptual causes, the reader arrives
at each king's perception of reality. We still reason about people
in the same way. We still infer what people think of as reality from
the people they choose to surround themselves with. We assume
mutual interests, aspirations, codes, ways of seeing the world.
Perceptual causes, therefore, whether common-nature based or
individual based, shape Chaucer's descriptions of the two companies of men. His larger point, once again, is that whether one sees
reality as a nominalist or as a realist is not a matter of freedom in
the Christian sense. It is not what one will be judged on.

For Ockham and in the Franciscan tradition generally, everything in nature or in the mind is individual or singular. Universal
concepts arise in our minds because of the resemblance which, in
our individual experiences, individual substances and accidents
bear to one another. But the reality is the individual. Here is
Chaucer's description of Lygurge's men. They are each described
individually ("som," MnE 'one'):

> With hym ther wenten knyghtes many on [i.e., one];
> Som wol ben armed in an haubergeoun,
> And in a brestplate and a light gypoun;

And som wol have a paire plates large;
And som wol have a Pruce sheeld or a targe;
Som wol ben armed on his legges weel,
And have an ax, and som a mace of steel. (2118–24)

In this company, the individuals exist separately. Chaucer here describes five, implying the rest would be similarly perceived, as individuals. Further, each man occupies a separate individual clause or phrase; each therefore exists grammatically as a separate individual substantive (e.g., substance). Moreover, these men are each specifically individualized on the basis of their separate individual choices—an haubergeoun, a Prussian shield, and so on—choices presumably made on the basis of their different individual experiences and reflecting their different individual wills ("wol," "wol"). Indeed, Chaucer makes absolutely clear that in this passage individual choice is the issue by ending it with an explicit summary: "Armed were they, as I have yow told, / Everych after his opinioun" (2126–27). In this company, therefore, as throughout voluntarist nominalism, perceptual focus is on the individual. Further, in this description Lygurge's men precede and follow him in a disorganized manner unusual in a medieval set piece (2117–27, 2153–54). The result is, although these individuals do have a clearly discernible leader, even if he does not go first, the group *qua* group lacks definition or clear outline. In the way they precede and follow their leader, the viewer's perception of them as a group is indirect, 'confused,' a "route" (2153), precisely Ockham's description of the way people perceive universals.[65] For each of these men, therefore, inclusion in this group is secondary to his existence as an individual.

For Aquinas, on the other hand, and in the medieval realist tradition generally, the key concepts are group, hierarchy, and telos. Emetreus's men follow their leader, their description enclosed within his and following his in a properly ranked hierarchical fashion:

An hundred lordes hadde he with hym there,
Al armed, save hir heddes, in al hir gere,
Ful richely in alle maner thynges.

For trusteth wel that dukes, erles, kynges
Were gadered in this noble compaignye,
For love and for encrees of chivalrye. (2179–84)

These men appear only as plurals. They are armed as a group, bare-headed as a group, motivated as a group, and all lumped together into a single group-noun subject without even a conjunction to divide them, "dukes, erles, kynges" (2182, a most unusual construction for Chaucer[66]). Except for Emetreus himself, the passage contains no individuals and no implied individual choices. Rather, his men are all united under the common telos, love and chivalry. In Emetreus's company, therefore, it is the group that really exists, along with the subsidiary groups into which it is subdivided, but its individuals are not individually perceived. Their existence has to be inferred, Thomist perception theory precisely: the intellect knows directly the abstracted *species* (common nature, universal); its knowledge of individuals is indirect.

In these two portraits, for the reader who reasons to their causes (Act 3 of the mind model), Chaucer has summed up the essential points of the realist/nominalist controversy in just eighteen lines— twelve for the nominalists (2118–27, 2153–54) and six for the realists (2179–84). The quarrel, it becomes clear, is not in Reality itself but in the rival perceptions of it. Moreover, at the end of the whole champions' passage, he quietly puts the two rival sides back together again in a single, offhand, subordinate phrase:

And in this wise thise lordes, *alle and some,*
Been on the Sonday to the citee come
Aboute pryme, and in the toun alight. (2187–89,
emphasis added)

The phrase "alle and some" (MnE 'one and all') was already petrified in Chaucer's day; its repetition here, following hard on three "all's" in two lines on Emetreus's company and five "som's" in six lines on Lygurge's, is a striking final reprise of the contrast between the two rival scholastic perceptions of reality, the realists' all and the nominalists' one.

Reasoning to causes from Chaucer's descriptive details in the portraits of these two rival kings—details of their physical appearances, their possessions, and their companies of men—has provided the reader with a good grip on the three core issues in scholastic metaphysics (Causation, Being, and Reality) from the rival positions of the two opposing systems, voluntarist and intellectualist. And the result in fourteenth-century terms is—all the questions those people at Oxford and Paris and Cologne have been debating for so long are not what real people need to be concerned about. All those differences between Lygurge and Emetreus—as to prime faculty, as to oneness of the soul, as to unicity or plurality of forms, as to actuality of prime matter, and so on—all those differences are natural; they pertain to pagans as well as to Christians; vis-à-vis Christian choice they are irrelevant. As pagans, Lygurge and Emetreus are just fulfilling their own natures. Lygurge's natural substance is one hundred percent voluntarist, Emetreus's one hundred percent intellectualist. In these two portraits, not a cause is out of place. There are no anomalies, no incongruities, no evidence of free choice in the Christian sense.

Indeed, when one really ponders them, it becomes clear that the Knight has presented these two kings as opposite extremes. Lygurge is overly primitive, Emetreus overly decorated. Bulls, bearskin, huge lumps of gold set with bright stones, and great muzzled hunting dogs do not suggest their owner has much concern with sustained conceptual thought. And diapered gold horsecloth, pearl-encrusted cashmere, ruby-sparkling mantelet, and fresh-smelling laurel wreath do not suggest *their* owner has much sense of purpose, much serious concern about what he is supposed to be doing here in Athens.

—Little interest in conceptual thinking on one side,
—Little sense of sustained purpose on the other.

Why does the Knight exaggerate in this way? The inference to causes (continuing with Act 3) that now comes to mind is a generalization: that when the human will is totally in charge it can run to barbarism, as does Lygurge; and when the human intellect is totally in charge it can run to surface glitter, as does Emetreus. From this a further inference follows (one that Chaucer's characterization of Theseus has already validated): that the better relationship between these two metaphysical faculties, rather than rivalry, rather than the primacy of either over the other, would be one of mutual cooperation. In this view, as suggested in these two portraits, the will supplies the mind with power, depth, and direction; the intellect supplies organization and an understanding of causes. Both are valuable. Indeed, if the issue were not pagan self-fulfillment, as in these portraits, but Christian trying-to-be-better, cooperation between the two faculties would seem to be most desirable, as Chaucer demonstrates with Theseus. With regard to the metaphysical battles and the rivalries of the university friars, therefore, Chaucer may be suggesting the same—cooperation, and the resulting freedom to serve something better.

This, then, is Chaucer's *sophisma* on Act 3 of the 3-Acts thinking process model. Here in the Knight's Tale, of course, the subject matter has been the two pagan romance kings, but given a theme of rivalry (rather than, say, complementarity or indifference), just about any rivalry would do—farmer versus commodity broker, new critic versus deconstructionist, Monopoly versus Trivial Pursuit. For purposes of constructing a pair of *sophismata* on reasoning to causes in which the chosen theme is rivalry (but without, of course, attempting a Chaucerian-type deep structure demystification of metaphysics), the key components are:

—Two figures from different species of the same genus.
—An understanding of their Aristotelian causes.

Difficult to construct? About equal to a good game of chess, and offering many of the same kinds of pleasures.

FURTHER CHAUCERIAN COMMENTARY ON LOGIC

Exploratory thinking by means of the four causes can be rich and revealing, as just shown. But actual scientific demonstration (valid reasoning from first principles) is binary. Thus, as he did in the Venus/Mars and Diana *sophismata* passages, so too here: Chaucer inserts into these two portraits small but logically devastating disproofs of binary-type either/or thinking.

Traditionally, logic had two standard disproofs—self-contradiction, which the narrator does 'accidentally' in the Lygurge passage, and *reductio ad absurdum,* which the narrator does literally in the Emetreus passage. In the description of the "route" surrounding Lygurge, written according to the nominalist perception of reality as shown earlier, each man is individualized by his own particular choice of armor (haubergeoun, gypoun, Prussian shield, and so forth). Yet, the Knight remarks innocently as he pauses before his summary, "ther is no newe gyse that it nas old," thus 'inadvertently' asserting the universality of all those existentially individualizing choices. The form of this disproof is again another perfect contradiction, a universal negative "no newe gyse" against a series of particular affirmatives "som wol . . . som wol . . . som wol." As for Emetreus, on the other hand, whose company of men is described according to the realist perception of reality as shown earlier, the items in his own personal description are ordered unusually: his personal description concludes with the lily-white eagle on his hand, which is immediately followed by the description of his hundred lords, which is immediately followed by the couplet about his lions and leopards. The result of this ordering is that the reader receives the momentary but delightfully absurd impression that Emetreus's noble company of "dukes, erles, kynges," brought here "for love and for encrees of chivalrye," actually functions to separate his pet bird from his tame jungle cats. Both passages thus contain logically rigorous disproofs of their own informing notions: the considered choices of a bunch of rugged individualists turn out to be the same old "gyse"; and a noble company of the highest chivalric ranks and motives is reduced to separating a bird from some cats. In the real world, Chaucer suggests, human beings perceive *both* individuals and groups, priority depending on circumstance.

By way of concluding summary to the portraits of these two kings, in their descriptions Chaucer has presented us with—in the subject matter, pagan romance epitomes of the two rival metaphysical systems, of which Palamon and Arcite earlier were only instances; in the intricately paralleled contrasts of descriptive details, an experiential double *sophisma* on mental Act 3, inference to causes; and in the descriptions of the two companies of men, witty

III. Thinking Processes and Language Use

disproofs of their own notions of perceiving reality. In short, once again: pagan subject matter, scholastic definition, and comic refutation.

Now, lumping all five of these passages together—the descriptions of the temples of Venus, Mars, and Diana, and of the champion-kings Lygurge and Emetreus—it also seems to me that, for his own trivium-trained audience, in the course of spoofing the scholastic interpretation of the thinking processes, among other things, Chaucer actually goes after the so-called Laws of Thought themselves. These three laws are considered to ground the whole enterprise of logic. They are defined by Boruch Brody in the *Encyclopedia of Philosophy* as follows:

> *Laws of thought.* Three laws of logic that were traditionally treated as basic and fundamental to all thought. They were
> (1) *the law of contradiction,* that nothing can be both P and not-P;
> (2) *the law of excluded middle,* that anything must be either P or not-P; and
> (3) *the law of identity,* that if anything is P, then it is P.[67]

Analytic philosophers still regard these as the very basis of human rationality. Well, here is what happens when Chaucer puts the three of them out for testing in his real world. As just shown, in Chaucer's description of Lygurge's men, individual choices turn out to be both individuating and not-individuating. That disposes of the law of contradiction. Regarding the astrological prediction in Mars's paintings discussed earlier, in real life Julius will be slaughtered and Antony won't, but Nero will be a little of both, slaughtered and not-slaughtered. That disposes of the law of excluded middle. And finally, Lygurge and Emetreus are absolutely, perfectly, consistently human in every way; indeed, each of them embodies *universal* human nature; and yet they are opposed in every respect. That disposes of the law of identity. Any logician would no doubt attack these disproofs of the Laws of Thought by first pointing out that logic does not deal with actual cases in the real world; and, of course, that is precisely one of Chaucer's *sententiae* in these *sophismata*. Logic is artificial, a human construction subject to human manipulation. It is, therefore, not pure, not objective, and not universal; it therefore cannot produce certitude about real human beings in the real world. No matter who is using it, poet or scholastic, logic is always artifice.

Finally, like the glowing multi-paneled stained glass sequences in some Gothic cathedrals, each of these five long descriptions from Part III of the Knight's Tale is rich in itself as well as fitting richly into its larger groupings and the longer overall narrative. Three subjects have been foregrounded in these five passages: suffering, rivalry, and thinking processes. In the three temples the reader has seen every kind of human suffering—inward, outward, and unjust. One question has been strongly raised—as to the cause/purpose/ result of human suffering. In the portraits of the two kings the reader has seen emblems of every kind of human rivalry. One question has been strongly implied—as to the difference to the real world of pagan self-fulfilling rivalries versus the cooperations of Christian free choice. And, finally, by means of the *sophismata* sequence, the reader has undergone experientially the three separate thinking processes. One question has been strongly suggested—as to the adequacy of the 3-Acts model in describing the processes of the human mind. Chaucer closes Part III with Saturn's monologue. In it, the next chapter will show, he magnifies the questions as to human suffering and natural rivalries, raising them to the cosmic level; but at the same time he resolves the question as to the mind model's adequacy by adding subjectivity as a component of universal human nature.

CHAPTER

5

Saturn:
Chaucer's Sophisma
on Human Subjectivity

IN THE KNIGHT'S TALE, Saturn is Chaucer's addition.[68] There is no such character in the *Teseida*. Since Chaucer's Venus, unlike Boccaccio's, does not wield physical power (as shown earlier, her power works inwardly, inside the beholder's mind), she cannot reasonably sponsor a knight in a physical combat. Chaucer therefore adds to Boccaccio's plot the planet who can best provide his Venus with the power over physical matter she lacks—the outermost, most powerful planet, the Greater Infortune, Saturn. In his monologue closing Part III, Chaucer characterizes his Saturn as a typical anthropomorphic pagan deity, completely convinced of his own great powers, easily swayed by his "doghter's" tears, and totally indifferent to the human pain he causes.

At the same time, Chaucer shapes Saturn's monologue to form the final *sophisma* on thinking acts and language use in the Knight's Tale, a *sophisma* putting forward his own thoughtful solution to the deficiencies of the scholastic model. In this monologue, to the traditional three thinking activities of simple apprehension of objects, judgment of complex propositions, and reasoning, Chaucer adds affections, historicity, allusions, and blind spots. These too are active powers in natural (i.e., fallen) thinking. Chaucer's final *sophisma* thus presents the reader with an experiential definition of real human subjectivity. First I will show that Chaucer has shaped Saturn's monologue to include each of the three traditional thinking acts. Then I will show Chaucer's additions to the three acts. And finally I will show that, apparently in order to establish subjectivity as a real universal (i.e., two instances), Chaucer has interlocked his two very different resolution-figures: both Saturn and Theseus manifest recognizable subjectivity, the former fulfilling his own nature, the latter becoming better.

Saturn's speech is divided into two parts, self-description (2453–69) and promise to Venus (2470–78). Much of Saturn's self-description is in the form of a list of objects, to be perceived as if by simple apprehension (i.e., Act I again):

> Myn is the drenchyng in the see so wan;
> Myn is the prison in the derke cote;
> Myn is the stranglyng and hangyng by the throte,
> The murmure and the cherles rebellyng,
> The groynynge, and the pryvee empoysonyng; . . . (2456–60)

> Myn is the ruyne of the hye halles,
> The fallynge of the toures and of the walles
> Upon the mynour or the carpenter. . . . (2463–65)

> And myne be the maladyes colde,
> The derke tresons, and the castes olde; (2467–68)

The customary figures Saturn lists here are like those of Venus; they are abstractions: "the drenchyng," "the stranglyng," "the pryvee empoysonyng," and so on. The combination of singular noun (in this case, gerund) with timeless present tense ("myn is . . .") makes these objects seem like personifications, but they are in fact universals of actions. What the reader does grasp here by means of his physical senses are not the actions themselves, but the places and objects in and on which these shadowless universals perform their work: "the see so wan," "the throte," "the toures," and so on. Thus Saturn's customary figures, like Venus's, are universals rather than particularized individuals, but unlike those of Venus, they do have power over corporeal matter. In this respect, they are like those of Mars. With regard to noise, Saturn lists the universals of murmuring and grumbling. Like Venus with her "allas's," the noises associated with him are quiet. Any louder noises of his victims would be muffled, by the sea or inside the strangled throat, just as any bodies of his victims would be hidden from view, inside the prison or under the fallen walls. With his lack of visible blood and gore and lack of piercing screams and outcry, in this regard Saturn is again more compatible with Venus than with Mars. So far as suffering is concerned, Saturn, again like Venus, has a list of symptoms—"the maladyes colde, the derke tresons, and the castes olde," each with its particularizing adjective and each pluralized so that the reader's mind cannot turn it into a personification. These constructions parallel Venus's "the broken slepes," "the sikes colde," and so on. Samson, the one victim Saturn identifies by name, was actually trapped first by Venus, although Saturn claims credit for his demise. Thus, in the kinds of objects he lists for the reader's apprehension, Chaucer allies his pagan-romance Saturn with his Venus, but in the fact that they are objects in a list for the reader to apprehend simply, they are part of his final *sophisma* on thinking processes. In his model of the human mind, therefore, Chaucer does include Act 1.

Next, Saturn puts forward four propositions in his self-description; apparently these are to be cognized as if by Act 2, judgment of complex propositions.

Proposition

My cours, that hath so wyde for to turne,	1
Hath moore power than woot any man. (2454–55)	
I do vengeance and pleyne correccioun,	2
Whil I dwelle in the signe of the leoun. (2461–62)	
I slow Sampsoun, shakynge the piler; (2466)	3
My lookyng is the fader of pestilence. (2469)	4

All four propositions concern Saturn's power. In the Knight's Tale, he, like Mars, wields his power through the stars of the physical universe. The question is, does he wield it freely, as he claims to here? Actually, as shown earlier, the fires on Diana's altar had predicted his solution a hundred lines before he found it himself in that "olde experience" of his (2331–40, 2443–46). Moreover, a Saturnian champion had shown up to help Palamon three hundred lines before Venus appealed to Saturn for his help (2128, 2438). Still, in this speech, Saturn obviously believes he is a free agent.

To solve this contradiction, the reader must reason to causes, that is, put aside Act 2 for a moment and cognize by means of Act 3. Chaucer helps by enclosing the little six-line subsection requiring inference with a rare (for Chaucer) initial rhyme ("I do" and "I slow"):

> I do vengeance and pleyn correccioun
> Whil I dwelle in the signe of the leoun
> Myn is the ruyne of the hye halles
> The fallyng of the toures and of the walles
> Vpon the mynour or the carpenter
> I slow Sampson shakyng the piler . . . (2461–66 MR)

Two allusions are involved here: Samson's death and the sign of the lion. With regard to Samson's death, the Lord himself always dealt directly with Samson. Samson was consecrated to the Lord from before his conception; and until he lost his hair (the sign of his consecration) through his own foolishness and lust and in spite of repeated warnings, the Spirit of the Lord moved directly in him, especially when he was involved with Philistines. At the end, eyeless in Gaza but with his hair starting to regrow, Samson prayed to the Lord for strength, vengeance, and death, and (exactly like Chaucer's two young knights) he received precisely what he prayed for. For Saturn to claim credit for his death here in the Knight's Tale is preposterous. At most, Saturn could have been only a subsidiary agency fulfilling the prescribed course of the Lord. And second, with regard to the "signe of the leoun," Johnstone Parr has shown that "vengeance and correction are not to be found as peculiar to Saturn in the astrological manuals, and that the planet is not often said to be more malignant in Leo than in other signs."[69] The question arises, then, what does the "signe of the leoun" refer to? Immediately preceding a reference to Samson's end, the possibility arises of a deliberately equivocal reference to Samson's beginning and his lion riddle. The whole story comprises Chapter 14 of the Book of Judges. It begins with Samson falling in love with a Philistine woman, *quod res a Domino fieret, et quaereret occasionem contra Philisthiim*; it contains a lion that Samson slays whose carcass later swarms with bees whose honey Samson eats; and it ends with Samson, *irruit itaque in eum spiritus Domini,* killing and despoiling thirty of the Philistine men in order to fulfill ironically the terms of the riddle game which the Philistines had freely entered into with him and then cheated in order to win.[70] In the Samson story, the 'sign of the lion' is the sign of the Lord's occasion. In his monologue here in the Knight's Tale, Saturn clearly intends the "signe of the leoun" to carry astrological meaning, the same kind of meaning he finds in Samson's death. But reference to 'the sign of the lion,' followed by reference to high halls, falling towers, and Samson shaking the pillar, can also bring to the reader's mind the story of Samson's first move and first victory against the Philistines, just as reference to his death can bring to the reader's mind his last move and final victory over them. And, as in the Lygurge/Emetreus *sophismata,* inference from the fact that animals and planets can act only naturally (i.e., not freely) back to their First Cause corroborates the solution to the contradiction about his power from which we started. The solution is, the Knight's Tale Saturn is not free. He wields his great power on earth in ignorance of the Divine Providence whose natural instrument he really is.

As a result, returning now to the four propositions in Saturn's self-description, the first on his wide course is True (at least it was in Chaucer's time); the third claiming credit for Samson's death is False; and the other two on vengeance and pestilence are problematic (at least for a twentieth-century reader at this stage of our knowledge). In any event, however, the result is that in Saturn's monologue all three thinking acts have been shown to be present: lists of objects for simple apprehension, complex propositions for judgment, and reasoning to causes. By scholastic thinking, these are the universal thinking acts, common to all men of all times and places.

Let us turn now to Chaucer's additions: affections, historicity, allusions, and blind spots. The point here is that these additions add natural human subjectivity. Today we are accustomed to think of characters in terms of whether or not they have been individualized, but that is too strong a term for what Chaucer does here. In philosophic terms, all Chaucer needs to demonstrate in order to break out of (refute) the universality tradition is particularity—particular knowledge, particular age, particular family, and so on. To say that Saturn has been individualized would be an overstatement. But it is easy to show that he has been particularized—as a delightfully pompous, indulgent, elderly grandfather figure.

In Chaucer's time, Saturn was the slowest moving of the planets; and there is a correspondingly slow, ponderous quality to his monologue, achieved partly by its splendidly sententious opening ("My deere doghter Venus" followed by sixteen lines of solemn pronouncements), partly by the repeated long vowels and nasals of "myn," and partly by the syntactic inversions with their linguistically-mandatory pauses for displacement:

> Myn is the drenchyng in the see so wan;
> Myn is the prison in the derke cote;
> Myn is the stranglyng . . . (2456–58)

The slow, measured quality thus achieved amplifies this Saturn's awesome sense of self-importance. In the first seventeen lines of his monologue, every sentence and two of the phrases begin with "I," "my," or "myn"; and most of these instances stand at the head of their lines. In the speech as a whole, these three self-important words appear fourteen times. Twenty of the lines are directly concerned with his exercise of power. In short, Saturn is not unimpressed with his own earthshaking responsibilities. In addition, he is a most indulgent grandfather. His affection for Venus is manifested in the last nine lines of his speech, where, after subjecting her (and us) to this long self-satisfied preamble on his power, he finally promises to do as she asks, as fond grandfathers faced with weeping granddaughters usually do.

> Now weep namoore, I shal doon diligence
> That Palamon, that is thyn owene knyght,
> Shal have his lady, as thou hast him hight.

III. *Thinking Processes and Language Use*

Though Mars shal helpe his knyght, yet nathelees
Bitwixe yow ther moot be som tyme pees,
Al be ye noght of o compleccioun
That causeth al day swich divisioun.
I am thyn aiel, redy at thy wille;
Weep now namoore, I wol thy lust fulfille. (2470–78)

This final subsection for Venus herself both begins and ends with a comforting 'now weep no more.' In it Saturn tells Venus not once but three times that he will do her will, both for her own sake and for the sake of the neighbors (2476). Thus Saturn's monologue shows us a natural (i.e., fallen) mind at work—a mind with real thinking (i.e., more than the 3-Acts model), real speech (with tones, phrasing, repetitions, and inversions), real pomposity, real affection, real blindness about the relationship between human suffering and divine causes, and with allusions to a real miracle. Among other things, Chaucer has given Saturn affections (for both himself and his granddaughter); historicity (particular places, particular times,[71] specific activities, a particular family); and allusions and blind spots that establish a particular stock of knowledge. All these play an active, shaping part in his thinking processes in this speech. Saturn is not individualized in modern terms, but he is certainly particularized in the terms of the fourteenth century. His is a natural subjectivity—he fulfills his own inclinations. He knows nothing higher.

Above all, the Knight's Tale portrait of Saturn is shaped by Chaucer's decision to insert the whole issue of subjectivity, both its thinking processes and its language use, into the universal psychology of his time. In the pagan romance narrative, Saturn's presence in the Knight's Tale is necessitated by Chaucer's characterization of Venus as outwardly inactive and therefore needing help in the tournament. But the fact that Saturn appears in the form of a dramatic monologue, rather than, say, a temple description and statue, is necessitated by Chaucer's larger Part III point: immaterial subjectivity is real; it shapes our thoughts and behaviors; it must, therefore, on truth grounds, be included in any adequate theory of universal human psychology.

However, there is more. Chaucer has interlocked the two resolutions, Theseus and the *disputatio* on faculty psychology with Saturn and the *sophismata* sequence on thinking processes. First, Saturn is interlocked into the faculty psychology debate by his particular deficiencies. The evils Chaucer depicts in his Knight's Tale characterization stem from two specific underlying lacks, one in his intellect, the other in his will. Overall, Saturn's behavior in the Knight's Tale is appalling, as is his general characterization throughout medieval astrology. Of the seven planets, Saturn is the worst, the greatest "infortune." He has the widest course of power and the greatest range of evils. And he is disgustingly secret, burrowing in and around here and there, plotting silently behind everyone's back. Aspects of his particular characterization here in the Knight's Tale, however, result from two unusual underlying lacks. First, Saturn does not know his place in the universe. He does not know there is a Prime Mover, and as a result, he does not realize that his own actions in some way follow from it. This deficiency in his intellect causes his pride, his pomposity. And second, he doesn't care about the consequences of his actions on any beings beyond his own immediate circle. He does not care how much suffering his movements cause others, either directly or inadvertently. Not knowing and not caring are, therefore, major facets of his Knight's Tale characterization—in scholastic terms, the one a deficiency of his intellect, the other a deficiency in the affections of his will.

As for Theseus, on the other hand, although his characterization as resolution figure of the will/intellect *disputatio* focused primarily on freedom and learning to be better, he is interlocked into the sequence of *sophismata* by Chaucer's emphasis on his subjectivity, especially in the second half of Part II (1663–1880).[72] After Theseus condemns the two young knights to death and hears the ladies plead, the reader listens in on twenty-four lines of his inward thought processes as he reasons to himself in his mind and in his heart, universalizing the two knights' behavior, considering the plight of women, and lecturing himself on how lords should behave (1760–84). This is followed by forty more lines of Theseus's outward subjectivity, as he speaks about the God of Love's power,

the foolishness of his servants, for example these two, the oblivi-
ousness of their quarry, and the reasons for forgiving them (1785–
1825). This is then followed by another forty lines spelling out not
for himself, but for the two young knights, the ladies, and the
reader, the terms of what he convinces everybody is a fair resolution of the problem (1829–69). In short, Chaucer is presenting to
us here, at great length, examples of a man's inward subjectivity
and outward subjectivity, and juxtaposing them with a sample of
explicit outward communication, in a full spectrum of thinking
acts and language uses, both inward and outward. These lines do
not individualize Theseus, although they make him seem remarkably human. Rather, given the context of a philosophical *disputatio*
about universal human nature, in which, as discussed in Chapter
2, Theseus's mind is shown to be free and to learn from its particular
experiences, these lines universalize subjectivity. They formally
include subjectivity (the particularity of one's thinking processes
and language use) within Chaucer's own embodiment of universal
psychology.

To conclude here, Saturn resolves the 3-Acts *sophismata* sequence
in the Knight's Tale transept, so to speak, just as Theseus resolved
the will/intellect faculty *disputatio* in its side aisles. Saturn's portrait
argues that human subjectivity must be included in any universal
psychology on the basis of truth. His particularity is real. Theseus's
portrait argues that human subjectivity must be included in any
universal psychology on the basis of virtue. This is because, if
freedom is liberation of the subjective mind to find, know, honor,
and serve something higher than itself (and this *is* what happens to
Theseus in the tale), then, on ethical grounds too, subjectivity must
be part of any practical theory of universal human nature. As a
result, Chaucer's universal psychology incorporates subjectivity
on the bases of both truth, the object of the intellect, and value,
the object of the will.

6

The Method of a Universal Psychology: Logic versus Experience

THE TITLE OF this chapter is another gestalt figure. Depending on the ground one is using for context, the method of a universal psychology may be the methodology of the investigator, as he or she goes about selecting the objects to be studied and the questions to be asked, formulating principles, collecting data, accepting certain kinds of evidence, rejecting others, and setting the standards of acceptable proof. Or, on the other hand, the method of a universal psychology may be the methodology of its Maker, the methodology by which its Maker offers to improve and save it. The former methodology is scientific, searching for objective new knowledge about finished facts; the latter methodology is humanistic, fostering the ongoing development of individual human beings. Chaucer's universal psychology is doing both.

The Knight's Tale *disputatio* and *sophismata* have suggested major flaws in scholastic methodology. They have suggested that inadequacies arise in traditional scholastic theorizing, intellectualist and voluntarist alike, from two fundamental mistakes in their method: their over-reliance on logic and their choice of the wrong aspects of the Divine Nature to use as starting point.

As to over-reliance on logic, both the *disputatio* and the *sophismata* sequence suggest that Chaucer understood formal logic well, found it valuable, and used it easily, but that he regarded absolute faith in it as unrealistic. On the one hand, the overall logic of Chaucer's

III. Thinking Processes and Language Use

approach is what turns the Knight's Tale into serious scholastic philosophy. As has been shown, the various concepts he uses (will, intellect, substance, prime matter, perception, and the like) and the literary forms in which he argues them (disputation and *sophismata*) are those of the scholastic philosophers. Further, the method by which he argues is logical. His paralleled contrasts and his minutely interlocking figures—and I am thinking here of the dozens, scores, hundreds of carefully chosen implications that dovetail exactly to form, for example, the truth table in the Diana passage, or the inference puzzles in the portraits of Lygurge and Emetreus, or the contrasts of causes versus judgments and choices in the speeches of the three principals, or the specialized free will and submission dictions attached to and then exchanged between the two young knights—this rigorous, quantitatively-based figurative logic, which Chaucer apparently devised for the Knight's Tale, possesses at least as much certitude as the literal logic of the scholastics. A professional logician, whether fourteenth-century or twentieth-century, would always be free to reject the Knight's Tale discussion, but I doubt she or he could refute it. Chaucer's arguments for freedom, for learning from experience, and for the subjectivity that makes them both possible, are logically sound.

On the other hand, and at the same time, Chaucer's Knight's Tale also undercuts every claim of traditional logic to be anything more than a man-made invention, a useful tool for manipulating abstractions, totally at the beck of its fallible human users, dependent for its value not on the nature of ultimate metaphysical reality, but merely on the skill, intelligence, judgment, and—most difficult of all to apprehend and eliminate—the personal values of its human users. The Knight's Tale shows, for example, that even the axioms of traditional logic are to some degree subjective. People choose whether to believe that the conjunction of a True and a True automatically produces a True, just as they choose whether to believe that the fierce pagan goddess of chastity and the hunt might actually take pity on an unchaste woman. People choose, further, whether to believe that one faculty is or should be superior to the other, just as they choose which faculty it should be. Such choices are based on subjectively-held values prior to the "objectivity" of logic, the Knight's Tale suggests. The influence of prior values explains how different scholastic thinkers, using the same logic, could come to competing conclusions about psychology, just as the influence of their faith in scientific demonstration explains how they could overlook the remarkably binary results of their metaphysics. As a thinking, analyzing, composing, and persuading tool, logic is invaluable, as the Knight's Tale shows; but as the single tool for developing an adequate theory of universal psychology, logic is not enough. It is necessary but not sufficient.

Here the question of Chaucer's own audience arises again. What of all this logic and anti-logic would they have understood? I think they would have recognized fairly easily the will/intellect embodiments, the 3-Acts mind model sequence, and the suggested return to the freer, more traditonal and Boethian psychology. These ideas were part of their culture. As for the details of the Part III *sophismata* sequence, my own sense is that they would have understood the major issues. For that matter, any twentieth-century reader, once clued in to the thinking theories, is going to notice immediately the difference between lists of objects and summaries of stories. Perhaps only the university educated would have been able to appreciate fully the demystification of scholastic metaphysics in the descriptions of Lygurge and Emetreus; but surely any medieval reader would have caught immediately, on first reading, the som-som-som of the nominalists as opposed to the all-all-all of the realists in the descriptions of their companies of men, as well as the Saturnian/Martial and griffin/lion contrasts in their own physical descriptions. As to Chaucer's examples of formal logic, both its use and its undercutting, my feeling is that his audience would have understood a good deal. Some of the Knight's Tale anti-logic smacks of generations of schoolboy wit and wisdom. Nero's death, particularly, sounds like a well-honed, highly treasured grammar-class joke, one that would have produced the same glee, no doubt, as our own generation experienced on proving that $1 = 0$ in algebra class. Today, unfortunately, there is apparently no way of ascertaining the schoolboy jokes of Chaucer's day. My intuition says there are a good number of them in the Knight's Tale his own audience recognized with delight.

III. Thinking Processes and Language Use

But, in any event, whatever they were, and however much or little Chaucer's own audience would have recognized or understood, does not change the logic and anti-logic that is actually there in the tale. Too many variables interlock to be explained away simply as chance or *aventure*. Chaucer's Knight's anti-logic suggests that the scholastics' theorizing has relied too heavily on logic and not enough on pondering their own outward experiences and inward thoughts.

Similarly, as to choice of starting point for a science of human nature, the Knight's Tale suggests, one should pick carefully the aspects of the Divine Nature one chooses to use. No doubt it is true, as the Bible says, that human beings are made in God's image; but God lacks ignorance, weakness, and malevolence. He has no need to change, no need to become better. He certainly has no need to be saved. Therefore, important differences exist, one might say, between God and man. Historically, the scholastic will/intellect debate was as much about the nature of God as of man. Indeed, twentieth-century historians of philosophy tend to focus the debate almost entirely on God. The scholastic philosophers, on the other hand, apparently reasoned back and forth between the two in order to parallel the concepts in which the natures of both were thought about. Since the scholastics thought of God as a separate, immaterial entity, they tended to think of the immaterial human soul in the same way. And since they thought of God as existing outside the processes of moment-by-moment, day-by-day change and development, they tended to think of human souls as likewise. They tended to think that the important things about human beings were the things in them that were separate and alike-in-everybody and not subject to change, for example their inborn faculties; and thus they dismissed from their thinking the subjectivity and daily social experiences of individual human beings. Reinforcing this dismissal was the fact that speculation in these two areas, individual subjectivity and daily social interaction, was by definition not universal and therefore could not produce, so they thought, the scientific certitude they respected.

Chaucer, on the other hand, was apparently fascinated by individual subjectivity and the effect of daily social experience on it.

(It would not be difficult to argue, I think, that this is the major subject of the *Canterbury Tales* taken as a whole, the give-and-take relationship between social interaction on the one hand, and individual subjectivity [its values, motives, languages, and thinking processes] on the other.) Chaucer therefore starts his theory of universal psychology from two other aspects of God, not from his separateness and immutability, but rather from his subjectivity and social interaction in this world of time and process and change. In the Bible, God walks around in Eden in the cool of the day. He takes sides. He takes part in the world. He fasts. He preaches. He teaches. He sometimes speaks figuratively, in parables. God makes time and worldly experience for us to learn to be better in, the Knight's Tale characterization of Theseus proposes. Living in the world therefore has the possibility of immaterial value for us, as it did for Theseus. This difference in methodology—in formulating the Divine Object to be studied and reasoned from, whether abstracted unchanging Universal or particular Individual active within the created world—accounts for many of the differences between Palamon and Arcite on the one hand, and Theseus on the other. As a result, as embodiments of universal psychologies, where Palamon and Arcite often seem fixed, Theseus seems real. As he wavers between condemning and pardoning the two young knights in Part II, his subjective thinking processes are lifelike. And as he realizes during Part IV that in this world there are always going to be discrepancies between intention and outcome, his change in style of thinking and, as a result, in style of ruling is motivated in a subtle, lifelike way. As the starting point for a theory of universal human nature as it exists in this real world, the Knight suggests, it makes more sense to start with what we know of real Human Nature as it was incarnated in this real world.

From the humanist point of view, belief in a purely objective methodology is like belief in an absolutely certain result—on the one hand a will-o'-the-wisp, on the other potentially dangerous if accepted uncritically. Scholastic scientists believe pure objectivity is possible; humanists do not. Philosophically speaking, at least from the humanist point of view, how is it possible to be completely objective about a world one is inside of and cannot escape?

III. Thinking Processes and Language Use

or about a culture one is inside of? or about a language one is inside of? Some degree of objectivity is always achievable, of course, and one should try for whatever degree is appropriate to the matter at hand; but absolute objectivity about anything important can never be achieved in this life. It is simply not possible. The human mind is too restless, too powerful. In the modern scientific world, the dream of pure objectivity finally died with Heisenberg. As he showed, in concrete physical fact one cannot totally escape one's point of view, no matter how one shifts it, no matter where one stands. Nor, Chaucer implies in the Knight's Tale, can one totally escape one's particular values and personal knowledge or lack of it. If anyone is capable of objectivity about the world, it should be Saturn in the Knight's Tale, since, although he is inside the sphere of the universe, he is the furthest removed from the world. Yet during the Saturn passage in Part III, in what seems to be a four-teenth-century disproof in Ptolemaic terms of the possibility of absolute objectivity, Chaucer shows that there is more to thinking than the rational, objectifiable processes of the scholastic 3-Acts model. Before the passage, Chaucer's Knight implies that Saturn's solution to the strife between Venus and Mars will be impartial:

> . . . the pale Saturnus the colde,
> That knew so manye of aventures olde,
> Foond in his olde experience an art
> That he ful soone hath plesed every part.
> As sooth is seyd, elde hath greet avantage;
> In elde is bothe wysdom and usage. (2443–48)

During his monologue, however, his own simple apprehension of objects, judgment of complex propositions, and inference to causes are shown to be shaped by his own particular subjectivity—his own pomposity, affection for Venus, ignorance of the higher divine, and indifference to human pain. Thus, as Ockham would put it, a different Saturn might have found (or thought he found) a different solution. In a Christian context, like the claim of scientific certitude discussed earlier in the chapter on goals, the claim of pure objectivity in method can be damaging. People who believe in objectivity always think they have it, and the belief can restrict their openness to the ideas and feelings of others. Rather than learning, belief in total objectivity can promote ignorance. Rather than empathy, it can promote indifference. Rather than humility, it can promote pride. Chaucer's Saturn exhibits all three.

As a result of his changes in basic methodology—less faith in logic and a different (and more traditional) Divine Role-Model—in addition to arguing for total freedom, Chaucer's universal psychology adds to the universal psychology of the scholastics three key, interrelated (and quite Boethian), humanist methods: process, subjectivity, and figurative language.

Process is necessary to the concepts of both learning and change. Universals, obviously, never change; immutability is part of their definition. In this respect, they are very Greek. In a Christian humanist context, on the other hand, the possibility for people to change, hopefully for the better, has to be considered a universal. It therefore must be included in any theory of psychology. The difficulties the scholastics experienced in trying to include day-to-day change within their universal psychologies were touched on earlier. Among other things, those difficulties account for the miraculous quality of the personality changes in the Part III prayers, when, like a comic-opera changing of the guards, Palamon suddenly about-faces from demanding to submissive and Arcite suddenly about-faces in the opposite direction, from passive to assertive. Those two surprising reversals suggest that, for Chaucer, the kind of radical change both scholastic psychologies postulate is too sudden, too sweeping, and not well motivated. This is not true of Chaucer's theory of psychology, however. His Theseus undergoes equally radical change, from outwardly precipitate to inwardly thoughtful, but it takes place slowly and almost imperceptibly, over a long period of years; and although his changes are sweeping, they are well motivated from specific incidents in his own personal experience. Theseus is only one instance, of course, and he is a theoretical rather than "real" character; but in some of Chaucer's "real" characters—the Wife of Bath, say, or the Pardoner or the Reeve—Chaucer makes sure that what his reader sees will not seem a sudden characterization sprung full blown. Rather, such characters seem to be the realistic outcome of a long, slow, steady process of repeated incidents of a certain type in their individual histories, and of repeated choices as to the meaning of those incidents. Thus, as discussed earlier in Chapter 2 on Theseus, Chaucer's theory of universal psychology includes a universal *process*—experience in this world—which every human being undergoes. In Chaucer's psychology, worldly social interaction is the Maker's methodology, the process by which the Maker provides for every individual a constant, continuing, sometimes painful pressure to make meaning of his or her experiences, and, therefore, provides a constant continuing opportunity for individual thought, judgment, choice, and, hopefully, change for the better.

Subjectivity, as already shown, is the second key humanist method Chaucer adds to scholastic psychological theory. Theseus's subjectivity as revealed in his Prime Mover speech resulted, at least in part, from the processes of his own day-to-day social interaction with other human beings, including the ladies-in-black and carnage at Thebes and his close friendship with Arcite and evaluation of Palamon, as well as his own thinking, feeling, and judging about those interactions, his choices as to what to make them mean, and finally his own subsequent behavioral choices as a result of those meanings. Subjectivity and the process of particular worldly experiences are thus central methodological concerns for Chaucer as "maker." Further, unlike the two scholastic psychologies, Chaucer's psychology is quite open. It does not specify which faculty, will or intellect, is or should be prime in any particular individual, suggesting a process of cooperation depending on context instead. Nor does it specify either path to virtue, willing submission to the divine or rational ordering of the faculties, although Theseus does seem to achieve both. And it leaves open and unspecified the way in which human souls are individuated as they come into the world, whether *ab initio* or on combining with prime matter or by particular prime matter. And it further leaves open and unspecified God's way of working in the world, whether by distant natural cause or special personal intrusion as well and/or others. All these questions, the Knight's Tale implies, are interesting to think about, but given the natural differences between people, they are probably not capable of resolution in this world. That being the case, future speculation might focus more profitably on questions about subjectivity. For example, what are the interrelationships between the incidents of our own personal experience, the subjective knowledge we receive and make from them, and our resulting concepts, judgments, and behavior. If we learn from our own particular experiences, can we still be totally free and therefore totally responsible? In short, by emphasizing process and subjectivity in his theory of universal psychology, Chaucer is actually arguing for a return to the humanist concerns of traditional pastoral Christianity.

Figurative language use, a third key humanist element Chaucer adds to the psychological theory of his own time, had been an important methodology in traditional prescientific Christianity. Indeed, in view of the figurative language used throughout the Bible, it had been a methodology favored by God himself. The difficult passages of the Bible had traditionally been regarded as pluses, put there by their Author for individual readers to interpret subjectively with effort, pleasure, and profit at whatever level was appropriate for their understanding at the time. Indeed, the principal methodology of traditional biblical exegesis had consisted of these same three components—the learning process, subjectivity, and interpreting figurative language. Increasingly, however, from the twelfth century on, the literalizing, objectifying, universalizing tendency of Aristotelian science had shifted the point of biblical interpretation from the effect of the passage on its reader to the exact meaning of the text. Difficult passages were to be rendered not intelligible by the levels of interpretation, but correct by the new sciences of grammar, logic, and signification. In the course of time, as traditional exegetical interpretation of the Bible was devalued, so too was allegorical interpretation of the texts of the classical poets.[73] During the twelfth century, the literal sense became the only "objective" sense; and thus in the thirteenth century, apparently in order to keep the figurative passages of the Bible valuable, Aquinas wound up defining them as literal too. Under these historical circumstances, Chaucer's Knight's Tale constitutes a rigorously argued revalidation of figurative language as a method for conveying and/or discovering and/or evoking

III. Thinking Processes and Language Use

important truths, a revalidation which also revalidates personal experience as a method for conveying and/or discovering and/or evoking important truths, spiritual, intellectual, and ethical. The tale's romance fiction is pagan; yet embedded in it the reader discovers, first, well-known scientifically-demonstrated scholastic truths set forth in well-known scholastic genres; and then discovers, second, that their resolutions consist of scientific demonstrations of well-known and long-valued *humanist* truths. The precision of thought and language in the Knight's Tale is that of a scholastic *summa*. In it Chaucer's manipulation of simultaneously presented multiple meanings is a linguistic tour de force. In extended verbal virtuosity I know of nothing to equal it, especially the Part III *sophismata*. In these passages, Chaucer first demonstrates that, as a methodology, figurative language can convey exactly the same truths as literal language can, with the same degree of certitude and a good deal more succinctly. And then he shows that figurative language can in fact convey a good deal more.

Chaucer's is a universal psychology that is good for people to know. Rather than limiting their freedom, dismissing their personal experiences, and spurning their subjectivity, it foregrounds their individual value as human beings and their potential for development. Indeed, it is itself fostering the positive development of individual human beings. Further, although written for a Christian audience, it is a universal psychology not limited to Christians. All three principals are pagan, yet Palamon and Arcite become theoretically "parfit"; Theseus (more realistically) simply becomes better. Theories of this magnitude cannot be proven, of course; but with its emphasis on two things all of us do know—the fact of inward human subjectivity and the fact of outward social experience—Chaucer's universal psychology seems much more general, much more inclusive, and yet much more realistic than the theories of the scholastics who preceded him. In this, of course, he profited from their thinking as well as learned from their mistakes; and in this also he leads the way into the humanism of the Renaissance, with its rejection of abstract universals and the methodology of logic, and its focus on human experience of itself in the real world.

SECTION IV

Universal Psychologies: Makers and Contexts

— ADDING REALITY —

CHAPTER 7. The Knight

CHAPTER 8. The Pilgrimage Reality

CHAPTER 9. Chaucerian Didacticism

BACKGROUND

Chaucer apparently thought the "making" of a universal psychology to be a process both more personal and more social than the scholastics did and than we do now. Today, most of us would expect a psychological theory of this magnitude to be constructed by social scientists in a university laboratory situation, working from statistical data gathered in carefully controlled experiments on patients, volunteers, graduate students, and mice. All very logical, all very replicable. In this regard, the objective, abstractive spirit of the scholastic scientists, of Aquinas, Scotus, Ockham, and their contemporaries, lives on. Given the shifts in start-point from written authority to living organism, and in methodology from verbal to quantitative logic, much of twentieth-century psychological science is not very different from that of Chaucer's time. The goal is still discovery of new truth of universal scope; the method is still rational abstraction.

Actually, however, such scientifically-constructed psychologies are but the tip of the iceberg. In actual fact, universal psychologies are being constructed by all of us, in our minds, from everything that happens to us, every day of our lives. Our own experiences with people teach us what they are like. Our experiences with people at home, at work, at play, in social life and literature and art, cause each of us to generalize about people and to construct subjectively our own universal psychologies. In this sense, we are all makers. This is the Chaucerian insight that has him begin the *Canterbury Tales* with his Knight's Tale. In this way of thinking, the very first theory of universal psychology was constructed by God; Adam was its first embodiment; and human beings have been emulating both divine activities ever since, creating new human beings with our bodies, obviously, but also, each of us individually, creating our own idea of human nature in our mind, that is, "making" our own subjective universal psychologies on which we then base our everyday expectations, conversations, and actions vis-à-vis others. This is another reason why Chaucer's inquiry into human nature, as evidenced in the Knight's Tale, shifts focus from the outward objective ontology the scholastics studied to the inward subjectivity of the individual human mind in the course of its day-to-day existence and development. Instead of asking, "Is man free?" Chaucer asks, "What effect does Arcite's belief that he is not free have on his behavior?" In this way Chaucer raises the question not of belief in the abstract, but of individual human beliefs—where do they come from? why this belief rather than that? why does one man believe he is free and another believe he is not? By adding subjectivity to his universal psychology, then, Chaucer moves the making of a universal psychology out from the academic cloister and into the real world. Here, as Chaucer shows, rather than just another abstract hypothesis, a theory of universal psychology becomes an instrument of great temporal power, capable of doing immense harm or immense good to the human beings who believe in it.

For example, in the real world, individuals who believe they are free/capable/responsible behave very differently from individuals who believe they are not free/capable/responsible. In Part I, when he believed himself bound by the stars, Arcite sat and complained about them; in Parts III and IV, however, now believing himself free, he prays, wins the tournament, and, as he dies, finally comes to value Palamon as Palamon deserves. Contrariwise, in Parts I and II, when Palamon believed himself free and capable, he prayed, made plans, and finally escaped; but in Part IV, believing himself no longer free and responsible, after losing the tournament he gives up on Emelye and goes quietly home to Thebes. Theseus, on the other hand, believes himself free/capable/responsible throughout; during the first half he thoughtlessly caused a lot of unnecessary suffering; during the second half he realizes it and tries to do better. Chaucer's point in these instances is that our own subjective beliefs as to whether or not we are free/capable/responsible—i.e., our own individual theories of universal psychology—exert a profound influence on our behavior. Thus, Chaucer suggests, making our own theory of universal psychology is an extremely important activity for each of us individually. When someone teaches us that we are not free/capable/responsible, whether by reason of some "natural necessity" or some "divine revelation," something is wrong. In a Christian context, we are being mistaught.

Similarly, as with makers, so with background circumstances. Chaucer apparently conceived the context of a universal psychology differently than the scholastics did and somewhat differently than humanists do today. We no longer try to think of human nature as set off in a vacuum, completed, abstracted from real life, as the scholastics seem to have done. For Chaucer as for most twentieth-century humanists, the context of a universal psychology is the real world. One's conception of "the real world," however, will shape one's notion of the freedoms and choices it offers. Chaucer's sense of the universe being somewhat different from ours, his freedoms and options will be somewhat differently conceived from ours.

Today, when we look up into the sky and think of outer space, we think of blackness, silence, deep cold, endless reaches and endless time, of isolation and alienation. For us, outer space is scary and is hostile to human life. The later medieval "sense" of the universe was quite different. When Chaucer looked up into the sky and thought of outer space, he thought of a considerably cozier cosmos. He looked up through at least eight gleaming translucent concentric spheres, each enclosing the earth within its heavenly brilliance, each revolving around the earth at the benevolent behest of the great Prime Mover, all eight together creating beautiful harmonies, raining down light and music and complex influences, mostly benign and all providential, all of this going on for the express benefit of human beings, including himself, for whose sake it was created in the first place. Two such different "senses" of the universe—one endlessly, vastly indifferent; the other closed and infinitely caring—will naturally generate, in spite of our using the same words, two very different "senses" of metaphysical freedom. We today tend to think of metaphysical freedom as open, endless, and isolated, like our sense of space. As a result, for most of us metaphysical choice has become a personal decision that can be postponed indefinitely until convenient (so long as it is made before death); and it has come to seem a kind of voluntary limitation, so to speak, by which one closes off some options. We oppose this freedom to various kinds of determinism, biological and social, of which the subject has little if any knowledge and over which no control. Judging from the conclusion of the Knight's Tale, however, Chaucer thought of metaphysical choice differently. He thought of freedom as enclosed, ordered, and hierarchical, like the medieval sense of outer space. As a result, for him, metaphysical choice is free but it is not isolated and it cannot be postponed. One is constantly choosing, every day, whether to accept/submit-to universal order or add to universal disorder, whether to submit to God or to some form of negation, error, sin. According to this way of thinking, God provides this harmonious, hierarchical universe for us to live in. We can freely accept its order or we can rebel against it. We can "maken vertu of necessitee" or be "rebel . . . to hym that al may gye" (3041, 3046). God likewise provides this land, this city, this way of life, these neighbors, this event or experience to each of us, all of this as opportunities for us to think about and learn from. Man is a learning animal. Hopefully, she or he will choose to learn to behave better, will choose to know, honor, and serve something higher.

In the Knight's Tale, Theseus is provided with the context, the people and events, that enable him to choose to learn to be better:

Destiny, "ministre general" of God's "purveiaunce," apparently brings him to the grove where Palamon and Arcite are fighting, sends the champions, provides the fury that causes the death of his close friend, and so on. At the end, in his Prime Mover speech, Theseus freely accepts his place in the universe as he now understands it, an understanding he "made" subjectively for himself out of generalizing from his own experience. In this speech, after defining and tracing the fair "cheyne of love" from the First Mover down into the world, and after outlining the essential orderliness of being in this world, Theseus advises his listener to accept this universal order as he himself has accepted it: "And take it weel that we may nat eschue, / And namely that to us alle is due" (3042–43). And, later, ". . . after wo I rede us to be merye, / And thanken Juppiter of al his grace" (3068–69). Earlier in the tale Theseus's free choices had led to disorder; here at the end, his free choices are within the order of things, the fair chain of love, as he has come to understand it. He has come to know and appreciate something higher than his own self-fulfillment.

To us, this closed, ordered, hierarchical universe may seem a very providential context in which to try to work out a realistic theory of universal psychology, especially one centered on total freedom, but this is apparently the context in which Chaucer believed a truly responsible theory of universal psychology had to be placed. Chaucer's is a very social theory. It makes people responsible not only for their own thinking, but also, at least partially, for the ideas they cause in their children, their spouses, their neighbors, their customers, their friends and acquaintances. In this quite Boethian way of thinking, God provides us with the context of this world and our experience in it in order to give us the opportunities we need to learn freely.

CHAPTER

7

The Knight

IN CHAUCER SCHOLARSHIP, the Knight himself has ordinarily taken a back-seat to his tale. Thus, as published interpretations of the tale grew gloomier over the past few decades, under influence of erasures in the order/disorder paradigm, so comments on its teller grew negative. Now, however, as critics have begun to focus instead on historical context and psychological concerns, commentary on the Knight and interpretation of the details of his General Prologue portrait have once again become positive.[1] Earlier I showed that the injustice in the Knight's Tale constitutes only its pagan narrative, that Boethian Providence is actually present and active throughout, benevolently drawing all the tale's suffering out to final good. On that basis, the recent return to the literal, unironic, idealistic reading of the Knight's General Prologue portrait is well warranted, a return to the reading that says the Knight is exactly what Chaucer says he is, a man who, ". . . fro the tyme that he first bigan / To riden out, he loved chivalrie, / Trouthe and honour, fredom and curteisie," a man who has fought worthily in "his lordes werre," and a man who ". . . nevere yet no vileynye ne sayde / In al his lyf unto no maner wight" (44–71). I wish to show now that the Knight is indeed characterized as this kind of man.

Actually, it is difficult in literary criticism today to know how to talk analytically about the characterization of a figure in a medieval work, particularly a character presented within the fiction as a "real person," as Chaucer presents his Knight. No longer do we speak of imaginary characters, since we recognize that no characters are fully imaginary. Nor, on the other hand, do we know any more what a "real person" is—one with center, or without? And if without, then with what?—language, historicity, . . . ? Similarly, the answers to traditional-type questions are not particularly revealing. The Knight's character is presented by direct exposition in the General Prologue, by dramatic action in a few of the links, and, within the fiction, by dramatic speaking as teller of his tale. He receives plenty of authorial comment, all good, but perhaps intended ironically. He is certainly more than two-dimensional, but difficult to think of as a fully-rounded three. He does not "develop" during the *Tales,* yet his final actions do surprise, at least in the twentieth century. Every "successful" fictional character, so they say, is a fusion of universal and particular, yet with regard to the Knight, who may or may not be "successful" but is certainly unforgettable, exactly what that universal is, and whether the particular is positive or negative, seems to be problematic. Given all these scholarly complexities, it seems best to talk here about what seems to be "there" in the *Tales* as a whole, in the context of the interpretation of his tale just presented.

THE KNIGHT AS MAKER

The Knight and his son are the only nobles on the pilgrimage, an interesting statistic. His is the first portrait in the General Prologue, and his is the first tale in the *Canterbury* collection, more interesting statistics. These alone suggest it unlikely that he is just a pilgrim among pilgrims and his tale just a tale among tales.

During the *Canterbury Tales,* Chaucer develops the reader's perception of the Knight in a typically scholastic twofold manner, combining increasing specification (from abstraction to particularity) with increasing contradiction (from warrior to peacemaker). Much of this is accomplished by manipulating the reader's point of view: where the narrator seems to stand in terms of what he sees, there too stands and sees the reader; what the narrator looks at and how he reacts, so too looks and reacts the reader. We saw

Chaucer using this technique earlier. In the temple and champion descriptions, for example, the reader seems to be standing still in Venus's temple and moving about in Mars's; on seeing Diana's paintings the reader is drawn in to blaming Diana for all the suffering; and on seeing Lygurge's alaunts the reader immediately takes a close look at safety precautions, whereas he sees Emetreus's lions and leopards without a second thought. In somewhat the same subtle way, Chaucer develops our perception of the Knight, from abstract concept to total particularity.

In order of revelation, Chaucer gives us first the distant idealized formal General Prologue portrait of the Knight as universal Christian warrior; then closer a momentary glimpse of the Knight as universal father served by respectful son; then even closer the Knight as the "goode man" who welcomes the cut that designates him (not unexpectedly) as first teller; and now we see into his mind through the story he tells, a teaching story defining universal human nature in a pagan setting, optimistic in spite of its woe, and trusting Providence even while acknowledging the reality of human suffering and rivalry. Then later we see the Knight come to the aid of the Pardoner to spare him further humiliation, and finally we see the Knight come to everybody's aid by interrupting the Monk. By starting his Knight far off, and then bringing him closer and closer and finally showing him interacting with the others, Chaucer materializes his Knight for the reader from distant, abstract, universal ideal into real particularity, into a flesh-and-blood human being active and responsible in this world.

On the standard *Canterbury Tales* issue of tale/teller match, there is much in the interpretation I am suggesting that makes this tale particularly suitable for this teller.[2] Some of the judgments made in the tale one would expect from a knight such as that described in the General Prologue, a worthy, intelligent, thoughtful, experienced, devoutly religious soldier, a man who has spent a lifetime serving the great medieval Christian ideal of religious chivalry, despite its decline into cynicism, Latin church imperialism, and greed. First, in the pagan narrative, his Theseus learns lessons that a man like the Knight would have learned on crusade. A man like Chaucer's Knight, for example, would have witnessed repeatedly, as does Theseus, the decline of "heigh" intent into "wrecched" actualizations. He would have learned quickly, as does Theseus, that once started, physical violence is difficult to stop. He would have come to value highly, as does Theseus, the kind of practical wisdom one gains from living actively in the world, from having to make hard decisions and then live with their outcomes. And he would have learned also (contra Egeus) that in the real world there is joy and solace as well as sadness and pain. Further, some of the judgments in the tale's embedded scholastic material are also appropriate for a fourteenth-century knight-crusader. For one thing, the teller seems to regard the speculations of the university friars as intellectually interesting but factional, and as lacking an appreciation of the complexity of real human beings and the real world. For another, he is both amused and concerned by theories about real people and the real world that result from logical demonstration based on *a priori* principles. Both judgments, rightly or wrongly, still characterize the opinions of people who work in the "real world" as to the theories of university academics. Thus these occupationally suitable judgments and opinions—about the decline of high intentions and the persistence of physical violence, and about the complexity of human nature and of life in the real world as opposed to their abstract simplification—characterize the experienced Crusader/Knight of the General Prologue as an appropriate teller for the complex story of Palamon, Arcite, and Theseus. Certainly no one else on the pilgrimage could qualify.

Further, Chaucer combines several other, ordinarily contradictory, qualities in this one knight. Possibly he was trying to characterize him as a "real person." Possibly he was trying to make several abstract points at the beginning of the *Tales* by means of his highest ranking pilgrim. In any event, in this one character, Chaucer believably combines an overriding optimism about human nature and the divine purpose; a surpassing knowledge of contemporary scholastic psychology and poetics; and a lifetime devoted to slaughter on the battlefield.

When one puts together the Knight's General Prologue portrait as a superlatively worthy crusader and man, with his tale of Palamon, Arcite, and Theseus which finally (despite all the suffering) ends well, with the respect accorded him by the Host and the other pilgrims, with his peacemaking after the Pardoner's Tale and interruption of the Monk's—when one puts all this together, the striking thing about this Knight turns out to be his philosophical optimism, his insistence on finding an essential goodness in things, even the most painful or degraded, and his apparent conviction that no matter how bad things may seem, Providence is at work drawing them out to some good end. How is one to evaluate this optimism, so unexpected in a man so experienced? In traditional roadside-drama terms, is this the simple childhood faith of an old-fashioned crusader, held in spite of every evidence to the contrary? Or, is it the hard-won belief of a seasoned campaigner, maintained in spite of years of warfare, disillusion, and disappointment? Or, on the other hand, is Chaucer making an abstract point about the nature of reality itself in the voice of his most authoritatively experienced pilgrim?

The Knight's optimism is evident in his deep affection for human nature, in his ability to value opposing points of view and praise what is good in each of them, and in his ability to withhold negative judgments. So far as one can tell from his tale, from the absence in its human characters of evil motives or malicious behavior (except possibly Creon, whose side of the story we never get), the teller truly believes that human nature is essentially good, that most people do intend well, regardless of how things work out. So far as one can tell from his telling, the Knight respects those scholastic theories, overdeveloped as they may be, enjoys the two exemplary if unrealistic young knights they produce, relishes responding to them with the verbal razzle-dazzle of the temples he concocts and the champions he causes, enjoys the hustle and bustle of the tournament preparations, pities Arcite as he dies unaware of the beautiful *visio* that awaits him, joys in Palamon as he returns "sor-wefully" to Athens unaware of the bliss that awaits him, listens approvingly to Theseus as he delivers his magnificent Prime Mover speech, and likes him immensely as he steps down unpretentiously at its end with those final simple lines to Palamon. Thus the teller of the Knight's Tale enjoys human beings and human life, in spite of the suffering. This affectionate respect for all things human, which Chaucer says has characterized the Knight all his life (GP 70–71), is what causes the Knight to quiet the general laughter at the Pardoner and to put an end to the spiritually misleading stories of the Monk. The teller of the Knight's Tale doesn't love just the abstraction "human nature"; rather, he loves the human nature in real people, both in his tale and in the links. As a result, he looks for the good in people. He can, therefore, value different kinds of people for what is individually good in each of them, as he values Arcite's intelligence and Palamon's sense of justice, as he values early Theseus, prone to haste and violence but meaning well, and as he values later Theseus, wiser although still not perfect. And because he is an optimist about the divine purpose—in his tale the hidden hand of Providence brings everything to good: Arcite receives grace, Theseus achieves wisdom, and Palamon marries Emelye—the teller of the Knight's Tale does not indulge himself in negative judgments. In fact, his ability to withhold negative judgments is what enables him to find some good in everybody, even the Monks and Pardoners of this world. The interesting thing is, these three qualities—love for human nature, flawed though it is; ability to discern what is good; and withholding premature negative judgments—these three qualities we associate both with the Divine Nature itself and with the very best in human nature. Here at the beginning of the *Canterbury Tales,* Chaucer's Knight sets a very high standard of being and behavior toward other people.

At first, the Knight's thorough impartial knowledge of the major scholastic theories of his time comes as a surprise. One expects a man like Chaucer's Knight to be well read in tales and treatises on chivalry and travel and warfare. But his expertise on both the substance and the style of the best scientific psychology of the period is most unexpected. By Chaucer's time, scientific substance had been refined down to unchanging, endlessly divided universals; scientific style had been distilled into a literalized, formidably technical diction, set forth in a sequence so artificially stuctured that the nonexpert reader soon loses the point of an argument among the answers to its objections. The general reader of Chaucer's time must have approached a scholastic treatise with the same enthusiasm a general reader of our own time musters for, say, Wittgenstein. The same enthusiasm and, no doubt, the same terrible reverence. Speaking for myself, I find Wittgenstein painful to read. I feel guilty about it. I know I should be fascinated. In principle I am. When I hear people mention his name, I listen for clues to substantiate and possibly add to my knowledge. But read him again? Never. The time and effort invested were not worth the enlightenment received. Awe and avoidance express my feelings exactly, and with Wittgenstein the fate of my soul is not at stake (so far as I know). Think, however, how an ordinarily devout middle-class Christian of Chaucer's time must have felt about the scholastic theological experts at Oxford and Paris, about their abstruse Latin arguments, claims of certitude, and notorious arrogance. No doubt a terrible reverence. Moreover, this ordinarily devout Christian may well have believed the fate of his or her soul *was* at stake. One reason, I think, why Chaucer's Knight, speaking not in Latin but in the vernacular, thoroughly demystifies scholastic metaphysics in his tale, is this larger social and very human context. Doing so to the degree the Knight's Tale does—defining clearly and accurately for the interested and able reader the basic scholastic notions of Being, Causation, and Reality that underlie their psychological theories—was not necessary for Chaucer to make the argument for his own universal psychology. Rather, the demystification is an unexpected gift from Chaucer to his fellow lay Christians, the gift of knowledge. Chaucer's Knight knows his philosophy well and shares it.

A third quality Chaucer assigns to his Knight—or perhaps a third point he wants to make here at the beginning of the *Canterbury Tales*—is that this particular Knight has devoted a lifetime to killing people on the edges of Christendom.[3] He has been at fifteen "mortal batailles," each of which could have lasted anywhere from a day to a year or more; has fought in at least a dozen widely scattered places on heathen borders; and three times at Tramyssene fought in lists, apparently representing his side, and "ay slayn his foo." It is true that feelings about killing may have been different then, that "war was the normal condition of society in medieval Europe," and that, according to Augustine, the soldier who strikes down his enemy from benevolence and pity acts in accordance with Christ's teaching.[4] On the other hand, Chaucer's Knight is also presented as a thoughtful optimist; and people who love human nature as it is, who are more amused than annoyed at its foolishness, who believe it can learn to be better, and who trust that Providence really does draw things out to good ends, do not ordinarily spend their lives killing other people. Usually they either give up killing or give up optimism. In his tale, Chaucer's Knight demonstrates repeatedly how to hamonize oppositions by finding them alike on higher levels—hunting dogs and jungle cats, but both pets; inductive and deductive, but both modes of thinking; voluntarist and intellectualist, but both worthy young men. Also in his tale, physical violence is something his Theseus learns to rise above. Yet this particular Knight keeps going back to the killing. Why does he do it? Out in the field, does a man like this try to unite the warring sides on some higher level, say a natural theology of some kind, and kill only when he fails? (In his tale, he saves the righteous pagan.) Or does he kill because he was born to killing in a closed-class society? (The righteous pagans in his tale were pre-Christian.) Since all the battles named in his portrait were to defend Christendom, and since he now is en route to Canterbury, he is apparently a devout Christian. Does he therefore spend his life killing people because he has made the kind of hard choice an active man must make and live with—optimist or philosopher, he is a crusader and the heathen are on the border? Or, on the other hand, rather than particularly characterizing his Knight, is Chaucer's primary point in these details, here at the beginning of the *Canterbury Tales,* that living as a Christian is serious business; that the final inevitable outcome will be eternal life or eternal death.

Let us turn now from these three points Chaucer has made with the characterization of his Knight—as one who is optimistic about human nature; as one who demystifies the scholastics' metaphysics and modifies their psychologies to reestablish the traditional Christian psychology of freedom and ethical choice; and as one who kills heathen—let us turn now to his traveling companions.

The General Prologue catalog of pilgrims begins with the three-some of father, son, and silent retainer. In these opening portraits, at the same time that the Knight, Squire, and Yeoman are being characterized literally as "real person" pilgrims en route to Canterbury, I wish to show that nonverbal suggestions are being inserted into the reader's mind that, at the same time, they are also more. In these three portraits, as he often does, Chaucer has it both ways.

Throughout the thirty-six lines of the Knight's General Prologue portrait, with his love for all that was best in chivalry, his lifetime of service "in his lordes werre, / . . . As wel in cristendom as in hethenesse" (I, 49), and his genuine humility, the Knight seems too ideal to be real. Chaucer materializes him, however, from distant admirable abstraction into real being by means of his fresh young son and alert armed retainer. All three members of this group are described directly by the details of their appearance and past and present behavior, and they are also described indirectly, almost subliminally, by means of the narrator's point of view. The narrator, and therefore the reader, keeps a respectful distance from this Knight. He sees the Knight whole, from far enough off to see all his horses at once; and the details of his biography are summarized as if gleaned from a knowledgeable third person. The pilgrim-narrator did not sit right across the table from this Knight observing his table manners, nor did he stand chatting with him later about the decline of chivalry. The Squire, however, we meet close up; we see his curly locks and embroidered flowers; and he is so delightfully young and eager and open and talkative and inexperienced and gay, that as one looks at him and chats with him, as the pilgrim-narrator seems to have done, one feels again the tremendous pleasure of a parent watching a child grow up well. In the final couplet of the Squire's description,

> Curteis he was, lowely, and servysable,
> And carf biforn his fader at the table, (99–100)

the Knight suddenly comes to life, not as a warrior, but as a father well served by an obedient son. Moreover, judging from the unexpected combination of the boy's flowery attire and respectful demeanor, this is a father who has raised his son well. The obedience and humility suggest he brought the boy up in his own traditional values; the fashionable attire and courtly accomplishments suggest that although the boy now lives in a different world, the Knight is trusting him to sort out his own values, not trying to force him back. Their relationship here suggests to the reader that the Knight is a man to be trusted. This brief picture of father and son is followed immediately with the striking portrait of their silent, purposeful, heavily armed retainer. Although we see him very close up, from the feathers on his arrows to the Christopher shining on his chest, we learn absolutely nothing more about him, not even whether or not he really is a forester (117). The description reads as if the narrator stood right next to him and tried to engage him in conversation but failed. This Yeoman is apparently not a man to be distracted. Rather, he seems totally intent on everything going on around him and ready for any contingency. One suspects he is there not to look after the needs of the battle-hardy father so much as to watch out for and serve the lovely young son.

This initial threesome of distant father, fresh young son, and silent capable retainer may be perceived by the reader as composed of fictional "real person" pilgrims en route to Canterbury. By poetic implication, however, whether by Being or merely by participation, it may be perceived as more.[5] My own feeling is that, here at the beginning of his last and most ambitious work, Chaucer is having it both ways.

In some sense, of course, any real crusader participates in the nature of the Divine Crusader, so to speak, meting out eternal death to the heathen. Likewise, any wise and loving father participates in the nature of the Divine Father, just as any obedient son participates in the nature of the Divine Son and any faithful retainer participates in the nature of the Divine Spirit. This is simply standard medieval realism. On the other hand, in these three opening portraits, what we know about the father we seem to have learned from the son; and what we know about the retainer is only what we see. Although I certainly do not suggest that Chaucer intends these three to be perceived as the three Persons of the Trinity, on the other hand, more than ordinary participation does seem to be going on, at least by implication, in their General Prologue portraits. The hints are there, but they are no more than hints. Their importance depends on the reader's point of view. In addition, of course, Trinitarian resonances, not emphatic but certainly explicit, continue in their tales. The Knight's Tale defines universal human nature—creates it, so to speak—in the characterization of Theseus, as totally free in its mind and therefore totally responsible, and as being put here on this postlapsarian earth in order to learn to be better. The Squire's Tale of allusions and miracles is unexpectedly cut off. And the Yeoman, of course, never speaks in his own voice; he has no tale of his own.

The tale Chaucer's Knight "makes" can be read with pleasure and profit from many points of view: pagan romance, scholastic treatise, humanist manifesto, handbook for princes, ethical manual, logic and meta-logic textbook, compendium of verbal techniques, and more. Meanings in Chaucer come on Porphyrean trees, as they do in most Gothic artworks, and knowledge depends enough on the individual reader that one is free to make many choices. But on all levels, so far as I can tell, the Knight's tone is friendly and patient, his wit gentle and teasing, and his criticisms both fair and constructive. His final conclusions, however, are practical and they are very hard. Among them are: total freedom of one's mind; full thoughtful responsibility for the effects of one's ideas and actions on others; peaceful acceptance of natural human differences; and always, the choice to behave better. Day-to-day choice is the hard edge of medieval Christianity, and the Knight who advises it is a killer when he has to be, a point Chaucer makes twice: "mortal batailles" and "ay slayn his foo" (61, 63). Not surprisingly, the Knight's final message on all levels is charity: to thank God for his many kindnesses (3069)—the way Providence watches over us, bringing us to good, and the minds with which he has graced us so that we may learn—and to get together peacefully with and foster our neighbor, *or else.*

THE KNIGHT AS PART OF THE PILGRIMAGE FRAME

In the overall framework of the *Canterbury Tales,* Chaucer balances the beginning against the ending as the many against the one, the responsible humanist fostering others against the individual penitent taking responsibility for himself or herself. In complex ways ranging from explicit to merely allusive, the General Prologue portraits, Knight, and Knight's Tale at the beginning function as complements to the Parson, Parson's Tale, and Retraction at the end.

Like most works of Gothic high art, the *Canterbury* tales are structured as separate compartments enclosed within a multiple, sometimes interlocking, system of frames. Outermost there is the pilgrimage frame, consisting of the General Prologue at the beginning and the Retraction at the end. In this first frame, the catalog of pilgrim portraits at the beginning, headed by the Knight's, puts forward a spectrum of the many, varied, marvelously particularized human "weyes" of this world, human beings of every kind, with all sorts of typically different worldly occupations, histories, and personalities. Chaucer's Retraction at the end, by way of complement, puts forward a model for the one saving way to the next world, a model of gratitude, good will, prayers, penitence, and grace.[6] In this frame, the humanist many is in balance with the penitent one.

Next in are the two outer framing tales, the Knight's at the beginning, the Parson's at the end. In this context, the Knight's Tale demonstrates scientifically two things: *(a)* The validity of the many—the existence in this created world of more than one good kind of person, more than one legitimate way of thinking, more than one approach to language use, more than one source of valuable experience; and *(b)* the freedom of the many to choose how and what to learn from their experiences—human minds are not constrained by logical consistency, nor by natural appetites or influences, nor by providential direction. It follows, then, that in this world there are going to be many sorts of human beings learning many sorts of lessons from many sorts of experiences. By way of complement, the Parson's Tale at the end focuses down narrowly on the one: one sure aspect of every person—the sinner; one necessary lesson for every person—penitence; one certain purpose for everyone—getting safely to the next world. As the Parson says,

Manye been the weyes espirituels that leden folk to oure Lord Jhesu Crist, and to the regne of glorie. / Of which weyes,

ther is a ful noble wey and a ful covenable, which may nat
fayle to man ne to womman that thurgh synne hath mysgoon
fro the righte wey of Jerusalem celestial; and this wey is cleped
Penitence. (78–80)

What we have here at the end of the *Canterbury Tales* is another
hard edge of medieval Christianity, that one really certain way. It
explains the harsh personality of the snibbing Parson and the hard
choices of the killer Knight on the edges of Christendom, keeping
the heathen out. Judging from his tale, Chaucer's Knight loves
human beings dearly, but they are in this world free and able to
learn. And eventually they are going to have to take responsibility
for themselves, each one, individually.

The two tales differ greatly in style. The Knight's Tale is figurative, many-levelled, intellectually exciting, and very much of this
world—sparkling burgundy and speculative caviar. The Parson's
Tale, on the other hand, seems to be scholastically-inspired pastoral
theology, painstakingly practical but well pointed toward the next
world—brown bread and cold water. Yet their structural relationship is fairly explicit: according to the first tale, human beings are
free to choose; according to the last tale, they must choose.[7] Further, the Parson's Tale, like the Knight's, is making a comment
about language use. Although the Parson is not a university scholastic, neither is he a friend of fables. Not for him "swich
wrecchednesse," not alliteration, not "rym," not any such pagan
"draf" as the Knight told (X, 31–44). The Parson insists instead
on sowing good literal "whete," and that is what Chaucer gives
him, by the wagonload. For people unable or unwilling to learn
from figures and parables, from pagan romances, from mirrors for
princes, beast fables, Breton lais, allegories, fabliaux, saint's lives,
their own experiences and the experiences of others (after all, in
their medlies of meanings these can be difficult to decipher), for
people who really need their knowledge presented literally, Chaucer graciously provides even for them in his final tale. The Parson's
Tale is a literal-minded manual for the confession and penance that
are certainly necessary and needed, couched in the clearest, the
most flat-footed, single-layered, scientific kind of prose—abso-

lutely logical and thoroughly consistent; comprised of definition, division, classification, enumeration, predication, and consequence. It is uncharitable to consider the Parson's Tale dull. The fact is, many people in this world really prefer this kind of thinking and language use. Read any *summa*. Read any journal. Read Wittgenstein. A wise and loving maker provides for every kind of pilgrim, even the literal-minded, since the final destination will be theirs, each of them individually, "cristendom" or "hethenesse."

The two tellers, obviously, differ greatly in personality, social class, and background. Yet in some ways they are remarkably similar. Both are experienced, both practical, both active rather than cloistered. The more-than-human figurative resonances in the portraits of Knight, Squire, and Yeoman are balanced by the best-of-human literal resonances in the portraits of Parson and Plowman. Again, Chaucer is having it both ways. Both Knight and Parson are actually presented, literally, as "real person" human beings, although the Knight is too good to be true and therefore often read ironically, and the Parson is too good to be pleasant and therefore often read defensively.[8] In sum, as guides on this pilgrimage, the Knight, with his intelligence, optimism, and faith in human nature, is perhaps the perfect maker to bring us into this world. But the Parson, with his less tolerant ear, sharper tongue, and strict, absolutely literal approach to the "weyes espirituels," is perhaps the safer maker to lead us out of it.

8

The Pilgrimage Reality

CHAUCER ALSO CHANGES the context in which a scientific theory of universal psychology is to be constructed and tested, from the quiet world of logical abstraction to the busy, bustling world of real human living. His own theory, embodied in Theseus as universal, argued that all human beings are totally free in their minds (traditional) and that they learn from their own individual experiences (new). But in the rest of the *Canterbury Tales,* he puts this general theory of human nature out for testing in what purports to be a real pilgrimage through the real world with real people. Immediately, as suggested earlier, there is a problem: Is total freedom of mind possible if people learn from their own individual day-to-day experiences?

First let us look at Chaucer's insistence on the reality of the *Canterbury* pilgrimage, and then at the problems a good theory encounters in a real world context.

Chaucer no doubt chose a real pilgrimage as the frame for his great work about human nature because he saw real life as a pilgrimage—as a journey through place and time toward a supernatural destination, and as a journey taken not individually but by groups of people traveling together, "by aventure yfalle / in felaweship" (25–26). Chaucer's pilgrimage is, therefore, presented not as a personification allegory and not as a quest and not as a dream vision, but as a real pilgrimage with a group of real people.

Unlike Dante, Chaucer sets his epic in this world and peoples it for the most part with ordinary middle-class folk. Unlike the abstract creations of the scholastics, Chaucer's pilgrims interact with each other. Unlike the characters of the mystery plays, what Chaucer's pilgrims say and do is in immediate response to what is going on around them, and as a result is personal and unpredictable.[9] And unlike the Italian humanists of his time, Chaucer pleads no special knowledge or consideration for poets; like the others in his *Tales* and in the real world, he too is a pilgrim traveling in the group. In this way of thinking, the real world is the world of pilgrimage on which we are all faring together, each of us traveling in a group composed of some family, some friends, some associates, and some strangers, "yfalle togidre by aventure."

As one result, Chaucer's universal psychology is a social theory. By adding subjectivity and learning processes to the universal psychologies of his time (we see into Theseus's subjective mind, and we watch him in the process of coming to decisions), Chaucer includes within his own theory interaction with other people. In his psychology, people learn from each other. They therefore have a responsibility for what they purposely or inadvertently teach each other. It is true that knowledge depends partly on the knower; and it is also true (according to this way of thinking) that God will draw all things out to good. Nevertheless, Chaucer's theory suggests, people have some responsibility for the ideas and images they put into each other's minds. Life is a pilgrimage on which we travel in groups, not one by one, and we learn from each other as we go. This is why Chaucer's *Canterbury Tales'* pilgrimage is so social. His people interact with and respond to each other. They not only teach and enlighten each other, however; they also manipulate, mislead, misunderstand, bully, tease, divert, charm, swindle, and manage each other. And more. In short, they are a real group. And, in Chaucer's theory, they are individually responsible to each other for their behavior as a group. The Knight's termination of the Monk's tales and his peacemaking between Pardoner and Host not only set an example; they suggest that individually the pilgrims have something yet to learn about responsible group behavior.

Chaucer's pilgrimage context for the making and testing of a universal psychology not only adds real group dynamics to the traditionally solitary scholastic context, it also adds the tangible temporal real world. His *Canterbury* pilgrims travel together through real places in real time. England; Canterbury itself; the Tabard in Southwerk; Deptford and Greenwich and "it is half-wey pryme" (A, 3906); fourteen lines to reveal that it is actually ten A.M. on the morning of April 18th (B, 1–14)—references like these to real places and real times are scattered tantalizingly here and there in the links. Whatever the final arrangement of such references would have been, Chaucer clearly intended to anchor the *Canterbury Tales* in the actual places and times and daily physical lives of his own audience. The real English world is very perceptible in the *Canterbury Tales*.

Inside the Knight's Tale, for this same reason, Chaucer sometimes foregrounds real world activities in order to contrast them against the timeless, placeless, actionless void of the scholastics' theories. As a rule, the passages on the generally bleak story of Palamon and Arcite are less tangible physically and less pressured temporally than are the passages on the noisy, bustling, feasting, dancing Athenian court. Theseus's is a world more real, Chaucer thus suggests, than the theoretical world of the two theoretical young Thebans. For example, following the artificially constricted set-piece descriptions of Part III, by way of contrast Chaucer opens Part IV with a burst of real-life details: the first forty lines present a world in which people go to bed at night to get some rest when they have to get up early (2490); where harness clatters, spears have to be nailed and lanyards laced (2492, 2503–4); where horses gnaw on golden bridles, armorers race to and fro, people gather by threes and tens to debate an outcome, and strangers are identified by their black beards and bald heads (2506–7, 2517–18); and where a battle axe has real weight (2520). All this crowded movement, busy noise, constantly shifting texture, and vivid sense of minutes passing and things to be done, all this overwhelming physicality and temporality is what causes the opening of Part IV to seem like a great explosion of life after Part III.[10] Amid the pressures of worldly time, place, and physicality, Chaucer suggests, is where people really work out their own individual universal psychologies, both what they themselves are and what they think all people are. Hence, if a psychological theory is to be accurate and therefore useful, the real world is where it has to be developed.

And finally with regard to reality of context, Chaucer's *Canterbury* pilgrimage is made by characters presented as real people. They come from real places, have real occupations and real histories, and have real subjectivities. The Clerk is from Oxford, the Shipman probably from Dartmouth, Alison is from near Bath. The Miller and the Reeve seem to have known each other previously; the Man of Law seems to have read a lot of Chaucer and even more of Gower. Tantalizing hints are scattered here and there linking the descriptions of Chaucer's real-seeming pilgrims with actual persons living in his England and well known to his audience.[11] Whatever the extent of these allusions in particular cases, Chaucer clearly intended to evoke from his reader the general notion that his pilgrims were to be perceived as potentially real people, rather than, say, as personifications or symbols or the bloodless stereotyped figures of French fabliaux. And Chaucer gives some of his pilgrims real subjectivity. Scholars might disagree as to the amount, but all would concede, I think, that the Miller, Reeve, Wife of Bath, Friar, Clerk, Pardoner, Prioress, Monk, Canon's Yeoman, Host, and Parson all possess at least some recognizably human subjectivity. More than this in terms of the reality of individual characters, however, the unfinished state of the center of the *Canterbury Tales* makes difficult to ascertain.

Nonetheless, one thing Chaucer was doing in the unfinished center, it seems to me, was using the real world context to test his universal psychology. A good theory is a remarkable achievement in itself, even in a vacuum. One value of a good general theory is that it gives other thinkers something to think against; a better general theory can then be worked out in the ensuing dialogics between good general theory and real individual instances. Chaucer's is the best (i.e., most responsible, most workable) theory of human nature with total freedom I have ever seen—but it *is* a deductively developed theory. Even the best of theories needs testing in the real world, to see what it really says and does to people. Chaucer was well aware of this; in the Knight's Tale, for example, one major motif was the difference between intentions and outcomes. As a result, it seems to me likely that in the center of the *Canterbury Tales* what Chaucer was doing was making, retelling, and shaping stories and then matching them up with this pilgrim or that to see what would happen, what each would do to the other when so joined, no doubt tinkering, amplifying, and deleting as ideas developed and changed. One of the great pleasures of writing, it seems to me, is the discovering that it makes happen, especially the discovering of complexities that "click" together. Differences of opinion aside, we all know a successful "real person" fictional character when we read one; we recognize such a "real" character intuitively. It is much more difficult, however, to specify explicitly exactly what it is that makes this or that character seem "real," and, additionally, what this specification in any particular instance would imply for a general theory of psychology. Chaucer's unfinished center thus may have been in the process of discovering "right" matches of characters with stories, matches that would test/prove his psychological theory in intellectually interesting ways. This theory-testing seems to me as good a conjecture as any as to Chaucer's general aim in the unfinished middle of the *Tales*. The Knight's Tale has the twofold subject of psychology and poetics; I conjecture that the *Canterbury Tales* as a whole has the same twofold subject—the psychology of the pilgrims and the poetics of their stories and the way the two fit together, amplifying and refracting each other.

A real world context can be rough on a good theory. The core of Chaucer's theory of universal psychology is the fact of human subjectivity. One pole of this subjectivity is the total freedom of human beings to find, know, and serve something better than themselves; another pole, however, is their natural propensity to learn from their own individual experiences. Unfortunately, when tested out in the real world of hierarchical social relationships, the two poles are not necessarily compatible in complex ways that Chaucer appears to have been working on but not to have worked out. For example, what if I am a young idealistic monk, not too bright, perhaps, but well-meaning and well-built, and my abbot assigns me the job of outrider for the monastery lands? Given such important responsibilities as these for the welfare of my order, how long can my inward mind stay separate, totally free, from the pleasurable social and materialistic practicalities of my daily duties? Or, what if I am a young girl, married off (willingly or unwillingly) to a rich old man at age twelve (some six to ten years younger than the usual marital age)? Given the physical realities of my daily existence with such a husband, how can my inward mind become or stay so separate, so totally free from my outward life that it can respond to everything that happens to me with patience, charity, and goodness? The traditional Christian humanist answer to such examples was quite clear: since knowledge depends on both knower and known, no matter how corrupting the experience I undergo, I am still totally free, totally separate and able in my own inward mind, to come to a different meaning than the simple obvious direct reaction, whatever that might be. I am always free to reject corruption and be better. The Divine can, therefore, justly hold me responsible—apparently—for doing exactly what I am being taught to do by my daily experiences, as did these two, idealistic young monk and twelve-year-old bride. Something is wrong here.

No doubt Chaucer is questioning some specific social practices of his own day (wealthy monasteries, May/January marriages). And he is obviously rejecting the excuses of coercion, ignorance, and so on offered by the scholastics. Instead, and more speculatively I think, one thing he may be suggesting is that since human nature both exists in a social context and learns from its experiences in it, that therefore human beings bear some responsibility for the experiences they give to each other, however customary or casual such experiences may seem at the time. People do bear some responsibility for the images and ideas they put and do not put into each other's minds, especially, considering the fates of the little clergeon in the Prioress's Tale and of Virginia in the Physician's Tale, for the images and ideas they put and do not put into the minds of the very young. Chaucer's developing universal psychology is, thus, considerably more social—and socially responsible— than the other psychologies of his day and of our own. In the real world, Chaucer suggests, to some degree, people create each other's subjectivities. Yet what this suggestion would have done to his universal theory is difficult to say. Would he, sooner or later, have modifed his insistence in the Knight's Tale argument for total human freedom of both will and intellect? Would he, like the scholastics, have watered down total individual responsibility? I doubt it.

Empirical observation, the method of the modern scientist, has always underlain the art of the poet. An eye for detail, a feel for pattern, a sense of the significant—these are the tools of the good observer, whether poet or scientist. Empirical science had already begun developing in the thirteenth century, under the impulse of Robert Grosseteste, Peter de Maricourt, Roger Bacon, and the general Franciscan emphasis on the individual and on actual experience. Thus, Chaucer's moving the context of scientific psychology out from the universal void and into the everyday real world accords with the growing empirical spirit of his time. Today, a good scientific theory combines real world observation with logical construction, as does Chaucer's; its formulation is essentially simple, as is Chaucer's (human minds are free and learn); and even as it resolves some problems it brings other interesting new possibilities to light, as does Chaucer's (subjectivity, the effects of day-to-day experience on the mind, relationship between language use and thought). Thus Chaucer's concern throughout the *Canterbury Tales,* evidenced not only in the carefully constructed *disputatio* and *sophismata* of the Knight's Tale, but also in the years of thoughtful empirical observation that must have preceded the characterizations of his other pilgrims, is scholastic/scientific as well as humanist. He is trying to understand and formulate previously unarticulated truths about universal human nature, but he is also trying to do so in a way that will foster responsibly the development of individual human beings.

CHAPTER

9

Chaucerian Didacticism

SINCE NESTED WITHIN the medievalized pagan romance that is Chaucer's Knight's Tale are the two university teaching genres, the *disputatio* and the *sophismata* sequence, the New-Critically forbidden question is here legitimate: What does this first of all the *Canterbury* tales set out to teach? What didactic context does Chaucer want to establish for the rest of his tales and links? Like the Cathedral at Canterbury, like the Towneley Cycle plays, like *The Vision of Piers Plowman,* the Knight's Tale puts forward a whole hierarchy of ideas and experiences for the reader to profit from if she or he so chooses, a hierarchy focusing on new aspects of and clothing in new garments the kind of traditional moral and spiritual knowledge that in every culture every generation must learn for itself anew. The material being rich, a final reprise is in order.

The most noble lesson in the Knight's Tale, in the context of Chaucer's own time, is that, in theory, the human mind is free and learns from its own experiences; ideally, it learns to honor and serve something higher than its own nature, and as a result to do good unto others. This is the *determinatio* to the disputation embodied in the three central characters, begun with the debate between Palamon (representing the Augustinian-Franciscan primacy of the will) and Arcite (representing the Aristotelian-Thomist primacy of the intellect) and resolved with the more lifelike figure of Theseus, in whom both faculties are free and function together harmoniously. At the end, because he is free to learn from events in his own life, Theseus has become a better man; albeit still a pagan, he accepts a higher order than his own making and behaves better toward others. Making possible this most noble lesson of freedom and opportunity for every human soul are the supporting arguments for individual subjectivity and figurative language use. First, without individual subjectivity, freedom of the individual human mind is not possible, nor is learning from its own experience. This is why individual subjectivity as the fourth and shaping mental reality was added to the scholastic 3-Acts mind model by the *sophismata* sequence in Part III: To simple aprehension of objects, judgment of complex propositions, and inference to causes, Saturn's monologue added the shaping effects of his own immaterial subjectivity (his particular affections, historicity, knowledge, and blind spots), an addition second-instanced by the immaterial subjectivity displayed in Theseus's Part II monologue. And second, without figurative language use as valid, the only important knowledge is going to be knowledge conveyed in literal language. If that were the case, then learning anything important from experience would not be possible. This is why figurative language use is validated as vehicle for important truths, in order to validate all experience as vehicle for important truths. For this reason important scholastic truths are conveyed by figuring them in the depictions of Palamon and Arcite and in the descriptions of the temples and champions (just as important ethical truths are conveyed in the figurative language of the *Aeneid* and important spiritual truths in the figurative language of, for example, the biblical parables). Whether presented figuratively or literally, the Knight's Tale shows, any truth will depend also for its realization on the subjective mind of its individual perceiver. Overall, therefore, the Knight's Tale bears the same twofold focus as the *Canterbury Tales* overall: one on human nature including individual subjectivity (as in the personalities of its pilgrims—how are they free? what do they think and mean?); and the other on all kinds of language use (as in their byplay and tales).

Yet, caveat lector! What the Knight's Tale teaches by means of its two teaching genres is PURE THEORY. It is Chaucer's *universal* psychology, arrived at *deductively,* by reasoning down from prior notions about the human nature of Christ, in whose image (according to this theory) human nature can re-create itself—Christ's subjectivity, Christ's use of figurative language, and Christ's free choice to serve something higher than his own human nature and as a result to minister to his fellow human beings. This is the psychological context Chaucer sets for the rest of the *Canterbury Tales:* an ideal of individual human possibility derived deductively from the nature of Christ, to be tested, however, in the real world of Chaucer's own time, a fallen world of power often corrupt and people often misguided but of joy and gentilesse as well. To the extent that the Knight's Tale is satire, its targets are the factionalism, pagan metaphysics, and literalizing poetics of the university scholastics. To the extent that the Knight's Tale is humanist, its purposes are traditional—a return to the humane subject matter and noble discussions of earlier literature, whether pagan or Christian, to human virtue, freedom, knowledge, and, above all, to the nature of the human mind.

Chaucer's theory of psychology is unifying. Whereas for the Dominicans intellect is the highest human power, and for the Franciscans will (affection and choice) is the highest human power, Chaucer finds their common, even higher, harmonization in the human ability to learn. In the Knight's Tale, real learning is both intellectual and volitional. Theseus becomes more just as well as more thoughtful. His changes—from polytheist to monotheist, from precipitately physical tyrant to parliamentary ruler, from valuing a man for his lineage and riches to valuing also his constancy, from victorious man of arms to more conciliatory man of mind—these changes all involve elements from both sides of the nave. According to Chaucer's theory of human nature, affections and judgment as well as information and methodologies are learned (an insight few developmental psychologists of our own day would reject). In the context of Chaucer's theory, therefore, all art is didactic. This is not because of artist's or maker's intentions (intentions always differ from outcomes), but because human beings are animals who learn—who are by nature constantly making meaning out of whatever they are perceiving at any given moment. Whether the meaning they make is good or is bad depends partly on them, of course (knowledge always depending to some degree on its knower), but in fact meaning is always being made. Further, if all art is didactic, so too is all science, and so too then are the two scholastic psychologies. Their scholastic makers no doubt intended only a search for certain truth, and no doubt with the best of intentions. Nevertheless, from such theories real people make their meanings, uncertain though they may be. And theories that limit any part of one's metaphysical freedom and responsibility—whether of intellect or will, of means or end—are going to be taken by those who believe in them as behavioral warrants for doing whatever they feel like doing (passivity, adultery, betrayal, whatever) and then passing the buck—to the stars, to superior beings (divines, experts), to natural appetites or social customs, to wherever the theories suggest. According to the Bible, God did not do this—and here I believe I am following Chaucer's thought when he characterized his Knight with participatory Trinitarian implications—God told people they were individually responsible for what they do. Furthermore, God spent his time on earth teaching by means of parables and examples as well as literal precepts, and fostering people's ethical and spiritual development in the course of dispensing objective new truths. For Chaucer at the beginning of the *Canterbury Tales,* I think it safe to say, because human beings are animals who learn, everything is didactic. In principle at least, life is a school in which by nature the pupils are free, programmed to learn, and responsible for what they teach each other.

Life in this world is a school. To this way of thinking, rather than a pilgrimage of woe or a display of divine power, life here is a period of benevolent freedom in which we are offered opportunities to learn to be better. Whether it succeeds, however, is up to each of us and all of us. If this was Chaucer's thought here at the beginning of the *Canterbury Tales,* then he was positing two ideas unusual in his own time about learning from experience:

(a) that human beings have individual knowledge, learned from the things that have happened to them even when no lesson was planned or expected; and

(b) that some things of great intelligible value can be learned only through social interaction with real people in the real world.

The Knight's Tale puts forward these unusual ideas in theoretical terms, as was shown; the remainder of the *Canterbury Tales,* I would suggest, considers them again in practical terms. The larger context of both (and a major and well-known concern in all areas of later fourteenth-century thought) was as to the value of actual experience. Further, both ideas would traditionally have been discussed as subtopics of the active/contemplative and authority/experience debates. Thus, by approaching them psychologically, Chaucer is coming at them from a direction new in his time.

First, when people expect to learn, they obviously do. People learn from going to school, but schools are planned, and they have teachers and canonical texts. What is learned is what is expected. People also learn by apprenticeship and repeated practice, but again, the procedure is planned and an instructor is present and one knows what one is supposed to be learning. Further, Augustine speaks of the pleasure of figuring things out for oneself, of the importance of engaging the mind, but the context he speaks in is attempting to understand the Bible. Again, one is consciously intending to learn and one knows generally what is expected. Cathedrals were planned as three-dimensional books which people read in order to learn, but again the lessons were set and traditional; people knew pretty much what they were expected to find. Humanist poetics likewise were predicated on the pleasure of finding moral and spiritual kernels within fictional figures, but here again, the context was looking for and finding an expected traditional kind of knowledge.

The idea that ordinary people also learn important things from the unplanned transitory events of their daily, seemingly uneventful, public and private lives is quite different. The knowledge they learn this way is going to be *individual* knowledge (as touched on earlier). It is not planned, not expected, and not supervised; and it is not necessarily going to be traditional or even socially acceptable knowledge; but it is going to influence importantly their behavior and therefore their lives. (Witness once again the Monk and the Wife of Bath.) In the abstract, perhaps, the notion of important individual knowledge seems obvious, but in real life it is by no means so simple as it sounds. Nor is such knowledge necessarily easy even for its knower to understand or articulate. Consider what a child learns from physical or psychological abuse. Consider what you yourself have learned from some trauma, a death perhaps, or an injustice or betrayal. Consider also what you have learned from driving the freeway each morning, from dealing with the local post office, or from sitting on a grants committee. *This* is individual knowledge. This is why Chaucer adds subjectivity to his theory of universal psychology. Knowledge depends on both known and knower, of course, so to some degree the individual does choose what she or he learns from everyday happenings. But the point is, human beings do learn from them. Important knowledge. The acquisition and effect of this individual kind of knowledge is, I suggest, one major topic of the *Canterbury Tales* as a whole. In the Knight's Tale *disputatio,* there is no way of knowing how Palamon learned to conform his will to the divine will nor how Arcite learned to get his faculties in order; unlike Boccaccio, Chaucer sends both of them back to Thebes for the year before the tournament and thereby leaves unanswered the question the two scholastic psychologies leave unanswered. Theseus, however, learns valuable individual knowledge by living through and generalizing from the unexpected outcome at Thebes and the unexpected outcome of the tournament. At the time, the knowledge he gained was, at first, subjective, imperfect, and uncertain. Notice, however, that Chaucer has him reason by means of it to man's first discovery of the great Prime Mover and of the fair chain of love—thereby pointing out that all *auctoritee,* even the greatest, begins as someone's individual knowledge.

This practical behavioral individual kind of knowledge which Theseus gains by learning from his own life was and still is normally dismissed by scholastic scientific philosophers as rationally uncertain and therefore not really valuable. That outcomes can be terrible, that longstanding devotion has worth, that parliaments can be helpful—this kind of knowledge is not scientifically demonstrable. Once again, the criterion of absolute logicality generates a conclusion that is not incorrect as regards real life, but merely inadequate. A purely rational creature who insisted on certain knowledge as the only real knowledge would be unable to learn much by living with real people in the real human world; indeed, he or she would probably be unable to function. This is because the real human world, according to this way of thinking, was designed by its Maker as a school for real human beings, not for purely rational creatures. Real human beings acquire irrational and uncertain but nevertheless important meanings from all the things that happen to them in the unpredictable social world in which they live.

The second unusual life-as-school idea that Chaucer posits speculatively in the Knight's Tale is that some things of great intelligible value can be learned only through personal experience in the real human world. To that idea Chaucer's scholastic (and cloistered) contemporaries no doubt would have replied—of course, things worked out that way for Theseus, but Theseus was noble as well as universal, and besides, this is the fourteenth century when all the important intelligible things like Prime Movers and chains of being have already been discovered and can now be better known through studying the *auctoritees*. All the important discoveries nowadays are being made at the universities, they would no doubt have claimed, by proposition and syllogism, and are certified by scientific demonstration. On the contrary, Chaucer shows in the Knight's Tale, some important lessons can be learned only by personal experience. Some are hard and serious; some lighthearted and laughing; aspects of both are nonliteral.

One hard serious lesson people learn only by experience, the Knight's Tale suggests, is a healthy skepticism toward theories about human beings grounded on logic alone. For example, recall the *sophismata* sequence in the Part III temple and champion descriptions. In these, rather than just defining the scholastic 3-Acts thinking processes, Chaucer makes his readers experience them. We readers must apprehend simple objects abstractively and intuitively in the temples of Venus and Mars; we readers must judge complex propositions for their truth values in the temple of Diana; and we readers must infer many different instances of the four causes, one by one, this aspect and that, if we wish to cognize completely the champions Lygurge and Emetreus. In other words, Chaucer does not allow us to listen passively to the abstract definitions of the *auctoritees* as to how our own minds and language work. He insists we actually experience those definitions. Here in these first five set pieces, he makes us try on for ourselves the accepted scholastic interpretations of the thinking activities of the mind. "Well, how do they fit?" he seems to say; "do these cover adequately the way *your* mind works? Do *you* apprehend, judge, and reason according to the model? And does nothing else go on in *your* mind?" And then, because it is one thing to feel uncomfortable in ready-to-wear garments cut to abstract measurements, and quite another to pinpoint accurately their deficiencies, he closes Part III with Saturn's marvelously self-centered monologue. Reading this, I think, we are all much more comfortable. This, we recognize as we read it, feels more like a *real* mind working. In other words, here in Saturn's monologue, the 3-Acts mind model works because Chaucer has added the other human mental processes to it—affections, historicity, allusions, repetitions, and blind spots. The 3-Acts theory thus becomes another logically grounded theory that is not incorrect as far as it goes, but simply inadequate. The human mind is more. Chaucer's readers, however, after first reading the descriptions, then realizing from the syntax what Chaucer was doing with them, then figuring them out and experiencing the flash of recognition that would have come with *understanding* the conceptual process they were undergoing, would be unlikely ever again to swallow uncritically a purely logical claim about the way their own minds worked or about the way they should use their own language. Rationality is a valuable tool, as is logic, they would have learned, but in the real world their usefulness is limited (in fact, the limits of both reason and logic was another major discussion in all areas of fourteenth-century thought). Thus, Chaucer suggests, a healthy, self-confident, show-me attitude toward the "demonstrated" theories of experts can be learned only by practical experience, by testing a few such "certain" theories in the real world and watching some of them fail.

A second serious lesson that can be learned only through worldly experience has to do with values. Chaucer suggests that there can be complicated differences between a virtue in the abstract and its manifestation in a real person in the real world. For example, in the Knight's Tale, Chaucer's characterization of Emelye stresses her absolute innocence. She is markedly different from Boccaccio's knowledgeable, self-conscious young heroine. As revealed in her prayer, Chaucer's Emelye is pious, chaste, fearful, obedient, and above all trusting. She is both an idealized romance heroine and a pathetic prize being fought over by powerful forces beyond her understanding or control. No one in the tale considers her wishes; no one human even speaks to her except Arcite just before he dies. In the real world, Emelye's would be a pitiful situation. Because there is no positive evil in the Knight's Tale, however, she gets off unhurt. The belief that innocence/ignorance/incapacity of this magnitude is a virtue is a subject that Chaucer returns to again and again in the *Canterbury Tales* in more practical, realistic contexts. In the Prioress and in her tale and in the Franklin's and Physician's Tales, for example, Chaucer may be suggesting that this kind of innocence is dangerous: on the one hand, it is so easily victimized; on the other, it can, albeit unintentionally, cause great suffering. Innocence in the abstract seems lovely and fragile, like a delicate flower. But is it a virtue? Or, possibly, in the real world, is it a deficiency (in the Thomistic sense), a lack of some natural good that rightfully pertains to being human? Virtues can be tested only by experience in the real world, Chaucer suggests. That is how one learns what they really do to people.

Some other important lessons gainable only by experience, the Knight's Tale implies, rather than negative or critical, are affirmative. For example, if it is possible to learn a genuine affection for people unlike ourselves, it will have to be learned through social experience and example. It will not be learned, at any rate, by studying scholastic authorities. The fact is, people are not all cut to one type. From our own personal experience we all know that in some people, as in Arcite, intellect is prime. These people ask questions, make lists, figure out reasons, and explain them at length. In other people, as in Palamon, will is prime. These people intuit situations, make moral and emotional judgments, and put practical matters first. In the Knight's Tale, the undisputed existence of the two different types establishes scientifically (i.e., according to the logic of their own proofs) the legitimate plurality of human types, and, as a result, the social need for peaceful accommodation to natures other than our own. This is a need the scholastic philosophers were clearly unable to recognize in their own univeral psychologies, and the reason is not difficult to find. Figure 8, dated around 1410, is a charming illumination from the Boucicaut Master's Book of Hours, showing the four mendicant orders in the roundels; reading clockwise down from the top are depicted the Cistercians, the Franciscans, the Augustinians, and the Dominicans. It is a sad fact of life in this fallen world that, no matter how brilliant, a universal psychology worked out by a man who restricts his acquaintance to men who mirror his own personality, values, and daily concerns is not going to be universal. It is going to be similarly restricted. To achieve the approval of Franciscan thinkers, one must put obedience before one's own rationality; to achieve the approval of Dominican thinkers, it would be the other way around. Notice that all the tempering qualifications generalizations this broad certainly deserve will not obscure their fundamental truth: there are more kinds of human nature than our own in this created world.

Recognition that the two polarities, intellectualist and voluntarist, do exist in human nature is or should be commonplace: Lunete and the Lady Laudine. Square and Thwackum. Walter Shandy and Uncle Toby. Agatha Christie and Dashiell Hammett. In recorded history the two types go back at least as far as Greek rationalism and Hebrew justification; and, because human types are going to hold for human groups as well as human individuals, conflicts between the two polarities are evident today, as no doubt in Chaucer's time, in every kind of human institution, from family structures at odds between reasoning and obedience to aesthetic disciplines at odds between formalism and expressionism. Always,

Figure 8. Boucicaut Master. The Mendicant Orders, c. 1410. Illumination from Book of Hours, MS 1176. Bibliothèque Nationale, Paris.

within every entity, there will be the tug between reasoning and intuition, between order and affection, between prediction and freedom, between those who believe they have discovered the way to certain truth and those who believe that truth is always relative to the means by which it is found. On the intellectualist side lie abstraction, orderly sequence, rule-governed regularities, and the possibility of science; on the voluntarist side lie individual identity, emotions, free choice, and the possibility of ethics.

In the medieval period, although he did characterize their leaders as exchanging compliments, even Dante did not try to unify the two rival types. Their representative orders remain separate even in the Sphere of the Sun, where they are portrayed with a remarkable evenhandedness: Aquinas praises St. Francis and laments the sad state of his own Dominicans; whereas Bonaventure praises St. Dominic and deplores the sorry condition of his Franciscans.[12] Writing the Knight's Tale some three generations later, however, Chaucer offers a unifying resolution. Rather than privileging either faculty, Chaucer posits will/intellect relations along a bipolar spectrum ranging from competition at the extremes (Lygurge, Emetreus; Palamon, Arcite) to cooperation at the center (Theseus). As a result, Chaucer's is a truly universal theory of psychology, one capable of peacefully including within its parameters people of every possible personality type. The Knight himself, later in the links, peacefully includes even the Pardoner:

> But right anon the worthy Knyght bigan,
> Whan that he saugh that al the peple lough,
> "Namoore of this, for it is right ynough!
> Sire Pardoner, be glad and myrie of cheere;
> And ye, sire Hoost, that been to me so deere,
> I prey yow that ye kisse the Pardoner.
> And Pardoner, I prey thee, drawe thee neer,
> And, as we diden, lat us laughe and pleye." (VI, 960–68)

A genuine affection, empathy, or at the least, a courteous tolerance for people unlike ourselves can only be learned, Chaucer suggests, through social example, through experience with the diversity of real people in the real world.

And finally, some other important lessons obtainable only through personal experience, the Knight's Tale suggests, are light-hearted and laughing. For example, a sense of humor must be learned with other people. Palamon and Arcite are at all times serious and literal-minded, as are their respective psychologies. Theseus, on the other hand, can also be ironic and playful, as can the Knight himself. In fact, humor, playfulness, and wit are essentially social. They require multiple points of view. They ordinarily arise in the presence of a sudden unspoken understanding between two or more minds. They require a shared knowledge, norm, or expectation against which something incongruous or unexpected can suddenly break out.[13] Much of the pleasure of laughter itself is due to that flash of silent community with others that takes place at the moment of recognition, that silent connection which strengthens our social affections with the group and with human bonds in general, regardless of presence, as in Escher draw-ings, and regardless of time, as in the pleasure we receive from Chaucer himself. As a result, the laughing and lighthearted must be learned through personal experience with other minds. And further, they are never simply literal. They always require at least two levels simultaneously: the shared understanding and the unex-pected breakout. For example, in Part III of the Knight's Tale, Diana's temple paintings are pitiful, the four Ovidian stories so full of suffering and so terribly unjust. Then one day, quite unexpect-edly, they turn into a perfect truth table! I am still moved by the injustice, but now Chaucer and I also share a joke at the expense of the scholastic logicans. Similarly, Arcite's prayer to Mars for the use of Emelye's beauty (2385) is obnoxiously self-centered and sexist. Then one day, quite unexpectedly, it turns into an accurate portrayal of the Aristotelian ethic of self-perfection. Now I empa-thize with Arcite's plight and no longer resent his sexism. Instead Chaucer and I share a joke at the expense of pagan ethics. This playful kind of wit is social; it requires at least two minds, two points of view, to achieve the pleasure of the unexpected. And since it depends on shared but unspoken knowledge, it can never be simply literal.

Further, take the Knight's Tale itself as social and as teaching its reader to laugh. It is a stunning piece of work. As one mulls it over, as idea after idea, correspondence after correspondence, layer after layer become clear, one's reaction moves from sorrow and empathy to amusement, from sadness to intellectual recognition and sometimes to outright laughter. When responding to humor in literature, instances of actual laughter ordinarily take two or three comic recognitions in quick succession (as in the Miller's Tale denouement). I will try to do two in the Knight's Tale justice, based on your and my knowledge, shared with Chaucer, of the scholastic denigration of figurative language and antique poems: "Fie! Disgusting stories, every one of them! Ancient pagan lies!"

First, Chaucer starts off the *Canterbury* catalog of pilgrims with that striking group of three—father, son, and silent retainer—which he allusively connects in subtle participatory ways to the figures of the Holy Trinity. Then he has that idealized First-Person father-figure start the tales themselves off by "authoring" a pagan romance depicting an ancient world of meaningless human suffering and divine injustice, but a world which this father-figure shows improving—he moves its belief from polytheist to monotheist, and he moves its ruler from arbitrary violence to thoughtful parliamentary procedure. This story is, therefore, more than just an ordinary pagan romance. This pagan romance tells what actually happened! Well then, in that case, it *was* divinely authored. . . . Mirabile! that disposes of the scholastic claim that the figurative language in Scripture is the one acceptable case because God wrote it. God wrote pagan romance too.

Further, embedded within this romance and hidden hardly at all from its fourteenth-century reader is the psychological debate embodied in the rival figures of Palamon and Arcite—the scholastics' favorite debate; indeed, the debate containing the scholastics' most scientifically demonstrated and therefore absolutely certain truths; and isn't it interesting that some demonstrated absolutely certain truths are incompatible. Can it be that demonstration offers a "medley of meanings"? Can it be that logic lies? . . . Marvelous! That disposes of the scholastic charge that figurative language lies because it produces multiple meanings. Literal language produces multiple meanings too.

Life is a school, the Knight's Tale suggests, a period of benevolent freedom in which we are offered opportunities to become
better. Some of its lessons, as just shown, can be learned only by
personal experience, experience in figuring out causes, in testing
theories against reality, and in establishing and enjoying community with others. If this is so, then—and Chaucer may be implying
or he may be teasing, who can say for sure?—figurative literature,
rather than the lowest form of logic, may be the highest. Like life
itself, it presents to its pupils a medley, out of which they are free
to make their own individual meanings, as befits people who are
going to be held individually responsible for their own thoughts
and actions and behavior toward others.

There are many kinds of didacticism.[14] During the Gothic period,
artists continued to utilize the traditional didactic techniques that
had come down to them—of allusion, iconography, and exegesis
to teach directly, and of allegory and figures to teach indirectly by
first pleasurably engaging their audience's imagination. In addition,
however, apparently capitalizing on the Gothic belief that the mind
contains an appetite for knowledge and a natural rationality, some
of the high scholar-artists chose to engage their audience's mind
intellectually to a degree unknown either before or since in Western
art. From the implications of their interpretation of the 3-Acts
thinking model, that the mind is constantly active and innately
knowledge-seeking, and that when confronted with at least two
instances of an idea or thing, rather than simply accepting it passively, the mind would, by nature, think about it actively and
rationally, these scholar-artists developed to a fine art the Gothic
technique of figural triangulation. Rather than let their audience
interpret their fictions freely in the traditional Augustinian manner,
in any direction whatsoever so long as it eventually arrived at some
notion of morality or charity, these scholar-artists utilized multiple
instances to triangulate their audience more surely toward the
complex meanings they hoped it would discover and make. Jean,
Dante, Langland, and Chaucer all chose different kinds of didacticism and different kinds of direct meaning-statements, but all
four display also the same head-spinning profusion of multiple

IV. Makers and Contexts

instances, correspondences, connections, parallels, repetitions, variations, harmonizations, oppositions, and counter-instances that makes Gothic high literature so rich; and as a result, although all four make liberal intermittent use of the affections, the appeal of all four is finally to the intellect. After the third or fourth reading, the works of all four become sets of multi-level, rather chess-like problems to be solved, fascinating mind-puzzles to be pondered and pieced together, objects every aspect of which promises to become meaningful if only the right set of keys can be found.

Yet, even more than most Gothic high artists, all of whom provide unexplained correspondences and unanswered questions, Chaucer makes his reader's mind do the work. He salts his writing with suggestions, implications, and allusions that raise his reader's expectations, and then omits the intellectual connections and moral judgments his reader anticipates, thereby suggesting his reader make them. But to do this kind of thinking well is hard. It is the hardest work we have to do in this life. In fact, it is the means by which we learn how to learn from our own individual experiences. Yet things are so much easier when other people figure them out for us, so why not let them do so? Chaucer's ingenuous narrator functions often to provide the second logically-necessary instance, the second point of view, that will push the reader to an intellectual response rather than a symbolic one, a learning response rather than an acquiescing one. It is so much easier to agree with people like the Monk than to think critically about the relevance of Austyn's rule in times like these, so much simpler to condemn the Wife of Bath than to understand her, and so much more pleasant simply to admire the Prioress, who is really a lovely woman, than to figure out her shortcomings. By insisting that his reader do the thinking, but at the same time giving her or him a little unobvious help by means of his multiple instances and uncritical narrator, Chaucer is performing the function of a good father, somewhat like his Knight, keeping people aware that choices are being made, but letting them arrive at their own values freely—letting them decide whether to fulfill their own natures or honor and serve something higher.

APPENDIXES

APPENDIX A

Chaucer's Exchange of Dictions
between Palamon and Arcite

AS SET FORTH toward the end of Chapter 1, at any given time throughout the tale, Palamon's and Arcite's metaphysical status as to freedom or submission is indicated by means of the type of diction associated with each at that time: physically evocative diction indicates freedom; non-physical diction indicates submission to an outside power. This plan contains only two qualifications, both of them also logical and systematic. First, the word "herte" can have both physical and non-physical reference. As a result its use is not significant in the exchange of diction. And second, the presence or threat of physical violence overrides the assignment of the non-physical submission diction. This is because in this world our bodies, like those of beasts, *can* do whatever they are physically capable of doing; it is our minds that can restrain them, our minds therefore that make us able to choose whether to submit or to act freely. Returning to the exchange, here are the appropriate word lists. In building this "figurative demonstration," Chaucer contrasted words signifying four basic categories of experience: physical attributes, physical movements, noise, and pain.

PHYSICAL ATTRIBUTES

In Part I, Palamon casts his *"eye"* (1077), *blenches* (1078), is hurt throughout his *"ye"* into his *"herte"* (1096–97), falls on his *"knees"* (1103), and knits his *"browes tweye"* (1128). His *"bittre, salte teeres"* (1280) wet the *"pure fettres"* on his *"shynes grete"* (1279), the fire of jealousy starts up within his *"brest"* and seizes him by the "herte" (1300), and he is damned to be dead *"in cheynes and in fettres"* (1343). Arcite's only physical attributes in Part I are in connection with

Theseus's sentence of death if he violates his exile: *"heed"* (1215), *"nekke"* (1218), and *"heed"* (1344).

In Part II, the technique is reversed. Arcite receives the physical description while Palamon has physical attributes only in connection with potential or actual physical violence. Arcite's *"eyen"* become hollow (1363) and his *"hewe"* fallow (1364) while suffering in Thebes. After his decision to return to Athens the physical details mount up: *"colour"* (1400), *"visage"* (1401), *"face"* (1403), *"array"* (1408), physical build: "For he was *yong* and *myghty* for the nones, / And therto he was *long* and *big of bones"* (1423–24), and *"tonge"* (1438). Palamon's only physical attributes in Part II are the *"dredeful foot"* (1479) on which he steals through the grove and his *"face"* (1578) when he challenges Arcite.

In Part III, other than four references to his heart (2213, 2220, 2229, 2256), Palamon is given only his *"bittre teeris"* (2225) and the *"armes"* in which he wants Emelye (2247). Arcite's *youth* is mentioned twice (2379, 2393), his *"strengthe"* twice (2399, 2401), he has *"myght"* (2380), heart (2371), and *beard, hair,* and *hand* (2415, 2428).

In Part IV, Arcite has a *helmet* (2676), *head* (2689, 2875), *breast* (2691, 2743, 2753, 2799), *blood* (2693, 2745), *face* (2677, 2693), heart (2683, 2695, 2744, 2765, 2775, 2804, 2805), *trunk* (2746), *lungs* (2752), *muscles* (2753), *feet* (2799), *arms* (2801), *eyes* (2806, 2807), *breath* (2806), *corpse* (2819), *hands* (2874, 2876), *gloves* (2874), *crown* (2875), *sword* (2876), *visage* (2877), and *body* (2940). Physical details for Arcite cease with his funeral. Palamon's only physical description in Part IV until after the funeral preparations is in connection with the physically violent tournament (*face, flesh,* and heart: 2586, 2640, 2649). But after Arcite's death, Palamon again, as in Part I, receives physical attributes: *beard* and *hair* (2883), *black clothes* (2884, 2978), and *tears* (2884).

To summarize (keeping in mind the qualification that anything connected with physical violence receives physical attributes), Palamon is described with physical attributes only in Part I and in Part IV after Arcite's death. The only exceptions to this are his tears and arms in his prayer to Venus in Part III. This plan is exactly reversed for Arcite. Arcite is described with physical description only in Parts II and III and in IV up until his funeral. (That Arcite is given no physical attributes after his funeral is not necessarily dictated by the plot; Boccaccio followed his Arcita after death, and Chaucer's Arcite is spoken of after the funeral.)

The foregoing list necessarily omits much of the context in which the references occur. And one must admit that it is sometimes difficult to know exactly how to interpret the evocative qualities of a word. However, these lists do provide logical, objective evidence, statistically far beyond the possibility of chance, as to how Chaucer wished his audience to conceive his characters. Palamon and Arcite are each to be conceived, right from the start, as rigidly one-sided, at least in this respect, and as passing from one extreme to the other during the action from Part I to Part III.

PHYSICAL MOVEMENT

In Part I, Palamon's "wone" in prison is to go *roaming to and fro* (1064–65, 1071; this is one reason Chaucer's Palamon sees Emelye first), whereas Arcite apparently just sits (1080). Palamon *casts* his eye upon Emelye (1077), whereas Arcite just *observes* her ("espye," 1112). Palamon *falls to his knees* to pray (1103), whereas Arcite just *speaks with a sigh* (1117). On Arcite's release from prison, Palamon *makes* such sorrow that the tower resounds (1277–78), whereas Arcite merely *suffers* it inwardly (1219–20). Thus, in Part I, Palamon moves around and is described with physically active verbs, whereas Arcite's outward physical activity is kept to a minimum.

Arcite's outward physical activity begins when, after Mercury's prompting, he decides to return to Athens in Part II. He *starts* after his dream (1393), *catches* a mirror (1399), an idea *runs* him in his mind (1402), he *changes* his array (1408), *clothes* himself as a laborer (1409), *goes* to Athens (1413), *goes* to court (1414), *proffers* his service to "*drugge and drawe*" (1415–16), and *falls in* with the chamberlain (1418). "Wel koude he *hewen* wode, and water *bere*" (1422). In Athens he does hard physical labor and rises quickly by merit in both speech and deeds (1438 and thereafter) to become Theseus's chamber squire. One May morning, he *rises* (1499), remembers his purpose in Athens, and *rides* out on a fiery courser to *play* (1503). Then he *sings* loudly (1509), *starts hastily* from his horse (1513–14), and—recalling Palamon's customary prison behavior in Part I—goes *roaming up and down* (1515). He *falls* into a study (1530), sighs, *sits down* and laments (1541 and thereafter), *falls down* in a trance, and *starts up* (1572–73). His remaining physical activity after this, during Palamon's challenge and their duel, is necessitated by the possible physical consequences. Conversely, Palamon in Part II spends seven years *sitting* in prison ("seten," 1452). He moves actively during his prison break, *fleeing* (1475) and *stalking* (1479), but once safe in the grove, he is twice described as *sitting still* in his bush (1517, 1527). The rest of his physical activity in Part II is in connection with the challenge and duel. To summarize, in Part II, except for situations of potential or actual physical violence, Arcite is now the one described with active verbs and active physical movement, whereas Palamon's outward physical activity is kept to a minimum. In terms of their relative physical activity, the reader's final sight of the two separately, at the close of Part II: "Who *looketh lightly* now but Palamon? / Who *spryngeth up* for joye but Arcite?" (1870–71, emphasis added), is just the opposite of the initial sight of them in Part I, where Palamon was roaming to and fro and Arcite was outwardly still.

During the prayers of Part III, Palamon is physically very subdued. He takes twelve lines to get to Venus's temple (2209–20), whereas Arcite takes only six to get to the temple of Mars. He *kneels* during his prayer (2219). The actual details of his rites are specifically suppressed (2262–64). Venus's statue merely *shakes* and makes a sign for him (2265–66), whereupon he goes home "with glad herte" (2270). Conversely, Arcite's physical movement in Part III is forthright. He speaks his prayer to Mars "right thus" (2372). He *heaves up* his hand and *casts* more incense into the fire (2428–29). The doors and their rings *clatter* "ful faste" in response for him (2422–23), the fires *burn brighter* (2425–26), and the statue *rings* its hauberk (2431). And finally, Arcite *fares* home "as fayn as fowel is of the brighte sonne" (2437). During Part III, vividly perceptible physical movement is associated with Arcite; slow, subdued movement with Palamon.

After the tournament in Part IV, Palamon "moste *abyde*" by the stake (2650), while Arcite "*priketh*" along the field (2678). (Neither idea appears in the *Teseida:* there Palamon is simply borne out of the fray and quickly disarmed, "e tratto fuor della crudel mislea, / e sanzo alcuno indugio disarmato" [VIII, 122]; and as for Arcite, the fury goes to the field "lá dove Arcita correva festante" and stands in the path of his horse [IX, 7].) Palamon has no more physical movement until he comes woefully to ride in the funeral procession (2882), but at the end, summoned by Theseus, he comes hastily ("in hye," 2979) back to Athens. Arcite's illness is described with physically active verbs (swell, increase, corrupt, and so on, 2743 and thereafter), and his active movement ceases with his death. (In the *Teseida,* Arcite continues to receive active verbs after his death: volando, ammirava, ascoltando, volse a rimirare, e seco rise, dannando, sortio [XI, 1–3].) In Part IV, then, active physical movement is Arcite's until his death, after which it is returned, as in Part I, to Palamon.

To summarize, in Part I Palamon moves around actively and is described with physically active words. But after he chooses Emelye as his final goal at the beginning of Part II, his physical activity in the remainder of the poem is slow and subdued, except during scenes directly related to physical violence, until he returns to Athens hastily at the end. Conversely, Arcite's physical activity is quite subdued in Part I. But after he decides to return to Athens in Part II, vigorous physical movement and physically active verbs are associated with him until his spirit changes house in Part IV.

NOISE

Loud noise is associated with Palamon in Part I, with Arcite in Parts II and III and until his death in IV, after which it is returned to Palamon.

In Part I, on first seeing Emelye, Palamon cries "A!" (1078). When his cousin is released from prison, "Swich sorwe he [Palamon] maketh that the grete tour / Resouneth of his youlyng and clamour" (1277–78). He makes no loud noise again until his howl after Arcite dies (2817). Conversely, Arcite merely sighs (1117) on first seeing Emelye, and he suffers quietly, compared to Palamon, when he is released from prison: "He wepeth, wayleth, crieth pitously; / To sleen hymself he waiteth prively" (1221–22). In Part

II, however, he sings loudly (1509) and lustily (1529). In Part III, his champion's voice is as a trumpet thundering (2174), whereas Palamon's champion is conspicuously silent. Mars answers Arcite's prayer by clattering the temple doors, ringing his hauberk, and murmuring, whereas Venus merely shakes and makes a silent sign for Palamon. After the tournament is over and Theseus awards Emelye to Arcite,

> Anon ther is a noyse of peple bigonne
> For joye of this, so loude and heighe withalle,
> It semed that the lystes sholde falle. (2660–62)

After his accident, Arcite is carried to Theseus's palace, "alwey criynge after Emelye" (2699). But after his death, Chaucer's Arcite (unlike Boccaccio's) is absolutely silent.

QUALITY OF PAIN

The diction used for descriptions of pain causes the same contrast, based on whether or not a physical body is evoked in the mind of the reader. Palamon's pain in Part I and Arcite's in Part III are phrased in such a way as to suggest that a physical body is being physically hurt; the imagery is that of a stab, a sting, or a burn. Conversely, Arcite's pain in Part I and Palamon's in Part III are generalized; the person as a whole is hurt, rather than a particular part of his body with a particular kind of pain, or he suffers negatively, through deprivation, rather than positively through some ill.

When Palamon first sees Emelye, "he bleynte and cride, 'A!' / As though he *stongen were unto the herte*" (1078–79). He himself describes the physical passage of the feeling through his body: "But I was hurt right now *thurghout myn ye / into myn herte*" (1096–97). Conversely, with Arcite's first sight of her,

> . . . hir beautee *hurte* hym so,
> That if that Palamon was wounded sore,
> Arcite *is hurt* as muche as he, or moore. (1114–16)

He himself describes the feeling as general, encompassing his self as a whole: "The fresshe beautee *sleeth me* sodeynly / Of hire . . ."

(1118–19). Near the end of Part I, in his speech bewailing his plight after Arcite's release, Palamon is interrupted by a specifically physical kind of pain: ". . . the *fyr* of jalousie *up sterte / Withinne his brest*, and *hente him by the herte*" (1299–1300). At the same point in Arcite's rhetorically paralleled speech, a vast generalization is used to describe his own situation of deprivation:

> But I, that am exiled and bareyne
> Of alle grace, and in so greet dispeir,
> That ther nys erthe, water, fir, ne eir,
> Ne creature that of hem maked is,
> That may me helpe or doon confort in this,
> Wel oughte I sterve in wanhope and distresse.
> Farwel my lif, my lust, and my gladnesse! (1244–50)

In Part I, love causes them both to suffer, but Palamon suffers specifically physical, particularized kinds of pain, a sting or a clutch, whereas in the first Arcite as a whole is hurt, and in the second he is deprived rather than actively, physically injured.

In Part II, the situation begins to be reversed. Each knight begins to receive the kind of pain originally assigned in Part I to the other. Palamon's pain is now generalized.

> In derknesse and horrible and strong prisoun
> This seven yeer hath seten Palamoun
> Forpyned, what for wo and for distresse. (1451–58)

Palamon feels "double soor" and "hevynesse"; love destrains him, and he is a prisoner. When he is described with physically particularized pain, it is immediately followed by physical description, movement, and challenge to physical combat:

> This Palamoun, that thoughte that *thurgh his herte*
> He *felte a coold swerd sodeynliche glyde*,
> For ire he *quook*, no lenger wolde he byde.
> And whan that he had herd Arcites tale,
> As he were wood, *with face deed and pale*,
> He *stirte hym up* . . . (1574–79)

In his challenge, however, he himself generalizes his pain: "Al this peyne and wo." As for Arcite, he begins Part II with the generalized pain of deprivation:

So muche sorwe hadde nevere creature
That is, or shal, whil that the world may dure.
His slep, his mete, his drynke, is hym biraft,
That lene he wex and drye as is a shaft; (1359–62)

But later, after he finally remembers why he returned to Athens, "the poynt of his desir" (1501), then he begins to be described with the sharply physical imagery: "To sleen me outrely, / Love hath his *firy dart so brennyngly / Ystiked thurgh my trewe, careful herte*" (1563–65).

In the prayers of Part III, the diction is completely reversed from what it was in Part I: Arcite now speaks of specifically physical pain, being burned, whereas Palamon's suffering is now generalized.

Arcite: For thilke peyne, and *thilke hoote fir*
          In which thow whilom *brendest* for desire, (2383–
          84)

          For *thilke fyr* that whilom *brente* thee,
          As wel as *thilke fyr now brenneth me,*
          And do that I tomorwe have victorie. (2403–5)

Palamon: Allas! I ne have no langage to telle
          Th'*effectes* ne the *tormentz* of myn helle;
          Myn herte may *myne harmes* nat biwreye. (2227–29)

In Part IV, aside from the violent tournament, so far as diction indicating pain is concerned, Palamon is described with the adjective "woful" (2882) and the adverb "sorwefully" (2978), both indicating generalized emotional pain. And Arcite, finally, in his death-bed speech, is described with diction indicating the same generalized kind of pain: "my sorwes smerte," "the wo," and "the peynes stronge" (2766, 2772).

In summary, except for circumstances of physical violence, Palamon's pain in Part I and Arcite's in Part III are specifically physical; Arcite's in Part I and Palamon's in Parts II and III are generalized.

Interestingly, in addition to its philosophical significance, mentioned earlier, Chaucer's qualification regarding physical violence in this exchange-of-diction system supports an inference often made (but difficult to prove) about him as a person—that he had an intense dislike of physical violence.[1] In systematically overriding the freedom/submission schema throughout the tale with active, physically evocative diction whenever physical violence is threatened or present, Chaucer seems to be saying that, in this world, the positive physical violence of one human being against another is always a freely made choice. Certainly, for human beings, there is nothing in either natural necessity or divine revelation and the sacramental system to encourage us to such behavior. There are better ways to resolve things.

In addition to its function of signifying the two young knights' status as to metaphysical freedom or submission, this exchange of diction is also interesting for what it reveals of Chaucer's techniques as a poet. To see multiple instances of so many different and unusual verbal techniques turns the tale, at times, into a veritable handbook for poets.

APPENDIX B

Use of Boethian Phrases and Ideas in Theseus's Prime Mover Speech

THESEUS'S SPEECH has so often been read as a Chaucerian summary of Boethian thought, rather than as the artful Chaucerian characterization it is, that a detailed comparison of the appropriate passages from the two works may be helpful. In fact, the Prime Mover speech does contain free-standing ideas and phrases from the *Consolation,* most of them ancient and traditional, but Chaucer uses them to form a pre-Christian cosmology for Theseus different from Boethius's cosmology in the *Consolation.*

Theseus's speech is ordinarily said to derive particularly from Book IV, prose 6 and meter 6, and Book II, meter 8. These *Consolation* passages and the Prime Mover speech both consider the same general topics of earthly order, of the Being who first established it, and of untimely human death, but as I will now show, they differ sharply in their specific approaches and implications.

EVIDENCE OF ORDER

Boethius:		Theseus:
Orderly harmony	versus	*Orderly corruption*

In Book II, meter 8, Philosophy praises the orderly *harmony* by which the world moves through its changes and by which the competition of things is held in balance—the competition of seeds, of sun and moon, of sea and land, of people, couples, friends. Love is the force both physical and spiritual which holds all these competing things together. In the Prime Mover speech, on the other hand, Theseus praises the orderly *corruption* of all earthly things—the oak wastes, likewise the stone, the river runs dry, the great towns wane, people die (2994–3034). On earth the physical duration of all these things is limited in an orderly way; this shows the existence of order in the universe, and therefore the existence of a stable eternal First Mover.

Thus both passages serve to demonstrate order in the universe, but order of two very different kinds: The source of Boethius's notion of order is love, both spiritual and physical. The source of Theseus's notion of order is the regular, predictable, physical decline and death of all the individual entities of this world.

NOTIONS OF THE SUPREME BEING

Boethius:		Theseus:
Individually loving		*Distant, stable,*
caretaker	versus	*eternal First Mover*

As a whole, Book IV of the *Consolation* is devoted to showing that the evil in the world is only apparent. In prose 6, Philosophy describes the Supreme Being as a personal deity, a "ruler and healer of minds," who directs all natures individually towards the good.[2] All things, she tells Boethius, from the movements of the stars to the individual acts and fortunes of men, are bound in an unbreakable web of causes; and regardless of how confused, disordered, or unjust things may seem to a human observer, God is arranging what is fitting for every single human being: "The whiche God, whan he hath byholden from the hye tour of his purveaunce, he knoweth what is covenable to every wight, and lenyth [grants/allows; lends/gives] hem that he woot that is covenable to hem" (notice the present tense: "quod convenire novit accommodat").[3] In meter 6, as she discusses the return of all things to their source, Philosophy again uses the present tense: "Among thise thinges sitteth the heye makere, kyng and lord, welle and bygynnynge, lawe and wys juge to don equite, and governeth and enclyneth the brydles of thinges. And tho thinges that he stireth to go by moevynge, he withdraweth and aresteth" ("sedet," "flectit," "concidat," and "sistit").[4] Thus the *Consolation* notion of the Supreme

Deity is of an all-powerful personal caretaker presently active in the world and bringing each of us individually toward the good.

The First Mover of Theseus's speech, on the other hand, at one time ordered the elements and established durations for this world, but that was all in the past (notice the past tense: "made," "was," "wiste," "mente," and so on, 2986–99); he paid then and still pays no attention whatsoever to individual beings in this world, functioning now (present tense, 3035–38) only as their source and final end.

Thus once again, Theseus's meaning is not the Boethian meaning. His Prime Mover is far away in time and space, and now is simply the source and end of all things, not their individually caring guide.

FAME

	Boethius:		Theseus:
	Dying gloriously	versus	*Dying young*

In Book IV, prose 6, while speaking of the different fortunes that Providence metes out to human beings, Philosophy says that "many other folk han bought honourable renoun of this world by the prys of glorious deth" ("Nonnulli venerandum saeculi nomen gloriosae pretio mortis emerunt").[5] The passage makes one think of heroic warriors defending mountain passes and of early Christians martyred for their faith. Arcite's death, however, was not at all glorious or even necessary; it was unjust and ugly. He was thrown by his horse through no fault of his own after winning a tournament, and he died slowly and painfully of infection. His funeral was glorious, but the credit there belongs to Theseus, not to Arcite. What Theseus actually praises, as he tries to find some virtue in this necessity, is not Arcite's dying gloriously but Arcite's dying young:

> And certeinly a man hath moost honour
> To dyen in his excellence and flour,
> Whan he is siker of his goode name;
> Thanne hath he doon his freend, ne hym, no shame.

And gladder oghte his freend been of his deeth,
Whan with honour up yolden is his breeth,
Than whan his name appalled is for age,
For al forgeten is his vassellage. (3047–54)

From the human point of view within the tale, Arcite's death is not glorious; it is a waste. Only when Theseus puts it in the context of Arcite's larger "welfare" (3063) does his death become humanly acceptable.

Thus Chaucer's use of Boethian phrases and constructions in the Prime Mover speech is never a simple summary reference to the *Consolation*. Rather, each allusively Boethian phrase or construction carries its own ordinary Middle English meaning in the context in which Chaucer uses it. The result is to characterize Theseus (Chapter 2) as a man who has generalized from his own painful experiences of the difference between high intention and harsh this-world outcome to the existence and some understanding of the Being who first ordered it. Theseus's Prime Mover is not the Christianized prime mover of Boethius's *Consolation*. Rather, it is the pagan prime mover, source and end of all things. Theseus becomes a monotheist, and he learns to recognize and accept his place within the larger order of things, but he does not become a Christian.

APPENDIX C

Thinking Act 3—Inference to Causes:
Sample Analyses of Lygurge/Emetreus Possessions

AS SHOWN IN Chapter 4, systematic causal analysis of the possessions of each rival king—his choice of crown, gold, gems, cotearmure, conveyance, and household animals—reveals his kind of human substance (form, prime matter, and manner of combination), whether voluntarist or intellectualist. Creating the paralleled pairs of contrasting possessions for these two kings so that readers could easily infer this metaphysical kind of information seems to have been done by using Aristotle's four analytic causes, at least in the initial stages of writing. The paired contrasts are as to: *(1)* whether the item's natural physical matter is treated as actual (voluntarist) or as potential, i.e., mere substrate for change (intellectualist)—*material cause*; *(2)* whether the item's maker expended primarily brute physical force (voluntarist) or primarily technical or intellectual skill (intellectualist)—*efficient cause*; *(3)* whether the item appears to be still close to its original, natural state (voluntarist) or to have been changed so as to be apprehended as something quite different (intellectualist)—*formal cause*; and *(4)* whether the item appeals affectively to the will as something to be acquired or avoided (voluntarist) or appeals first to the intellect as aesthetically or intellectually interesting (intellectualist)—*final cause*. Sample analyses follow for the crowns and household animals, with formal causes on the left and material, efficient, and final causes on the right.

The challenge in forming such contrasted pairs of possessions is to pick items that can be appropriately fitted in all four causal categories. However, the basic contrasts shown in the samples opposite

Appendix C

LYGURGE

gold wreath (crown)	original qualities little changed, emphasis on mass, weight	matter as actual
	primitive technology: melting and molding	means: more power than intellect
	great, easily negotiable wealth	appeal to will as a good to acquire

alaunts (household animals)	original qualities little changed, emphasis on size, strength	matter as actual
	primitive technology: muzzles, collars with turrets	means: physical power
	savagery, function to drag down large game	appeal to will as something to fear

EMETREUS

laurel garland (crown)	original quality as leafy greens fundamentally changed	matter as potential
	technology: development of an intellectual tradition	means: intellect
	symbolic value only (intrinsically worthless)	appeal to cognitive intellect

lions and leopards (household animals)	original wild natures drastically changed, completely tamed	matter as potential
	technology: highly sophisticated methods of taming	means: intellect
	docility, reliability (allowed to run unrestrained), no function specified	primary appeal to cognitive intellect as marvel of skill

are only the beginning of Chaucer's technique; each pair can additionally be considered in far greater depth. For example, each king has a cote-armure.

> Lygurge: In stede of cote-armure over his harnays,
> With nayles yelewe and brighte as any gold,
> He hadde a beres skyn, col-blak for old. (2140–42)

> Emetreus: His cote-armure was of clooth of Tars
> Couched with perles white and rounde and grete;
> (2160–61)

Let us look just at the material causes of these two items. In fact, the materials of which both cotes-armure were made are entirely of animal origin, but Lygurge's was wild, Emetreus's mostly domesticated. Chaucer's contrasts here are of mass and weight and layer, of technological sophistication, of degree of change from natural state, and of faculty appeal. To make Lygurge's cote, someone killed a bear, skinned it, cured it by fairly simple methods since it has apparently changed color with age ("col-blak for old"), and polished its claws. To make Emetreus's cote, on the other hand, so many technologies were expended that the original worms, goats, and oysters that produced its component materials hardly even enter one's mind. Cloth of Tars was a rich, costly Oriental fabric of woven silk and cashmere. Silk is produced by silk-moth larvae spinning their cocoons; in order to retain the cocoon as one long strand, the larvae were killed; then the cocoons were soaked, unreeled, and several strands twisted together into thread strong enough for weaving. Similarly, cashmere is the downy fleece underlying the long coarse outer hair of the cashmere goat, also from the Orient. It too has to be formed into strands. Gathering and blending these two types of threads into "clooth of Tars" (Tarsia in Turkestan) suggests a high degree of technological organization and skill. Further, Emetreus's pearls were first formed by tropical sea oysters, enclosing foreign substances that had got inside their shells, perhaps a tiny parasite or grain of sand, within a coat of nacre, the substance secreted to line their shells. These too had to be expertly harvested. And finally, couching these large round pearls into a soft silky fabric could not have been an easy task. In sum, pondering just the material causes of the cotes-armure of these two kings reveals important aspects of the personal taste of each man, and thus of their respective metaphysical forms. Pondering the causes of the other contrasted pairs of possessions can be equally revealing. My point is not only that the details of these portraits reveal a good deal about each man; they also reveal a good deal about Chaucer's ways with words, his own language use.

NOTES

Section I. Introduction
    1. Elizabeth Salter, *Chaucer: The Knight's Tale and the Clerk's Tale* (New York: Barron's, 1962), pp. 22, 13, 19, 32, 33. In the most recent reading of the tale of which I am aware, a paper prepared for the August 1988 Sixth International Congress of the New Chaucer Society, Winthrop Wetherbee makes of this "double vision" as it is fought out in the mind of the Knight the central battleground of the story: In the Knight's Tale "an optimistic depiction of chivalric heroism is tempered by a lurking awareness of other, darker aspects of life which are an inherent part of its classical subject matter, but which the chivalric program that governs it tends always to suppress or marginalize. . . . In the Knight's Tale [this awareness] is made to surface as if against the will of narrator who has a powerful professional investment in the optimistic, 'romance' version of his story, and whose suppression of historical and psychological reality, while largely unwitting, is also to a certain extent a deliberate, political gesture" ("Romance and Tragedy in the Knight's Tale: Chaucer's Dark Statius," p. 3).
    2. Charles Muscatine, *Chaucer and the French Tradition: A Study in Style and Meaning* (Berkeley: Univ. of California Press, 1957), pp. 175, 180–81.
    3. Terry Jones, *Chaucer's Knight: The Portrait of a Medieval Mercenary* (Baton Rouge: Louisiana State Univ. Press, 1980), pp. 141–43.
    4. Larry Sklute, *Virtue of Necessity: Inconclusiveness and Narrative Form in Chaucer's Poetry* (Columbus: Ohio State Univ. Press, 1984), pp. 102, 96, 129, 79.
    5. Helen Cooper, *The Structure of the Canterbury Tales* (Athens: Univ. of Georgia Press, 1984), p. 240.
    6. Judith Ferster, *Chaucer on Interpretation* (Cambridge: Cambridge Univ. Press, 1985), pp. 23, 44, 156.
    7. V. A. Kolve, *Chaucer and the Imagery of Narrative: The First Five Canterbury Tales* (Stanford: Stanford Univ. Press, 1984), pp. 86, 90.

8. E. D. Hirsch, Jr., *Validity in Interpretation* (New Haven: Yale Univ. Press, 1967), p. 75.

9. Roughly one-quarter of the tale's critics have either alluded to the genre problem directly, or, as a result of the subjects they do discuss, indicated some uncertainty about the nature of this particular "romance." In chronological order, Hoxie Neale Fairchild speaks of its "allegorical implications" ("Active Arcite, Contemplative Palamon," *Journal of English and Germanic Philology* 26 [1927]: 292). Howard Rollin Patch comments that, "if the *Knight's Tale* must be a romance, I would say that it is after the manner of the English Cycle" (*On Rereading Chaucer* [Cambridge, Mass.: Harvard Univ. Press, 1939], p. 210). Charles Muscatine feels it is only "nominally a romance"; instead it is "rather a sort of poetic pageant" (*Chaucer and the French Tradition*, pp. 175, 181). Richard Neuse believes it to be a kind of fusion of classical epic and chivalric romance ("The Knight: The First Mover in Chaucer's Human Comedy," *University of Toronto Quarterly* 31 [1962]: 301). Bernard Huppé resolves the combination of love story, philosophical questions, and "comic deflations" by reading it as "a venture in . . . high comedy" (*A Reading of the Canterbury Tales* [Albany: State Univ. of New York Press, 1964], p. 54). Judith Scherer Herz feels that the "combination of romance and reality in the *Knight's Tale* remains a striking contradiction" ("Chaucer's Elegiac Knight," *Criticism* 6 [1964]: 224). Paul G. Ruggiers speaks of it both as a "didactic romance" and as "a kind of quizzical and thought-provoking literary type" somewhere between tragedy and serious comedy (*The Art of the Canterbury Tales* [Madison: Univ. of Wisconsin Press, 1965], pp. 152, 158). Robert S. Haller regards it as a classical epic in which love has become "the means whereby the cosmic and political implications of the epic are conveyed" ("The *Knight's Tale* and the Epic Tradition," *ChRev* 1 [1966–67]: 68). Robert M. Jordan feels that the tale "celebrates rationality" as the ruling force throughout the universe (*Chaucer and the Shape of Creation* [Cambridge, Mass: Harvard Univ. Press, 1967], p. 153). P. M. Kean terms the love story "the pretext for a philosophical poem," one that generalizes rather than particularizes, something nearer "the type-situation of, for example, the morality play" (*Chaucer and the Making of English Poetry* [London: Routledge and Kegan Paul, 1972], vol. 2, *The Art of Narrative*, pp. 2–3). Kathleen A. Blake regards the Knight's rhetorical style as suited for employment in a "futile . . . scholastic quibble" ("Order and the Noble Life in Chaucer's *Knight's Tale?*" *Modern Language Quarterly* 34 [1974]: 5). And finally, Paul A. Olson says that "clearly, the Knight's Tale is an epic or heroic song" which becomes "a serious critique on English policy to create peace within and abroad" (*The "Canterbury Tales" and the Good Society* [Princeton: Princeton Univ. Press, 1986], pp. 62, 65).

10. Indeed, one major argument for the tale's generic identification as a romance is the quantity and quality of its paralleled contrasts with Chaucer's fabliaux. For extended discussion of the parallels between the Knight's Tale and the Miller's Tale, see C. David Benson, *Chaucer's Drama of Style: Poetic Variety and Contrast in the Canterbury Tales* (Chapel Hill: Univ. of North Carolina Press, 1986), Chap. 4; between the Knight's Tale, the Miller's Tale, and the Reeve's Tale, see Olson, *The "Canterbury Tales" and the Good Society*, pp. 49–84.

11. See Anthony Kenny and Jan Pinborg, "Medieval Philosophical Literature," *CHLMP*, pp. 20–34, for description, history, influence, and bibliographical references on the disputations.

12. Norman Kretzmann, "Syncategoremata, Exponibilia, Sophismata," *CHLMP*, p. 234. These discussions are still not widely understood. Dorothy L. Sayers, for example, recalls the time that a "glib speaker entertained his audience (and reduced the late Charles Williams to helpless rage) by asserting that in the Middle Ages it was a matter of faith to know how many archangels could dance on the point of a needle. I need not say," she continues, "that it never was a 'matter of faith'; it was simply a debating exercise, whose set subject was the nature of angelic substance: were angels material, and if so, did they occupy space? The answer usually adjudged correct is, I believe, that angels are pure intelligence, not material, but limited, so that they may have location in space but no extension. An analogy might be drawn from human thought, which is similarly non-material and similarly limited. Thus, if your thought is concentrated upon one thing—say, the point of a needle—it is located there in the sense that it is not elsewhere; but although it is 'there,' it occupies no space there, and there is nothing to prevent an infinite number of different people's thoughts being concentrated upon the same needlepoint at the same time. The proper *subject* of the argument is thus seen to be the distinction between location and extension in space; the *matter* on which the argument is exercised happens to be the nature of angels (although, as we have seen, it might equally well have been something else)" ("The Lost Tools of Learning," *National Review*, January 19, 1979: 92–93).

13. Kenny and Pinborg comment that "many *sophismata*, especially from Paris in the latter half of the thirteenth century, are in the form of regular disputed questions" ("Medieval Philosophical Literature," p. 24); and in a recent unpublished paper entitled "Methods of Teaching Dialectic," Alfonso Maierú concludes that "From the literature that has come down to us it is, in fact, possible to argue that the disputation exercises for the logicians consisted *mainly* of sophisms" (delivered at the Twenty-third International Congress of Medieval Studies, Western Michigan University, Kalamazoo, May 1988, emphasis added).

14. To avoid sexism in pronouns and common nouns is difficult in a medieval context, because often the medieval writers intended the sexism. As a result, it would be misleading to adopt contemporary nonsexist usage indiscriminately. In this book, I will do my best both to be accurate to the medieval thinkers as I understand them and to stay within contemporary nonsexist standards of good usage whenever the context allows.

15. R. W. Southern, *The Making of the Middle Ages* (New Haven: Yale Univ. Press, 1953), pp. 49–50.

16. Jane Chance outlines the defense of classical poetry against charges of blasphemy by both pagan and Christian critics ("The Origins and Development of Medieval Mythography: From Homer to Dante," in *Mapping the Cosmos,* ed. Jane Chance and R. W. Wells, Jr. [Houston: Rice Univ. Press, 1985], esp. pp. 38–45).

17. *Familiares* (10.4), as translated by Concetta Carestia Greenfield, *Humanist and Scholastic Poetics, 1250–1500* (Lewisburg: Bucknell Univ. Press, 1981), p. 99.

18. "Poets are liars, as the proverb has it," *Commentary in Metaphysics,* 63, as quoted in Umberto Eco, *Art and Beauty in the Middle Ages,* trans. Hugh Bredin (New Haven: Yale Univ. Press, 1986), p. 106. Marcia L. Colish summarizes the several different medieval views of poetry: "All of them possess classical antecedents. All of them contain the implicit idea that poetry, as a form of communication, can be judged according to rhetorical canons, although the type of rhetoric in each case may differ. Thus, medieval poetics can assume a sophistical, or purely technical orientation, in which primary stress is placed on decoration and style. Or, it can assume a broader, antisophistic orientation in which the good, the true, and the eloquent are linked and applied to poetry, by way of criticizing existing poetry or by way of establishing norms for the poetry that ought to be written. Some medieval theorists hold the view that poetry is wholly or partially false or fictitious, an interpretation which implies that poetry is didactic and persuasive. Thus, some of them regard the characters, plot, or stylistic accoutrements of a poem as fictitious veils which stand between the reader and an edifying inner core. These fictitious veils may be pulled aside by literary analysis or left clothing the core of the poem, depending on the literary astuteness of the reader. For the less sophisticated reader, the veils may be regarded as a lure, a sugar coating over the pill within, which makes the edification provided by the poem more palatable. The more skillful reader will regard the veils as a series of obstacles, and his enjoyment of the poet's message will be enhanced by his feeling of success in having met and solved them. Alternatively the fictitious veils may be thought of as a shield protecting an esoteric inner truth from profane eyes, ensuring that it will be detected only by initiates whose intellects are equal to the task of penetrating the veils.

Finally, following the tradition established by Plato when he ejected the poets from his *Republic* and seconded by Augustine in his *Confessiones*, some medieval theorists thought that poetry was entirely false and fictitious in the ideas and attitudes it put forth, and that it was dangerously seductive on account of its beauty" (*The Mirror of Language: A Study in the Medieval Theory of Knowledge* [New Haven: Yale Univ. Press, 1968], pp. 227–28). In the thirteenth century, Colish continues, "the view that poetry has no claims to truth was quite popular. It can be found in the works of the Franciscans Robert Grosseteste and St. Bonaventura, as well as in the works of the Dominicans Albertus Magnus and Thomas Aquinas" (p. 236).

19. Thomas Aquinas, *Summa theologiae* (New York: Blackfriars, 1967–76), Ia, 1.10: "Now because the literal sense is that which the author intends, and the author of holy Scripture is God who comprehends everything all at once in his understanding, it comes not amiss, as St. Augustine observes, if many meanings are present even in the literal sense of one passage of Scripture." Further, Eco points out that "in holding that natural objects have an allegorical significance only in the context of Scripture," Aquinas "broke with tradition": He reduced the cosmic allegory of Augustine and earlier thinkers to biblical allegory; natural objects and arts were to have "only a literal meaning" (Eco, *Art and Beauty*, p. 63).

20. See discussion in Greenfield, *Humanist and Scholastic Poetics*, especially pp. 17–40. This kind of science ultimately derives from the methods of Socrates and Aristotle, according to which one searches for new truths by questioning and challenging everything, free of dogma, recognizing reason as the only authority. C. H. Lohr contrasts this idea of "science," imbued with the spirit of freedom, curiosity, and criticism, with the traditional idea of "science" which it began to replace in the thirteenth-century universities, the idea that science was the transmission of traditional wisdom to God's children, concerned not with discovering any new knowledge, but rather with the unveiling and if need be harmonizing, in a spirit of reverence and faith, of truths already known, concealed within the words of the sacred texts ("The Medieval Interpretation of Aristotle," *CHLMP*, pp. 80–98). Ernst Curtius discusses the changeover in "Poetry and Scholasticism, in *European Literature and the Latin Middle Ages*, trans. Willard Trask (New York: Harper and Row, 1963), pp. 480–84.

21. Judson Boyce Allen has shown that "the later medieval theory of literature presumes that the content of literature is radically grounded in ethics" (*The Ethical Poetic of the Later Middle Ages: A Decorum of Convenient Distinction* [Toronto: Univ. of Toronto Press, 1982], p. 289). Further, "this medieval doctrine [that "poetry is to be classified as ethics"] flatly contradicts purely aesthetic approaches to literature, unless they are un-

dertaken merely as the first step in an analysis of rhetorical effectiveness—that is, as the first step in an analysis of poetic consideration, expressive power, or heightened language as these relate to and demonstrate ethical values" (p. 38).

22. There is still no accepted definition of "mind." Writing in 1967 for the *Encyclopedia of Philosophy,* Jerome Shaffer comments: "The fact of the matter is that there does not as yet exist a very satisfactory account of our concept of the mind. We know that for each person a series of mental changes occurs, but if we try to say exactly what it is that changes we fall into utter obscurity; if we take the mind to be simply the collection of those changes, we seem to be leaving out precisely what ties them together into the mind. Because of this inability to say what a mind is, many philosophers prefer to speak not of minds as such but simply of mental facts, mental states, mental properties, mental acts, mental processes, mental events, etc." ("Mind-Body Problem," *EP* 5: 337).

23. The development of universal psychologies in the twelfth and thirteenth centuries parallels in striking ways the development of universal grammars during the same period. Both were, of course, due to the same phenomenon: the universalizing tendency of the incoming Aristotelian science overwhelming the fostering-the-individual preoccupation of traditional Christian humanism. The heady delights of theory, one might say, overcame the mundane demands of practical day-to-day pedagogy.

Medieval grammatical theory descended ultimately, as did so many theories, from the Greeks, from Plato and Aristotle of course (among other things Plato justified the separation of noun and verb), but much more importantly, from the Alexandrians of the first centuries B.C. and A.D., with their word-class system and their emphasis on literary rather than spoken language. In the late days of the Roman Empire, Donatus in Rome and Priscian in Constantinople continued the Alexandrian approach in Latin (Priscian's grammar has survived in more than a thousand manuscripts). About the development of early medieval grammatical theory, not much is known, except that it was certainly not pursued as an Aristotelian-type science. Quite the contrary. Until the eleventh century, G. L. Bursill-Hall tells us, grammar was defined, taught, studied, and practiced as "the art of speaking and writing correctly and the art of interpreting the poets" (*Speculative Grammars of the Middle Ages* [The Hague: Mouton, 1971], p. 5). However, with the rise of the universities, grammar became both professionally seductive and scientized. Reading and writing Latin—the "universal" language—became the gateway to every kind of higher learning and profession; and at the same time, with the introduction of logic into grammatical theory, the long battle began between the humanistic "authors" schools of Orleans and Chartres versus the scientific, search-for-new-truth "logic" school of Paris. As a result, according to Bursill-Hall, "By 1215, classical authors were absent from the Arts course in the University of Paris and by 1255, only Donatus and Priscian remained of the ancient Latin authors; the plain fact is that the classical literary tradition which had been so superbly fostered by the cathedral schools of Chartres and Orleans died of sheer starvation, because the ideas which the study of Aristotle produced became too absorbing to allow the study of the classical authors to remain important. Grammar, the weathervane of intellectual change, turned from the study of literature to a logical science, a speculative philosophical discipline, and its problems were no longer solved by reference to the best Latin literature but by logic" (pp. 24–25). The Modistae, the northern grammarians of this period, sought the one universal grammar, which they believed they would find not in particular languages here or there but in the rational structure of universal reality.

24. The most comprehensive theory of mind now current, albeit almost totally cognitive, is that of Howard Gardner, proposed in *Frames of Mind: The Theory of Multiple Intelligences* (New York: Basic Books, 1983).

25. Wilhelm Windelband, *A History of Philosophy,* trans. James H. Tufts (1901; reprint, New York: Harper Torchbooks, 1958), vol. I, *Greek, Roman and Medieval,* p. 303, emphasis added.

26. Ross Arthur elucidates, with examples, the semantic nature of medieval logic in "The *Pearl*-Poet as Master of Logic," *English Studies in Canada,* forthcoming.

27. J. A. Weisheipl, "Scholastic Method," *NCE* 12: 1145.

28. Aquinas, *Summa theologiae,* Ia, 1.10.

29. This comparison is made in O. B. Hardison's General Introduction to his selections of "Medieval Literary Criticism," in *Classical and Medieval Literary Criticism,* ed. Alex Preminger, O. B. Hardison, Jr., and Kevin Kerrane (New York: Ungar, 1974), p. 294.

30. To Chaucer as courtier, writer, and reader, I hope to persuade the reader to add (by the end of this book) Chaucer as Christian humanist. Robert W. Ackerman has shown that in his works taken as a whole, Chaucer demonstrates a sound knowledge of the church and the church system, of the saints and of the Old and New Testament personages, and an "awareness of the theological debates of his period," concluding that his works are "in the mainstream of Christian culture of the late Middle Ages" ("Chaucer, Church, and Religion," in *Companion to Chaucer Studies,* rev. ed., ed. Beryl Rowland [New York: Oxford Univ. Press, 1979], pp. 33, 35).

31. Charles A. Owen, Jr., has repeatedly called our attention to the unfinished state of the manuscripts (see "The Alternative Reading of *The*

Canterbury Tales: Chaucer's Text and the Early Manuscripts, " *PMLA* 97 [1982]: 237–50).

32. J. A. W. Bennett, *Chaucer at Oxford and at Cambridge* (Toronto: Univ. of Toronto Press, 1974), p. 63.

33. Israel Gollancz, "Strode, Ralph, " *Dictionary of National Biography* (1921–22), 19:58. The same doubts as to whether the poet Chaucer was the tax collector/diplomat Chaucer exist as to whether the philosopher Strode was the London lawyer Strode. See Paul Strohm, "Chaucer's Fifteenth-Century Audience and the Narrowing of the 'Chaucer Tradition,' " *Studies in the Age of Chaucer* 4 (1982): 12–13.

34. Paul Vincent Spade, "Insolubilia, " *CHLMP,* p. 249.

35. Gollancz, "Strode, " p. 58.

36. Donald R. Howard cites several medieval references to Chaucer as a philosopher and discusses generally the philosophical positions in *Troilus* ("The Philosophies in Chaucer's *Troilus,*" in *The Wisdom of Poetry,* ed. Larry D. Benson and Siegfried Wenzel [Kalamazoo: Medieval Institute Publications, 1982]). Sheila Delany explicates some significance of four-teenth-century scholastic philosophical changes for a contemporary poet interested in the human personality ("Undoing Substantial Connection: The Late Medieval Attack on Analogical Thought, " *Mosaic* 6 [1972]: 31–52). Robert Stepsis, Joerg O. Fichte, and Russell A. Peck, among others, have already argued for Chaucer's familiarity with and use of scholastic philosophical ideas in his poetry, especially those of Ockham (Stepsis, "*Potentia Absoluta* and the *Clerk's Tale,*" *ChRev* 10 [1975]: 129–46; Fichte, "Man's Free Will and the Poet's Choice: The Creation of Artistic Order in Chaucer's *Knight's Tale,*" *Anglia* 93 [1975]: 335–60; Peck, "Chaucer and the Nominalist Questions, " *Speculum,* 53 [1978]: 745–60).

37. Bennett, *Chaucer at Oxford,* pp. 75, 66.

38. Robert O. Payne has shown that Chaucer "expressed in his poems . . . a great deal of serious *independent* thought about the questions which had been central to nearly all Christian considerations of poetry and rhetoric from Augustine's time to his own" ("Chaucer and the Art of Rhetoric, " in *Companion to Chaucer Studies,* rev. ed., ed. Beryl Rowland [New York: Oxford Univ. Press, 1979], p. 56, emphasis added).

39. Renate Haas suggests that in the Monk's Tale Chaucer is experi-menting "critically with the current concept of tragedy, " at that time much under discussion in the fashionable literary circles of Italy ("Chau-cer's *Monk's Tale:* An Ingenious Criticism of Early Humanist Concep-tions of Tragedy, " *Humanistica Lovaniensia* 36 [1987]: 44).

40. C. David Benson argues that the *Tales* "is a collection of absolutely different kinds of poetry, " that the "central achievement" of the *Tales* is its "radical stylistic variety" ("The *Canterbury Tales:* Personal Drama or

Experiments in Poetic Variety?" in *The Cambridge Chaucer Companion,* ed. Piero Boitani and Jill Mann [Cambridge: Cambridge Univ. Press, 1986], pp. 107, 105.

41. See note 31 above.

42. Ruggiers, *Art of the Canterbury Tales,* p. 12; see esp. pp. 3–15 for a discussion of Chaucer's interest in and approach to character in the *Tales.*

43. J. A. Burrow, *Ricardian Poetry* (New Haven: Yale Univ. Press, 1971), pp. 69–78.

44. Elaine Showalter, "The Feminist Critical Revolution" (in *The New Feminist Criticism,* ed. Elaine Showalter [New York: Pantheon, 1984], p. 4). In "Aristotle's Sister," Lawrence Lipking traces the charge back through the centuries. "Women, male critics like to say, consistently fail to maintain 'aesthetic distance' " (in *Canons,* ed. Robert von Hallberg [Chicago: Univ. of Chicago Press, 1984], p. 93).

45. Robert M. Jordan, *Chaucer's Poetics and the Modern Reader* (Berkeley: Univ. of California Press, 1987), pp. 5–21.

Section II. Faculty Structure

1. For a full history of psychology, from the pre-Socratics to the early twentieth century, see R. S. Peters, ed., *Brett's History of Psychology,* rev. ed. (Cambridge, Mass.: MIT Press, 1962).

2. Both the term *faculty* and the entities it implies are beginning to be revived; see Noam Chomsky, *Knowledge of Language* (New York: Praeger, 1986); and Jerry A. Fodor, "The Present Status of the Innateness Controversy," in *Representations: Philosophical Essays on the Foundations of Cognitive Science,* ed. Jerry A. Fodor, pp. 257–316 (Cambridge, Mass.: MIT Press, 1981).

3. For full discussion and historical tracing of the two overlapping traditions, see E. Ruth Harvey, *The Inward Wits* (London: The Warburg Institute, University of London, 1975).

4. See Edwin Clarke and Kenneth Dewhurst, *An Illustrated History of Brain Function* (Berkeley: Univ. of California Press, 1972), fig. 57.

5. Regarding use of the term *Augustinian* here and throughout, since Augustine was the seminal thinker of the Western Christian church, every Western Christian can be accurately termed an Augustinian in some sense; and, of course, Augustine in this sense was one of the great influences on Aquinas. In the thirteenth century, however, in response to the new "Aristotelianism," a new "doctrinal amalgam" of notions Augustinian in origin took shape, mostly among the Franciscans, which has since come to be known as "scholastic Augustinianism." Among its characteristic theses were the primacy of the will, the oneness of the soul, the plurality of forms, and the interdependence of philosophy and theology (see Rob-

ert P. Russell, "Augustinianism," *NCE,* 1: 1065–66). The term *Augustinian* will be used throughout in this sense. Of course, the same kind of specification is necessary for the term *Aristotelian.* It is safe to say that every major scholastic thinker was Aristotelian in some ways (this is especially true of Ockham), but the term will be reserved here for the Aristotelianism ordinarily associated with Aquinas and the Dominicans.

6. Etienne Gilson, *The Christian Philosophy of St. Augustine,* trans. L. E. M. Lynch (New York: Random House, 1960), p. 223.

7. Aquinas, *Summa theologiae,* Ia, 75.1–6; 77 (see Etienne Gilson, *The Christian Philosophy of St. Thomas Aquinas,* trans. L. K. Shook (New York: Random House, 1956), pp. 201–6.

8. Bonaventure, for example, teaches that the faculties are really distinct from each other, although not really distinct from the soul. Rather, they are consubstantial with the soul, in the genus substance not *per se* but *per reductionem;* see Clement M. O'Donnell, *The Psychology of St. Bonaventure and St. Thomas Aquinas* (Washington, D.C.: Catholic Univ. of America Press, 1937), pp. 53–58.

9. In postmedieval times, as physical science has replaced metaphysical, the immaterial faculties of the soul (like the soul itself) have ceased to be objects of serious scientific study; and in the academic world today they exist mainly in speculative philosophy, especially that of Kant and his followers. Its physical faculties, on the other hand, barring the recent brief aberration of behaviorism, have had a continuous scientific history right down to the present. In the seventeenth century, the *sensus communis,* imagination, and memory were moved from the ventricles of the brain to its structures, and scientific interest began to focus on the cortex. In the eighteenth century, "animal spirits" were replaced by "nerve fluid" (to no real gain in scientific value). Modern science of the brain really began toward the end of the eighteenth century with Gall's theory of phrenology, which localized in different parts of the cortex all the various intellectual, moral, and emotional qualities of the mind (a real advance at the time, since many people were still using other locations, for example, siting the emotions in the abdomen; see Raymond E. Fancher, *Pioneers of Psychology* [New York: W. W. Norton, 1979], pp. 43–59). Today the theory that the brain is physically structured in separate parts which perform particular functions is termed "vertical structuring" by some cognitivists, in order to contrast it against the more holistic theories of people like Piaget, who posit very general structures such as perception and memory as functioning "horizontally" across the brain for a wide range of tasks and contents (Jerry A. Fodor, *The Modularity of Mind* [Cambridge, Mass.: MIT Press, 1983], pp. 10–23, terms slightly adapted). This present-day contrast between the notion that the mind is organized by distinct parts or functions as opposed to the notion that the mind is

essentially a unified whole has shown up in most if not all of the new disciplines concerned with cognition. Conceptually, it is a most interesting reappearance in physicalist terms of the ancient immaterialist contrast between separated Aristotelian faculties and undivided Augustinian soul.

10. Windelband, *History of Philosophy*, I: 328–29.

11. For discussion, see J. B. Korolec, "Free Will and Free Choice," *CHLMP*, pp. 629–41.

12. See Gilson, *Augustine*, pp. 132–36, 130–32, 143–64; Frederick Copleston, *A History of Philosophy* (1950; reprint, New York: Doubleday, Image Books, 1962), 2, 1: 96–99.

13. For brief overview, see Copleston, *History of Philosophy*, 2, 2: 262–64 and 3, 1: 113–15. For Duns Scotus, see *Oxon.*, IV, d. 49, qu. ex latere (*Opera omnia* [1891; reprint, Farnborough, England: Gregg International Publishers, 1969], 21: 123–70); for analysis, see Robert Prentice, "The Voluntarism of Duns Scotus as Seen in his Comparison of the Intellect and the Will," *Franciscan Studies* 28 (1968): 63–103. For discussion, see Bernardine M. Bonansea: although "Scotus' voluntarism is a well-balanced doctrine in which intellect and will are each one assigned their specific role," Scotus consistently taught the "superiority of the will over the intellect," the doctrine "which takes its concrete form in the affirmation that love is above knowledge" ("Duns Scotus' Voluntarism," *Studies in Philosophy and the History of Philosophy*, 1965: 112–13). For William of Ockham, see *In II Sent.*, q. 20 (*Opera theologica* [St. Bonaventure, N.Y.: Franciscan Institute, 1967], 5: 435–47). For discussion, see David W. Clark: since the human soul has no parts or distinct faculties, "the primacy of intellect or will is a false question"; the terms simply connote "different acts of the soul." Although Ockham agrees with Aquinas that "rational activity is primary because knowing what is desirable must precede any real desire," he also agrees with Scotus "that volition is the more perfect (i.e., the more complete) action since will-acts include both cognitive and affective aspects" ("Ockham on Human and Divine Freedom," *Franciscan Studies* 38 [1978]: 132, 133). See also Gordon Leff: for Ockham, "in its nominal definition as that by which the soul wills, the will is nobler than the intellect because it is nobler to love than to know" (*William of Ockham* [Manchester: Manchester Univ. Press, 1975], p. 537).

14. For Scotus, see C. Balić, "Duns Scotus, John," *NCE*, 4: 1104, and Efrem Bettoni, *Duns Scotus*, trans. and ed. Bernardine Bonansea (Washington, D.C.: Catholic Univ. of America Press, 1961), pp. 153–59, 160–82. For Ockham, see Ernest A. Moody, "William of Ockham," *EP*, 8: 307b–308a, and Clark, "Ockham on Freedom."

15. For Scotus, see Julius R. Weinberg, *A Short History of Medieval Philosophy* (Princeton: Princeton Univ. Press, 1964), pp. 231–32; for

Ockham, see Moody, "William of Ockham," pp. 313–15. According to Copleston, Ockham "thought of the theory [of divine ideas] as implying a limitation of the divine freedom and omnipotence, as though God would be governed, as it were, and limited in His creative act by the eternal ideas or essences. Moreover . . . he thought that the traditional connection of the moral law with the theory of divine ideas constituted an affront to the divine liberty: the moral law depends ultimately, according to Ockham, on the divine will and choice. In other words, for Ockham there is on the one hand God, free and omnipotent, and on the other hand creatures, utterly contingent and dependent. True, all orthodox Christian thinkers of the Middle Ages held the same; but the point is that according to Ockham the metaphysic of essences was a non-Christian invention which had no place in Christian theology and philosophy" (*History of Philosophy*, 3, 1: 62–63).

16. Windelband comments: Scotus teaches that the good "is good only because God has willed and commanded it, and Occam adds to this that God might have fixed something else, might have fixed even the opposite as the content of the moral law. . . . [Hence] the good cannot be an object of natural knowledge, for it might have been otherwise than it is; it is determined not by reason, but by groundless will. Nothing, so Pierre d'Ailly teaches with extreme consistency, is in itself, or *per se*, sin; it is only the divine command and prohibition which makes anything such— a doctrine whose range is understood when we reflect that, according to the view of these men, God's command becomes known to man only through the mouth of the Church" (*History of Philosophy*, 1: 332–33).

17. For Scotus, see *Ord.*, I, d. 48, qu. unica (*Opera omnia*, ed. Carlo Balić [Vatican Scotistic Commission, 1963], 6: 387–89). For discussion, see Bettoni: "Only the man who ordains all his actions to God respects and realizes in himself the proper hierarchy of values that lead to God. Man's will finds its basis and model in the divine will" (*Duns Scotus*, p. 169). For Ockham, see *Quodl.*, III, q. 14 (*Opera theologica*, 9: 253–57). For discussion, see Leff: "moral acts owe their virtue to conforming to God's decrees. First among them is to love God above all, which is expressed in loving whatever God wills to be loved (and hating whatever he wills to be hated)" (*William of Ockham*, p. 480).

18. Aquinas, *Summa theologiae*, Ia, 79–82, note esp. 82.3. For discussion, see Appendix 8 ("Will") of this volume (11) of the Blackfriars *Summa*, by Timothy Suttor, who points out that for Thomas, "Appetite is a passive power" (Ia, 80.2), and who deplores the modern "confusion of will with freedom. . . . St. Thomas held not only that the will is necessitated by its nature to certain desires, but also that an act of knowledge exercises causality in every act of will" (IaIIae, 914 ad. 1; 17.5 ad. 2). Vernon J. Bourke similarly interprets this aspect of Thomas's position:

"Choice is an act of the human will, performed under the specifying direction of the human intellect. Materially, choice belongs to the will; formally, it pertains to reason" (*Will in Western Thought* [New York: Sheed and Ward, 1964], p. 68; for extended discussion, see esp. pp. 63–69).

19. Natural causation is characteristic of the Aristotelian conception of the universe: events follow from their causes unless impeded by other causes. As a result, science for Aristotle was the systematic search for causes. Similarly for Aquinas, any influence on being was regarded as a cause. For overview of causal analysis, see G. F. Kreyche, "Causality," *NCE*, 3: 342–47.

20. For example, see Aquinas, *Summa theologiae*, IIaIIae, 141.1 and 4; for discussion, see Gilson, *Aquinas*, pp. 263–64.

21. For Thomas, everything in the universe, by reason of its form, is a "participation in the highest intelligible, God." To know a thing is the noblest way to possess it, and this is done by possessing its form, its immaterial perfection. Thus the object of knowledge becomes part of the knower intelligibly, in somewhat the same way the prey becomes part of the lion and the grass part of the steer materially. As a result, "to know is to be in a new and richer way than before" (Gilson, *Aquinas*, p. 224), since one's own form has been increased, in a way, by the form of the object known. In this theory of knowledge, the more one knows, obviously, the more perfections one possesses, or is. According to "St. Thomas . . . 'The ultimate perfection to which the soul can reach is that in it there be found the whole order of the universe and its causes. This, according to the philosophers, is the ultimate end of man' [*De ver.* 2.2]" (George C. Reilly, "Knowledge," *NCE*, 8: 224). Moreover, in Thomas, lack of certain types of knowledge, when due to negligence, can be the indirect cause of sinful behavior: "One is obliged to know certain things because if he does not know them he cannot correctly carry out his duties. Thus all men are obliged to know the basic truths of faith and the general principles of right and wrong, while each man is obliged to know the duties of his state in life" (Aquinas, *Summa theologiae*, IaIIae, 76.2). Thus, for Aquinas, human beings have certain responsibilities to use the intellect God gave them; for discussion, see Gilson, *Aquinas*, pp. 223–35, 259–64. Chrétien's Perceval is the great example of one justly punished for his ignorance, Chrétien's Yvain of one justly punished for his negligence.

22. Aquinas draws a real distinction between the soul and its faculties, and for him the faculties are arranged in a natural hierarchy which the intellect should rule. On the level of intellective experience he distinguishes two kinds of intellect (one abstracts, the other knows), and an intellective appetite, which he also calls the will. On the level of sensory experience he distinguishes two kinds of appetite: the concupiscible

(which tends toward the easily attainable good) and the irascible (which tends toward the dangerous or difficult good). The various passions— love, joy, hope, hatred, anger, courage, and so on (the content of the will in the Augustinian psychology)—are attributed to these sensory appetites when their object is on the level of sensory experience (*Summa theologiae,* Ia, 79, 80, 81, 82; for natural virtue, see Ia, 95.1 and 2; IaIIae, 56.3, 4, 5, 6; for supernatural virtue, see IaIIae, 63, 109, 110, 112.1). For discussion, see Gilson, *Aquinas,* pp. 259–64 on acquired natural virtue, pp. 337–50 on infused supernatural virtue.

23. Reproduced in Richard Marks and Nigel Morgan, *The Golden Age of English Manuscript Painting, 1200–1500* (New York: George Braziller, 1981). p. 75.

24. A. C. Spearing, ed., *The Knight's Tale* (Cambridge: Cambridge Univ. Press, 1966), p. 28.

25. With regard to differentiation between the two young knights, there is now general agreement on the notion that they are in most, if not all, respects remarkably similar. Critical disagreements arise mainly with regard to what, if anything, is the single quality of differentiation between them, or with regard to the moral judgments their behavior is intended to elicit from the reader. First (and chronologically), are Palamon and Arcite equally worthy and not significantly differentiated (J. R. Hulbert, "What Was Chaucer's Aim in the *Knight's Tale?*" *Studies in Philology* 26 [1920]: 377–80; H. S. Wilson, "*The Knight's Tale* and the *Teseida* Again," *University of Toronto Quarterly* 18 [1949]: 143; Charles Muscatine, "Form, Texture, and Meaning in Chaucer's *Knight's Tale,*" *PMLA* 65 [1950]: 923, 25; Paull F. Baum, *Chaucer: A Critical Appreciation* [Durham, N.C.: Duke Univ. Press, 1958], pp. 96–104; E. Talbot Donaldson, ed., *Chaucer's Poetry: An Anthology for the Modern Reader* [New York: The Ronald Press Co., 1958], pp. 903–4; Herz, "Chaucer's Elegiac Knight," p. 220; Joseph Westlund, "The *Knight's Tale* as an Impetus for Pilgrimage," *Philological Quarterly* 43 [1964]: 531; Ruggiers, *Art of the Canterbury Tales,* pp. 157–58; Charles A. Owen, Jr., "The Problem of Free Will in Chaucer's Narratives," *Philological Quarterly* 46 [1967]: 438; Jordan, *Chaucer and the Shape of Creation,* pp. 156, 172–73; Robert B. Burlin, *Chaucerian Fiction* [Princeton: Princeton Univ. Press, 1977], pp. 100–101; Derek Pearsall, *The Canterbury Tales* [London: George Allen and Unwin, 1985], p. 130)? Or does each knight embody a worthy half of a two-part standard, whether the Active-Contemplative service of God (Fairchild, "Active Arcite, Contemplative Palamon," p. 292; Albert H. Marckwardt, *Characterization in Chaucer's Knight's Tale,* University of Michigan Contributions in Modern Philology, no. 5 [Ann Arbor: Univ. of Michigan Press, 1947], p. 23), or the battlefield-bower service of the lady (W. H. French, "The Lovers in the *Knight's Tale,*" *Journal of English and Germanic*

Philology 48 [1949]: 327–28), or the lover-warrior aspects of chivalry (Patch, *On Rereading Chaucer,* p. 206; J. Don Vann, "A Character Reversal in Chaucer's *Knight's Tale,*" *American Notes and Queries* 3 [May 1965]: 131; Donald R. Howard, *The Idea of the Canterbury Tales* [Berkeley: Univ. of California Press, 1976], pp. 234–37; Alfred David, *The Strumpet Muse* [Bloomington: Indiana Univ. Press, 1976], pp. 81–83; A. J. Minnis, *Chaucer and Pagan Antiquity,* Chaucer Studies no. 8 [Cambridge: D. S. Brewer and Rowman and Littlefield, 1982], pp. 111–16)? Or are the two of them disrupting the natural unity in the conventional order of things (Robert J. Blanch and Julian N. Wasserman, "White and Red in the *Knight's Tale:* Chaucer's Manipulation of a Convention," in *Chaucer in the Eighties,* ed. Julian N. Wasserman and Robert J. Blanch [Syracuse: Syracuse Univ. Press, 1986], p. 176)? Or are they instead differentiated in terms of their personalities (Robert Kilburn Root, *The Poetry of Chaucer: A Guide to Its Study and Appreciation,* rev. ed. [1934; reprint, New York: Peter Smith, 1950], pp. 169–70; Peter Elbow, *Oppositions in Chaucer* [Middletown, Conn.: Wesleyan Univ. Press, 1973], pp. 75–78) or their gods (Minnis, *Chaucer and Pagan Antiquity,* pp. 109, 134–36)? Or, on the other hand, are Palamon and Arcite both imperfect, and again not significantly differentiated (Edward B. Ham, "*Knight's Tale* 38," *English Literary History* 17 [1950]: 259; John Halverson, "Aspects of Order in the *Knight's Tale,*" *Studies in Philology* 57 [1960]: 609, 613–14; Neuse, "The Knight," p. 309; Allen C. Koretsky, "The Heroes of Chaucer's Romances," *Annuale Mediaevale* 17 [1976]: 23, 33; Christel van Boheemen, "Chaucer's *Knight's Tale* and the Structure of Myth," *Dutch Quarterly Review of Anglo-American Letters* 9 [1978]: 176–90; Edward C. Schweitzer, "Fate and Freedom in *The Knight's Tale,*" *Studies in the Age of Chaucer* 3 [1981]: 43–44)? Or do they both act dishonorably (T. K. Meier, "Chaucer's Knight as 'Persona': Narration as Control," *English Miscellany* 20 [1969]: 18), or are they both prime examples of cupidinous behavior (D. W. Robertson, Jr., *A Preface to Chaucer: Studies in Medieval Perspectives* [Princeton: Princeton Univ. Press, 1962], pp. 110, 466; Huppé, *A Reading of the Canterbury Tales,* pp. 68–69; Richard L. Hoffman, *Ovid and the Canterbury Tales* [Philadelphia: Univ. of Pennsylvania Press, 1966], p. 48; W. F. Bolton, "The Topic of the *Knight's Tale,*" *ChRev* 1 [1966–67]: 225; Jeffrey Helterman, "The Dehumanizing Metamorphoses of the *Knight's Tale,*" *English Literary History* 38 [1971]: 494–95)? Or is one concupiscent, the other irascible (Olson, *"Canterbury Tales" and the Good Society,* p. 65)? Or is Arcite perhaps the worthier of the two (J. S. P. Tatlock, *The Mind and Art of Chaucer* [Syracuse: Syracuse Univ. Press, 1950], p. 96), or is Palamon the more worthy (Percy Van Dyke Shelly, *The Living Chaucer* [Philadelphia: Univ. of Pennsylvania Press, 1940], pp. 236–38; William Frost, "An Interpretation of Chaucer's Knight's Tale," in *Chaucer Criti-*

cism: The Canterbury Tales, ed. Richard J. Schoek and Jerome Taylor [Notre Dame: Univ. of Notre Dame Press, 1960], pp. 101–2, 104–5; Rodney Delasanta, "Uncommon Commonplaces in *The Knight's Tale,*" *Neuphilologische Mitteilungen* 70 [1969]: 684–89; Douglas Brooks and Alastair Fowler, "The Meaning of Chaucer's *Knight's Tale,*" *Medium Aevum* 39 [1970]: 135–37)? Or do they both start out in error, and then both develop in some ethical or intellectual or ironic way (Robert M. Lumiansky, *Of Sondry Folk: The Dramatic Principle in the Canterbury Tales* [Austin: Univ. of Texas Press, 1955], pp. 40, 47; Haller, "*Knight's Tale* and the Epic Tradition," p. 82; F. Anne Payne, *Chaucer and Menippean Satire* [Madison: Univ. of Wisconsin Press, 1981], pp. 226–30)? In any event, in spite of the wide range of opinion as to the moral standing and personal qualities of these two young knights, each commentator seems to feel that, within the purview of his or her own interpretative system, the two in final analysis are much alike.

26. With regard to simplification, although Chaucer presents the various scholastic issues accurately, by presenting them in the form of direct contrasts he does simplify into oppositions what was really more a question of "science" developing within two different traditions over a long period of time toward the same goal. This common purpose can be seen, for example, in the frequency with which each of these thinkers tried to find middle positions between those of their predecessors. Thus, on the nature of "free choice," Bonaventure cites the positions of Alexander of Hales and Thomas Aquinas and "attempts to reconcile these two diverging opinions" (O'Donnell, *Bonaventure and Aquinas,* p. 93). On whether the will is moved by its object or by itself, Scotus took "a stand between two extreme positions," that of Godfrey of Fontaines (a strong intellectualist) and that of Henry of Ghent (a leading voluntarist); and on the nature of beatitude he took "a somewhat middle position" between Albert the Great and Bonaventure on the one hand and Aquinas on the other (Bonansea, "Scotus' Voluntarism," pp. 109, 120–21). In the debate as to the primary faculty of the soul, Ockham can be regarded a "mediator" between "Thomistic 'rationalism' and Scotistic 'voluntarism' " (Clark, "Ockham on Freedom," p. 132). History, however, rarely memorializes middle positions as such. Since the human intellect seems to work better with oppositions (to be discussed in Section III), by presenting them embodied as opposites, Chaucer has made these two fascinating philosophical psychologies accessible to the general reader in a way no scholastic treatise possibly could.

27. Debate is argumentation according to rules: about taking turns, being able to speak at length without interruption, receiving equal time and treatment, avoiding digression, and submitting to judgment by an impartial third party on a higher level. Thus, the very form of the Knight's

Tale strongly suggests the regular Middle English literary debate genre, especially that of the "unresolved debates" such as *The Owl and the Nightingale* (in which the debate is embedded in a bird fable) and *Winner and Waster* (in which the debate is embedded in a chronicle romance). For general discussion of the literary debates, see Francis Lee Utley, "Dialogues, Debates and Catechisms," in *A Manual of the Writings in Middle English 1050–1500,* ed. Albert E. Hartung, vol. 3, pt. 7 (New Haven: Connecticut Academy of Arts and Sciences, 1972); Thomas H. Bestul, *Satire and Allegory in "Wynnere and Wastoure"* (Lincoln: Univ. of Nebraska Press, 1974); Kathryn Hume, *The Owl and the Nightingale* (Toronto: Univ. of Toronto Press, 1975); and Thomas Lloyd Reed, Jr., "Middle English Debate Poetry" (Ph.D. diss., University of Virginia, 1978).

28. The historical backgrounds of these two different notions of the divine economy—the one transcendent and associated with Aquinas; the other present in the world and associated with Bonaventure and the Franciscan tradition—are traced by Ewart H. Cousins ("St. Bonaventure, St. Thomas, and the Movement of Thought in the 13th Century," in *Bonaventure and Aquinas: Enduring Philosophers,* ed. Robert W. Shahan and Francis J. Kovach [Norman: Univ. of Oklahoma Press, 1976], pp. 15–23), back to the Islamic/Aristotelian backgrounds of thirteenth-century Western thought on the one hand, and to the Greek Christian fathers and their Trinitarian processions on the other.

29. God as First Mover, Producer, Being, Value, and Purpose; see Vernon J. Bourke, "Thomas Aquinas, St.," *EP,* 8: 110–11.

30. A key Ockhamist distinction, brought forward from the thirteenth century and Scotus, to reconcile God's unlimited freedom with the natural order we see all around us in the world, is the distinction between his *absolute* power and his *ordained* power. William J. Courtenay explains it: "Both the natural laws of the physical universe and those of the sacramental system of salvation within the church are contingent on God's will, which is one with his reason. On the other hand, divine freedom should not be so stated as to undermine the regularity and reliability of the physical and spiritual worlds, limit unduly the integrity and freedom of man, or compromise the notion that God will reward human effort in attaining salvation. . . . Outside of his ordination, or the plan that God has established for his creation, God was and is free and unlimited, save by the principle of noncontradiction (that he cannot make contradictories true at the same time). God could have arranged things differently; there is no necessity that stands over him, determining his actions from without. Yet *from* the area or sphere of absolute possibility (*de potentia Dei absoluta*) God has chosen to implement or realize a lesser number of possibilities, which he has put into operation, in time, through his ordination (*de potentia Dei ordinata*), and which he continues to uphold despite

his freedom to do otherwise. If one considers divine power in and of itself (simply or absolutely), without regard for what God has in fact chosen to do, then it appears to be almost limitless. If one reflects on the orders God has established for nature and grace, then divine power appears *self*-limited. Occasional miraculous suspensions of the ordained laws of nature and grace are not *absolute* actions but foreordained reminders that those laws are *gifts,* not absolutely necessary relationships" (*Schools and Scholars in Fourteenth Century England* [Princeton: Princeton Univ. Press, 1987], pp. 211–12).

31. The difference between the two conceptions of the divine, Arcite's as opposed to Palamon's, reflects somewhat the difference between pre- and post-1277 theologizing. William J. Courtenay points out that "the stress on omnipotence and divine power, the stress on the covenantal nature of man's relation with God, the continual use of Biblical (especially Old Testament) examples in the writings of Ockham and Biel, all mark a re-emphasis on the Judeo-Christian conception of God in contrast with the more distant and more mechanistic deity of Latin Averroism as influenced by Aristotle's Prime Mover . . . this trend back to a Biblical conception of God was stimulated by the condemnations of 1277 and represents a reaction to Greco-Arabian necessitarianism. Ockhamism was only one part of that changing conception of God, although one of the more visible and important parts" ("Nominalism and Late Medieval Religion," in *The Pursuit of Holiness in Late Medieval and Renaissance Religion,* ed. Charles Trinkhaus and Heiko A. Oberman [Leiden: E. J. Brill, 1974], p. 58).

32. Because in the Augustinian-Franciscan psychology the soul is a unity consisting of memory, intellect, and will, one speaks here of functions rather than separate faculties. Bourke distinguishes historically eight different and complexly interacting notions of "will" in Western usage: intellectual preference; rational appetite; freedom; dynamic power; seat of the affections; source of law; consensus of the people; and reality itself (*Will in Western Thought*). The first six of these above reflect the very difficult process involved in assimilating to the earlier simpler Augustinian conception, the more complex Greek notion of rational appetite, with its claim that some psychic functions are natural (i.e., not subject to choice), some deliberated.

33. Aquinas, following Aristotle, accepted certain kinds of analogical knowledge, reasoning that while it might be imperfect and inadequate, such knowledge would not be false; for discussion, see Copleston, *History of Philosophy,* 2, 2: 71–78. Scotus and Ockham, however, rejected such knowledge. In the Knight's Tale, Arcite draws three analogies: in 1177–80, we strive as did the hounds; in 1181–82, love's decisions are made like royal decisions; and in 1261–65, in this world we fare like drunkards. All

three are true analogies in that they point out relationships of likeness. Palamon's only similar type of comparison in the tale turns finally into one of unlikeness: in his Part I lament (1307–21) he parallels the circumstances of man and sheep, but finds man's worse in that he will suffer after death.

34. In the assumption of each that his rival should be behaving according to his own standard, the two knights are following the examples set by the theories of the orders whose psychologies they embody. No doubt a young man of a primarily intellectual bent, seeking to join an order, would naturally be drawn to Dominic's focus on things cognitive; and a young man of a primarily affective bent, seeking to join an order, would naturally be drawn to Francis's focus on love. The natural result would be that, cloistered off with people of similar bents, when fashioning their images of universal human nature theorists on each side would assume their own natures to be representative of all human natures and ultimately of the Divine Nature as well.

35. Aquinas, *Summa theologiae*, IaIIae, 1.7 and 13.3. The reasoning is that only if one perceives some imperfection in an object can one deliberate about desiring it; for discussion, see Copleston, *History of Philosophy*, 2, 2: 99–101.

36. For extended discussion of the concepts of natural law and positive law, see John A. Alford, "Literature and Law in Medieval England," *PMLA* 92 (1977): 941–51.

37. Scotus, *Oxon.*, II, d. 25, q. unica (*Opera omnia*, 13: 196–227). For Scotus, the will has a double tendency: one natural and therefore passive and self-perfecting and, obviously, not free; the other active and essentially free, even to the choice of its own ultimate end, *Oxon.*, IV, d. 49, q. 10 (*Opera omnia*, 21: 317–88); for discussion, see Bernardine Bonansea, *Man and His Approach to God in John Duns Scotus* (Lanham, Md.: Univ. Press of America, 1983), pp. 51–89, 44–50. For Ockham, see *In I Sent.*, d. 1, q. 6 (*Opera theologica*, 1: 486–507); for discussion, see Arthur Stephen McGrade, "Ockham on Enjoyment," *Revue Metaphysics* 37 (1981): 723.

38. Palamon's characterization according to the voluntarist psychology explains the puzzling parallel construction in line 1339:

> The somer passeth, and the nyghtes longe
> Encressen double wise the peynes stronge
> *Bothe of the lovere and the prisoner.*
> I noot which hath the wofuller mester. (1337–40, emphasis
>   added)

As it stands, Chaucer's line implies that Palamon does not love Emelye as much as Arcite, and, of course, that is precisely the point: Palamon here is still retaining his metaphysical freedom; he has not yet chosen Emelye as his final goal. Moreover, the fact that Palamon is still retaining his freedom gives added point to the *demande d'amour* with which Chaucer ends Part I. Chaucer's closing chiasmus is thus between a voluntarist knight whose essential "mester" (OED, s.v. "mister," III, need or necessity) is freedom, whereas he is condemned to jail; as opposed to an intellectualist knight whose essential "mester" is the *visio essentiae* of his lady, whereas he is banished from her sight (see the discussion at subhead 5, "Ethical Development: Arcite and the *visio divinae essentiae*" in this chapter).

39. Scotus, *Oxon.*, III, d. 19, q. unica (*Opera omnia*, 14: 709–28); *Rep.*, IV, d. 28, no. 6 (*Opera omnia*, 24: 377–78): for discussion, see Copleston, *History of Philosophy*, 2, 2: 268–70. Ockham too treated of the possibility of hatred of God; see Philotheus Boehner, *Philosophical Writings, a Selection: William of Ockham* (Indianapolis: Bobbs-Merrill, 1964), pp. xlviii–l.

40. See Berard Vogt, "Metaphysics of Human Liberty in Duns Scotus," *Proceedings of the American Catholic Philosophical Association* 16 (1940), esp. 30–31; and Allan B. Wolter, "Native Freedom of the Will as a Key to the Ethics of Scotus," in *Congressus Scotisticus Internationalis* (Rome: Societas Internationalis Scotistica, 1972), pp. 359–70.

41. "Encumbered" is a legal term; in context here it means that, in Palamon's opinion, the two do not hold legal right to their own lives (see *Black's Law Dictionary*, 4th ed., s.v. "encumbered").

42. Gilson, *Aquinas*, pp. 187–89.

43. See Gilson, *Aquinas*, pp. 351–56.

44. Walter Clyde Curry, *Chaucer and the Mediaeval Sciences* (1926; New York: Barnes and Noble, 1960), p. 147.

45. Moody, "William of Ockham," 8: 307.

46. "Adoon" may be a play on Adonis/Adonai, one of the Hebrew names for God (literally "lord"); the word *Adonai* appears in the Wyclif Bible, in Lydgate's *Pilgrimage*, and in the Towneley Plays (see MED).

47. See Sir James George Frazer, *The Golden Bough*, 3d ed. (New York: Macmillan, 1935), i: 28–29. Boyd Ashby Wise points out several instances in the *Thebaid* of promises of hair and beard to gods (*The Influence of Statius upon Chaucer* [Baltimore: J. H. Furst, Co., 1911]).

48. See Edward Dennis O'Connor, "Immaculate Conception," *NCE*, 7: 380.

49. Copleston remarks that "one of Ockham's main preoccupations as a philosopher was to purge Christian theology and philosophy of all traces of Greek necessitarianism, particularly of the theory of essences, which in his opinion endangered the Christian doctrines of the divine liberty and omnipotence. His activity as a logician and his attack on all

forms of realism in regard to universals can thus be looked on as subordinate in a sense to his preoccupations as a Christian theologian. This is a point to bear in mind. Ockham was a Franciscan and a theologian" (*History of Philosophy*, 3, 1: 60).

50. Today, rather than a "religion," we would term Theseus's belief a monotheistic natural philosophy, just as we do Boethius's system in the *Consolation;* but in Chaucer's time the term *natural philosophy* meant what we would now call physics and natural science. In scholastic times, the idea of a natural religion (as opposed to a positive or revealed religion) was of a religion completely dependent for its content on reasoning from the structural uniformities and orderly processes we see all about us in the natural world to conclusions about life, mind, value, happiness, and final purpose, and on to philosophical knowledge of God (that he exists, is one, and so on).

51. J. Stephen Russell, in *"Lege caritate legem caritatem"* (paper written for the Midwest Modern Language Association convention, Minneapolis, November 1989), argues that reading in any other fashion, and particularly reading in the modern nonallegorical "objective" fashion, was really unknown to Augustine and his age. For Augustine, existence itself was thematized by the Father's law of charity. Literal was not antonymous with allegorical, but rather all texts were coverings for ideas, and the extent to which one veil was more or less figurative was only a matter of degree. The Knight's Tale suggests that Chaucer did expect his late medieval reader to read for inner truths.

52. Chaucer's Saturn does not know it, but he is at most a secondary cause, as will be shown in Chapter 5.

53. The astrological identification of the two champion-kings is discussed in Chapter 4. Walter Clyde Curry showed that Chaucer depicted Lygurge as a man born under the influence of Saturn and Emetreus as a man born under the influence of Mars (*Chaucer and Sciences*, pp. 130–37 and 154–63).

54. In addition, of course, grace in Thomism is a participation in the Divine Being, a further assurance that the person who receives grace will receive bliss (Gilson, *Aquinas*, pp. 343–50).

55. Ockham, *Ord.*, d. 17, q. 1 (*Opera theologica*, 3: 440–66); for discussion, see Leff, *William of Ockham*, pp. 472–75. For that matter, immortality itself for Scotus is not scientifically demonstrable, *Oxon.*, IV, d. 43, q. 2 (*Opera omnia*, 20: 34–65); it is a matter of revelation rather than reason. For discussion, see Bettoni, *Duns Scotus*, pp. 86–92.

56. To regard Arcite's desire for Emelye as sinful, as some critics seem to do, does not accord with the philosophical psychology by which he is characterized. Gilson comments on the Thomistic view of pleasure, passion, and love: "whatever their causes or effects, the moral values of

pleasures depends upon that of the loves from which they result. All sense pleasure is good or evil according to whether or not it is in accord with the demands of reason. In morals, reason is nature. Man remains, therefore, in the norm and in order while he is taking sensible pleasure from an act in agreement with moral law. Good pleasures only become better by being more intense; the bad only become worse. Thomistic morality is, accordingly, frankly opposed to that systematic destruction of natural tendencies which is often considered characteristic of the medieval mind. Nor does it even include that hatred of sense pleasures in which some would find the specific difference between the Christian spirit and Greek naturalism" (*Aquinas,* p. 281). Further, after discussing briefly each of the passions individually, Gilson concludes: "Such are the basic passions which are, as it were, the matter on which the virtues are exercised. In themselves passions are neither good nor bad. The Stoic notion of the wise man as one whom no passions ever disturb is a grand ideal but hardly a human one. To be completely free of passion, we should have to be without a body, to be something more than just a man. . . . For the soul to be united to its body and to feel its organic modifications in a sensible way is no malady. It is absolutely normal. Morally speaking, passions are neutral. If they get out of reason's control, they become real maladies. On the contrary, it is normal that in a completely regulated moral life, nothing in man escape reason's rule. To say that man must pursue truth with his whole soul is to say that he must pursue it with his whole body, for the soul does not know without the body. Similarly, man must pursue good with his whole body, if he wishes to pursue it with his whole soul. . . . Practical wisdom does not exclude the passions but busies itself with regulating, or ordering and using them. The passions of the wise man are an integral part of his moral life" (pp. 285–86).

57. Speculation as to what Chaucer found so interesting in the *Teseida* that caused him to "translate" it depends, clearly, on one's interpretations of both works. Plots that can accommodate two equally worthy heroes, a necessity for a debate romance, are rare. Moreover, the *Teseida*'s resolution results from prayers contrasted on the basis of means and ends, just as the two psychological theories contrasted their notions of human freedom. In addition, although Boccaccio's two young men are not consistently distinguished or significantly allegorized in the text, in his glosses to their prayers in Book VII Boccaccio allegorizes at great length the houses, personifications, and appurtenances of Mars and Venus into representing the irascible and concupiscible appetites respectively. Boccaccio's psychology here is very elementary (Mars = irascible appetite = anger; and Venus = concupiscible appetite = lascivious love); and the conflict between the two sides is brief, settled even before Emilia's prayer

in the same book. But *if* Chaucer knew the glosses (Piero Boitani, in *Chaucer and Boccaccio* [Medium Aevum Monographs, n.s. 8. Oxford: Society for the Study of Medieval Languages and Literature, 1977], pp. 113–16, argues that he did; William Coleman, in "Boccaccio's Commentaries on *Il Teseida:* The Question of Chaucer's Manuscript Once More" [address delivered at the New Chaucer Society, Fifth International Congress, University of Pennsylvania, Philadelphia, March 23, 1986]), argues that he did not), it is possible that, coupled with the contrast of means and end, they could have suggested to him the idea of opposing the two sides on a larger scale in some kind of psychological debate. Chaucer's further borrowings from Boccaccio beyond the plot incidents consist of innumerable brief allusions, phrases, comparisons, and mannerisms which in Boccaccio are unsystematic, repetitive, and mostly decorative. These Chaucer cuts, pares, systematizes, and then puts to his own uses, much as he does with similar elements from Boethius. For detailed summary in English of the *Teseida,* see Robert A. Pratt, "The Knight's Tale," in *Sources and Analogues of Chaucer's Canterbury Tales,* ed. W. F. Bryan and Germaine Dempster (1941; reprint, New York: Humanities Press, 1958). For English translation of the *Teseida,* see Bernadette Marie McCoy, trans., *The Book of Theseus* (New York: Medieval Text Association, 1974); for a comprehensive study of Chaucer's use of the *Teseida,* see Boitani, *Chaucer and Boccaccio.*

58. The notion that Emelye is a goal rather than a person, at least so far as Palamon and Arcite are concerned, is one of the few areas of real agreement in Knight's Tale criticism. Thus, in chronological order, although Fairchild feels that Emelye personally desires to be a nun so far as the two knights are concerned, throughout his interpretation he conflates love of Emelye with love of God ("Active Arcite, Contemplative Palamon," p. 290). Root remarks that "She is the golden apple of strife, and later the victor's prize; but . . . she *does* nothing" (*The Poetry of Chaucer,* p. 171). Her character is realized "only in its effect upon others." Muscatine argues that "the lady in the *Knight's Tale* is merely a symbol of the noble man's desires" (*Chaucer and the French Tradition,* p. 185). Donaldson says that "The heroine Emily is a symbol of the loveliness life and society have to offer, but her effect is generalized: she is beautiful, therefore lovable" (*Chaucer's Poetry,* p. 904). Halverson says that "Emelye is scarcely a character at all; she is a goal, a final cause" ("Order in the *Knight's Tale,*" p. 621). Neuse comments that "Emily's character is hardly the kind to inspire a noble passion. . . . she is after all merely the prize for which men fight" ("The Knight," p. 309). Morton W. Bloomfield says that "Emily is little more than a bone over which the dogs fight. We are told about her beauty; we do not see it" ("Authenticating Realism and the Realism of Chaucer," *Thought* 39 [1964]: 349). Huppé suggests that

she fills an "emblematic role as a gift of fortune" (*A Reading of the Canterbury Tales*, p. 71). Ruggiers says "it must be stated that Chaucer intended the deflation of Emily's character and performance since she is merely the instigator of the conflict" (*Art of the Canterbury Tales*, p. 157). Allen Barry Cameron comments that Emily functions both allegorically as "a personification of man's idea or goal, of perfecting himself," and symbolically "as a symbol of psychological and cosmic order, as natural woman, as object of courtly love and member of society, and finally as an exemplar of Fortune" ("The Heroine in *The Knight's Tale*," *Studies in Short Fiction* 5 [1967–68]: 122, 127). David argues that "Chaucer has deliberately refrained from bringing her fully to life. She is never . . . permitted to become more than the type of the ideal courtly heroine" (*The Strumpet Muse*, p. 80). John M. Fyler says "she is reduced to a passive responder to events beyond her control" (*Chaucer and Ovid* [New Haven: Yale Univ. Press, 1979], p. 139). Cooper comments that Chaucer "defines Emily as the ideal romance heroine *par excellence*, unsurpassable in beauty and symbolic association, and so the inevitable object of the cousins' adoration" (*Structure of the Canterbury Tales*, p. 95). Pearsall finds Emily "is reduced to a cipher, a mere trigger for impulse in others" (*Canterbury Tales*, pp. 131–32). Blanch and Wasserman regard Emelye as a symbol of "harmony and unity" ("White and Red in the *Knight's Tale*," p. 175). Lorraine Kochanske Stock suggests that "Chaucer's characterization of Emelye conflates aspects of the two antithetical goddesses, Flora and Diana," thus giving her "an iconlike character" ("The Two Mayings in Chaucer's *Knight's Tale*: Convention and Invention," *Journal of English and Germanic Philology* 85 [1986]: 210, 208). C. David Benson regards her characterization as "simple and idealized" (*Chaucer's Drama of Style*, p. 76). The only major exception to critical unanimity about Emelye is that of Meier: "the most serious fault of the character analysts [of the *Knight's Tale*] is their insistence on treating Emelye as an abstraction; . . . It is certainly true that we catch very few glimpses of her personality, . . . but those few glimpses show her as being passionately involved" ("Chaucer's Knight as 'Persona,' " p. 11–12).

59. Thomas H. Luxon has shown that a striking number of the tonal shifts in the tale actually involve the use of proverbial expressions, requiring the reader suddenly to jump from empathizing with the particular experience being narrated to the deflationary notion that this particular experience is after all a representative experience, part of the common experience of all human beings (" 'Sentence' and 'Solaas': Proverbs and Consolation in *The Knight's Tale*," ChRev 22 [1987]: 94–111).

60. Chaucer uses the word *chastity* in this sense at least three times: Physician's Tale, VI, 43; Summoner's Tale, III, 1936 and 1940.

61. Cousins, "St. Bonaventure, St. Thomas," pp. 15–20. For St. Fran-

cis, all of nature had been sanctified by the Incarnation; see Edward A. Armstrong, *Saint Francis: Nature Mystic* (Berkeley: Univ. of California Press, 1973), p. 144. For Bonaventure, see *In I Sent.*, d. 3, pars 1 (*Opera omnia*, 1: 62–63) and the discussion in Cousins. For Scotus on *haecceity*, see *Oxon.*, II, d. 3, q. 6 (*Opera omnia*, 12: 127–59); for discussion, see Bettoni, *Duns Scotus*, pp. 60–65; on the Incarnation see *Oxon.*, III, d. 7, q. 3 (*Opera omnia*, 14: 348–60); for translation and comment, see Allan B. Wolter, "Duns Scotus on Predestination of Christ," *The Cord* 5 (1955): 366–72. For Ockham on the divine liberality, see Moody, "William of Ockham," p. 316, and Leff, *William of Ockham*, pp. 614–43; on intuitive cognition see Sebastian J. Day, *Intuitive Cognition* (St. Bonaventure, N.Y.: The Franciscan Institute, 1947), pp. 143–200.

62. In the *Roman de la Rose*, Chastity is always treated as a personification. She is characterized in a variety of ways, depending on the speaker, but most commonly she is the object of Venus's continuing hostility and the refuge of those unfortunates who have nowhere else to turn. In the *Romaunt*, allusions to "werreying" on Chastity appear in lines 3699 and 3917.

63. Actually, the practice of Aristotelian demonstrative science varied from philosopher to philosopher during the course of the Middle Ages. For discussion, see Eileen Serene, "Demonstrative Science," *CHLMP*, pp. 496–517, who concludes by suggesting that perhaps the very "malleability" of demonstrative science accounts for some of its popularity.

64. Augustine's famous example was chosen by D. W. Robertson, Jr., to open his watershed chapter on "Some Principles of Medieval Aesthetics" (in the *Preface to Chaucer*, pp. 53–54): Speaking of the pleasure that can arise from obscurity, St. Augustine "begins by calling attention to a general situation which he first describes in literal terms and then in the figurative language of the Canticle of Canticles. There are, he says, holy and perfect men whose example enables the Church to rid of superstitions those who come to it, so that they may be incorporated into it. These faithful and true servants of God, putting aside the burdens of the world, come to the holy laver of baptism, and ascending thence, conceiving by the Holy Spirit, produce a twofold fruit of charity. This fact stated in these literal terms is less pleasing than the same fact revealed in the Scriptures where the Church is being praised as a beautiful woman (Cant. 4. 2): 'Thy teeth are as flocks of sheep, that are shorn, which come up from the washing, all with twins, and there is none barren among them.' St. Augustine assures us that for a reason he does not understand holy men are more pleasingly described for him as the teeth of the Church, which cut off men from their errors and soften them so that they may be taken into the body of the Church. Moreover, he joyfully recognizes them as sheep, which, having been shorn of the burdens of

the world, come up from the washing of baptism bearing the twin loves of charity, the love of God and of one's neighbor for the sake of God. And this is true even though the figurative expression says nothing which is not said in the literal expression."

65. For Aristotle and some others, the heart was the site of the intellect. In the tale, Chaucer locates the intellect of Arcite, the Aristotelian-Thomist knight, in his heart (pt. 11. 2803–5).

66. Carl Lindahl describes the characteristics of Chaucer's "listening communities" in *Earnest Games* ([Bloomington: Indiana Univ. Press, 1987], pp. 161–65). The effect of Chaucer's own audience on the poems he wrote should also be considered here. Paul Strohm draws a complex relationship between the dissolution of Chaucer's own circle of listeners and friends, the changing popularities of various *Canterbury* tales, and political and social changes in England in the fifteenth century, and shows that whereas Chaucer's own audience, the people he wrote most directly for and read directly to, apparently enjoyed being surprised "by new turns of plot and ways of shaping material and challenged by interrogation of received beliefs and values," two generations later Chaucer's audiences were more drawn to "familiar materials treated within stable generic frames and to thematic reaffirmation of divine, social, and inner hierarchies" ("Chaucer's Audience," p. 27). A superior poet does not *need* a superior audience, perhaps. But one wonders whether Chaucer would have, could have, written the poems he did for the later audience.

67. The characterization of Theseus is generally regarded as the most realistically human of the three principal characters, but is he the agent of God's foresight (Frost, "Interpretation of Chaucer's Knight's Tale," pp. 106–7; Baum, *Chaucer: A Critical Appreciation,* pp. 97–98; Ruggiers, *Art of the Canterbury Tales,* pp. 161–62; Jordan, *Chaucer and the Shape of Creation,* p. 156; Koretsky, "Heroes of Chaucer's Romances," pp. 40–41; Boheemen, "Chaucer's *Knight's Tale,*" pp. 178, 189; Olson, *"Canterbury Tales" and the Good Society,* p. 82); the admirable normative figure of the tale (Muscatine, "Form, Texture, and Meaning," pp. 923, 25; Halverson, "Order in the *Knight's Tale,*" pp. 614, 619; Hoffman, *Ovid and the Canterbury Tales,* p. 46; Kean, *Chaucer and the Making of English Poetry,* pp. 18–19; Minnis, *Chaucer and Pagan Antiquity,* pp. 121–28), or a fully human, noble, medieval ruler (Root, *Poetry of Chaucer,* p. 171; Tatlock, *Mind and Art of Chaucer,* pp. 96–97; Donaldson, *Chaucer's Poetry,* pp. 904–5; Elbow, *Oppositions in Chaucer,* pp. 79, 82, 86; Spearing, *The Knight's Tale,* p. 27)? Or is he, too, flawed: indecisive, inefficient, or partially blind (Dale Underwood, "The First of *The Canterbury Tales,*" *English Literary History* 26 [1959]: 466; Meier, "Chaucer's Knight as 'Persona,'" p. 18; Blake, "Order and the Noble Life," pp. 9, 14, 18–19; Stewart Justman, " 'Auctoritee' and the *Knight's Tale,*" *Modern Language Quarterly,* 39

[1978]: 8–10)? Or does he have mixed and dubious motives (Henry J. Webb, "A Reinterpretation of Chaucer's Theseus," *Review of English Studies* 23 [Oct. 1947]: 289; Neuse, "The Knight," pp. 305–6)? Or does he too develop in a positive direction during the course of the tale, into a more worthy ruler (Haller, "The *Knight's Tale*," p. 82; Merle Fifield, "The *Knight's Tale:* Incident, Idea, Incorporation," *ChRev* 3 [1969]: 95; Thomas A. Van, "Theseus and the 'Right Way' of the *Knight's Tale*," *Studies in the Literary Imagination* 4 [1971]: 99–100; John Reidy, "The Education of Chaucer's Duke Theseus," in *The Epic in Medieval Society,* ed. Harald Scholler [Tübingen, 1977], p. 394; John P. McCall, *Chaucer among the Gods: The Poetics of Classical Myth* [University Park: Pennsylvania State Univ. Press, 1979], p. 67; Traugott Lawler, *The One and the Many in the Canterbury Tales* [Hamden, Conn.: Archon, 1980], p. 93)?

68. A final goal in this individual sense is really foreign to pagan Greek thought, which tends to be cyclical and necessitarian. So far as one can tell, Aristotle's active intellect which survives death is not an individualized principle, nor is Plato's rational soul.

69. For example, Book III, m. 9, Loeb ed., pp. 270–75; see also III, m. 12, pp. 298–99, and IV, m. 6, pp. 372–75.

70. Not all human beings learn as profoundly as Theseus, of course. Arcite's death, for example, provokes only a thoughtless pagan response from the Athenian women, one that denies him any transcendent value: " 'Why woldestow be deed,' thise wommen crye, / And haddest gold ynough, and Emelye?' " (2835–36). It provokes only a similarly thoughtless pseudo-Christian response from Egeus, a response that denies the process of living in this world any transcendent value: "This world nys but a thurghfare ful of wo, / And we been pilgrymes, passynge to and fro. / Deeth is an ende of every worldly soore" (2847–49). Pearsall (*The Canterbury Tales,* p. 123) remarks that "surely life's pilgrims should be going somewhere, not passing *to and fro?*" Theseus, on the other hand, shows by example how much and how deeply a truly thoughtful well-intentioned human being can learn from even the most dreadful, the most heartbreaking worldly experience.

71. Edith Hamilton writes that in classical legend Theseus was the great Athenian hero. For them he was "a wise and disinterested king"; for them he became the founder of Athenian liberty, voluntarily resigning his royal power and organizing a commonwealth in which citizens gathered and voted (*Mythology* [New York: New American Library, 1969], p. 152). Since Chaucer adds the parliament to Boccaccio's story, one assumes that this aspect of the Theseus legend came down through the medieval channels.

72. Richard Firth Green shows that Arcite's "meteoric" rise, not in Boccaccio, from the most menial of household servants ("page," often a

kitchen boy) to Theseus's close personal servant in only a year or two, would have been regarded by Chaucer's own audience as pure romance fantasy. One possible interpretation, Green suggests, is that Chaucer intended this as an "idealizing" of the Athenian court as a place in which one could rise by merit ("Arcite at Court," *English Language Notes* 18 [1981]: 251–57).

73. Beryl Rowland, in *Blind Beasts* (Kent, Ohio: Kent State Univ. Press, 1971), devotes a chapter to the hare; and the OED entries reveal the intimate connection between "cuckoo" and "cuckold." Here in the Knight's Tale, in the paintings of Venus, a cuckoo sits on Jealousy's hand (1930).

74. Greenfield (*Humanist and Scholastic Poetics,* p. 112) comments on the rationalizations made by the Italian humanists, especially Boccaccio (*Gen. Deorum,* Bk. 11), of the "confusion" in ancient poetry of Jupiter with the "True God."

75. "Chaucer is the most notably feminist author in English until Richardson, and has had few rivals since," Derek Brewer remarks ("Gothic Chaucer," in *Geoffrey Chaucer,* ed. Derek Brewer [Athens: Ohio Univ. Press, 1974], p. 18), and I believe most Chaucerians would agree with him. Consequently, it seems unlikely that Theseus's sexism was not deliberate on Chaucer's part.

76. John of Salisbury, for example, points out that in the *Timaeus* Plato understood and taught the doctrine of the Trinity (*Policraticus,* ed. Murray F. Markland [New York: Ungar, 1979], Book VII, Ch. 5, p. 103). For general discussion, see Minnis, *Chaucer and Pagan Antiquity,* esp. Ch. 2, "The Shadowy Perfection of the Pagans."

77. Armand Maurer, "Ockham on the Possibility of a Better World," *Medieval Studies* 38 (1976): 307.

78. P. L. Heath, "Experience," *EP,* 3: 156–57. See also Aristotle, *Posterior Analytics,* II, 19 (Loeb ed., pp. 254–61). The terms *unplanned* and *transitory* are being used here to distinguish this kind of experience from both formal schooling and training by apprenticeship on the one hand, and from deliberately repeated actions intended to build up habits or lasting dispositions of the soul on the other.

79. For Aquinas the value of experience would seem to mean the value of repeated positive acts by which one deliberately seeks to form an inward disposition, a habit for one's general behavior (see Gilson, *Aquinas,* pp. 256–58). For Ockham, Rega Wood tells me, the notion of experience seems very close to the notion of empirical evidence; it establishes what is actual. In his theory of perception, experience is the repeated intuitions at different times of an object by which one recognizes that the object one is experiencing at this time resembles previous such objects (see Moody, "William of Ockham," 309–10).

80. John H. Fisher has marshaled some evidence for a secular and egalitarian ethic in the *Canterbury Tales:* the unusual opening of the catalog of pilgrims, with a knight and squire rather than a member of the clergy; the relative paucity in the *Canterbury Tales* of ecclesiastical categories compared to other estates lists; the choice of the publican Host as master of ceremonies on a pilgrimage to the most sacred shrine in England; and the emphatic focus on natural (rather than inherited) nobility in the tales of both the Wife of Bath and the Clerk ("Chaucer's Prescience," *Studies in the Age of Chaucer* 5 [1983]: 3–15). The suggestion I am making here, that Chaucer included a learning ability in his theory of universal human nature (i.e., not just noble human nature), would be additional evidence for such an ethic.

81. Jill Mann, in *Chaucer and Medieval Estates Satire* (Cambridge: Cambridge Univ. Press, 1973, pp. 10–16, 202), speaks in passing of the "sense of daily work" the reader receives from the portraits.

82. Karl Joachim Weintraub, *The Value of the Individual* (Chicago: Univ. of Chicago Press, 1978), pp. 49–71.

83. Inconsistencies in the characterizations of the two young knights have been pointed out by Baum, *Chaucer: A Critical Appreciation,* p. 93; Jordan, *Chaucer and the Shape of Creation,* pp. 172–73; and Meier, "Chaucer's Knight as 'Persona,' " pp. 12–13, among others. The only explicit suggestion of some kind of exchange is that of Vann, "A Character Reversal in Chaucer's *Knight's Tale,*" p. 131.

84. The strong debate in thirteenth-century philosophy and later as to the principle of individuation evidences the scholastic scientists' serious recognition of the phenomenon as well as the difficulty they had in accounting for it. For Aquinas, matter is the principle of individuation (that is, I differ from my fellow human beings by reason of the different matter, *materia quantitate signata,* of which we are composed). For Bonaventure, individuation arises from the union of matter and form, personality when the form is a rational form. For the Scotists, the soul itself is individualized and substantialized by a positive entity, *haecceitas,* before its relation to a body. For the Ockhamists, of course, no principle of individuation was needed because every being is individualized by reason of its actual existence. For general discussion, see J. R. Rosenberg, "Individuation," *NCE,* 7: 475–78. For technical discussion see Jorge J. E. Gracia, *Introduction to the Problem of Individuation in the Early Middle Ages* (Washington, D.C.: Catholic Univ. of America Press, 1984). For discussion of the medieval sense of the individual in poetry and in art, see Robert W. Hanning, *The Individual in Twelfth-Century Romance* (New Haven: Yale Univ. Press, 1977), and Colin Morris, *The Discovery of the Individual: 1050–1200* (1972; reprint, New York: Harper Torchbooks,

1973). For discussion of Chaucer's principles of individuating his characters, see Mann, *Chaucer and Medieval Estates Satire,* pp. 187–91, 289–91.

85. For further discussion, see John Macquarrie, *In Search of Humanity* (New York: Crossroads, 1983), passim.

Section III. Thinking and Language

1. "Language use" is a much larger concept than "language." In our time the term "language" has come to signify a system of verbalized signs, or a system of words and grammars, or a system of conventionalized signs and differences—in short, it means an abstract "other." "Language use," on the other hand, signifies language as lived experience. As well as the above, it includes conversation; it includes letter-writing and story-telling; it includes teaching; it includes giving one's word; it includes the unreliability of reasoning (as we rationalize our values, beliefs, desires, errors, and guilts); and it includes the way we, whether through carelessness, fatigue, change of interests, or ignorance, allow and encourage significations to change over time. Language use was not an abstraction for Chaucer. He refers to it in everything he writes. See, for example, Liam O. Purdon, "Chaucer's 'Lak of Stedfastnesse,' " which shows Chaucer addressing explicitly these same concerns (in *Sign, Sentence, Discourse,* ed. Julian N. Wasserman and Lois Roney [Syracuse: Syracuse Univ. Press, 1989], pp. 144–52).

2. Louis Ceci, "The Case for Syntactic Imagery," *College English* 45 (1983): 436–37. R. A. Shoaf comments that "language reduces experience to meaning" (*Dante, Chaucer, and the Currency of the Word* [Norman, Okla.: Pilgrim Books, 1983], p. 12).

3. In the medieval period, the word *sophisma* seems to have had both wide and narrow meanings. It could refer to a whole class of different kinds of logical/verbal conundrums (including problems of pronoun reference; insolubles; problems of change and gradation as in acceleration/deceleration, increase/decrease, beginning/ending, knowledge/doubt; and so on); or it could refer to just one kind of conundrum (as I use it throughout this book). Further, in the case of the one kind, it could refer to the "whole development consisting of the *sophisma* sentence, hypothesis, proof, disproof, and resolution," or it could refer simply to the "*sophisma* sentence" alone (Edith Dudley Sylla, "The Oxford Calculators," *CHLMP,* p. 559) as I use it throughout this book, albeit Chaucer's six *sophismata* are considerably longer than the sentence or two one usually finds in the scholastic examples). For helpful discussions, see Paul Spade's introduction to *William Heytesbury: On "Insoluble Sentences"—Chapter One of His "Rules for Solving Sophisms,"* (Toronto: Pontifical Institute of Mediaeval Studies, 1979), and Alan R. Perreiah's introduction to *Paulus*

Venetus' "Logica Parva" (Washington, D.C.: Catholic Univ. of America Press, 1972). Writing about the fourteenth-century Oxford Calculators, Edith Dudley Sylla comments: "Although the extant university statutes and other evidence for fourteenth-century Oxford are frustratingly full of gaps, it appears . . . that at Oxford there were disputations *de sophismatibus,* which were understood mainly as aids to learning logic, which were held (or called) *in parviso,* and which were primarily intended for advanced undergraduates, who were called *sophistae* because of their participation in these disputations" (p. 545).

4. Paul Vincent Spade, "Roger Swyneshed's *Obligationes:* Edition and Comments," *Archives d'histoire doctrinale et littéraire du moyen age* 144 (1977): 244–45.

5. E. J. Ashworth, "The Treatment of Semantic Paradoxes from 1400 to 1700," *Notre Dame Journal of Formal Logic* 13 (1972): 39.

6. Norman Kretzmann, "The Logic of Instantaneous Speed," lecture delivered at the Institute on Medieval Philosophy, Cornell University, July 22, 1980.

7. Kretzmann, "Syncategoremata, Exponibilia, Sophismata," *CHLMP,* pp. 234–40.

8. Even in the thirteenth century, Eco points out, Gothic sculptors understood subjective points of view. For example, "the statues in the King's Gallery in Amiens Cathedral were designed to be seen from a floor thirty metres below: the eyes were placed far from the nose, and the hair sculpted in great masses. At Rheims, statues on the spires have arms that are too short, backs that are too long, lowered shoulders, and short legs. The demands of objective proportion were subordinated to the demands of the eye. In practice, then, artists were aware of the subjective element in aesthetic experience and made allowance for it" (*Art and Beauty,* p. 66). Martin Stevens suggests that the Ellesmere supervisor and illustrator responded to Chaucer's focus on the subjectivity of his pilgrim-tellers ("The Ellesmere Miniatures as Illustrations of Chaucer's *Canterbury Tales,"* *Studies in Iconography* 7–8 [1981–82], esp. 121–26).

9. Aristotle, *De Anima,* Bk. III, Ch. 5, in *Introduction to Aristotle,* trans. Richard McKeon, 2d ed., rev. and enlg. (Chicago: Univ. of Chicago Press, 1973), p. 231.

10. Ibid., pp. 233–34.

11. Thomas Aquinas, *Commentary on the Posterior Analytics of Aristotle,* trans. F. R. Larcher (Albany, N.Y.: Magi Books, 1970), pp. 1–2. In his preface to Larcher's edition, J. A. Weisheipl explains the context in which Aquinas was working as follows: "In studying methodology, or the common logic of all the sciences, Aristotle and those after him followed a logical order which considered problems arising from each step of logical thinking. The scholastics thought they had found this order in the

various books of logic. Thus according to St. Thomas (Foreward) the predicables (in the *Isagogy* of Porphyry) and the categories (in the *De praedicamentis* of Aristotle) deal with universals that are begotten by the first act of the mind. Propositions, or enunciations (in the *Peri hermenias* of Aristotle) deal with constructs of various types of judgments in the second act of the mind. These two areas of logical investigation are prior to the analysis of reasoning itself, the third act of the mind. St. Thomas recognized that there are two types of analysis, or resolution, to be considered: the formal structures of reasoning, which Aristotle discusses in the *Prior Analytics,* and the material structure of the premises, which can be of three kinds, namely necessary and scientific (considered in the *Posterior Analytics*), probable and dialectical (considered in the *Topics*), and erroneous and false (considered in the *Sophistici Elenchi).*"

Possibly because of their very simplicity, the 3-Acts were capable of great elaboration. Steven P. Marrone, in *William of Auvergne and Robert Grosseteste* (Princeton: Princeton Univ. Press, 1983), shows that in early thirteenth-century speculation, the problem of defining knowable truth was central and exciting, and that all this scientific discussion seems to start from the epistemological implications of the 3-Acts model. Chaucer's interest in the model, however, is psychological rather than simply epistemological.

For extended discussion of each of the three acts, see the Blackfriars edition of the *Summa theologiae,* 12, "Human Intelligence," which contains Ia, 84–89, Aquinas's discussion of knowledge; in this volume see Appendixes 2–4 by Paul Durbin, the translator, one on each of the three acts: "The Simple Understanding of *Quidditas,*" "Complex Knowledge, the Second Act of the Mind," and "Reasoning: Demonstrative and Dialectical."

12. See John F. Boler, "Intuitive and Abstractive Cognition," *CHLMP,* pp. 460–78, for summary of the positions and complexities of this issue; and Day, *Intuitive Cognition,* for extended discussion.

13. The similarity of the mental process involved in Act 3 to Augustine's famous definition of how a sign works is striking: a sign is "a thing which causes us to think of something beyond the impressions the thing makes upon the senses" (*De doctrina Christiana,* trans. D. W. Robertson, Jr. [Indianapolis: Liberal Arts Press, 1958], p. 34).

14. Serene, "Demonstrative Science," p. 497.

15. Curry, *Chaucer and the Mediaeval Sciences,* pp. 130–37.

16. In Chaucer studies, drawing comparisons between Gothic art and literature has been illuminating. Highly influential have been D. W. Robertson, Jr.'s *Preface to Chaucer;* Robert Jordan's *Chaucer and the Shape of Creation;* and V. O. Kolve's *Chaucer and the Imagery of Narrative.* My concern here is to point out what John Fleming ("Chaucer and the Visual

Arts of His Time," in *New Perspectives in Chaucer Criticism*, ed. Donald M. Rose [Norman, Okla.: Pilgrim Books, 1981], pp. 121–36) calls "mental habits" that the literary artist shared with the visual artist of Chaucer's time.

17. See Gilson, *Aquinas*, pp. 230–31, for discussion.

18. Florence H. Ridley, "Chaucerian Criticism: The Significance of Varying Perspectives," *Neuphilologische Mitteilungen* 81 (1980): 131–41, and Russell Peck, "Public Dreams and Private Myths: Perspective in Middle English Literature," *PMLA* 90 (1975): 461–68, argue the pluralist case for medievalists. Paul B. Armstrong, "The Conflict of Interpretations and the Limits of Pluralism," *PMLA* 98 (1983): 351–52, argues it in terms of contemporary critical theory; Louise M. Rosenblatt, in *The Reader, the Text, the Poem* (Carbondale: Southern Illinois Univ. Press, 1978), argues it in terms of reading theory. Jay Dowling has pointed out to me that among contemporary theories of cognition, Piaget's notions of "assimilation" and "accommodation" express this kind of give-and-take between subject and object, and Jung's notion of typical reliance on one or the other process likewise attempts to capture the genesis of individual differences in cognition. For exposition of medieval allegory before the rise of critical theory, see especially James I. Wimsatt, *Allegory and Mirror* (New York: Pegasus, 1970), and Robert P. Miller, "Allegory in the *Canterbury Tales*" (in *Companion to Chaucer Studies*, ed. Rowland, pp. 326–37).

19. I am, of course, simplifying here for the sake of expository clarity. Abstractive knowledge is actually more complicated. In Aquinas, for example, a particular corporeal object acts upon the outward senses, causing an image (phantasm) to arise in the imagination. Since the immaterial rational soul cannot be directly affected by a material thing, the active intellect illuminates and abstracts from the phantasm its universal (i.e., its form or intelligible *species*) and by it produces in the passive (potential) intellect the *species impressa*. The reaction of the passive intellect is the *species expressa*, that is, the universal by which the mind knows. After this, the intellect turns again to the phantasm and in this way has a reflexive knowledge of the particular object (since it now possesses an understanding of its form). Thus the mind has direct knowledge of the universal, indirect knowledge of the particular (see *Summa theologiae*, Ia, 84 and 86). The point here, however, is that Act 1 is passive; barring a miracle, the normal mind adds no knowledge to it.

20. Aristotle *De Anima*, Bk. III, Ch. 7 (McKeon ed., pp. 234–35).

21. J. F. Donceel, in "Knowledge, Process of" (*NCE*, 8:230–32), explains immaterial knowledge as follows: First, "every material object possesses many forms—usually one substantial form and a multiplicity of accidental forms. The substantial form makes the object be what it is,

whereas the accidental forms make it be such and such a thing of this kind. Thus a young black cat is a cat because of its substantial form, and it is young and black because of its accidental forms, say size and black color. In the process of cognition these forms, while existing physically, or ontologically, in the extramental object, enter the knowing subject and become, intentionally, his own forms. They do not become the forms of that subject physically, since this would make the subject become ontologically whatever he knows—e.g., a man would thus become a young black cat. But the forms become intentionally his, and he becomes intentionally whatever he knows" (p. 231b). And second, God "not only possesses knowledge; He *is* knowledge. . . . since God is also infinite and pure being, it follows that being in its fullness is consciousness, self-awareness, and knowledge. . . . The degree of knowledge a being possesses corresponds to the degree of being with which it is endowed. The more it is being, the more and the better it knows" (p. 231a).

22. Dante, *The Paradiso,* trans. John Ciardi (New York: New American Library, 1970), p. 364.

23. Sayers, "Lost Tools of Learning," pp. 91, 92. Jurgen Herbst argues for a resurrection of the medieval "Acquisition of Basic-Skills" approach to the undergraduate curriculum on the basis of its democratic value to the society ("The Liberal Arts: Overcoming the Legacy of the Nineteenth Century," *Liberal Education* 66 [1980]: 36–38). See William Ragsdale Cannon, "Genesis of the University" (in *Contemporary Reflections on the Medieval Christian Tradition,* ed. George H. Shriver [Durham, N.C.: Duke Univ. Press, 1974]), for a traditional, comprehensive account of the history and development of medieval higher education.

24. Sayers, "Lost Tools of Learning," p. 99.

25. R. P. Petri Berchorii, *Ovidius Moralizatus,* trans. William Reynolds (Ph.D. diss., University of Illinois, 1971), throughout. For example, "Therefore, because I have seen that Scripture uses fables to communicate natural or historical truths, it has seemed proper to me that after my moralization of the properties of things and of the works of nature *I* moralize the fables of poets so that through *man-made* fictions *I* may be able to *confirm* the mysteries of morals and faith" (pp. 33–34, emphasis added). Making the same point in a slightly different vein, Richard Dwyer shows that medieval literary art is a social art, that medieval scribes participated in a "continuous re-creation" of literature transmitted by manuscript, and that appreciating the efforts of "inspired scribes" at "filling in the gaps" in the records "is critical to a proper appreciation of one of the ways medieval man created literature" ("The Appreciation of Handmade Literature," *ChRev* 8 [1974]: 221–41). Jane Chance discusses the many different types, systems, and practices of allegorizing in "Medieval Mythography."

26. Rosenblatt puts forward the "transactional theory" of literary interpretation, a two-way process involving complex interdynamics between literature and text, in which the text is "simply paper and ink" until a literary work is evoked from it in the mind of the individual reader (*Reader, Text, Poem,* lx). Susan R. Suleiman classifies current audience-oriented theories into six "self-reflexive" kinds—rhetorical; semiotic and structural; phenomenological; subjective and psychoanalytic; sociological and historical; and hermeneutic—describes them at length, and finds in their common focus on the interaction between observed and observer a relationship to the twentieth-century principles of relativity and uncertainty ("Introduction: Varieties of Audience-Oriented Criticism," in *The Reader in the Text,* ed. Susan R. Suleiman and Inge Crosman [Princeton: Princeton Univ. Press, 1980]). On the other hand, Jane P. Tompkins argues that over the long run of history (except for the medieval period, which is silently passed over), the focus of literary criticism, and therefore by implication the purpose of literary authors, has shifted, from the rhetorical effects of literature on the political, social, and moral behavior of the audience and on the techniques by which the writer could influence them, the focus of ancient, Renaissance and Augustan criticism, to the modern focus on meaning, interpretation, universal (i.e., noncontroversial) values, and private aesthetic experience as an end in itself, divorced from political life and direct social and moral action (i.e., this is the focus of all modern criticism whether formalist or reader-response). Overall, she argues, the historical change in criticism, and by implication literature, has been away from social *action* and *doing* to individual *meaning* and *being* ("The Reader in History," in *Reader-Response Criticism,* ed. Jane P. Tompkins [Baltimore: Johns Hopkins Univ. Press, 1980], pp. 201–32).

27. Raymond J. McCall, *Basic Logic,* 2d ed. (New York: Barnes and Noble, 1967), p. xix.

28. Aristotle, *De Anima,* Bk. III, Ch. 3 (McKeon ed., pp. 223–24).

29. Irma Brandeis, *Ladder of Vision* (Garden City, N.Y.: Doubleday Anchor, 1962). Farinata, pp. 47–52; Sordello, pp. 80–88.

30. The presumably deliberate gaps in Chaucerian characterization have been commented on by many. Florence H. Ridley remarks that "Chaucer involves the reader by imposing upon him the burden of creation" ("Questions without Answers—Yet or Ever?" *ChRev* 16 [1981]: 103).

31. Ernst Cassirer, *Language and Myth,* trans. Susanne K. Langer (New York: Dover, 1953), p. 32.

32. Paul T. Durbin, in *Summa theologiae,* 12, app. 4, "Reasoning," p. 176.

33. Tzvetan Todorov discusses the changes during the past century in the way literary specialists have come to think about literature, its

"scientization," so to speak, as opposed to the thousands of years in which literature was regarded as a discourse about the human world and its values ("Poetic Truth: Three Interpretations," F. W. Bateson Memorial Lecture, *Essays in Criticism* 38 [1988]: 95–113); Brice R. Wachterhauser summarizes current philosophical thinking (since Descartes) on the effects of one's language and historicity on one's perception of art and literature (in the introduction to *Hermeneutics and Modern Philosophy* [Albany: State Univ. of New York Press, 1986]); D. W. Robertson, Jr., in *Preface to Chaucer,* surveys the rich contextual background in which Chaucer wrote and his own readers read and understood him.

34. Much has been written about the sources, meaning and style of the four gods of the Knight's Tale. Their sources in classical literature have been studied (Hoffman, *Ovid and the Canterbury Tales,* pp. 71–95; Kean, *Chaucer and the Making of English Poetry* 2: 1–52; Linda Tatelbaum, "Venus' Citole and the Restoration of Harmony in Chaucer's *Knight's Tale,*" *Neuphilologische Mitteilungen* 74 [1973]: 649–64; Georgia Ronan Crampton, *The Condition of Creatures* [New Haven: Yale Univ. Press, 1974], pp. 99–110) as have their sources in medieval astrology (Curry, *Chaucer and the Medieval Sciences,* pp. 119–54; Chauncey Wood, *Chaucer and the Country of the Stars* [Princeton: Princeton Univ. Press, 1970], pp. 62–76). Suggestions as to their "meaning" in the tale fall generally into three types: (*a*) those which see the four as together presenting a grievous image of the human condition, even as contributing to a subsurface pattern of disorder that runs throughout the poem (Frost, "Chaucer's *Knight's Tale,*" p. 110; Muscatine, *Chaucer and the French Tradition,* pp. 177–82; Westlund, "The *Knight's Tale* as an Impetus for Pilgrimage," pp. 529–32; Spearing, *The Knight's Tale,* pp. 54–66; Blake, "Order and the Noble Life," pp. 7–8, 12–19); (*b*) those which see the first two or three portraits as either abstractions or psychological projections of the emotions of the two young knights and their lady—usually love or passion, anger or destruction, and denial of life or a combination of virginity and fertility (Ruggiers, *Art of Canterbury Tales,* p. 156; Kean, *Chaucer and the Making of English Poetry,* 2, p. 5; Crampton, *The Condition of Creatures,* p. 70; Alan Gaylord, "The Role of Saturn in the *Knight's Tale, ChRev* 8 [1974]: 174–75, which also contains an excellent review of scholarship on the gods; John Gardner, *The Poetry of Chaucer* [Carbondale: Southern Illinois Univ. Press, 1977], pp. 249–53); and (*c*) one which combines both types into complex dual allegorizations of the four gods and the four classical virtues (Venus = concupiscence and temperance, Mars = irascibility and fortitude, Jupiter = will and justice, and Saturn = intelligence and prudence) so as to set forth an overall mythologization of virtue (McCall, *Chaucer among the Gods,* pp. 63–86). Discussions of their style have examined their rhetorical symmetry, their sound and sense of

"movement," their prison and animal imagery, their structuralistic use of cultural oppositions, and their handling of the narrator's point of view (Muscatine, *Chaucer and the French Tradition*, pp. 175–90; Stephen Knight, *Rymyng Craftily* [Sydney, Aust.: Angus and Robertson, 1973], pp. 145–51; Crampton, *The Condition of Creatures*, pp. 99–110; Frederick Turner, "A Structuralist Analysis of the *Knight's Tale*," *ChRev* 8 [1974]: 279–96; Howard, *Idea of the Canterbury Tales*, pp. 231–37).

35. Other than Curry's astrological commentary (*Chaucer and the Mediaeval Sciences*, pp. 130–37, 154–63), surprisingly little has been written about the details of the two kings' descriptions. Commentators generally agree that the two portraits function symbolically in the tale: either they evoke a single thematic abstraction ("magnificence" in the noble life, Muscatine, *Chaucer and the French Tradition*, pp. 177, 182; or "the animal in man," Spearing, *Knight's Tale*, pp. 69, 178–79); or they evoke a pair of related but opposing elements in such an abstraction (the Saturnian as opposed to the Martian in the human personality, Brooks and Fowler, "Meaning of Chaucer's *Knight's Tale*," p. 134; or the lion as opposed to the griffin in mortal combat, Rowland, *Blind Beasts*, pp. 46–48.)

36. The conventions of Modern English punctuation are misleading in these *sophismata*. We capitalize individual personification, but do not capitalize universals or common nouns that refer to individuals, thus reducing our possibilities of verbal allusion to binary either/or choices, and therefore obscuring, for example, the ontological similarity between Chaucer's "Beautee and Youthe" (1926) and "strengthe ne hardynesse" (1948), as well as that between "The crueel Ire" (1997) and "The colde deeth" (2008). For that reason, I have occasionally changed the familiar Robinson capitalization in the citations. In this passage from the Mars description, neither of the either/or choices offered by modern capitalization is really apt. In "The Knight's Tale, 2639" (*ChRev* 21 [1986]: 133–41), Emerson Brown demonstrates at length the problems modern punctuation can create: with comma, Emetreus intervenes and stabs Palamon apparently in the back [dastardly]; without comma Emetreus intervenes when Palamon is stabbing Arcite [chivalrously].

37. The classical Square of Opposition appears as follows; strictly speaking it pertains to two propositions which, having the same subject and predicate, differ in quality or quantity or both. Opposing Chaucer's two descriptions here starts with: (1) Venus rules the world, or, It is not the case that Venus rules the world; and (2) Mars will cause these events in the world, or, It is not the case that Mars will cause these events in the world; and then their opposition follows in the obvious way. Contradictories cannot be jointly true or false: the truth of a given proposition implies the falsehood of its contradiction; its falsehood implies the contradictory is true.

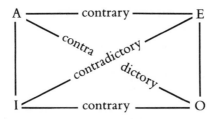

A = universal affirmative (all X's are Y's)
E = universal negative (no X's are Y's)
I = particular affirmative (some X's are Y's)
O = particular negative (some X's are not Y's)
The vowels are taken from the words *affirmo* and *nego*.

By way of contrast to Chaucer's lines, in the case of a universal affirmative and a particular negative, some X's still may be Y's. Edith Dudley Sylla shows that logic "held in the medieval university the place that mathematics holds in the modern university: it was considered the basic key to many other areas of knowledge" ("Autonomous and Handmaiden Science," in *The Cultural Context of Medieval Learning,* ed. John Emery Murdoch and Edith Dudley Sylla [Dordrecht: D. Reidel, 1975], p. 351).

38. The word *champarty* (literally, OF "field-part") was a feudal law term and remains today a law term in English. In Chaucer's time it had two meanings: In French feudal law it signified a division of the produce of land whereby the landlord received a fixed share. In this case, the image in Chaucer's four lines is that of Venus as a landholder, and these six qualities receiving no share of her produce. In English law it signified an arrangement by which a person not naturally concerned in a lawsuit helped one side to win in return for a share of the proceeds, and it was illegal, considered to be a form of bribery. In this case, the image in Chaucer's four lines is that of Venus as a scrupulous lord, whom Intelligence, Riches, Looks, Power, "Sleighte," and Hardiness cannot bribe. The larger question being raised here is as to what causes people to fall in love: is falling in love a totally inward, autonomous impulse, as these lines seem to claim, or is love subject to influence from the outer physical world (from outwardly perceived qualities such as Power, Beauty, Wealth, Courage, and so on)? The word *champarty* is listed in these various senses in the dictionaries of Godefroy, Tobler-Lommatzsch, and Littré, and in Modern English in Black's and Ballentine's law dictionaries. See Du Cange for historical entries.

39. The problem is as to the logical status of future contingents and the range and validity of the principle of excluded middle. The conclusion to Mars's paintings raises the same problems as Aristotle's famous sea battle in Chapter 9 of the *De Interpretatione* (trans. Ackrill [Oxford, 1963],

pp. 52–53), problems considered by Aquinas and Ockham and others and still under discussion today. See A. N. Prior for summary discussion and short bibliography including scholastic references ("Logic, Many-Valued," *EP*, 5: 1–5).

40. Suetonius, *The Lives of the Caesars* (Loeb ed.), vol. 2, Bk. 6, 47, 49, pp. 172–79.

41. The "first serious medieval attempt to argue that bivalence is not a fundamental logical principle" was apparently that of Peter Aureoli (d. 1322); for discussion see Calvin Normore, "Future Contingents," *CHLMP*, p. 370. Elsewhere Chaucer tells all three stories more in accord with the histories: Julius and Nero in the Monk's Tale (VII, 2695–710, 2519–50) and Antony in the *Legend of Good Women* (657–62).

42. Albert E. Blumberg, "Logic, Modern," *EP*, 5: 14–18. C. S. Peirce traced the use of truth-matrices as far back as the Megarians, c. 400 B.C. (I. M. Bochenski, *A History of Formal Logic,* trans. Ivo Thomas [Notre Dame, Ind.: Univ. of Notre Dame Press, pp. 17, 115).

43. Faulty and misleading implications of exactly these types constituted a major portion of scholastic logic studies. For example, the kind of inaccuracy in the Callisto summary—omitting Juno and Jove as causes—falls under the paralogism of "treating more than one question as one." William of Sherwood, for instance, after noting that a question and a proposition are one and the same, says that in this case, "The deception comes about because a proposition that is more than one seems to be one, and one responds to it with a single response. For example: 'Are Socrates and Plato at home?' (when the one has gone out and the other has not). If one says 'yes,' then Socrates, who is not at home, is at home. If one says 'no,' then Plato, who is at home, is not at home. . . . To a proposition that is more than one, one must respond with more than one response." William regards this as a form of Equivocation (*William of Sherwood's Introduction to Logic,* trans. Norman Kretzmann [Minneapolis: Univ. of Minnesota Press, 1966], pp. 165–66). The kind of inaccuracy in the Meleager story, the use of the pronoun "hym" with a misleading antecedent (Meleager rather than the boaster), William treats under the "properties of terms." He asks whether the expression " 'woman, who has damned us, has also saved us' (*mulier que damnavit salvavit*)" can be true. It cannot, he says, because "the purpose of a relative pronoun is to bind the succeeding part of the sentence to the same suppositum with which the sentence began (*Item relativum ad hoc est, ut continet sequentem sermonem ad idem suppositum, de quo processit sermo*). But [if 'woman' is replaced] by the name of one and the same suppositum [i.e., both 'Eve, who has damned us, has saved us' and 'Mary, who has damned us, has saved us' are false, and, *a fortiori,* so are all other such instances] [the expression] is false (*Sed de nomine eiusdem suppositi est*

secundus sermo falsus); therefore it is absolutely false"(pp. 114–15). Logic of this kind was part of the trivium in Chaucer's day, and fallacies such as these would have been known to every schoolboy.

44. Ovid, *Metamorphoses,* trans. Frank Justice Miller, Loeb Classical Library (Cambridge, Mass.: Harvard Univ. Press, 1916), Bk. 2, 409–531.

45. Ibid., Bk. 1, 452–567.

46. Ibid., Bk. 3, 138–258.

47. Ibid., Bk. 8, 267–546.

48. In a "controlled" experiment, I equipped my then fifteen-year-old resident poet with the Diana description, an explanation of truth tables, and the truth table for "and," and asked her to produce a *sophisma*. She started out working with comic strip characters, then tried fairy tales, but then decided a single "authoritative" text was a necessity; she chose the Old Testament and I Middle-Englished the result.

> Ther saw I how the wif of Haranes Lot
> Whan that Satanas to Sodom put a halt
> Was turned from woman til a pilere salt
> And stod ther after on the wey to Zoor
> Thus was it writen I kan seye yow no moor
> Her doghtres ben scapen for they looked to-heed
>   Ther saw I Pharao with his first-born deed
> I mene nat Satanas broghte things til this hedde
> But Egiptes ruler whiche that Moyses fledde
>   Ther saw I Job his liflyhed made noght
> For cause that Satanas him to been blasphemour soght
> I saw his camailles goots sheepe oxen dede
> Likewise his sons and doghters yet unwedde
>   And on the wal another tale was tolde
> How Joseph by his bretheren false was solde
> By force a thral to Egipte then to goe
> For which Satanas wroghte hir children woe

Her comment afterward was, it's easy when you know what you have to do. Elapsed time: less than three hours.

49. The woman in Chaucer's statue is not traditional iconography. Other than this scene in the Knight's Tale, so far as I have been able to determine, there seem to be only two representations in European art before the twentieth century of a woman in hard labor onstage, so to speak: The Woman Clothed with the Sun in the Apocalypse, Rev. 12: 1–7, 13–17, and Aldhelm's Riddle 90, the Woman in Labor with Twins. A few others may exist, but the point is, traditional iconography kept women in such circumstances offstage. Moreover, Chaucer explicitly

points out that this unusual statue is rendered realistically, in living, three-dimensional color: "Wel koude he peynten lifly that it wroghte; / With many a floryn he the hewes boghte" (2087–88). One infers that the reader is intended to ponder the woman's predicament realistically. Both figures, of course, are Chaucer's invention; this statue does not appear in the *Teseida*.

50. Chaucer likewise organizes the descriptions of the statues of Venus and Mars as two-part visual propositions: Venus's proposes that "Love is blind," and Mars's proposes that "War turns men into food for beasts."

51. The notion that two True's automatically produce a True was apparently under attack during Chaucer's time. Ralph Strode, for example, writing in the context of obligation literature, defends the traditional view but observes that "not a few sophisters" attack it, commenting: "Many people . . . thought that they demonstrated conclusively from the common rules that a copulative was to be denied, such as the one just proposed, each part of which was nevertheless to be granted. And likewise they grant the disjunctive opposite of such a copulative, while denying each of its parts. By this means not a few sophisters are given courage to admit cases like 'Everything in this house is a donkey'. Along with this, when 'You are standing in this house' is proposed, they grant it. But when from these things it is concluded that you are a donkey, they grant the consequence and deny the antecedent. And when it is asked 'In virtue of which part?,' they say that it is neither in virtue of the major nor in virtue of the minor, but in virtue of the whole copulative composed of them, which is the antecedent. They say that this is false and irrelevant since it is composed of a posited falsehood and an irrelevant truth, as was said in the beginning. Therefore, although this view is now upheld by many people, it could deservedly be called sophistical, since it appears to be valid but is not valid" (as quoted by Spade, *"Obligations,"* p. 338). The Knight's Tale would number Chaucer among those "sophisters."

52. B. M. Ashley, "Final Causality," *NCE*, 5: 915. See G. B. Kerferd, "Aristotle," *EP*, 1: 156–57, for full definitions of the four causes and discussion of Aristotle's use of them as an analytic system.

53. Leff, *William of Ockham*, pp. 614–43.

54. These same antagonisms appear in the *Metamorphoses*, Bk. 4, 22, referring to a story Chaucer possibly had in mind when composing these portraits: Lycurgus, an ancient king of Thrace, opposes and is destroyed by young Bacchus/Dionysus, who is returning from India in triumph, with leaves in his hair, in a chariot drawn by tame lynxes. Ovid's point is their religious rivalry, a further type of basic human antagonism Chaucer may be including, by opposing Lygurge's name against Emetreus's country of origin, laurel wreath, and tame lions.

55. Amplifying Curry's discussion of physiognomy, John Block

Friedman describes a subtype he labels affective physiognomy, in literature ordinarily reserved for aristocratic characters, which uses facial color, color changes, and eye movements to indicate the state of the inward mind ("Another Look at Chaucer and the Physiognomists," *Studies in Philology* 78 [1981]: 138–52).

56. Rowland, *Blind Beasts,* pp. 46–48.

57. Louis Charbonneau-Lassay, *Le Bestiaire du Christ* (1940; reprint, Milan: L. J. Toth, 1974), pp. 365–77, gathers the griffin stories together and retells and reinterprets the story of Alexander. Griffins as rapacious creatures who tear men to pieces on sight are described by Isidore, *Etymologiarum Sive Originum,* vol. 2, XII, ii, p. 17; they were said to guard gold and gems and to kill all, good or bad, who sought to remove them. On this thought, Berchorius, *Ovidius Moralizatus,* Lib. X, Cap. XLVI, 3, p. 368, cites Ezechiel 21: *Occide in te justum, & impium,* and he either constructs or repeats an elaborate figure according to which the claws of the griffin represent the rigor of the justice of Christ himself, cutting down both the just and the unjust, and he remarks approvingly that the cup of doctrine may be offered from the claws of this kind of being. In Canto 29 of the *Purgatorio,* the triumphal chariot of the church is drawn by the Griffin representing Christ. For the "griffin eggs," see Joseph Braun, *Die Reliquiare des Christlichen Kultes* (Freiburg im Breisgau: Herder and Co., 1940), pp. 129–30, for the sacred; Charbonneau-Lassay, pp. 373–74, for the secular.

58. The story of the lion reviving his cubs appears in Aristotle, Pliny, and Isidore (XII, ii, 5), and was picked up and repeated in countless medieval bestiaries; *Physiologus: A Metrical Bestiary by Bishop Theobald,* trans. Alan Wood Rendell (London: John and Edward Bumpus, 1928), mentions a number of them. Berchorius (X, LVII, 3) supplies several symbolic interpretations, according to most of which the sleeping cub is humankind; the father lion who roars and rouses it is the Lord.

59. Copleston, *History of Philosophy,* 3, 1: 204, 212–13.

60. For all scholastics, the substantial form of the human composite was the rational soul. The soul's essential rationality is taught according to the Solemn Magisterium of the Church: " 'that man has one rational and intellectual soul' (Council of Constantinople IV in 870: Denz 657; there the doctrine of the two souls in man was condemned as heretical); 'that the rational or intellective soul is the form of the human body in itself and essentially' (Council of Vienne in 1312 against Peter John Olivi: Denz 902, cf. 900, 1440)." See P. B. T. Bilaniuk, "Theology of the Human Soul," *NCE,* 13: 462b. The scholastic question was, in this rational soul, which faculty, intellect or will, is prime?

61. Rowland, *Blind Beasts,* pp. 155–56.

62. Copleston, *History of Philosophy,* 2, 2: 142–43.

63. Katharine Everett Gilbert and Helmut Kuhn, *A History of Esthetics,* rev. ed. (London: Thames and Hudson, 1956), p. 141.

64. A. Robinson, "Substantial Change," *NCE,* 13: 771.

65. Weinberg, *History of Medieval Philosophy,* pp. 251–53.

66. Omission of the "and" in this triplet is not required by the meter, since the conjunction would normally elide anyway. The line is metrical with it or without it.

67. Boruch A. Brody, "Logical Terms, Glossary of," *EP,* 5: 67.

68. For review of scholarship on the Knight's Tale gods, see note 34 above, especially Gaylord and Kean on Saturn.

69. Wood, *Chaucer and the Country of the Stars,* p. 71 n. 38, commenting on pp. 307–14 of Johnstone Parr, "The Date and Revision of Chaucer's *Knight's Tale,*" *PMLA* 60 (1945).

70. Here is the riddle which Samson posed to the Philistines, along with its King James translation:

De comedente exivit cibus,
Et de forti egressa est dulcedo.
   Out of the eater came forth meat, and
   out of the strong came forth sweetness.

Here is Samson's first answer, itself a riddle, which Samson's wife tricked out of him after being threatened by her people:

Quid dulcius melle,
Et quid fortius leone?
   What is sweeter than honey? and
   what is stronger than a lion?

And here is the unspoken answer to this second riddle: Love.

71. The limiting (i.e., particularizing) effects on one's knowledge and perceptions of being within time, as Saturn is portrayed here, as opposed to being outside of time, were an important subject to Augustine and later thinkers. For extended discussion, see Eugene Vance, "St. Augustine: Language as Temporality," in *Mimesis: From Mirror to Method,* ed. John D. Lyons and Stephen G. Nichols, Jr. (Hanover: Univ. Press of New England, 1982).

72. Elbow discusses the richness of Chaucer's portrayal of Theseus's mental activities, *Oppositions in Chaucer,* esp. pp. 79–88.

73. See G. R. Evans, *The Language and Logic of the Bible* (Cambridge: Cambridge Univ. Press, 1985), pp. 42–50 esp.

Section IV. Makers and Contexts

   1. Brief remarks on the Knight's characterization are scattered throughout the enormous amount of commentary on the tale itself and

tend to reflect the interpretation of the tale with which they appear. Often the characterization, moral stature, and circumstances of Theseus correspond with those of the Knight. More lengthy, more explicit analyses of the Knight's situation and character have been offered by Muriel Bowden (1948) who reads the Knight as a human personification of the ideals of chivalry (*A Commentary on the General Prologue to the "Canterbury Tales"* [New York: Macmillan, 1948; reprint, 1967], pp. 44–73); Lumiansky (1955) who argues that the Knight, already established in his portrait as an outstanding warrior, is additionally characterized as unexpectedly philosophic in that he motivates his story throughout with Boethian elements (*Of Sondry Folk*); Neuse (1962) who argues that the Knight is a wise, prudent, ironic optimist ("The Knight"); Herz (1964) who argues that the Knight is a fighting man mainly interested in chivalric pageantry who really does not understand the seriousness of his tale ("Chaucer's Elegaic Knight"); Spearing (1966) who suggests that the Knight embodies the old-fashioned knighthood ideal but is touchingly innocent and unaware of the shadows his tale implies are part of the human condition (*The Knight's Tale*); Peter Beidler (1968) who argues that both the Knight and his tale are mature and wise ("Chaucer's 'Knight's Tale' and its Teller," *English Record* 18 [1968]: 54–60); Meier (1969) who argues that the Knight is a fundamental pessimist who stoically believes that all action is inconsequential in a world ruled by chance and misdirection ("Chaucer's Knight as 'Persona' "); Thomas J. Hatton (1969 and 1974) who argues that the Knight is truly worthy and wise, just as he is described in his portrait ("Chaucer's Crusading Knight, A Slanted Ideal," *ChRev* 3 [1969]: 77–87; "Thematic Relationships Between Chaucer's Squire's Portrait and Tale and the Knight's Portrait and Tale," *Studies in Medieval Culture* 4 [1974]: 452–58); Mann (1973) who argues that the Knight's General Prologue portrait conventionally establishes him in the chivalric literary tradition as a truly "parfit gentil" professional crusader (*Chaucer and Medieval Estates Satire*); Robert W. Hanning (1979–80) who argues that the Knight is a grim pessimist and inept amateur storyteller ("The Struggle Between Noble Designs and Chaos," *The Literary Review* 23 [1979–80]: 519–41); Christopher Watson (1980) who argues that the Knight is an enlightened pragmatist who appreciates order in spite of his awareness of the disorder in the evidence ("Chaucer's Knight and His Tale," *The Critical Review* 22 [1980]: 56–64); Jones (1980) whose book-length study amasses a wide array of historical evidence to argue for an ironic reading of both the Knight and his tale—that the tale is an antiwar, antityranny plea by the pilgrim who chose the pacifistic tale of Melibee for himself, and that the Knight is an "uncourtly, unphilosophical and totally unromantic professional soldier who nevertheless . . . yearns after the courtly trappings of knighthood but who has, himself, no courtly background, no education and little understanding of the ethical basis of courtly behaviour or the values that underpin the chivalric code" (*Chaucer's Knight*, p. 145); Kurt Olsson (1987) who argues that the Knight attempts to serve the common profit honorably if conventionally, but lacks insight into others, moral perspective, and spiritual intelligence ("*Securitas* and Chaucer's Knight," *Studies in the Age of Chaucer* 9 [1987]: 123–53); and finally, P. Olson (1986) who says that the Knight is presenting a veiled political suggestion about how peace with France is to be won ("*Canterbury Tales*" *and the Good Society*, p. 65); and Robertson (1987) who argues, against a detailed background setting forth English and French interest in and respect for chivalry and crusading efforts in the fourteenth century, that the Knight's portrait was written as a composite "exemplar" of English chivalry in Chaucer's own time, and was composed during the summer of 1394 in hopes of a peace with France and a joint crusade ("Probable Date and Purpose of *Knight's Tale*").

2. John Fyler argues for the appropriateness of the Knight-narrator in that he (the Knight) puts a kind of Ovidian "surrogate version" of himself (Theseus) inside his own poem: the two share certain characteristics, attitudes, and points of view (*Chaucer and Ovid*, pp. 138–47).

3. See John H. Pratt, "Was Chaucer's Knight Really a Mercenary?" (*ChRev* 22 [1987]: 8–27) for a thorough consideration of the places included in the Knight's General Prologue portrait and the economic facts of being a knight in Chaucer's time.

4. As cited in Jonathan Barnes, "Just War," *CHLMP*, p. 772.

5. The resonances hovering about this threesome are somewhat similar to those hovering about the Parson/Plowman twosome, make of them what one will. See Alan Gaylord for the problematic particulars and mixed and dubious motivations characterizing the principals of the "crusade" in which the Squire himself has already played some unspecified part, "in hope to stonden in his lady grace" ("Chaucer's Squire and the Glorius Campaign," *Papers of the Michigan Academy of Science, Art and Letters* 45 [1960]: 341–61). William B. McColly argues persuasively that the Yeoman-forester is actually an idealized figure of a high law enforcement official, and that his presence as retainer places the Knight within the ranks of the higher nobility, characterizing him as an idealized image of the baronial class ("Chaucer's Yeoman and the Rank of His Knight," *ChRev* 20 [1985]: 14–27).

6. Olive Sayce shows that the Retraction conforms to a traditional literary topos ("Chaucer's Retractions," *Medium Aevum* 40 [1971]: 230–40); Rodney Delasanta shows that it could be both, a personal statement as well as a topos ("Penance and Poetry in the *Canterbury Tales*," *PMLA* 93 [1970]: 240–47).

7. Mark Scarbrough argues that according to the Parson's Tale, "everyone must have a yoke; unlike oxen, however, everyone can choose the yoke. If one chooses sin, one is enslaved to sin. If one chooses God, one is in submission to God. For the Parson, it is delusional to believe in freedom from servitude" ("Closing the *Canterbury Tales* with a Question," paper delivered at the Twenty-first International Congress on Medieval Studies, Western Michigan University, Kalamazoo, May 1986, p. 5).

8. See Howard, *Idea of the Canterbury Tales,* pp. 378–79, for comment on the Parson's "astringent" characterization.

9. Speaking of the unpredictability of personal interactions, Hans-Georg Gadamer opens the third part of *Truth and Method* (London: Sheed and Ward, 1975) with the following: "We say that we 'conduct' a conversation, but the more fundamental a conversation is, the less its conduct lies within the will of either partner. Thus a fundamental conversation is never one that we want to conduct. Rather, it is generally more correct to say that we fall into conversation, or even that we become involved in it. The way in which one word follows another, with the conversation taking its own turnings and reaching its own conclusion, may well be conducted in some way, but the people conversing are far less the leaders of it than the led. No one knows what will 'come out' in a conversation" (p. 345).

10. The effect of release and freedom on the readers' sensibility here is similar to that achieved by Dante at the end of the *Inferno,* when the two travelers, climbing up from the constricted depths of darkness and dead air toward the round opening that brought "in sight the blest/ and beauteous shining of the Heavenly cars," finally walk out, "once more beneath the Stars" (Ciardi trans., p. 287).

11. John M. Manly, *Some New Light on Chaucer* (1926; reprint, New York: Peter Smith, 1952), throughout.

12. Aquinas: One, in his love, shone like the seraphim.
The other, in his wisdom, walked the earth
bathed in the splendor of the cherubim.
I shall speak of only one, though to extol
one or the other is to speak of both
in that their works led to a single goal.
(Dante, *Paradiso,* XI, 37–42)

Bonaventure: When one is mentioned the other ought to be;
for they were militant in the same cause
and so should shine in one light and one glory.
. . .
. . . He [God] sent His bride

> two champions by whose teachings and example
> the scattered companies [of the troops of Christ]
> were reunified. (XII, 34–36, 43–45)

Notice that in line placement in their respective cantos, Aquinas's praise is enclosed within Bonaventure's, and notice also the reverse paralleling of their thought structures (ibid., pp. 130, 140).

13. John Morreall combines features from the three traditional theories of laughter (superiority, incongruity, and relief) to create a single "new formula": "Laughter results from a pleasant psychological shift" (*The Philosophy of Laughter and Humor* [Albany: State Univ. of New York Press, 1987], p. 133).

14. Glending Olson, *Literature as Recreation in the Later Middle Ages* (Ithaca: Cornell Univ. Press, 1982), establishes that the traditional formula "sentence and solas" contained for the medieval writer and reader not one but three possibilities (sentence alone, solas alone, or both together), and that much medieval literature that we have dismissed as strictly "solas" literature would have been considered useful by the medieval writers and audiences themselves—as contributing to their physical and mental health, that is, even the fabliaux, to name but one genre, were written and read within a *utilitas* framework. Thus, to the generally accepted notion of useful (i.e., improving, uplifting) literature as being the explicit presentation of subject matter (whether moral or spiritual or intellectual), Olson has added a different *kind*—presentation of material to contribute to the physical and emotional health of one's audience, I am suggesting here in Gothic art the possibility of yet a third *kind* of useful approach— presentation of material to develop the mental skills of one's audience. The approach itself is probably related to that behind the manuals for other types of practical skills, such as hunting and arms and courtesy. Olson's book raises the possibility of multiple kinds and degrees of useful approaches, among them the possibility that there are other kinds of didacticism than that of the subject matter's meaning.

For the traditional opposition of didactic and mimetic in terms of subject matter, see Elder Olson, "A Dialogue on Symbolism" (in *Critics and Criticism: Ancient and Modern*, ed. R. S. Crane [Chicago: Univ. of Chicago Press, 1952], pp. 588–93); for general discussion of the didactic in literature, see John Gardner, *On Moral Fiction* (New York: Basic Books, 1978); and for a contrasting, more historically oriented view, see R. Barton Palmer, "The Problem with Gardner's *On Moral Fiction*," *Renascence* 34 (1982): 161–72.

Appendixes

1. For extended discussion, see R. F. Yeager, "*Pax Poetica*," *Studies in the Age of Chaucer* 9 (1987): 97–121.

2. Boethius, *Consolation,* IV, pr. 6, ll. 117–21, Loeb ed., p. 365.

3. Chaucer, *Boece,* IV, pr. 6, p. 369b, ll. 216–20; Boethius, *Consolation,* l. 123, Loeb ed., p. 364.

4. Chaucer, *Boece,* IV, m. 6, p. 371b, ll. 40–45; Boethius, *Consolation,* ll. 34, 35, 39, Loeb ed., p. 374.

5. Chaucer, *Boece,* IV, pr. 6, p. 370a, ll. 275–77; Boethius, *Consolation,* ll. 154–55, Loeb ed., p. 366.

WORKS CITED

Abbreviations

CHLMP   *Cambridge History of Later Medieval Philosophy*, edited by Norman Kretzmann, Anthony Kenny, and Jan Pinborg. Cambridge: Cambridge Univ. Press, 1982.

ChRev   *Chaucer Review*

EP   *Encyclopedia of Philosophy*, editor-in-chief, Paul Edwards. New York: Macmillan, 1967.

NCE   *New Catholic Encyclopedia*. New York: McGraw-Hill, 1967.

PMLA   *Publications of the Modern Language Association.*

Primary Works

Aristotle. *Aristotle's Categories and De Interpretatione.* Translated by J. L. Ackrill. Oxford: Clarendon Press, 1963.

———. *De Anima.* In *Introduction to Aristotle,* translated by Richard McKeon, 2d ed., rev. and enlg., pp. 146–245. Chicago: Univ. of Chicago Press, 1973.

———. *Posterior Analytics.* Translated by Hugh Tredennick. Loeb Classical Library. Cambridge, Mass.: Harvard Univ. Press, 1966.

Augustine. *De doctrina Christiana.* Translated by D. W. Robertson, Jr. Indianapolis: Liberal Arts Press, 1958.

Berchorii, R. P. Petri (Bersuire). *Opera Omnia.* Coloniae Agrippinae: J. W. Hirsch, 1730–31. Tomus Primus, Lib. X.

———. *"Ovidius Moralizatus of Petrus Berchorius:* An Introduction and Translation." Translated by William Reynolds. Ph.D. diss., University of Illinois, 1971.

Biblia Sacra juxta Vulgatam Clementinam. Rome: Desclee, 1956.

Boccaccio, Giovanni. *Teseida: delle Nozze d'Emilia.* Bari: Gius, Laterza and Figli, 1941.

Boethius. *The Consolation of Philosophy.* Translated by S. J. Tester. Loeb Classical Library. Cambridge, Mass.: Harvard Univ. Press, 1918, 1973.

Works Cited

Bonaventure. *Opera omnia*. Vol. 1, *In Primum Librum Sententiarum*. Quaracchi, 1882–1902.

Chaucer, Geoffrey. *The Text of the Canterbury Tales*. Edited by John M. Manly and Edith Rickert. Vol. 3. Chicago: Univ. of Chicago Press, 1940.

———. *The Works of Geoffrey Chaucer*, 2d ed. Edited by F. N. Robinson. Boston: Houghton Mifflin, 1957.

Chrétien de Troyes. *Perceval, or the Story of the Grail*. Translated by Ruth Harwood Cline. Athens: Univ. of Georgia Press, 1985.

———. *Ywain, the Knight of the Lion*. Translated by Burton Raffel. New Haven: Yale Univ. Press, 1987.

Dante Alighieri. *The Paradiso*. Translated by John Ciardi. New York: New American Library, 1970.

Duns Scotus, John. *Opera omnia*. Juxta editionem Waddingi xii tomos. Paris: L. Vivès, 1891. Reprint (in 26 vols.). Farnborough, England: Gregg International Publishers, 1969.

———. *Opera omnia*. Edited by Carolo Balić, et al. Vatican Scotistic Commission, 1950–73.

Fielding, Henry. *The History of Tom Jones, a Foundling*. New York: The Modern Library, 1950.

Isidori, Hispalensis Episcopi. *Etymologiarum sive Originum*. Edited by W. M. Lindsay, 1911. Reprint. Oxford: Oxford Univ. Press, 1957.

John of Salisbury. *Policraticus: The Statesman's Book*. Edited by Murray F. Markland. New York: Ungar, 1979.

Malory, Sir Thomas. *Malory: Works*. 2d ed. Edited by Eugène Vinaver. Oxford: Oxford Univ. Press, 1971.

Ovid. *Metamorphoses*. Translated by Frank Justice Miller. Loeb Classical Library. Cambridge, Mass.: Harvard Univ. Press, 1916.

Owl and the Nightingale, The. Edited by Eric Gerald Stanley. Manchester: Manchester Univ. Press, 1972.

Paulus Venetus' Logica Parva. Translated and commentary by Alan R. Perreiah. Washington, D.C.: Catholic Univ. of America Press, 1983.

Physiologus: A Metrical Bestiary of Twelve Chapters by Bishop Theobald, believed to have been Abbot of Monte Cassino 1022–35, printed in Cologne, 1492. Translated by Alan Wood Rendell. London: John and Edward Bumpus, 1928.

Roman de la Rose, by Guillaume de Lorris and Jean de Meun. *The Romance of the Rose*. Translated by Charles Dahlberg. Princeton: Princeton Univ. Press, 1971.

Sterne, Laurence. *Tristram Shandy*. Edited by Howard Anderson. New York: W. W. Norton, 1980.

Suetonius. *The Lives of the Caesars*. Translated by J. D. Rolfe. Loeb Classical Library. Cambridge, Mass.: Harvard Univ. Press, 1914.

Works Cited

Thomas Aquinas. *Aristotle's De Anima in the Version of William of Moerbeke and the Commentary of St. Thomas Aquinas.* Translated by Kenelm Foster and Silvester Humphries. New Haven: Yale Univ. Press, 1954.

———. *Commentary on the Posterior Analytics of Aristotle.* Translated by F. R. Larcher. Albany, N.Y.: Magi Books, 1970.

———. *Summa theologiae.* New York: Blackfriars, 1964–76.

Virgil. *The Aeneid.* Translated by C. Day Lewis. Garden City, N.Y.: Doubleday Anchor, 1953.

William Heytesbury: On "Insoluble Sentences"—Chapter One of His "Rules for Solving Sophisms." Translated and commentary by Paul Vincent Spade. Toronto: Pontifical Institute of Mediaeval Studies, 1979.

William of Ockham. *Opera theologica.* Vol. 1, *Scriptum in Librum Primum Sententiarum. Ordinatio:* Prologus et distinctio prima. Edited by Gedeon Gál and Stephano Brown. St. Bonaventure, N.Y.: Franciscan Institute, 1967.

———. *Opera theologica.* Vol. 2, *Scriptum in Librum Primum Sententiarum. Ordinatio:* Distinctiones secunda et tertia. Edited by Stephen F. Brown and Gedeon Gál. St. Bonaventure, N.Y.: Franciscan Institute, 1967.

———. *Opera theologica.* Vol. 3, *Scriptum in Librum Primum Sententiarum, Ordinatio:* Distinctiones 4–18. Edited by Girard J. Etzkorn. St. Bonaventure, N.Y.: Franciscan Institute, 1967.

———. *Opera theologica.* Vol. 5, *Quaestiones in Librum Secundum Sententiarum, Reportatio.* Edited by Gedeon Gál and Rega Wood. St. Bonaventure, N.Y.: Franciscan Institute, 1967.

———. *Opera theologica.* Vol. 9, *Quodlibeta Septem.* Edited by Joseph C. Wey. St. Bonaventure, N.Y.: Franciscan Institute, 1967.

William of Sherwood's Introduction to Logic. Translated by Norman Kretzmann. Minneapolis: Univ. of Minnesota Press, 1966.

"Wynnere and Wastoure." In *The Pelican Guide to English Literature.* Vol. 1, *The Age of Chaucer,* edited by Boris Ford. Penguin, 1954. Reprint. 1971.

Secondary Works

Ackerman, Robert W. "Chaucer, the Church, and Religion." In *Companion to Chaucer Studies,* rev. ed., edited by Beryl Rowland, pp. 21–41. New York: Oxford Univ. Press, 1979.

Alford, John A. "Literature and Law in Medieval England." *PMLA* 92 (1977): 941–51.

Allen, Judson Boyce. *The Ethical Poetic of the Later Middle Ages: A Decorum of Convenient Distinction.* Toronto: Univ. of Toronto Press, 1982.

Armstrong, Edward A. *Saint Francis: Nature Mystic.* Berkeley: Univ. of California Press, 1973.

Armstrong, Paul B. "The Conflict of Interpretations and the Limits of Pluralism." *PMLA* 98 (1983): 351–52.

Arthur, Ross G. "The *Pearl*-Poet as Master of Logic." In *English Studies in Canada*. Forthcoming.

Ashley, B. M. "Final Causality." *NCE* 5: 915–19.

Ashworth, E. J. "The Treatment of Semantic Paradoxes from 1400 to 1700." *Notre Dame Journal of Formal Logic* 13 (1972): 34–52.

Bakhtin, Mikhail. *Rabelais and His World*. Translated by Helen Iswolsky. Cambridge, Mass.: MIT Press, 1965.

Baldwin, Ralph. *The Unity of the Canterbury Tales*. Anglistica 5. Copenhagen: Rosenkilde and Bagger, 1955.

Balić, C. "Duns Scotus, John." *NCE* 4: 1102–6.

Ballentine's Law Dictionary. 3d ed. Rochester, N.Y.: Lawyers Cooperative Publishing Co., 1969.

Barnes, Jonathan. "The Just War." *CHLMP*, pp. 771–84.

Baum, Paull F. *Chaucer: A Critical Appreciation*. Durham, N.C.: Duke Univ. Press, 1958.

Baumgaertner, W. "Porphyrian Tree." *NCE* 11: 593.

Beidler, Peter. "Chaucer's 'Knight's Tale' and Its Teller." *English Record* 18 (1968): 54–60.

Bennett, J. A. W. *Chaucer at Oxford and at Cambridge*. Toronto: Univ. of Toronto Press, 1974.

Benson, C. David. *Chaucer's Drama of Style: Poetic Variety and Contrast in the Canterbury Tales*. Chapel Hill: Univ. of North Carolina Press, 1986.

———. "The *Canterbury Tales*: Personal Drama or Experiments in Poetic Variety?" In *The Cambridge Chaucer Companion*, edited by Piero Boitani and Jill Mann, pp. 93–108. Cambridge: Cambridge Univ. Press, 1986.

Bestul, Thomas H. *Satire and Allegory in "Wynnere and Wastoure."* Lincoln: Univ. of Nebraska Press, 1974.

Bettoni, Efrem. *Duns Scotus: The Basic Principles of His Philosophy*. Translated and edited by Bernardine Bonansea. Washington, D.C.: Catholic Univ. of America Press, 1961.

Bilaniuk, P. B. T. "Soul, Human, 5. Theology." *NCE* 13: 462–64.

Black's Law Dictionary. Rev. 4th ed. St. Paul, Minn.: West Publishing Co., 1968.

Blake, Kathleen A. "Order and the Noble Life in Chaucer's *Knight's Tale?*" *Modern Language Quarterly* 34 (1974): 3–19.

Blanch, Robert J., and Julian N. Wasserman. "White and Red in the *Knight's Tale*: Chaucer's Manipulation of a Convention." In *Chaucer in the Eighties*, edited by Julian N. Wasserman and Robert J. Blanch, pp. 175–91. Syracuse: Syracuse Univ. Press, 1986.

Bloomfield, Morton W. "Authenticating Realism and the Realism of Chaucer." *Thought* 39 (1964): 335–58.

Blumberg, Albert E. "Logic, Modern." *EP* 5: 12–34.

Bochenski, I. M. *A History of Formal Logic.* Translated by Ivo Thomas. Notre Dame, Ind.: Univ. of Notre Dame Press, 1961.

Boehner, Philotheus. *Philosophical Writings, a Selection: William of Ockham.* Indianapolis: Bobbs-Merrill, 1964.

Boheemen, Christel van. "Chaucer's *Knight's Tale* and the Structure of Myth." *Dutch Quarterly Review of Anglo-American Letters* 9 (1978): 176–90.

Boitani, Piero. *Chaucer and Boccaccio.* Medium Aevum Monographs, n.s. 8. Oxford: Society for the Study of Mediaeval Languages and Literature, 1977.

Boler, John F. "Intuitive and Abstractive Cognition." *CHLMP,* pp. 460–78.

Bolton, W. F. "The Topic of the *Knight's Tale.*" *ChRev* 1 (1966–67): 217–27.

Bonansea, Bernardine M. "Duns Scotus' Voluntarism." *Studies in Philosophy and the History of Philosophy,* 1965: 83–121.

————. *Man and His Approach to God in John Duns Scotus.* Lanham, Md.: Univ. Press of America, 1983.

Bourke, Vernon J. "Thomas Aquinas, St." *EP* 8: 105–16.

————. *Will in Western Thought.* New York: Sheed and Ward, 1964.

Bowden, Muriel. *A Commentary on the General Prologue to the "Canterbury Tales."* New York: Macmillan, 1948. Reprint. 1967.

Brady, Ignatius. *The Sources of Franciscan Spirituality.* Detroit: Duns Scotus College, 1952.

Brandeis, Irma. *The Ladder of Vision: A Study of Dante's Comedy.* Garden City, N.Y.: Doubleday Anchor, 1962.

Braun, Joseph. *Die Reliquiare des Christlichen Kultes und Ihre Entwicklung.* Freiburg im Breisgau: Herder and Co., 1940.

Brody, Boruch A. "Logical Terms, Glossary of." *EP* 5: 57–77.

Brewer, Derek. "Gothic Chaucer." In *Geoffrey Chaucer,* edited by Derek Brewer, pp. 1–32. Athens: Ohio Univ. Press, 1974.

Brooks, Douglas, and Alastair Fowler. "The Meaning of Chaucers' *Knight's Tale.*" *Medium Aevum* 39 (1970): 123–46.

Brown, Emerson, Jr. "The Knight's Tale, 2639: Guilt by Punctuation." *ChRev* 21 (1986): 133–41.

Bryan, W. F., and Germaine Dempster. *Sources and Analogues of Chaucer's Canterbury Tales.* 1941. Reprint. New York: Humanities Press, 1958.

Burlin, Robert B. *Chaucerian Fiction.* Princeton: Princeton Univ. Press, 1977.

Works Cited

Bursill-Hall, G. L. *Speculative Grammars of the Middle Ages: The Doctrine of "Partes Orationes" of the Modistae.* The Hague: Mouton, 1971.

Burrow, J. A. *Ricardian Poetry: Chaucer, Gower, Langland, and the Gawain Poet.* New Haven: Yale Univ. Press, 1971.

Cameron, Allen Barry. "The Heroine in *The Knight's Tale.*" *Studies in Short Fiction* 5 (1967–68): 119–27.

Cannon, William Ragsdale. "The Genesis of the University." In *Contemporary Reflections on the Medieval Christian Tradition,* edited by George H. Shriver, pp. 200–20. Durham, N.C.: Duke Univ. Press, 1974.

Cassirer, Ernst. *Language and Myth.* Translated by Susanne K. Langer. New York: Dover, 1953.

Ceci, Louis. "The Case for Syntactic Imagery." *College English* 45 (1983): 431–49.

Chance, Jane. "The Origins and Development of Medieval Mythography: From Homer to Dante." In *Mapping the Cosmos,* edited by Jane Chance and R. W. Wells, Jr., pp. 35–64. Houston: Rice Univ. Press, 1985.

Charbonneau-Lassay, Louis. *Le Bestiaire du Christ.* 1940. Reprint. Milan: L. J. Toth, 1974.

Chomsky, Noam. *Knowledge of Language: Its Nature, Origin, and Use.* New York: Praeger, 1986.

Clark, David W. "Ockham on Human and Divine Freedom." *Franciscan Studies* 38 (1978): 122–60.

Clarke, Edwin, and Kenneth Dewhurst. *An Illustrated History of Brain Function.* Berkeley: Univ. of California Press, 1972.

Coleman, William. "Boccaccio's Commentaries on *Il Teseida:* The Question of Chaucer's Manuscript Once More." Address delivered at New Chaucer Society, Fifth International Congress, University of Pennsylvania, Philadelphia, March 23, 1986.

Colish, Marcia L. *The Mirror of Language: A Study in the Medieval Theory of Knowledge.* New Haven: Yale Univ. Press, 1968.

Cooper, Helen. *The Structure of the Canterbury Tales.* Athens: Univ. of Georgia Press, 1984.

Copleston, Frederick. *A History of Philosophy.* Westminster, Md.: The Newman Press, 1950. Reprint. New York: Doubleday, Image Books, 1962.

Courtenay, William J. "Nominalism and Late Medieval Religion." In *The Pursuit of Holiness in Late Medieval and Renaissance Religion,* edited by Charles Trinkhaus and Heiko A. Oberman, pp. 26–59. Leiden: E. J. Brill, 1974.

———. *Schools and Scholars in Fourteenth-Century England.* Princeton: Princeton Univ. Press, 1987.

Works Cited

Cousins, Ewert H. "St. Bonaventure, St. Thomas, and the Movement of Thought in the 13th Century." In *Bonaventure and Aquinas: Enduring Philosophers,* edited by Robert W. Shahan and Francis J. Kovach, pp. 5–23. Norman: Univ. of Oklahoma Press, 1976.

Crampton, Georgia Ronan. *The Condition of Creatures.* New Haven: Yale Univ. Press, 1974.

Curry, Walter Clyde. *Chaucer and the Mediaeval Sciences.* 1926. 2d ed., rev. and enl. New York: Barnes and Noble, 1960.

Curtius, Ernst Robert. *European Literature and the Latin Middle Ages.* Translated by Willard R. Trask. 1953. Reprint. New York: Harper and Row, 1963.

David, Alfred. *The Strumpet Muse.* Bloomington: Indiana Univ. Press, 1976.

Day, Sebastian J. *Intuitive Cognition: A Key to the Significance of the Later Scholastics.* St. Bonaventure, N.Y.: The Franciscan Institute, 1947.

Delany, Sheila. "Undoing Substantial Connection: The Late Medieval Attack on Analogical Thought." *Mosaic* 6 (1972): 31–52.

Delasanta, Rodney. "Penance and Poetry in the *Canterbury Tales.*" *PMLA* 93 (1970): 240–47.

———. "Uncommon Commonplaces in *The Knight's Tale.*" *Neuphilologische Mitteilungen* 70 (1969): 683–90.

Donaldson, E. Talbot, ed. *Chaucer's Poetry: An Anthology for the Modern Reader.* New York: The Ronald Press Co., 1958.

Donceel, J. F. "Knowledge, Process of." *NCE* 8: 230–32.

Dowling, W. Jay, and Dane L. Harwood. *Music Cognition.* New York: Academic Press, 1985.

Du Cange, Charles Du Fresne. *Glossarium mediae et infinae latinitatis, conditum a Carolo Dufresne, Domino Du Cange.* Supplement by D. P. Carpenterii. Paris: Didot Fratres, 1842.

Durbin, Paul T. "Human Intelligence." Appendixes 1–4, in Thomas Aquinas, *Summa theologiae* 12: Ia, 84–89. New York: Blackfriars, 1964–76.

Dwyer, Richard A. "The Appreciation of Handmade Literature." *ChRev* 8 (1974): 221–41.

Eco, Umberto. *Art and Beauty in the Middle Ages.* Translated by Hugh Bredin. New Haven: Yale Univ. Press, 1986.

Elbow, Peter. *Oppositions in Chaucer.* Middletown, Conn.: Wesleyan Univ. Press, 1973.

Evans, G. R. *The Language and Logic of the Bible: The Road to Reformation.* Cambridge: Cambridge Univ. Press, 1985.

Fairchild, Hoxie Neale. "Active Arcite, Contemplative Palamon." *Journal of English and Germanic Philology* 26 (1927): 285–93.

Fancher, Raymond E. *Pioneers of Psychology*. New York: W. W. Norton, 1979.

Ferster, Judith. *Chaucer on Interpretation*. Cambridge: Cambridge Univ. Press, 1985.

Fichte, Joerg O. "Man's Free Will and the Poet's Choice: The Creation of Artistic Order in Chaucer's *Knight's Tale*." *Anglia* 93 (1975): 335–60.

Fifield, Merle. "The *Knight's Tale:* Incident, Idea, Incorporation." *ChRev* 3 (1969): 95–106.

Fisher, John H. "Chaucer's Prescience." *Studies in the Age of Chaucer* 5 (1983): 3–15.

Fleming, John V. "Chaucer and the Visual Arts of His Time." In *New Perspectives in Chaucer Criticism*, edited by Donald M. Rose, pp. 121–36. Norman, Okla.: Pilgrim Books, 1981.

Fodor, Jerry A. *The Modularity of Mind: An Essay on Faculty Psychology*. Cambridge, Mass.: MIT Press, 1983.

———. "The Present Status of the Innateness Controversy." In *Representations: Philosophical Essays on the Foundations of Cognitive Science*, by Jerry A. Fodor, pp. 257–316. Cambridge, Mass.: MIT Press, 1981.

Frazer, Sir James George. *The Golden Bough*. 3d ed. New York: Macmillan, 1935.

Friedman, John Block. "Another Look at Chaucer and the Physiognomists." *Studies in Philology* 78 (1981): 138–52.

French, W. H. "The Lovers in the *Knight's Tale*." *Journal of English and Germanic Philology* 48 (1949): 320–38.

Frost, William. "An Interpretation of Chaucer's Knight's Tale." In *Chaucer Criticism: The Canterbury Tales*, edited by Richard J. Schoeck and Jerome Taylor, pp. 98–116. Notre Dame: Univ. of Notre Dame Press, 1960. (First published in *Review of English Studies* 25 [1949]: 290–304.)

Fyler, John M. *Chaucer and Ovid*. New Haven: Yale Univ. Press, 1979.

Gadamer, Hans-Georg. *Truth and Method*. London: Sheed and Ward, 1975.

Gardner, Howard. *Frames of Mind: The Theory of Multiple Intelligences*. New York: Basic Books, 1983.

Gardner, John. *On Moral Fiction*. New York: Basic Books, 1978.

———. *The Poetry of Chaucer*. Carbondale: Southern Illinois Univ. Press, 1977.

Gaylord, Alan. "Chaucer's Squire and the Glorious Campaign." *Papers of the Michigan Academy of Science, Arts and Letters* 45 (1960): 341–61.

———. "The Role of Saturn in the *Knight's Tale*." *ChRev* 8 (1974): 171–90.

Gilbert, Katharine Everett, and Helmut Kuhn. *A History of Esthetics*. Rev. and enl. London: Thames and Hudson, 1956.

Gilson, Etienne. *The Christian Philosophy of St. Augustine.* Translated by L. E. M. Lynch. New York: Random House, 1960.

——. *The Christian Philosophy of St. Thomas Aquinas,* trans. L. K. Shook. New York: Random House, 1956.

Godefroy's *Dictionnaire de l'Ancienne Langue Française du IX au XV Siècle.* Paris: F. Vieweg, 1883.

Gollancz, Israel. "Strode, Ralph." *Dictionary of National Biography* 19 (1921–22): 57–59.

Gracia, Jorge J. E. *Introduction to the Problem of Individuation in the Early Middle Ages.* Washington, D.C.: Catholic Univ. of America Press, 1984.

Green, Richard Firth. "Arcite at Court." *English Language Notes* 18 (1981): 251–57.

Greenfield, Concetta Carestia. *Humanist and Scholastic Poetics, 1250–1500.* Lewisburg: Bucknell Univ. Press, 1981.

Haas, Renate. "Chaucer's *Monk's Tale:* An Ingenious Criticism of Early Humanist Conceptions of Tragedy." *Humanistica Lovaniensia* 36 (1987): 44–70.

Haller, Robert S. "The *Knight's Tale* and the Epic Tradition." *ChRev* 1 (1966–67): 67–84.

Halverson, John. "Aspects of Order in the *Knight's Tale.*" *Studies in Philology* 57 (1960): 606–21.

Ham, Edward B. "*Knight's Tale* 38." *English Literary History* 17 (1950): 252–61.

Hamilton, Edith. *Mythology.* New York: New American Library, 1969.

Hanning, Robert W. *The Individual in Twelfth-Century Romance.* New Haven: Yale Univ. Press, 1977.

——. "The Struggle between Noble Designs and Chaos: The Literary Tradition of Chaucer's Knight's Tale." *The Literary Review* 23 (1979–80): 519–41.

Hardison, O. B., Jr. "Medieval Literary Criticism." In *Classical and Medieval Literary Criticism,* edited by Alex Preminger, O. B. Hardison, Jr., and Kevin Kerrane, pp. 263–98. New York: Ungar, 1974.

Harvey, E. Ruth. *The Inward Wits: Psychological Theory in the Middle Ages and the Renaissance.* London: The Warburg Institute, University of London, 1975.

Hatton, Thomas J. "Chaucer's Crusading Knight, A Slanted Ideal." *ChRev* 3 (1969): 77–87.

——. "Thematic Relationships Between Chaucer's Squire's Portrait and Tale and the Knight's Portrait and Tale." *Studies in Medieval Culture* 4 (1974): 452–58.

Heath, P. L. "Experience." *EP* 3: 156–59.

Helterman, Jeffrey. "The Dehumanizing Metamorphoses of the *Knight's Tale.*" *English Literary History* 38 (1971): 493–511.

Herbst, Jurgen. "The Liberal Arts: Overcoming the Legacy of the Nineteenth Century." *Liberal Education* 66 (1980): 24–39.

Herz, Judith Scherer. "Chaucer's Elegiac Knight." *Criticism* 6 (1964): 212–24.

Hirsch, E. D., Jr. *Validity in Interpretation.* New Haven: Yale Univ. Press, 1967.

Hoffman, Richard L. *Ovid and the Canterbury Tales.* Philadelphia: Univ. of Pennsylvania Press, 1966.

Howard, Donald R. *The Idea of the Canterbury Tales.* Berkeley: Univ. of California Press, 1976.

———. "The Philosophies in Chaucer's *Troilus.*" In *The Wisdom of Poetry: Essays in Early English Literature in Honor of Morton W. Bloomfield,* edited by Larry D. Benson and Siegfried Wenzel, pp. 151–75. Kalamazoo: Medieval Institute Publications, 1982.

Hulbert, J. R. "What Was Chaucer's Aim in the *Knight's Tale?*" *Studies in Philology* 26 (1920): 375–85.

Hume, Kathryn. *The Owl and the Nightingale: The Poem and Its Critics.* Toronto: Univ. of Toronto Press, 1975.

Huppé, Bernard F. *A Reading of the Canterbury Tales.* Albany: State Univ. of New York Press, 1964.

Jameson, Fredric. *The Prison-House of Language: A Critical Account of Structuralism and Russian Formalism.* Princeton: Princeton Univ. Press, 1972.

Jardine, Lisa. "Humanism and the Teaching of Logic." *CHLMP,* pp. 797–807.

Jones, Terry. *Chaucer's Knight: The Portrait of a Medieval Mercenary.* Baton Rouge: Louisiana State Univ. Press, 1980.

Jordan, Robert M. *Chaucer and the Shape of Creation.* Cambridge, Mass.: Harvard Univ. Press, 1967.

———. *Chaucer's Poetics and the Modern Reader.* Berkeley: Univ. of California Press, 1987.

Justman, Stewart. " 'Auctoritee' and the *Knight's Tale.*" *Modern Language Quarterly* 39 (1978): 3–14.

Kean, P. M. *Chaucer and the Making of English Poetry.* Vol. 2, *The Art of Narrative.* London: Routledge and Kegan Paul, 1972.

Kenny, Anthony, and Jan Pinborg. "Medieval Philosophical Literature." *CHLMP,* pp. 11–42.

Kerferd, G. B. "Aristotle." *EP* 1: 151–62.

Knight, Stephen. *Rymyng Craftily.* Sydney, Australia: Angus and Robertson, 1973.

Kolve, V. A. *Chaucer and the Imagery of Narrative: The First Five Canterbury Tales.* Stanford: Stanford Univ. Press, 1984.

Koretsky, Allen C. "The Heroes of Chaucer's Romances." *Annuale Mediaevale* 17 (1976): 22–47.

Korolec, J. B. "Free Will and Free Choice." *CHLMP,* pp. 629–41.

Kretzmann, Norman. "The Logic of Instantaneous Speed." Lecture delivered at the Institute on Medieval Philosophy, Cornell University, July 22, 1980.

———. "Syncategoremata, Exponibilia, Sophismata." *CHLMP,* pp. 211–45.

Kreyche, G. F. "Causality." *NCE* 3: 342–47.

Ladner, Gerhart B. "Medieval and Modern Understanding of Symbolism: A Comparison." *Speculum* 54 (1979): 223–56.

Lawler, Traugott. *The One and the Many in the Canterbury Tales.* Hamden, Conn.: Archon, 1980.

Leff, Gordon. *William of Ockham: The Metamorphosis of Scholastic Discourse.* Manchester: Manchester Univ. Press, 1975.

Lindahl, Carl. *Earnest Games: Folkloric Patterns in the Canterbury Tales.* Bloomington: Indiana Univ. Press, 1987.

Lipking, Lawrence. "Aristotle's Sister: A Poetics of Abandonment." In *Canons,* edited by Robert von Hallberg, pp. 85–105. Chicago: Univ. of Chicago Press, 1984.

Littré, Émile. *Dictionnaire de la Langue Française,* vol. 10. Ed. intégrale. Paris: Jean-Jacques Pauvert, 1956.

Lohr, C. H. "The Medieval Interpretation of Aristotle." *CHLMP,* pp. 80–98.

Lumiansky, Robert M. *Of Sondry Folk: The Dramatic Principle in the Canterbury Tales.* Austin: Univ. of Texas Press, 1955.

Luxon, Thomas H. " 'Sentence' and 'Solaas': Proverbs and Consolation in *The Knight's Tale.*" *ChRev* 22 (1987): 94–111.

Macquarrie, John. *In Search of Humanity: A Theological and Philosophical Approach.* New York: Crossroad, 1983.

Maierù, Alfonso. "Methods of Teaching Dialectic." Paper delivered at the Twenty-third International Congress on Medieval Studies, Western Michigan University, Kalamazoo, May 1988.

Manly, John M. *Some New Light on Chaucer.* 1926, Reprint. New York: Peter Smith, 1952.

Mann, Jill. *Chaucer and Medieval Estates Satire.* Cambridge: Cambridge Univ. Press, 1973.

Marckwardt, Albert H. *Characterization in Chaucer's Knight's Tale.* University of Michigan Contributions in Modern Philology, no. 5. Ann Arbor: Univ. of Michigan Press, 1947.

Works Cited

Marks, Richard, and Nigel Morgan. *The Golden Age of English Manuscript Painting, 1200–1500*. New York: George Braziller, 1981.

Marrone, Steven P. *William of Auvergne and Robert Grosseteste: New Ideas of Truth in the Early Thirteenth Century*. Princeton: Princeton Univ. Press, 1983.

Maurer, Armand. "Ockham on the Possibility of a Better World." *Mediaeval Studies* 38 (1976): 291–312.

McAlpine, Monica E. *The Knight's Tale: An Annotated Bibliography*. The New Chaucer Bibliographies. University of Toronto Press. Forthcoming.

McCall, John P. *Chaucer among the Gods: The Poetics of Classical Myth*. University Park: Pennsylvania State Univ. Press, 1979.

McCall, Raymond J. *Basic Logic: The Fundamental Principles of Formal Deductive Reasoning*. 2d ed. New York: Barnes and Noble, 1967.

McColly, William B. "Chaucer's Yeoman and the Rank of His Knight." *ChRev* 20 (1985): 14–27.

McCoy, Bernadette Marie, trans. *The Book of Theseus: Teseide delle Nozze d'Emilia by Giovanni Boccaccio*. New York: Medieval Text Association, 1974.

McGrade, Arthur Stephen. "Ockham on Enjoyment—Towards an Understanding of Fourteenth Century Philosophy and Psychology." *Revue Metaphysics* 37 (1981): 706–28.

Meier, T. K. "Chaucer's Knight as 'Persona': Narration as Control." *English Miscellany* 20 (1969): 11–21.

Middleton, Anne. "The Idea of Public Poetry in the Reign of Richard II." *Speculum* 53 (1978): 94–114.

Miller, Robert P. "Allegory in the *Canterbury Tales*." In *Companion to Chaucer Studies*, rev. ed., edited by Beryl Rowland, pp. 326–51. New York: Oxford Univ. Press, 1979.

Minnis, A. J. *Chaucer and Pagan Antiquity*. Chaucer Studies no. 8. Cambridge: D. S. Brewer and Rowman and Littlefield, 1982.

Mitchell, Charles. "The Worthiness of Chaucer's Knight." *Modern Language Quarterly* 25 (1964): 66–75.

Moody, Ernest A. "William of Ockham." *EP* 8: 306–17.

Morreall, John, ed. *The Philosophy of Laughter and Humor*. Albany: State Univ. of New York Press, 1987.

Morris, Colin. *The Discovery of the Individual: 1050–1200*. 1972. Reprint. New York: Harper Torchbooks, 1973.

Muscatine, Charles. *Chaucer and the French Tradition: A Study in Style and Meaning*. Berkeley: Univ. of California Press, 1957.

———. "Form, Texture, and Meaning in Chaucer's *Knight's Tale*." *PMLA* 65 (1950): 911–29.

Neuse, Richard. "The Knight: The First Mover in Chaucer's Human Comedy." *University of Toronto Quarterly* 31 (1962): 299–315.

Normore, Calvin. "Future Contingents." *CHLMP*, pp. 358–81.

O'Connor, Edward Dennis, ed. *The Dogma of the Immaculate Conception: History and Significance.* Notre Dame, Ind.: Univ. of Notre Dame Press, 1958.

———. "Immaculate Conception." *NCE* 7: 378–82.

O'Donnell, Clement M. *The Psychology of St. Bonaventure and St. Thomas Aquinas.* Washington, D.C.: Catholic Univ. of America Press, 1937.

Olson, Elder. "A Dialogue on Symbolism." In *Critics and Criticism: Ancient and Modern,* edited by R. S. Crane, pp. 567–94. Chicago: Univ. of Chicago Press, 1952.

Olson, Glending. *Literature as Recreation in the Later Middle Ages.* Ithaca: Cornell Univ. Press, 1982.

Olson, Paul A. *The "Canterbury Tales" and the Good Society.* Princeton: Princeton Univ. Press, 1986.

Olsson, Kurt. "*Securitas* and Chaucer's Knight." *Studies in the Age of Chaucer* 9 (1987): 123–53.

Owen, Charles A., Jr. "The Problem of Free Will in Chaucer's Narratives." *Philological Quarterly* 46 (1967): 433–56.

———. "The Alternative Reading of *The Canterbury Tales:* Chaucer's Text and the Early Manuscripts." *PMLA* 97 (1982): 237–50.

Palmer, R. Barton. "The Problem with Gardner's *On Moral Fiction.*" *Renascence* 34 (1982): 161–72.

Parr, Johnstone. "The Date and Revision of Chaucer's *Knight's Tale.*" *PMLA* 60 (1945): 307–24.

Patch, Howard Rollin. *On Rereading Chaucer.* Cambridge, Mass.: Harvard Univ. Press, 1939.

Payne, F. Anne. *Chaucer and Menippean Satire.* Madison: Univ. of Wisconsin Press, 1981.

Payne, Robert O. "Chaucer and the Art of Rhetoric." In *Companion to Chaucer Studies,* rev. ed., edited by Beryl Rowland, pp. 42–64. New York: Oxford Univ. Press, 1979.

Pearsall, Derek. *The Canterbury Tales.* London: George Allen and Unwin, 1985.

Peck, Russell A. "Chaucer and the Nominalist Questions." *Speculum* 53 (1978): 745–60.

———. "Public Dreams and Private Myths: Perspective in Middle English Literature." *PMLA* 90 (1975): 461–68.

Peters, R. S., ed. *Brett's History of Psychology,* Rev. ed. Cambridge, Mass.: MIT Press, 1962.

Pratt, John H. "Was Chaucer's Knight Really a Mercenary?" *ChRev* 22 (1987): 8–27.

Pratt, Robert A. "The Knight's Tale." In *Sources and Analogues of Chaucer's Canterbury Tales,* edited by W. F. Bryan and Germaine Dempster, pp. 82–105. 1941. Reprint. New York: Humanities Press, 1958.

Prentice, Robert. "The Voluntarism of Duns Scotus as Seen in his Comparison of the Intellect and the Will." *Franciscan Studies* 28 (1968): 63–103.

Prior, A. N. "Logic, Many-Valued." *EP* 5: 1–5.

Purdon, Liam O. "Chaucer's 'Lak of Stedfastnesse': A Revalorization of the Word." In *Sign, Sentence, Discourse,* edited by Julian N. Wasserman and Lois Roney, pp. 144–52. Syracuse: Syracuse Univ. Press, 1989.

Reed, Thomas Lloyd, Jr. "Middle English Debate Poetry: A Study in Form and Function." Ph.D. diss., University of Virginia, 1978.

Reidy, John. "The Education of Chaucer's Duke Theseus." In *The Epic in Medieval Society,* edited by Harald Scholler, pp. 391–408. Tübingen, 1977.

Reilly, George C. "Knowledge." *NCE* 8: 224–28.

Ridley, Florence H. "Chaucerian Criticism: The Significance of Varying Perspectives." *Neuphilologische Mitteilungen* 81 (1980): 131–41.

———. "Questions without Answers—Yet or Ever? New Critical Modes and Chaucer." *ChRev* 16 (1981): 101–6.

Robertson, D. W., Jr. *A Preface to Chaucer: Studies in Medieval Perspectives.* Princeton: Princeton Univ. Press, 1962.

———. "The Probable Date and Purpose of Chaucer's *Knight's Tale.*" *Studies in Philology* 84 (1987): 418–39.

Robins, Robert H. *Ancient and Medieval Grammatical Theory in Europe.* London: Kennikat Press, 1971.

Robinson, A. "Substantial Change." *NCE* 13: 771.

Root, Robert Kilburn. *The Poetry of Chaucer: A Guide to Its Study and Appreciation.* Rev. ed. 1934. Reprint. New York: Peter Smith, 1950.

Rosenberg, J. R. "Individuation." *NCE* 7: 475–78.

Rosenblatt, Louise M. *The Reader, the Text, the Poem: The Transactional Theory of the Literary Work.* Carbondale: Southern Illinois Univ. Press, 1978.

Rowland, Beryl. *Blind Beasts: Chaucer's Animal World.* Kent, Ohio: Kent State Univ. Press, 1971.

Ruggiers, Paul G. *The Art of the Canterbury Tales.* Madison: Univ. of Wisconsin Press, 1965.

Russell, J. Stephen. "*Lege caritate legem caritatem:* Reading as Allegory in Saint Augustine." Paper written for the annual Midwest Modern Language Association convention, Minneapolis, November 1989.

Russell, Robert P. "Augustinianism." *NCE* 1: 1063–66.

Salter, Elizabeth. *Chaucer: The Knight's Tale and the Clerk's Tale.* New York: Barron's, 1962.

Sayce, Olive. "Chaucer's Retractions: His Conclusion of the *Canterbury Tales* and Its Place in Literary Tradition." *Medium Aevum* 40 (1971): 230–40.

Sayers, Dorothy L. "The Lost Tools of Learning." *National Review,* January 19, 1979: 90–99.

Scarbrough, Mark. "Closing the *Canterbury Tales* with a Question: 'By his free wyl' (X, 1012)." Paper delivered at Twenty-first International Congress on Medieval Studies, Western Michigan University, Kalamazoo, May 1986.

Scheps, Walter. "Chaucer's Theseus and the *Knight's Tale.*" *Leeds Studies in English,* n.s. 9 (1977): 19–34.

Schweitzer, Edward C. "Fate and Freedom in *The Knight's Tale.*" *Studies in the Age of Chaucer* 3 (1981): 13–45.

Serene, Eileen. "Demonstrative Science." *CHLMP,* pp. 496–517.

Severs, J. Burke. "The Tales of Romance." In *Companion to Chaucer Studies,* rev. ed., edited by Beryl Rowland, pp. 271–95. New York: Oxford Univ. Press, 1979.

Shaffer, Jerome. "Mind-Body Problem." *EP* 5: 336–46.

Shelly, Percy Van Dyke. *The Living Chaucer.* Philadelphia: Univ. of Pennsylvania Press, 1940.

Shoaf, R. A. *Dante, Chaucer, and the Currency of the Word.* Norman, Okla.: Pilgrim Books, 1983.

Showalter, Elaine. "The Feminist Critical Revolution." In *The New Feminist Criticism,* edited by Elaine Showalter, pp. 3–17. New York: Pantheon, 1984.

Sklute, Larry. *Virtue of Necessity: Inconclusiveness and Narrative Form in Chaucer's Poetry.* Columbus: Ohio State Univ. Press, 1984.

Southern, R. W. *The Making of the Middle Ages.* New Haven: Yale Univ. Press, 1953.

Spade, Paul Vincent. "Insolubilia." *CHLMP,* pp. 246–53.

———. "Roger Swyneshed's *Obligationes:* Edition and Comments." *Archives d'histoire doctrinale et littéraire du moyen age* 144 (1977): 243–49.

Spearing, A. C., ed. *The Knight's Tale.* Cambridge: Cambridge Univ. Press, 1966.

Stepsis, Robert. "*Potentia Absoluta* and the *Clerk's Tale.*" *ChRev* 10 (1975): 129–46.

Stevens, Martin. "The Ellesmere Miniatures as Illustrations of Chaucer's *Canterbury Tales.*" *Studies in Iconography* 7–8 (1981–82): 113–34.

Stock, Lorraine Kochanske. "The Two Mayings in Chaucer's *Knight's Tale:* Convention and Invention." *Journal of English and Germanic Philology* 85 (1986): 206–21.

Strohm, Paul. "Chaucer's Fifteenth-Century Audience and the Narrowing of the 'Chaucer Tradition.' " *Studies in the Age of Chaucer* 4 (1982): 3–32.

Suleiman, Susan R. "Introduction: Varieties of Audience-Oriented Criticism." In *The Reader in the Text,* edited by Susan R. Suleiman and Inge Crosman, pp. 3–45. Princeton: Princeton Univ. Press, 1980.

Suttor, Timothy. "Will." Appendix 8 in Thomas Aquinas, *Summa theologiae.* 11: 267. New York: Blackfriars, 1964–76.

Sylla, Edith Dudley. "Autonomous and Handmaiden Science: St. Thomas Aquinas and William of Ockham on the Physics of the Eucharist." In *The Cultural Context of Medieval Learning,* edited by John Emery Murdoch and Edith Dudley Sylla, pp. 349–96. Dordrecht: D. Reidel Publishing Co., 1975.

———. "The Oxford Calculators." *CHLMP,* pp. 540–63.

Tatelbaum, Linda. 'Venus' *Citole* and the Restoration of Harmony in Chaucer's *Knight's Tale.*" *Neuphilologische Mitteilungen* 74 (1973): 649–64.

Tatlock, J. S. P. *The Mind and Art of Chaucer.* Syracuse: Syracuse Univ. Press, 1950.

Tobler, Adolf, and Erhard Lommatzsch. *Altfranzösisches Wörterbuch.* Berlin: Weidmannsche Buchhandlung, 1936.

Todorov, Tzvetan. "Poetic Truth: Three Interpretations." F. W. Bateson Memorial Lecture. *Essays in Criticism* 38 (1988): 95–113.

Tompkins, Jane P. "The Reader in History: The Changing Shape of Literary Response." In *Reader-Response Criticism: From Formalism to Post-Structuralism,* edited by Jane P. Tompkins, pp. 201–32. Baltimore: Johns Hopkins Univ. Press, 1980.

Turner, Frederick. "A Structuralist Analysis of the *Knight's Tale.*" *ChRev* 8 (1974): 279–96.

Ullmann, Walter. *The Individual and Society in the Middle Ages.* Baltimore: Johns Hopkins Univ. Press, 1966.

Underwood, Dale. "The First of *The Canterbury Tales.*" *English Literary History* 26 (1959): 455–69.

Utley, Francis Lee. "Dialogues, Debates, and Catechisms." In *A Manual of the Writings in Middle English 1050–1500,* edited by Albert E. Hartung, vol. 3, pt. 7. New Haven: Connecticut Academy of Arts and Sciences, 1972.

Van, Thomas A. "Theseus and the 'Right Way' of the *Knight's Tale.*" *Studies in the Literary Imagination* 4 (1971): 83–100.

Vance, Eugene. "Saint Augustine: Language as Temporality." In *Mimesis: From Mirror to Method,* edited by John D. Lyons and Stephen G. Nichols, Jr., pp. 20–35, Hanover: Univ. Press of New England, 1982.

Vann, J. Don. "A Character Reversal in Chaucer's *'Knight's Tale.'* " *American Notes and Queries* 3 (May 1965): 131–32.

Vogt, Berard. "The Metaphysics of Human Liberty in Duns Scotus." *Proceedings of the American Catholic Philosophical Association* 16 (1940): 27–37.

Wachterhauser, Brice R. "Introduction: History and Language in Understanding." In *Hermeneutics and Modern Philosophy,* edited by Brice R. Wachterhauser. Albany: State Univ. of New York Press, 1986.

Wasserman, Julian N. "Both Fixed and Free: Language and Destiny in Chaucer's *Knight's Tale* and *Troilus and Criseyde.*" In *Sign, Sentence, Discourse: Language in Medieval Thought and Literature,* edited by Julian N. Wasserman and Lois Roney, pp. 194–222. Syracuse: Syracuse Univ. Press, 1989.

Watson, Christopher. "Chaucer's Knight and His Tale." *The Critical Review* 22 (1980): 56–64.

Webb, Henry J. "A Reinterpretation of Chaucer's Theseus." *Review of English Studies* 23 (Oct. 1947): 289–96.

Weinberg, Julius R. *A Short History of Medieval Philosophy.* Princeton: Princeton Univ. Press, 1964.

Weintraub, Karl Joachim. *The Value of the Individual: Self and Circumstances in Autobiography.* Chicago: Univ. of Chicago Press, 1978.

Weisheipl, J. A. "Scholastic Method." *NCE* 12: 1145–46.

Westlund, Joseph. "The *Knight's Tale* as an Impetus for Pilgrimage." *Philological Quarterly* 43 (1964): 526–37.

Wetherbee, Winthrop. "Romance and Tragedy in the Knight's Tale: Chaucer's Dark Statius." Paper prepared for the New Chaucer Society, 6th International Congress, University of British Columbia, August 1988.

Wilson, H. S. "*The Knight's Tale* and the *Teseida* Again." *University of Toronto Quarterly,* 18 (1949): 131–46.

Wimsatt, James I. *Allegory and Mirror: Tradition and Structure in Middle English Literature.* New York: Pegasus, 1970.

Windelband, Wilhelm. *A History of Philosophy.* Translated by James H. Tufts. Vol. 1, *Greek, Roman, and Medieval.* 1901. Reprint. New York: Harper Torchbooks, 1958.

Wise, Boyd Ashby. *The Influence of Statius upon Chaucer.* Baltimore: J. H. Furst Co., 1911.

Wolter, Allan B. "Duns Scotus, John." *EP* 2: 427–36.

———. "Duns Scotus on the Predestination of Christ." *The Cord: A Franciscan Spiritual Review* 5 (1955): 366–72.

———. "Native Freedom of the Will as a Key to the Ethics of Scotus." In *Congressus Scotisticus Internationalis* (Vienna, 1970): 359–70. Rome: Societas Internationalis Scotistica, 1972.

Works Cited

Wood, Chauncey. *Chaucer and the Country of the Stars.* Princeton: Princeton University Press, 1970.

Yates, Frances A. *The Art of Memory.* Chicago: Univ. of Chicago Press, 1966.

Yeager, R. F. *"Pax Poetica:* On the Pacifism of Chaucer and Gower." *Studies in the Age of Chaucer* 9 (1987): 97–121.

GENERAL INDEX

Abelard, Peter (d. 1142), 21
Abstraction vs. Reality, 130
Accidents and substance, 189, 193
Ackerman, Robert W., 296*n30*
Affectio justitiae. See Scotus, John
  Duns
Affections, 77–79
Albert of Saxony (d. 1390), 139
Albert the Great (d. 1280), 57,
  294*n18*, 305*n26*
Aldhelm (d. 709), 329*n49*
Alexander of Hales (d. 1245), 305*n26*
Alexander the Great, 191
Alexandrian grammarians, 295*n23*
Alford, John A., 308*n36*
Allen, Judson Boyce, 294*n21*
Analogies, 60–61, 307*n33*
Anima, 45
Anselm (d. 1109), 64
Aquinas, Thomas (d. 1274): on anal-
  ogy, 307*n33*; and Aristotle, 48, 50,
  52, 298*n5*, 299*n5*; on beauty, 196–
  97; on causation, 58, 145, 302*n19*;
  cosmology, 306*n28*; ethics, 66–71;
  faculty structuring, 302*n22*; on
  freedom, 62–63, 301*n18*, 305*n26*,
  308*n35*; on grace, 310*n54*; on happiness as final end, 62–63; as humanist, 14; on ignorance as defi-

ciency, 261; on individuation,132–
  33, 318*n84*; intellect nobler, 57; on
  knowledge, 127, 149, 151, 160–61,
  201–2, 302*n21*, 321*n11*, 322*n19*; on
  learning from experience, 123,
  317*n79*; on Mary, Immaculate
  Conception of, 78–79; and natural
  logic, 154; on natural virtue, 122;
  on poets as liars, 16, 293–94*n18*; on
  psychology, 21; on scriptural interpretation, 225, 294*n19*; on sense
  pleasures, 311*n56*; on 3-Acts thinking model, 142, 144–45, 159,
  320*n11*; on valid language use, 25;
  mentioned, 57, 227. *See also* Intellect, primacy of; Scientific demonstration
Argument of Knight's Tale (summary), 253–55
"Aristotelian," defined, 299*n5*
Aristotelian science: impact of,
  on Christian thinkers, 14, 47,
  50–51, 160; style of, 15; universalizing tendency of, 132–33, 225,
  295*n23*
Aristotle: on causes, 58, 185; ethics,
  26, 265; on knowledge, 145, 151,
  165; on prime mover, 114, 185;
  and scholasticism, 130, 296*n23*; and

316*n70*; conflict with freedom, 35, 225, 246, 249–50; to construct universal psychology, 228; in daily life, 93, 256–58, 317*n78*; freedom to, 243; as individuating, 33, 133–34; by nobility, 123–24; Ockham, 123, 317*n79*; opportunity for, 231; by ordinary people, 124–25, 127; from other people, 247; revalidated, 226, 254; sense of humor, 265; of *sophismata*, 164–65, 172, 183–84, 188, 259–61; summaries, 253–55, 267; as test of reasoning, 75, 221; as test of values, 261; Theseus and, 104, 106, 112, 113, 114–15, 119–20, 182, 223, 285; tolerance, 261–64; as universal process, 224. *See also* Freedom
—personal: fourteenth-century turn to, 51; revalidation of, 226, 253–55
Experiences, Providence as source of, 111

Fabliaux, 12, 29, 244, 249
Faculties: defined, 44–45; diagram, 46; history of, 45–48; modern theories of, 298*n2*, 299*n9*; in Thomism, 68, 302*n22*
Faculty psychologies, rival theories: defined, 21–22; freedom issue, 48–49; history, 44; overview of Knight's Tale disputation, 32–33; mentioned, 2, 10, 24, 218. *See also* Intellect, primacy of; Will, primacy of; Will/intellect debate
Faculty psychology: Chaucer's changes in (cooperation), 121–28, 204
Fairchild, Hoxie Neale, 4, 291*n9*, 303*n25*, 312*n58*
Fall, the: damaged man's nature, 71, 73; vs. freedom, 185; Scotus's theory, 90
Fancher, Raymond E., 299*n9*
Feminist theory, 39, 298*n44*

Ferster, Judith, 7, 9, 290*n6*
Fichte, Joerg O., 297*n36*
Fielding, Henry (*Tom Jones*), 262
Fifield, Merle, 316*n67*
Figurative language: in presenting philosophy, 36; revalidation of, 223, 226, 266, 267; scholastic disparagement of, 136, 172; scholastic use of, 136–39; summary of argument, 254; and traditional Christianity, 15, 221, 225. *See also* Defense of poetry
Final goals, 109, 316*n68*
Fisher, John H., 318*n80*
Fleming, John, 321*n16*
Fodor, Jerry A., 298*n2*, 299*n9*
Form: in knowledge, 69, 142–43, 302*n21*, 322*nn19, 21*; and substance/accident theory, 193–97; unicity vs. plurality of substantial, 47–48, 199, 298*n5*
Foucault, Michel, 40
Fourteenth-century philosophical concerns, 51
Fowler, Alastair, 305*n25*, 326*n35*
Francis, Saint, 90, 308*n34*, 314*n61*
Franciscan Order and Mary, 78–79
Franciscans and Augustinianism 298*n5*
Franciscan tradition: cosmology, 306*n28*; and created world, 90, 92; on justice, 64; individual, focus on, 92, 133, 200, 252; primacy of will, 255, 298*n5*; mentioned, 38. *See also* Will, primacy of
Frazer, Sir James George, 309*n47*
Free choice (*liberum arbitrium*). *See* Freedom
Freedom: Chaucerian, 33, 34, 35, 104, 106–12, 134, 223, 226, 242, 243, 253–55 (summary); Chaucer's foremost concern in Knight's Tale, xix, 93, 94–102; vs. determinisms, 96–97, 185–86, 192–93, 200, 203, 230; effect of belief in one's, 228–29; and language use, 136; to learn, 112, 121–22, 256; medieval Chris-

INDEX TO
THE KNIGHT'S TALE